T0293035

Cybersecurity Risk Management

Developments in Managing and Exploiting Risk

—

Volume I: Safety Risk Management
Volume II: Project Risk Management
Volume III: Organizational Risk Management
Volume IV: Socio-Political Risk Management
Volume V: Cybersecurity Risk Management

Editor-in-Chief
Kurt J. Engemann

Volume 5

Cybersecurity Risk Management

Enhancing Leadership and Expertise

Edited by
Kurt J. Engemann and Jason A. Witty

DE GRUYTER

ISBN 978-3-11-128601-3
e-ISBN (PDF) 978-3-11-128906-9
e-ISBN (EPUB) 978-3-11-128960-1

Library of Congress Control Number: 2024937160

Bibliographic information published by the Deutsche Nationalbibliothek
The Deutsche Nationalbibliothek lists this publication in the Deutsche Nationalbibliografie;
detailed bibliographic data are available on the Internet at http://dnb.dnb.de.

© 2024 Walter de Gruyter GmbH, Berlin/Boston
Cover image: Ignatiev/E+/Getty Images
Typesetting: Integra Software Services Pvt. Ltd.

www.degruyter.com

Kurt J. Engemann and Jason A. Witty
Advances in cybersecurity risk management

Introduction

Risk management deals with the dilemma of seizing new opportunities while simultaneously managing attendant undesirable consequences. Cyber threats are a persistent and ever-evolving risk that organizations and individuals must address proactively to minimize their exposure to potential harm. The fundamental components of cybersecurity can be broadly categorized into three areas: people, processes, and technology. These components work together to provide a layered approach to cybersecurity, which helps to mitigate risks and protect against threats. Cybersecurity has many positive benefits for individuals, organizations, and society as a whole, including protection of sensitive information, business continuity, protection of critical infrastructure, prevention of cybercrime, and protection of national security. There are also potential downsides associated with implementing a cybersecurity program. Some examples are: implementation costs, operational challenges, false sense of security, user resistance, and unintended consequences.

It is important for organizations to carefully assess and manage the risks associated with implementing a cybersecurity program, and to take a proactive and comprehensive approach to security that balances protection with practicality and efficiency. In this overview, we preview the book and its two main components: chapters covering fundamental concepts and approaches; and, chapters illustrating applications of these fundamental principles.

Fundamentals

Cybersecurity risk management is crucial in today's highly connected world, where personal, business, and government data are often vulnerable to a wide array of cyberthreats. The field of cybersecurity has evolved dramatically with the growth of the internet. The cyber threat environment has equally evolved from the early days of networked computers to the current landscape of highly sophisticated attacks, including the rise of ransomware and state-sponsored hacking. The cybersecurity field is extremely dynamic, with rapidly changing threats The chapter by Witty delves into various types of cyber threats, cybersecurity measures, and the importance of understanding and managing cybersecurity risks. It covers the role of public-private partnerships and information-sharing initiatives in combating cyberthreats and the importance of collaborative defense strategies. It also suggests that cybersecurity is a collective effort and

https://doi.org/10.1515/9783111289069-202

requires the use of established frameworks and standards, along with staying informed about threats through cyber-threat intelligence sharing processes.

Historically, cyber risk management has been perceived as merely forming a part of the overall enterprise risk function across all forms of organization, whether commercial, or governmental. Other risk areas, such as market and capital risks, have been perceived as having greater impact and thus greater resource allocation to the management of them. However, with major cyber breaches occurring, allied to increasingly punitive financial penalties and greater numbers of data privacy regulations, cyber has become a first level priority for all organisations.

Increasing technology dependence and management of upside and downside risks of adopting emergent technologies, such as within artificial intelligence and quantum computing, has increased the complexity of cyber risk management. Two approaches to this critical activity, which impact entity risk appetite setting and cyber threat control capabilities, are utilized by all entities with threat and mitigation data flowing between the hierarchical strata of organisations.

The chapter by King-Wilson discusses the importance of understanding the multi-facetted nature of cyber risks within a new technological environment. The options available in managing these risks requires an equivalent multi-dimensional approach and inputs for decision analysis and mitigation option generation. Yet the volumes of information upon which to form appropriate strategies and mitigating controls, requires an optimized model for such data use by each hierarchical level, in order to avoid error, personal interest influences, or being subsumed by too great a volume. Managing data types, their routing and utilization have become a crucial component of cyber and emergent technology risk management.

Amidst the expanding frontiers of cybersecurity, the integration of human factors engineering emerges as a transformative paradigm, blending the nuances of cognitive and physical ergonomics (Guastello, 2023).This synthesis leverages human factors methodologies, harmonized with cyberpsychology, to engender a deeper understanding of human interactions within cyber realms. Pivotal to this approach is the proactive mitigation of human error. In their chapter, Nobels and Robinson propose that through human factors, we can usher in an era of intuitive, human-centered cybersecurity by designing cybersecurity that inherently aligns with human tendencies. This paradigm champions the end-user, transforming traditional vulnerability points into robust defense nodes. Moreover, the actual potency of human factors engineering extends beyond system optimization. It galvanizes a profound behavioral shift, cultivating a proactive cyber ethos where individuals are not mere passive entities but active, informed, and conscientious participants. Thus, human factors engineering in cybersecurity does not solely bolster technological defenses; it fundamentally reshapes user interactions, fostering a holistic, secure digital environment.

The study of security and people represents a dynamic, interdisciplinary field, emphasizing behavior as both a vulnerability and an asset in securing information systems. Current works underscore the significance of human errors and behaviors as major security risks; it also reveals little empirical investigation into the relationships among features of the socio-organizational context, human factors, and security outcomes. Limited consensus on key definitions and testable frameworks may affect how practical implications from this research resonate. As such, the chapter by Krista Engemann draws from extant organizational research to introduce several considerations for the operationalization and measurement of the shared norms and values that are posited to influence desired, security-compliant behaviors. A review of the development of a facet-specific organizational climate demonstrates the potential in developing empirically-derived measures for cybersecurity theory and practice.

The chapter by Hetner focuses on providing guidance surrounding the importance of measuring, managing and reporting cybersecurity threats across today's modern business landscape. The focus is centered on various methodologies such as quantitative risk analysis which uses numerical values and models such as Annualized Loss Expectancy (ALE). This approach assesses financial, operational and business impacts, while incorporating qualitative risk assessments that evaluate risk factors introduced by cybersecurity threats. It's an approach heavily supported by the risk transfer markets and the boardroom community for effective cybersecurity risk governance and reporting.

Reporting to executive management and the board should not only cover cybersecurity maturity, vulnerabilities and technology-based capabilities but should also provide recommendations for enhancing cybersecurity capabilities that align with business strategies. This approach also captures the necessity for compliance with regulatory requirements when reporting to both internal and external stakeholders, and stresses the importance of embedding cybersecurity risk management into the overall business resiliency governance and risk management practices.

Cyber economics encompasses the economic aspects of cybersecurity and is a seismic shift from delivering technical jargon to the language of the business when discussing cybersecurity risk with enterprise risk management executives, the boardroom, and external stakeholders. Additionally, it calls for a focus on business impact analysis rather than tactical vulnerabilities, and stresses the importance of boardroom engagement as part of cyber risk governance and management. The new U.S. Securities and Exchange Commission's cybersecurity risk governance and disclosure rules requires companies to disclose their cybersecurity risk management and governance practices, and how cybersecurity incidents materially affect their business, operational, and financial condition (SEC, 2023).

Cybersecurity is ever increasingly becoming linked with artificial intelligence (AI). When discussing the dangers of AI through the lens of popular culture, it becomes evident how films, books, and television have not only entertained but also served as cautionary tales, reflecting societal anxieties and ethical quandaries regarding technological advancement. The portrayal of AI in popular culture ranges from benevolent helpers to existential threats, offering a rich tapestry through which to explore the potential risks associated with AI development.

One of the most enduring themes is the fear of AI surpassing human intelligence and becoming uncontrollable, a concept known as the "singularity." This is vividly illustrated in some movies in which an AI defense network becomes self-aware and decides to exterminate humanity to fulfill its programmed directive of preventing threats. Such narratives underscore the potential for AI systems to misinterpret their objectives, leading to unintended and possibly catastrophic outcomes.

In his chapter, Bernik addresses the challenges AI presents. The inclusion of data poisoning and social engineering in the discussion of AI dangers emphasizes the multifaceted nature of AI cybersecurity, encompassing both the integrity of the data that feeds AI systems and the human interactions that shape their use. It underscores the importance of a holistic approach to AI safety, including: ensuring data, designing AI systems to prevent manipulation through social engineering, fostering ethical standards that prioritize transparency and accountability, and establishing comprehensive regulatory frameworks.

Applications

The information security field has grown substantially over the past 30 years as systems have become more interconnected and the threat landscape has increased in breath and sophistication. Along with this progression, the Chief Information Security Officer's (CISO) role has had to evolve and adapt to the increasing demands to protect our organizations, customers and nations from criminal actors.

The chapter by Fitzgerald explores six distinct phases of the CISO evolution, whereby each phase adds to the cumulative role for the CISOs and their teams. While this is in part a historical perspective, it also serves as a blueprint for the future, as the successful CISO will quickly understand the importance that each phase brings to the job of the CISO today.

One could easily examine these phases and individual experience and develop a career plan to address the "gap areas" to develop competencies to become a complete CISO that is desired by their own organization and others. CISOs are not monolithic, but rather a heterogeneous group with different focuses and resulting experiences. By understanding the CISO history, we can seek out other CISOs and security professionals with different knowledge bases to educate and enhance our capabilities.

In his chapter, Hyat-Khan examines the escalating challenge of cybersecurity within the context of global information technology operations management governance, offering an analysis of the current landscape, historical developments, and future directions. The significant cyberattacks experienced by major institutions worldwide in recent years underscores the universal threat to data security. The response of the United States, particularly the implementation of the National Cybersecurity Strategy, emphasizes the critical role of cybersecurity in protecting the nation's economy, infrastructure, democracy, and personal data privacy. This extends to the need for robust national policies to combat cyber threats, especially in the face of advancements in quantum computing. The corporate sector's adoption of emerging technologies, highlights the essential role of IT governance in mitigating vulnerabilities, and increases the significance of advocating for a strategic approach that includes the creation of internal task forces and a universal culture of cybersecurity awareness.

Cybersecurity breaches continue to plague organizations, despite the availability of preventive measures such as patching vulnerabilities. The chapter by McKinney explores the root causes behind decision-making patterns that lead to cyber risk exposure and proposes practical strategies for mitigation. Drawing from empirical data and theoretical frameworks, including utility theory, the research examines why managers often neglect cybersecurity protocols, leaving their organizations vulnerable to attacks. The study delves into the psychological underpinnings of human decision-making, highlighting how optimism bias and the illusion of control contribute to a false sense of security. By understanding these cognitive biases, organizations can develop more effective risk management strategies and enhance their cyber resilience. Actionable recommendations aimed at promoting a culture of proactive cyber risk management emphasize the importance of informed decision-making and effective governance in safeguarding information assets.

Cybersecurity is vital for safeguarding privacy, accessibility, and information integrity, and emerging technologies can increase cybersecurity effectiveness. New AI techniques, which incorporate methods such as data mining and machine learning, create defensive as well as offensive capabilities. Data mining can be used in a beneficial manner to identify concealed patterns among vast amounts of data (Han and Tong, 2022), however, AI technologies also pose challenges, because in the wrong hands they may enable sophisticated cyberattacks based on deep fakes and misinformation dissemination. In their chapter, Engemann and Miller explore how AI impacts individuals' cybersecurity, by addressing classical security risks, AI-enabled threats, and defensive mechanisms. They discuss AI's role in threat detection, authentication, incident response, and recovery, and emphasizes the importance of balancing technological advancement with ethical considerations. Technical challenges are highlighted, including AI use by cybercriminals, use of public Wi-Fi, and expanding attack surfaces. Ethical challenges such as bias, accountability, and transparency are also addressed, along with privacy concerns evaluated through an organizational effectiveness model (Lyons, 2024). Future challenges facing AI in cybersecurity include controlling advanced AI systems to prevent unintended consequences and emergent behavior, and ensuring responsible AI development for individual cybersecurity.

Cyber threats are increasing as industries become more reliant on computers for their manufacturing and shipping functions, and include more chips in their products for wireless access and tracking. The chapter by Richardson, Soluade and Shin reviews cybersecurity, a major safety issue for airline operations, automobile distribution, and railroad operations. In the airline industry, the upgrade to the infrastructure of the National Airspace System, NextGen, is designed to move aircraft more efficiently throughout the United States. Currently, there are 164 airports utilizing different components of the new traffic-managed satellite-based system. In automobiles, the electronic control unit is increasing in complexity with new features that allow remote control of a car. This is exposing the car to theft as the auto moves through the supply chain from the manufacturer to the dealer. Railroad operations rely on different independent systems as the trains move around the country. For example, trains connect with state and local highway authorities to control highway traffic signals. Also, trains rely on inspection alerts when there is a malfunction indicated by the wheel impact load detector. This exposes the railroad to a cyberattack that could shut down the system.

Innovative information and communication technologies have pervaded the global health sector, and the proliferation of cyber-physical systems in hospitals around the world is testament to this reality. However, the increase in the number of cyber-attacks targeting such systems emphasizes the need for research-driven policy efforts aimed at curbing these outbreaks. The chapter by Ogu systematically investigates policy impera- tives for the security of cyber-physical systems and the information that they generate, especially in light of the convoluting factors and policy loopholes that have insured the success of recent cyber-attacks. Health sector security policy frameworks and recom- mendations are reviewed, with particular focus on those that pertain to the adoption, development and governance of eHealth amongst member states. The implications of policy insufficiencies and portended realities for global health security, suggest key areas of focus towards better securing cyber-physical systems.

Conclusion

Cybersecurity involves identifying and assessing potential threats and vulnerabilities, and implementing controls and countermeasures to mitigate or prevent them using technologies and strategies designed to protect computer systems. The most fragile part of a digital security system is the human element, necessitating that individuals reassess their role (Hong and Furnell, 2021). Cybersecurity is vital in all sectors be- cause a successful cyber-attack can have significant consequences for individuals, or- ganizations, and society as a whole.

References

Guastello, S. J. (2023). Human factors engineering and ergonomics: A systems approach. CRC Press.

Han, J., Pei, J., & Tong, H. (2022). Data mining: concepts and techniques. Morgan Kaufmann.

Hong, Yuxiang & Steven Furnell, (2021). Understanding cybersecurity behavioral habits: Insights from situational support, Journal of Information Security and Applications, Volume 57, 102710, ISSN 2214-2126, https://doi.org/10.1016/j.jisa.2020.102710.

Lyons, V. and Fitzgerald, T. (2024). The Privacy Leader Compass; A Comprehensive Business-Oriented Roadmap for Building and Leading Practical Privacy Programs. 1st Ed. CRC Press, Boca Raton, FL.

U.S. Securities and Exchange Commission. (26 Jul 2023). Cybersecurity Risk Management, Strategy, Governance, and Incident Disclosure. https://www.sec.gov/files/rules/final/2023/33-11216.pdf

Contents

Part I: **Fundamentals**

Jason A. Witty

1 Introduction to and brief history of cybersecurity risk management

1.1 Introduction

In today's world, technology use has become an integral part of the human experience. This has led to unprecedented conveniences and productivity, but also to a dramatic increase in the amount of personal, business and government data that is stored and transmitted online. Given the inherently internet-connected and many times, vulnerable, nature of the technologies we use every day, an incredibly complex and dynamic ecosystem of cyberthreats constantly requires an adequate understanding of cybersecurity risk management concepts.

This hyper-connected world has created a vast attack surface. Exceedingly well-funded adversaries have catalyzed the need to secure these systems over the last three decades. The field of cybersecurity is one of the most dynamic and high velocity fields you will ever study. It is a high velocity field (cyber) within another high velocity field (technology.) To be good at cybersecurity risk management, you must not only be knowledgeable in cybersecurity concepts, but you must also be very well educated on the technologies you are attempting to secure.

The word "secure" is interesting in of itself. Bruce Schneier (Schneier, 2019) famously said "Security is both a feeling and a fact. The feeling of security and the reality of security don't always match." His main point was that you can feel secure and not actually be secure, and you can also be secure and not feel like it. This phenomenon makes the field of cybersecurity risk management even more complex than it is inherently. We will elaborate on this throughout the book.

In the context of this complex, incredibly high velocity field, consider the recent explosive growth of Large Language Model (LLM) based Generative Artificial Intelligence. When OpenAI's ChatGPT was launched to the public Internet in late 2022, it quickly became the fastest technology adopted in the history of the world. It took a mere two months to grow from 1M visitors to 100M visitors between December 2022 and January 2023 (Milmo, 2023).

There is a saying in Chief Information Security Officer (CISO) circles – "Being a CISO is like being a weather predictor – except that you are trying to predict the weather on a planet that has a completely new type of weather every quarter, and none of the previous weather patterns ever go away."

ChatGPT's meteoric launch is a great example of "changing weather." Now practitioners suddenly need to consider things like: How will Large Language Models (LLMs) enable adversaries to be more successful? Since the models are constantly learning and re-learning, what if adversaries teach them super-bad habits? How good

https://doi.org/10.1515/9783111289069-001

are the guardrails that would limit that risk? Do they change dramatically from one LLM to another? What are the ethical/copyright/legal considerations of content output by a model trained off of data from the whole Internet? Is there a large difference between "consumer grade" LLMs and "commercial grade" LLMs? Do we block access to them for our corporate end-users until we figure all of this out? How do we safely enable LLMs, quickly, to ensure we don't stop potential business use that will drive new customer experiences, revenues, and efficiencies? How can LLMs enable cybersecurity practitioners to be "better, cheaper, faster"?

As a great example of the latter, in April 2023, we asked ChatGPT to define Cybersecurity and cite what aspects of the field are most important. Its reply was:

> Cybersecurity is the practice of protecting computers, servers, mobile devices, electronic systems, networks, and data from unauthorized access, use, disclosure, disruption, modification, or destruction. It encompasses the processes and technologies used to protect against both internal and external cyber threats and to ensure the confidentiality, integrity, and availability of data.
>
> Management of Cybersecurity risk is important for a variety of reasons, including:
> 1. **Protecting sensitive information**: Personal and business data is often stored and transmitted online, making it vulnerable to theft or unauthorized access. Cybersecurity measures are designed to protect this information from cyber criminals and other malicious actors.
> 2. **Maintaining privacy**: Cybersecurity measures help to maintain the privacy of individuals and organizations by preventing unauthorized access to personal and business data.
> 3. **Preventing financial losses**: Cyber attacks can result in significant financial losses for businesses and individuals. Cybersecurity measures help to minimize these losses by preventing cyber criminals from accessing sensitive financial information and disrupting business operations.
> 4. **Ensuring continuity of operations**: Cybersecurity measures help to ensure that critical systems and networks remain operational, even in the face of cyber attacks, to minimize downtime and disruption.
>
> Types of Cyber Threats:
> 1. **Malware**: Malware is malicious software that is designed to damage or disrupt computer systems. This can include viruses, worms, and trojan horses.
> 2. **Phishing**: Phishing is a type of social engineering attack that involves tricking individuals into revealing sensitive information or downloading malware.
> 3. **Ransomware**: Ransomware is a type of malware that encrypts a victim's data and demands payment in exchange for the decryption key.
> 4. **Distributed Denial of Service (DDoS)**: A DDoS attack involves overwhelming a network or website with traffic from multiple sources, making it unavailable to users.
> 5. **Advanced Persistent Threats (APTs)**: APTs are sophisticated and sustained cyber attacks that are designed to steal sensitive information from an organization.
>
> Cybersecurity Measures:
> 1. **Firewalls**: Firewalls are security systems that control incoming and outgoing network traffic based on predefined security rules.
> 2. **Antivirus and anti-malware software**: Antivirus and anti-malware software is designed to detect and remove malware from a computer or network.

3. **Encryption**: Encryption is the process of converting plain text into coded text to protect sensitive information from unauthorized access.
4. **Network security**: Network security refers to the measures taken to protect a computer network from unauthorized access, use, disclosure, disruption, modification, or destruction.
5. **User education and awareness**: User education and awareness programs are designed to educate individuals about cybersecurity threats and best practices for protecting against these threats.

Cybersecurity is a critical aspect of modern technology, and an understanding of cybersecurity concepts is essential for individuals and organizations that rely on technology. By understanding the types of cyber threats and the measures that can be taken to protect against these threats, individuals and organizations.

As a 30-year practitioner in the field, that's actually a fairly good summary – and it took all of 4 seconds to write that up. This new weather pattern is going to be transformative in the coming years and it will be crucial for cybersecurity professionals to understand how it works, how to safely enable its use, how it could help controls be more seamless (and automated), and how it might enable higher velocity decision making across the cybersecurity industry.

1.2 A brief history of information security / cybersecurity: The early days of the internet

To understand the present, it is usually helpful to understand the past. The information security industry has evolved dramatically with the growth of hyper-connected Internet networks in the past 40 years – but it wasn't always this way.

ARPANET officially went live in 1969 when two computers exchanged messages with each other between UCLA and the Stanford Research Institute (Shedden, 2014). Famously, that message was supposed to be "LOGIN", but the system crashed after the first two letters were transmitted. So the first message sent between two networked computers was literally "LO."

In the 1970s-1980s, computer interconnectivity was still limited and most of the compute resources that had the ability to network continued to belong primarily to governments and research universities. In that timeframe "information security" was mostly about controlling who had access to those systems, and once logged in, limiting what those users were entitled to do with it (if that was even a consideration.)

The first known computer virus, the so called "Creeper System", was released in 1971 (Rouse, 2011). It was created as an experiment by BBN Technologies in the United States, and worked by filling up the hard drive of an infected computer so that it could no longer operate.

Between 1980 and 1990, ARPANET connectivity grew substantially. By 1990, there were approximately 300,000 computers connected to each other (Solarwinds, 2010).

Much of this connectivity utilized acoustic coupler modems, or dedicated circuits at universities and government agencies.

During this period of connected-computer growth, the first self-replicating computer virus was released in 1982. The "Elk Cloner" copied itself into the boot sector of floppy disks used in Apple II computers.

The very first network-aware self-replicating worm-virus was released on ARPANET in 1988 (Uhde, 2017). The "Morris worm" was the first program that could automatically exploit "buffer overflow" vulnerabilities and then copy itself onto networked systems to replicate and propagate itself. While the worm's author, Robert Tappan Morris (then graduate student at Cornell University) had only intended to use the worm to gauge the size of ARPANET, the speed with which it propagated caused significant world-wide disruptions. It also resulted in Mr. Morris becoming the first person in history to be convicted under the Computer Fraud and Abuse Act (CFAA) of 1986 in the United States. He was sentenced to three years of probation, 400 hours of community service, and fined $10,050.

Between 1990–2000, the number of networked systems skyrocketed. In 1993, the National Center for Supercomputing Applications (NCSA) released the NCSA Mosaic web browser. This first web-browser is largely considered the birth of the modern world-wide web (Internet.) Prior to the web-browser, most networked systems access was done through command-line interfaces or rudimentary graphical user interfaces. The web-browser allowed for text and images to be presented utilizing standardized protocols and formats. Also in 1993, hackers from around the world decided to meet in person in Las Vegas at the first annual Defcon Hackers Conference. Mainstream movies "Sneakers" in 1992 and "Hackers" in 1995 glorified and popularized the exciting world of unauthorized computer access.

During this phase of the Internet's growth, segmentation of networks by utilization of firewalls and hardening of computer operating systems became incredibly important. So too was the detection of attacks in progress – network intrusion detection systems (NIDS) became popular. The goal of information security at that time was predominantly to "keep the bad guys out" of Internet-connected private networks. As companies started creating and publishing websites, it also became important to scan systems, networks, and applications for vulnerabilities that could potentially be exploited by adversaries.

By the year 2000, it is estimated that 361,000,000 (IWS, 2023) people were using the Internet. While the number of hackers on the Internet at the time is unknown, the motivation for hacking during this prior decade was mostly for street credibility, fame, notoriety, to make a political point (hacktivism) or simply because "information wants to be free."

Worm-viruses were also now becoming a tangible threat to network and systems availability during this period. In May of 2000, the ILOVEYOU virus became one of the first to spead by tricking users into opening what appeared to be an innocent text file, which actually had a ".txt.vbs" file extension that tricked most due to Windows default settings hiding the additional ".vbs" from end users. It infected over 10 Million Windows computers that were attached to the Internet at the time. It deleted data on the computers it infected as well as caused network interruption given its propagation speed (Wikipedia, 2024b).

In July of 2021, another very impactful network-worm was released: The Code Red Worm. This worm propagated by infecting vulnerable Microsoft Internet Information Server (IIS) webservers using a buffer-overflow vulnerability. It was one of the first worms to use time-based triggers to continue releasing its varying payloads. First, it infected the webserver and defaced its content, and copied itself to other webservers. Then It launched denial-of-service attacks from infected machines. After that, it was programed to "sleep" (Wikipedia, 2024a).

The concept of Denial-of-Service (DoS) attacks that exhaust compute resources to deny service to end-users or systems dates back to 1974, when a then 13-year-old David Dennis, managed to shut down 31 PLATO terminals by writing a script that repeatedly sent a problematic command (Wikipedia, 2024a).

Distributed Denial-of-Service (DDoS) attacks that utilize many computers to overwhelm the resources of a specific target then emerged in the 1990's. One of the first documented DDoS attacks happened against Internet Service Provider, Panix, in 1996. At that time, an attacker devised a new type of attack that would send on overwhelming number of TCP "SYN" (synchronize) packets from hundreds of other servers and workstations, to the victim servers, effectively clogging up Panix' network for 36 hours (Davis, 2021).

Hacktivism evolved as a new type of politically motivated hacking threat around this time as well. Hacktivist's motivation was predominantly to use computer networks to embarrass, harass, or shut-down a person, business, or government agency that they ideologically disagreed with. This took on many forms, including phishing attacks to steal credentials, exploitation of application-level vulnerabilities to steal data or infiltrate networks, "doxing" (publishing embarrassing or otherwise secret emails, files, etc.), online protests and disinformation campaigns, hacking of corporate or government social media accounts, hijacking or defacing website content, and of course, DDoS attacks that would shut down the victim's Internet presence.

At the end of the decade, in 2010, Internet-connected users had grown from 361 Million to around 2 Billion (IWS, 2023). This explosive growth created entirely new online business models, record profitability, unprecedented convenience and productivity, but also a massive attack surface for a now exponentially growing set of adversaries to exploit.

Towards the end of this decade is also when monetary motivation entered the adversarial consciousness. This was a game-changing development that would have far reaching implications to cybersecurity risk management efforts. In 2007, the "Zeus" and "Gozi" Banking Trojan malware families were first observed in the wild (Cohen, 2019). Both had the ability to exploit end-user systems to steal credentials, spoof bank websites or forms, perform online banking account take-over and send out unauthorized money transfers. Later versions were capable of auto-exploitation of systems based on the operating system and/or browser versions they were interacting with. Many other banking trojans also entered the market, given the successes the Zeus and Gozi teams were seeing. These highly funded organized-criminal banking trojan teams continued expanding their list of exploitable banks for many years, but then something interesting happened – they figured out it was too hard to keep track of thousands of different bank's login and credentialing/money movement capabilities, and instead re-focused down to the top 50 global banks. This allowed them to scale the malware much more effectively.

1.3 New weather: Destructive malware

While cyberattacks were still being done solely for fame and glory, hacktivists continued hacking for political reasons, organized crime hacking continued to make them a ridiculous amount of money, and government agencies now entered the news for using cyber-weapons to further their own objectives. Perhaps the most famous use of a government created cyber-weapon was the STUXNET worm, which was discovered in 2010 (Zetter, 2014) but was clearly operating on systems in 2009. STUXNET was specifically designed to destroy centrifuges being used by Iranian scientists to further the Iranian nuclear program at the Natanz uranium enrichment plant. It's highly specialized and highly effective payload was deployed and re-deployed multiple times over a roughly 18-month window and destroyed or degraded thousands of uranium centrifuges. This clearly had a significant impact on the development of Iran's nuclear program.

Two years later, in August of 2012, Saudi Aramco was attacked by sophisticated malware that destroyed or wiped the hard drives of 35,000 systems across its operations (Rashid, 2015). A group calling itself "Cutting Sword of Justice" claimed responsibility for the attack. U.S. sources attributed that to Iran.

The macro trend at this point in history, was that all of the previously seen adversarial activity and threats continued to happen, but the sophistication associated with militaries getting comfortable with use of cyber-weapons outside of wartime operations was starting to emerge.

Many cybersecurity companies were using the term "unprecedented" between 2011 and 2012. The number of new vulnerabilities published per month was unprecedented. The hyper-connected Internet was expanding at an unprecedented scale. The number of successful attacks on companies, individuals, and agencies was unprecedented. The use of cyber-weapons by militaries, publicly, was also unprecedented.

For the first time, the Verizon Data Breach Investigation Report of 2012 (Verizon, 2012) included attacks attributed to nation-state actors. It indicated that of 8% of breaches Verizon responded to that year were attributed to Nation States.

Fast forward a few years and something truly unprecedented happened in 2015. In February 2015, the Russian antivirus/cyberthreat company, Kaspersky, published a detailed analysis of a nation-state actor group they called "The Equation Group." (Kaspersky, 2015) Their analysis published 14 years' worth of trojans, techniques, and tradecraft associated with this actor group. They linked Equation Group to the Stuxnet Group and the Flame and Duqu malware. Although the Kaspersky report did not come out and say it, it is largely believed that the United States' National Security Agency (NSA) is synonymous the Equation Group (Zetter, 2015).

This is interesting in of itself, but then in August 2016, a group calling themselves The Shadow Brokers published a list of files, and some samples of malware and trojan-horse software it attributed to the NSA's Tailored Access Operations (TAO) group (Kumar, 2016a). The group was offering the tools at auction for 1 Million Bitcoins (worth approximately $568 Million at the time.) At this time, "Most cyber security experts, as well as former NSA contractor and whistleblower Edward Snowden, believes Russia to be behind the NSA hack" (Khandelwal, 2016).

After allegedly failing to get asking price, in December of 2016 (Kumar, 2016b), The Shadow Brokers then offered different stolen Equation Group (NSA) tools for sale on a dark-web site, ranging from 1 to 100 Bitcoins each. The exploit named "EternalBlue" was part of this auction. This is important, because that exploit was utilized in the devastating WannaCry ransomware attack that infected more than 200,000 computers in 150 countries between Friday May 12th and Monday May 15th, 2017 (ABC News, 2017).

The WannaCry ransomware attack was indiscriminate and impacted many type of organizations. However, perhaps the most concerning was that it affected at least 80 out of 236 NHS trusts (medical care facilities) in the U.K., impacting patient care and causing significant disruption to healthcare services. According to the U.K. National Audit Office's report on the attack, "Investigation: WannaCry cyber-attack and the NHS (Auditor General, 2017)," approximately one-third of NHS trusts in England were affected, with some hospitals forced to divert patients to other facilities. Page 11 of that report stated that "Since the attack occurred on a Friday this caused minimal disruption to primary care services, which tend to be closed over the weekend. Twenty of the 25 infected acute trusts managed to continue treating urgent and emergency patients throughout the weekend. However, five – in London, Essex, Hertfordshire, Hampshire and Cumbria – had to divert patients to other accident and emergency departments, and a further two needed outside help to continue treating patients. By 16 May only two hospitals were still diverting patients."

It is well-known in medical circles that the quality of care provided at a hospital also affects patient outcomes. Hospitals with lower quality care have been shown to have higher patient mortality rates. It is very clear that WannaCry caused significant communications, network, and systems outage at these hospitals, which clearly caused a severe impact of quality of the care they could provide. The world will likely never know how many patients would have died that weekend due to lack of care they otherwise may have received and how many hero doctors and nurses acted with haste to ensure that didn't happen.

The report "A retrospective impact analysis of the WannaCry cyberattack on the NHS", published in Nature Digital Medicine in 2019 (Ghafur, S. Kristensen, S. Honeyford, K. Martin, G. Darzi, A. Aylin, P., 2019), found no significant increase in mortality rates among patients treated at hospitals affected by the attack. However, the study did find that the attack had a significant negative impact on hospital activity, with a decrease in the number of outpatient appointments, elective admissions, and emergency admissions. What is clear is that even if patients didn't die as a result of the ransomware attack, they certainly could have.

On December 18th and 19th, 2017, the U.S. Government and then the U.K. Government publicly attributed the WannaCry ransomware attack to North Korean actors "The Lazarus Group"(Ahmad, 2017).

Let's summarize this series of events – Allegedly, the U.S. Government created and then left some zero-day cyber weapons somewhere that the Russian government could steal them. Those tools then wound up for sale in a Russian speaking Dark Web criminal forum. They were then, allegedly, sold to North Korean actors who then used them to create the WannaCry ransomware worm that shut down 300,000+ systems around the globe and came dangerously close to killing people in the U.K. when dozens of NHS hospitals were simultaneously shut down. The U.S. and the U.K. government then publicly attributed WannaCry to the North Korean state. Could you make up a more "Tom Clancy-like" story?

1.4 New weather: Crypto-ransomware

Meanwhile, as many governments were honing their use of cyber-weapons within military doctrine, organized crime was also seeing absolutely unprecedented success. In November 2022, Global Market Insights (GMI, 2022) released a report estimating that the global annual market value for cybersecurity products and services is approximately **$200 Billion** and is expected to grow to $900 Billion (10–15% CAGR) by 2032. However, As reported by Cybercrime Magazine on November 13, 2020, the venture fund Cybersecurity Ventures estimated the global cost of cybercrime at **$6 Trillion** in 2021, growing to $10.5 Trillion (15% CAGR) annually by 2025 (Morgan, 2020). The amount of funding that has gone into highly organized cyber-criminal groups is absolutely staggering.

Let's recap again. Adversaries originally attacked computers on the Internet for fame and glory. Then they figured out there was money to be made and started stealing personally identifiable information and selling it on the dark web. Around that time, it was also useful to attack networks to make a political point (hacktivism.) Next, there was roughly a decade of attacker focus on eCommerce / Banking trojans – account takeover and then illegal purchases or money movement through very advanced trojan software. Around that time, when attack tools were getting very sophisticated, nation-states were also using them to achieve military, intelligence, or economic objectives. Following in the footsteps of the various "data wiper" attacks successfully launched (allegedly) by the U.S., Iran, and North Korea, organized crime then birthed a new variant of that type of attack – ransomware.

Ransomware has been exceedingly successful business model to the dozens-to-hundreds of organized crime families that have been using it this decade. In the early days, tactics utilized by these groups focused on infecting as many devices as possible and then encrypting key documents or folders and demanding a ransom payment from the user, in exchange for a decryption key. This was a low-profit, high-turn business model (e.g. take a little from a lot of people.) However, the complexities of managing such a large robot-network of infected devices led to a re-shaping of the business model into one of high-profit, low-turn (e.g. take a lot from a smaller group of victims.)

The change in business model very quickly led to extreme income earned by holding corporate networks hostage and demanding the companies pay a ransom to become operational again. Many very high-profile companies fell victim.

This evolution in business tactics has created an extremely well-funded set of criminal adversaries and criminal partner organizations. As an example, GandCrab was a prolific ransomware-as-a-service operator between January 2018 and June 2019. In a surprise announcement in the summer of 2019, they "retired" after reportedly earning **$2B in Bitcoin** (Cimpanu 2019) ransom payments. While this spectacular number is widely thought to be an exaggeration, anti-malware company BitDefender "estimate[s] GandCrab has claimed more than 1.5 million victims around the world, both home users and corporations" (Botezatu, 2019)

GandCrab was also one of the first ransomware gangs to 1) realize their malware can attract a lot of "affiliates" who will carry out the actual attacks on behalf of the gang for a cut of the profit 2) implement "great customer service" to dramatically increase the ability to receive payments from victims, teaching them how to pay, walking them through the process, and even offering technical support and 3) partner with "Data Recovery Companies" to mask payment details in order to limit corporate reputation risk when making a payment (Botezatu, 2019).

Then in May of 2019, Maze ransomware quickly became one of the most prevalent and successful competitors to GandCrab. They were the first to partner with LockBit and Ragnar Locker teams to form a "Ransomware cartel" (TripWire, 2020). Maze was also one of the first to publicly publish stolen data if the victim didn't pay the ransom by their deadline. According to Heimdal Security (Dinu, 2022), some of their high-profile victims included Allied Universal, Hammersmith Research, Xerox, Cognizant, and LG Electronics.

In September 2019, cyber researchers witnessed the birth of yet another new group, Sodinokibi / REvil which initially caused major disruption to hundreds of dental practices (Ilascu, 2019) as well as 22 municipalities in Texas (Allyn, 2019). It is thought that this was a "re-branding" of much of the GandCrab ecosystem. On New Year's Eve, 2019, Travelex had many systems encrypted, prompting a shut-down of their world-wide network (Tidy, 2020). It is widely speculated that the attack was per-petrated by Sodinokibi / REvil. The gang initially asked for a $6 Million payment, and Travelex reportedly (Isaac, Ostroff, Hope, 2020) paid out $2.3 Million in Bitcoin to re-gain control of their network.

On November 3, 2020, Maze then announced their retirement. The highly orga-nized and resourced cartel claimed to have netted at least $100 Million (Sjouwer-man, 2020).

Given many corporate cyber-insurance policies typically cover the cost of ransom payments, a game-changing pivot in targeting started happening in 2021. During a fas-cinating interview with REvil's 'Unknown' actor on March 15, 2021, RecordedFuture's Dmitry Smilyanets asked 'Unknown' about the cartel's targeting of cyber insurers, so-liciting a reponse that ". . . this is one of the tastiest morsels. Especially to hack the insurers first – to get their customer base and work in a targeted way from there. And after you go through the list, then hit the insurer themselves" (Smilyanets, 2021).

In May of 2021, CNA Insurance fell victim to ransomware and paid a whopping ransom of $40 Million, according to Bloomberg (Mehrotra, Turton, 2021). The attack was reportedly conducted using "Phoenix CryptoLocker" (Gatlan, 2021), potentially by actor group "Evil Corp" Spadafora, 2021). At this point, it became very clear in the in-dustry that corporate Cyber Insurers were indeed being targeted. It also represented yet another interesting pivot in attacker tactics. This time, attackers broke into the network as usual, found the data they were looking for, exfiltrated that data, but then also found the backups of the data and deleted those, prior to detonating the malware. The ransom tactic then used "double extortion" to entice the company to pay in order to get control of their systems back, but also to pay to stop the gang from publicly releasing the data.

One of the most famous ransomware incidents also happened in May of 2021 – the Colonial Pipeline breach. This was notable not only because a large ransom was paid (nearly $5 Million) to the DarkSide gang (Ainsley, Collier, 2021), but also because the real-world impact of the incident was so high. Close to half of the U.S. East Coast temporarily ran out of fuel supply normally provided through the Colonial Pipeline.

In February of 2022, global insurer Aon also experienced a ransomware attack, but was able to promptly respond to it, stating that the incident "has not had a signifi-cant impact on the Company's operations" (Fadilpasic, 2022).

In May of 2023, the CL0P ransomware group (also known as TA505) moved to the front of the line as one of the most prolific groups, having compromised thousands of companies incredibly quickly. CL0P took many of the tactics used by LockBit, includ-ing the use of zero-day vulnerabilities to compromise targeted corporate networks. Among others, CL0P famously reverse engineered a corporate managed file-transfer supplier called MOVEit, discovering a remote command execution vulnerability that was previously unknown. Many companies had MOVEit installed and exposed to the Internet in order to move files to and from other suppliers or companies. This expo-sure led to a massive campaign to compromise all of those companies, install ransomware, and extort payments. CSO Online (Constantin, 2023) published that "NCC Group has recorded 502 ransomware-related attacks in July, a 16% increase from the 434 seen in June, but a 154% rise from the 198 attacks seen in July 2022. The CL0P gang was responsible for 171 (34%) of the 502 attacks while LockBit came in second with 50 attacks (10%)."

Later, in June of 2023, the U.S. Cybersecurity and Infrastructure Security Agency (CISA 2023) reported that "Beyond CL0P ransomware, TA505 is known for frequently changing malware and driving global trends in criminal malware distribution. Considered to be one of the largest phishing and malspam distributors worldwide, TA505 is estimated to have compromised more than 3,000 U.S.-based organizations and 8,000 global organizations."

1.5 New weather: Deep-fakes

It is hard to believe that as high velocity and high efficacy as ransomware is there are still many different types of new cyberthreats looming around the corner. While the ransomware gangs were making their millions off of Bitcoin and other crypto-payments, on July 11, 2017 University of Washington researchers announced (Langston, 2017) that they had successfully created a very believable deep-fake video of U.S. President Obama, utilizing hundreds of audio clips, photos, and videos of him. The computer-vision researchers, funded by Samsung, Google, Facebook, Intel and the UW Animation Research Labs, fed the audio into an algorithm that could create a synthetic voice, then used the photos and videos to create every conceivable facial expression and movement in a 3D video model. Using these models, the group was able to feed it text of what they wanted the video of the president to say, and created 4 very realistic, but fake videos of the President saying thing he never actually said.

There is generally a repeatable lifecycle of cyberthreat development. First, a group researches some new form of technology. Then that technology gets implemented. Then it gets adopted by companies and consumers. Then the threat groups figure out how to exploit it and/or use it for their criminal monetization or nation-state objective purposes. Then there is a cat and mouse game until some groups win, some groups lose, and the technology gets stronger and more secure or it fails to adapt and users stop using it. Between 2017 and 2019, there was a fair amount of theoretical discussion about what deep-fakes could do to the Internet, but threat groups hadn't really exploited it yet.

That changed in March of 2019 according to the Wall Street Journal (Stupp, 2019), when fraudsters, for the first time we know of, used a CEO's voice-clone to trick a subsidiary CEO into thinking he was speaking with his boss, and convincing him to subsequently transfer €220,000 out of the company. In this case, the story made the news, but the company's name was kept out of it.

In the first half of 2020, cybercriminals used an AI voice-clone deep-fake to fool a branch manager at a Hong Kong company whose headquarters was in Japan into a $35 million fraud scheme (Brewster, 2021). This was eerily similar to the March 2019 motus-operandi. Similarly, the companies involved were also shielded from the press.

By 2023, this threat moved from "difficult to execute and not really very believable" to "trivial to execute in a highly believable way", prompting the U.S. Federal Trade Commission to release an advisory on March 20, 2023 entitled *"Scammers use AI to enhance their family emergency schemes"* (Puig, 2023). Scammers are finding it very easy to trick grandparents into believing they are talking to their grandchild, having scooped up TikTok or other social media videos of the child and then feeding the audio into very cheap to use, but very high-quality voice-cloning tools.

While it will always be easier to trick a human into believing something than it is to trick a computer into believing something, and that is where attackers went first, it is also clear that this same technology is being utilized to fool voice authentication systems. Researchers from all around the world have already started testing this. As an example, on February 23rd, 2023, Joseph Cox wrote an article on Motherboard – Tech by Vice (Cox, 2023), detailing his ability to clone his own voice and then successfully authenticate to Lloyds Bank in the United Kingdom. Several other global financial institutions have had consumers test their own accounts in similar ways since then. It is worth noting that most of the high-profile claims by researchers at present also called in using the phone they had on record with the financial firm, and in some cases, also had to provide other identifiers. However, it is clear this is a risk that needs better mitigation.

Unlike many other social-engineering attacks, deepfake video and deepfake audio are likely to shake the root of trust on the Internet in the coming years, demonstrably adding to the threats of fake-news, fake-evidence, fake-sources, etc. and will create the need for better content provenance, video and audio source tagging, synthetic voice/video detection, and the ability to go the other way and prove a video or audio recording *isn't* a deepfake, when it claims someone did something they claim they didn't do.

1.6 New weather: Generative AI and Large Language Models

This author strongly believes that the public availability of Generative AI and Large Language Models (LLMs) is potentially the most transformative technology advancement since the NCSA Mosaic Web Browser moved connected networks from command-line only to a Graphical User Interface, thereby launching what we now know of as the Internet. We cover AI advantages and risks in detail in Chapter 6. It is clear that traditional Model Risk Management processes that can detect or manage bias, decision transparency, accuracy, model validation, model use monitoring, model input/output testing, training data security, and a number of other components still apply to LLMs, there are new things that need to be considered. For example, both traditional AI models and LLMs can make factual errors, but LLMs are more prone to generating creative and plausible but entirely fabricated text, even when prompted with factual queries. This "hallucination" (or technically, a confabulation) can mislead users and undermine the model's reliability.

One potential mitigation strategy for the hallucination problem is to use Transfer Learning (Hosna, Merry, Gyalmo, Alom, Aung, Zim, 2022) to teach an LLM about a specific topic (e.g. how insurance claims work) and then limit its ability to answer questions that are not related to that topic. Another is to have a human interpret results from an LLM prior to those results driving an action (AKA make the human decision-making process significantly faster but keep the human in the loop.)

Another big difference between traditional Data Models and LLMs is the size and scale of the training data. Both model types can perpetuate biases present in their training data. However, LLMs with massive datasets are arguably more susceptible to reflecting societal biases and stereotypes due to the sheer volume and variety of their training data.

Additionally, understanding how traditional AI models reach their decisions can be challenging, but LLMs pose an even greater explainability hurdle. Their black-box nature and complex internal processes make it difficult to trace how they generate outputs, hindering efforts to address potential biases or errors.

LLMs trained on vast datasets may also inadvertently generate text containing sensitive or private information gleaned from that data, causing privacy breaches or security concerns.

From a cyber-risk standpoint, LLMs have huge potential to accelerate the speed with which an analyst can react to a given threat or attack. They could potentially automate quite a lot of things that humans currently have to do manually. There are many positive cyberdefense use-cases to be explored.

However, LLMs also have the potential to learn or teach things usually restricted to militaries with strong international treaties and doctrines around them (e.g. how to build a nuclear weapon or how to create a human genome virus that only infects a certain demographic.) Consumer grade versions can also potentially leak corporate data, accelerate adversarial malware development, accelerate disinformation / information operations, and a number of other new risks.

For deeper analysis and additional mitigation strategies, many AI Safety / LLM Risk Management frameworks are currently emerging or already available in this space. Some examples include the Future of Life's Asilomar AI Principles (Future of Life, 2017), the U.S. National Institute for Standards and Technology (NIST) AI Risk Management Framework (NIST, 2023), Google's Responsible AI Framework (Google, 2023), and Microsoft's responsible AI framework (Microsoft, 2024).

1.7 New weather: Quantum computing

Quantum computing holds the potential to revolutionize many fields with its ability to perform calculations in fundamentally different ways than classical computers. Given the massive information storage of a single qubit in a quantum computer vs a single bit in a classical computer, quantum computers have the potential, over time, to be able to calculate thousands, tens of thousands, or even millions of times faster than current classic compute resources. While still fairly nascent, this has the potential to accelerate a large number of things that could be highly beneficial to the world. Some examples include simulating complex molecules and materials, designing new materials with specific properties, optimizing investment portfolios, solving complex optimization problems, and even creation of new AI algorithms.

However, like any other new technology, it can and will be used by legitimate organizations as well as nefarious adversaries. Perhaps the most concerning use of Quantum Computing is its potential ability to break our current asymmetric encryption algorithms. Consider that many governments around the world have the capability to record and store SSL/TLS encrypted Internet traffic. If they were able to decrypt all of that at a later date, this could have tremendous intelligence and counter-intelligence benefits (and risks.)

Estimating a precise timeframe for when quantum computers will be able to crack current asymmetric crypto algorithms is challenging due to ongoing research and technological advancements in both quantum computing and cryptography. However, it is clear that it will happen at some point. Various experts give diverse estimations, ranging from several years to a couple of decades, for when large-scale quantum computers capable of breaking asymmetric algorithms like Rivest-Shamir-Adleman (RSA), Elliptic Curve Cryptography (ECC), and Diffie-Hellman become a reality.

The U.S. National Institute of Standards and Technology (NIST) has set a timeline of 2024 to finalize post-quantum cryptography (PQC) standards to prepare for this potential vulnerability. On July 5th, 2022, NIST announced the first four approved algorithms (NIST, 2022): CRYSTALS-Kyber, CRYSTALS-Dilithium, FALCON, and SPHINCS+.

Academic Publisher "Scientific Research" published their Journal of Quantum Information Science Volume 13, No. 2 entitled "Navigating the Quantum Threat Landscape: Addressing Classical Cybersecurity Challenges" in June of 2023 (Sokol, 2023). Among other excellent facts, they shared that:

> In September 2022, as an extension of the national security memorandum released in May 2022, the [U.S. National Security Agency] (NSA) announced that [National Security Systems] (NSS) customers are to start migrating towards approved quantum-resistant algorithms – **CRYSTALS-Kyber and CRYSTALS-Dilithium – immediately** (NSA, 2022). The agency expects to fully use these algorithms by 2035. However, it is requiring all NSS services, equipment, and operating systems to initially support [Commercial National Security Algorithm Suite] (CSNA) 2.0 by 2025–2030, and shift to exclusive use of CSNA 2.0 by 2030–2033.

Clearly the U.S. and most other governments are taking the threat seriously. The good news is that these new quantum resistant algorithms will run on classic computers. However, they will need to be adopted by the technology supplier community and then by end-users. This will be a multi-year and even potentially multi-decade process the whole Internet community will need to participate in. This is why it is so important to start as soon as practical. Every crypto provider will need to be upgraded and every TLS / digital certificate will need to be replaced.

1.8 Risk management frameworks

Before we lead into Cybersecurity Risk Management, context is very important here. While it is very difficult to be precise with this measurement, we previously covered that in the year 2000, it is estimated that **361 Million** (IWS, 2024) people were using the Internet. As of December 2022, Internet World Stats estimates that **5.5 Billion** (IWS, 2024) people, or 69% of the world's population, use the Internet, slightly more than two decades later.

The number of devices which require protecting has also been growing at an absolutely staggering rate during that timeframe. The "Internet of Things" by itself (aka. devices that are not traditional desktop/laptop/servers) has grown to **15.14 Billion** devices in 2023 and is expected to be **29.42 Billion** by 2023, according to Statista (Statista, 2023). Further, according to Statista, the average number of devices and connections per user, globally, was 2.4 in 2018, which rose to 3.6 in 2023 (Statista, 2020). North American devices and connections in 2023 was estimated at a mind-blowing 13.4 (Statista, 2020) per person.

Please take a mental pause to consider all of the variables that we've described so far, and a few new ones, which are all important to managing cyber-risk:
- The world is hyper-connected in ways never contemplated by the human race and the vast majority of people on the planet not only connect to the Internet, but do so using multiple devices that need to be secured
- Most governments now have cyber tools as part of their military doctrine in some way. Some governments actively utilize sophisticated cyberweapons during peacetime to gather intelligence, create disinformation and sow civil unrest, evade sanctions, steal intellectual property, commit fraud, influence an election, or prepare the virtual battlefield for use in potential war-time objectives.
- Cybercriminal groups are funded in the hundreds of millions of dollars. They can afford things like 24x7 call-centers, offshore software development teams, online upskilling and learning management platforms, R&D teams, recruiters, affiliate partnerships and affiliate management programs, bullet-proof dark-web hosting (Norton, 2018) capabilities that law enforcement can't take down, hyper-anonymization services, military grade encryption and decryption capabilities, and even Customer Rela-

tionship Management platforms to keep tabs on which of their affiliates are grooming which corporate victims so that they attack in coordination. Groups with this much funding greatly resemble the budget and organization structure of your typical large company. Many of them have already surpassed the capabilities of younger Nation-State cyber actors.
- The technologies we need to secure are being invented and adopted at a pace never before seen in the history of mankind
- Countries and companies are digitalizing rapidly, reducing technology debt and adopting the newest, software-defined technologies
- Countries and companies are highly dependent on their supply-chains. Virtually none produce everything they need to operate.
- Artificial Intelligence capabilities and adoption rates are growing at an explosive rate, and can be used for good or evil.
- Quantum computing has the potential to make compute calculations 100,000, 1,000,000 or 10,000,000 times faster than current classical computers.

With these factors in mind, consider that one of the oldest and common equations for describing cybersecurity or information security risk is SANS' definition (SANS, 2012):

Risk = (threat x vulnerabilities x probability x impact)/countermeasures

Equations like this are very useful for Risk prioritization. However, to calculate the risk of something like "what is the risk my company will be down for multiple days/weeks because ransomware encrypted all of my key systems", one would have to understand that there is a "kill chain" associated with how ransomware works, a set of controls that could stop its effectiveness or fail to do so at each stage of that kill chain, and the humans, systems, and networks being attacked may have multiple vulnerabilities that could impact the probability of success. This is one of the things that makes calculation of true cyber risk very difficult – each variable has multiple variables, and they are changing constantly.

Let's say that ransomware happens in an eight step kill-chain:
1) Initial Access 2) Execution 3) Persistence 4) Escalation 5) Evasion 6) Collection 7) Exfiltration 8) Detonation.

The ransomware "threat" is likely high if your institution is profitable, connected to the Internet, and highly dependent on IT systems for its operations. But that threat is certainly higher if there is specific targeting of your industry vertical, like when multiple cartels were targeting dentists, hospitals, or insurance companies in specific campaigns between 2020–2023.

"Vulnerability" can take many forms at each stage of the kill-chain. In the "initial access" phase, users may have weak or shared passwords, or the institution may not have implemented multi-factor authentication (MFA), which could increase vulnerabilities associated with workforce account takeover. The same workforce could be vulnerable to thinking they are talking to the IT Help Desk, causing them to give away their credentials even if the institution used MFA. But the systems themselves could also have unpatched Internet-accessible Remote Code Execution vulnerabilities that could allow an adversary to compromise them and gain initial access that way. "Vulnerability" in this context has to be thought through broadly across people, process, and technology vulnerabilities.

"Probability" is closely related to threat and vulnerability – aka is the risk "rare", "happens occasionally", "happens sometimes", "happens frequently", or "happens constantly". All of those require thought about the inherent threats being faced, and the current state of play.

"Impact" is something one would think is fairly straight forward. But it actually requires knowledge of enterprise materiality for a Risk like ransomware to be calculated. For example, depending on the institution's size, scale, and profitability, losing $100 Million might be acceptable, or it could be devastating. What is a "big number" to the institution? From an integrity standpoint, what are impacts if your data isn't just unavailable, but its been corrupted? From an availability standpoint, if the institution could have all IT systems rebuilt from scratch in an hour, then the impact of them being compromised with ransomware might be relatively small. But if it would take a month to rebuild all systems, the impact could be devastating. Also consider the impact from a loss of trust / reputation impact standpoint – how many customer records stolen or deleted would be catastrophic? Impacts across business lines and to the institution as a whole must be thought through deliberately.

Finally, "countermeasures" is basically a calculation of the strength of the control environment against this specific kill-chain/threat.

In the "initial access" phase, if users were highly educated, skeptical, and utilized MFA for all systems access; and the inventory of all systems and assets exposed to the Internet has high integrity; and all Internet facing systems were rapidly patched so they were free from publicly known vulnerabilities, and application code was equally free from exploitable vulnerabilities; then these countermeasures could be quite strong at this phase.

At the "execution", "persistence" and "escalation" phases of the attack, if there are multiple layers of antivirus/antimalware in place; systems are hardened/configured to a secure baseline; proxy servers block executables being downloaded from the Internet from internal systems; firewalls prevent direct egress to the Internet without going through proxies; most users do not have privileged access; privileged accounts are "vaulted" and MFA is required to check those accounts out; and the network is well instrumented with 24x7 monitoring and threat hunting, then these countermeasures could be very strong.

Lastly at the "collection", "exfiltration", and "detonation" phases, if the institution has some form of event correlation and lateral movement (internal system to internal system) detection; some form of Security Orchestration and Automated Response (SOAR) system; well-tuned Data-Loss Prevention (DLP) technologies in place; proxies that block access to uncategorized / very new websites; and well tested, immutable and/or offline backups of all critical data and systems, then these countermeasures may work well to stop the threat.

As one can see, managing cyber risk can be a complex endeavor. However, in order to ensure countermeasures are as strong and as comprehensive as possible against a wide array of threats, there are many very excellent standards and frameworks that have emerged.

General-purpose Cybersecurity Frameworks:
NIST Cybersecurity Framework (CSF): Developed by the U.S. National Institute of Standards and Technology (NIST), the CSF is a voluntary, flexible framework offering best practices for identifying, protecting, detecting, responding to, and recovering from cyber incidents. It's highly customizable and applicable to organizations of all sizes and industries.

ISO 27001: This international standard specifies requirements for establishing, implementing, maintaining, and continually improving an information security management system (ISMS). It provides a structured approach to managing information security risks and ensuring compliance with legal and regulatory requirements.

CIS Controls: The Center for Internet Security (CIS) Controls framework consists of prioritized, actionable steps for mitigating common cyber threats. It's known for its focus on practical, cost-effective measures and is popular among smaller organizations.

Industry-specific frameworks:
SOC 2: Service Organization Controls 2 provides a standardized reporting framework for service providers who handle customer data. It's prevalent in cloud computing and other technology-related industries.

PCI DSS: The Payment Card Industry Data Security Standard (PCI DSS) focuses on securing payment card information. It's mandatory for organizations that store, process, or transmit credit card data.

HIPAA: The Health Insurance Portability and Accountability Act (HIPAA) protects the privacy of patient health information in the U.S. healthcare industry. HIPAA compliance is often achieved through frameworks like HITRUST CSF.

Additional frameworks:
MITRE ATT&CK: This framework catalogs different tactics and techniques attackers use, helping organizations anticipate and defend against specific threats.

COBIT: The Control Objectives for Information and related Technology (COBIT) framework provides a holistic approach to IT governance and aligns IT goals with business objectives.

To provide the most complete and comprehensive control / countermeasure coverage, many organizations assess their risks using one framework, but then supplement by mapping to and/or implementing additional frameworks. For example, a large scale technology provider who is constantly under attack by nation-state adversaries who are attempting to poison the code they provide to customers or subscribers, may implement the NIST CSF thoroughly, comply with PCI DSS where there is Debit/Credit card data, assess themselves using SOC2 in order to provide assurance to customers, and then utilize the MITRE ATT&CK framework to continuously assess and re-assess their abilities to adapt to advanced threats whose tactics change at high velocity. They may also subscribe to multiple external threat intelligence services that map to MITRE ATT&CK to ensure they have the latest on which adversaries are targeting them and which tactics, tools, and techniques are typically observed when they do.

1.9 Importance of public-private partnerships to manage cyber risk

This brings us to another simple rule of Cybersecurity Risk Management – it's a team sport. Given the volume and velocity of the threat, the constant change in the technology landscape, the accelerating capabilities of artificial intelligence, and the sheer number of attackers and groups involved, the best programs are highly threat informed, operationally collaborative with partner organizations and agencies, and consume standards-based automated threat intelligence that not only specifies observed tactics, tools, and techniques (TTPs), but also courses-of-action (CoAs) that can be taken automatically.

The concept of public-private partnership to combat cyberthreats is not new. In fact, on May 22, 1998 then U.S. President Bill Clinton signed Presidential Decision Directive 63 (PDD-63) (White House, 1998), which established the foundation for the creation of public-private Information Sharing and Analysis Centers (ISACs.) Since then, the U.S. Department of Homeland Security (DHS) has established 16 critical infrastructure sectors (CISA, 2024) and assigned a sector-specific agency to each:
1. **Chemical Sector** | Lead Agency: Department of Homeland Security (DHS) Chemical Facility Anti-Terrorism Program (CFATP)
2. **Commercial Facilities Sector** | Lead Agency: DHS Cybersecurity and Infrastructure Security Agency (CISA)
3. **Communications Sector** | Lead Agencies: DHS CISA and Federal Communications Commission (FCC)

4. **Critical Manufacturing Sector** | Lead Agency: DHS CISA
5. **Dams Sector** | Lead Agencies: DHS CISA and Federal Emergency Management Agency (FEMA)
6. **Defense Industrial Base (DIB) Sector** | Lead Agency: DHS CISA
7. **Emergency Services Sector** | Lead Agency: DHS CISA
8. **Energy Sector** | Lead Agencies: DHS CISA and Department of Energy (DOE)
9. **Financial Services Sector** | Lead Agencies: DHS CISA and Department of Treasury (Treasury)
10. **Food and Agriculture Sector** | Lead Agencies: DHS CISA and Department of Agriculture (USDA)
11. **Government Facilities Sector** | Lead Agencies: DHS CISA and General Services Administration (GSA)
12. **Healthcare and Public Health Sector** | Lead Agencies: DHS CISA and Department of Health and Human Services (HHS)
13. **Information Technology Sector** | Lead Agency: DHS CISA
14. **Nuclear Reactors, Materials, and Waste Sector** | Lead Agencies: DHS CISA and Nuclear Regulatory Commission (NRC)
15. **Transportation Systems Sector** | Lead Agencies: DHS CISA and Department of Transportation (DOT)
16. **Water and Wastewater Systems Sector** | Lead Agencies: DHS CISA and Environmental Protection Agency (EPA)

Ten of the 16 now have dedicated Information Sharing and Analysis Centers that allow sector-participants to rapidly share information about attacks, attackers, TTPs, CoAs, countermeasures and best-practices. This collective collaboration helps defenders "fight as a team", while also making it harder for the adversary to utilize the same technique on more than one victim institution at a time. Many of those ISACs have moved from U.S.-centric organizations to truly global organizations, better representing their participant institutions.

The U.S. Cybersecurity Information Sharing Act of 2015 (Congress, 2015) also created the concept of an Information Sharing and Analysis Organization (ISAO.) ISAOs can be made up of any affinity group that wants to share cyberthreat information with the protections afforded to them through the CISA-2015 provisions.

It is also quite a good idea to build relationships with Federal (e.g. FBI, Secret Service, NCA, MI5) and International (e.g. Interpol) Law enforcement. This can be very helpful day to day from an operational collaboration perspective but can also greatly improve response activities during an incident where an institution needs to involve them. Many federal agencies have formal information sharing or collaboration programs that institutions can elect to participate in. The FBI's Infragard (FBI, 2024) program is one such program, but there are many, many more.

Additionally, there are many commercially available solutions for tracking actor groups, TTPs, IoCs, and CoAs. Many of these services also watch for company-specific chatter on Dark-Web forums, data dump sites, or social media. Consumption of actionable cyberthreat intelligence can allow for early-warning of attacks about to happen, or the need to elevate monitoring or detection capabilities against a specific threat. This can have a dramatic effect on the management of the potential impacts of a given threat, while also improving the industry resilience posture as a whole.

1.10 Conclusion

In summary, as of the writing of this text, the internet is a really bad neighborhood. Fame-and-glory seekers, script "kiddies", password crackers, fraudsters, hacktivists, single criminals, highly organized criminal syndicates, and Nation-states are all utilizing advances in software and artificial intelligence to attack other countries, agencies, corporations, communities, and individuals. The tools they utilize have also gotten orders of magnitude easier to use, easier to purchase, and at the same time, much more high velocity, effective, and automated.

In order to comprehensively manage cybersecurity risk in such a high threat environment, companies must implement controls and countermeasures, based on well-established international frameworks.

Lastly, no one company, institution, or agency can do this alone. The importance of maintaining a threat-informed defense through consumption of external cyberthreat information sharing data cannot be underestimated.

References

ABC News. (2017, May 15). *A timeline of the WannaCry cyberattack.* https://abcnews.go.com/US/timeline-wannacry-cyberattack/story?id=47416785

Ahmad, T. (2017, Dec 19). *Foreign Office Minister condemns North Korean actor for WannaCry attacks.* Gov.Uk. https://www.gov.uk/government/news/foreign-office-minister-condemns-north-korean-actor-for-wannacry-attacks

Ainsley, J. Collier, K. (2021, May 13). *Colonial Pipeline paid ransomware hackers $5 million, U.S. official says.* NBC News. https://www.nbcnews.com/tech/security/colonial-pipeline-paid-ransomware-hackers-5-million-u-s-official-n1267286

Allyn, B. (2019, Aug 20). *22 Texas Towns Hit With Ransomware Attack In 'New Front' Of Cyberassault.* NPR. https://www.npr.org/2019/08/20/752695554/23-texas-towns-hit-with-ransomware-attack-in-new-front-of-cyberassault

Auditor General. (2017, Oct). *Investigation: WannaCry.*

Botezatu, B. (2019, Jun 17). *Good riddance, GandCrab! We're still fixing the mess you left behind.* Bitdefender. https://www.bitdefender.com/blog/labs/good-riddance-gandcrab-were-still-fixing-the-mess-you-left-behind/

Brewster, T. (2021, Oct 14). Fraudsters Cloned Company Director's Voice In $35 Million Heist, Police Find. https://www.forbes.com/sites/thomasbrewster/2021/10/14/huge-bank-fraud-uses-deep-fake-voice-tech-to-steal-millions/?sh=19e12c7a7559

Cimpanu, C. (2019, Jun 1). GandCrab ransomware operation says it's shutting down. ZDNet. https://www.zdnet.com/article/gandcrab-ransomware-operation-says-its-shutting-down/

CISA. (2023, Jun 07). #StopRansomware: CL0P Ransomware Gang Exploits CVE-2023-34362 MOVEit Vulnerability. Cybersecurity & Infrastructure Security Agency (CISA). https://www.cisa.gov/news-events/cybersecurity-advisories/aa23-158a

CISA. (2024, Apr 15). Critical Infrastructure Security and Resilience. Cybersecurity & Infrastructure Security Agency (CISA). https://www.cisa.gov/topics/critical-infrastructure-security-and-resilience

Cohen, R. (2019, Aug 09). Banking Trojans: A Reference Guide to the Malware Family Tree. F5 Labs. https://www.f5.com/labs/learning-center/banking-trojans-a-reference-guide-to-the-malware-family-tree

Congress. (2015). S.754 – To improve cybersecurity in the United States through enhanced sharing of information about cybersecurity threats, and for other purposes. United States Congress. https://www.congress.gov/bill/114th-congress/senate-bill/754

Constantin, L. (2023, Aug 23). *Clop ransomware dominates ransomware space after MOVEit exploit campaign.* CSO Magazine. https://www.csoonline.com/article/650272/clop-ransomware-dominates-ransomware-space-after-moveit-exploit-campaign.html

Cox, J. (2023, Feb 23). How I Broke Into a Bank Account With an AI-Generated Voice. https://www.vice.com/en/article/dy7axa/how-i-broke-into-a-bank-account-with-an-ai-generated-voice

cyber attack and the NHS. U.K. National Audit Office. https://www.nao.org.uk/wp-content/uploads/2017/10/Investigation-WannaCry-cyber-attack-and-the-NHS.pdf

Davis, R. (2021, Jan 15). *The History and Future of DDoS Attacks.* Cybersecurity Magazine. https://cybersecurity-magazine.com/the-history-and-future-of-ddos-attacks/

Dinu, C. (2022, Jun 7). *Maze Ransomware: Origins, Operating Mode, Attacks.* Heimdal Security. https://heimdalsecurity.com/blog/maze-ransomware-101/

Fadilpasic, S. (2022, Apr 14). *Insurance giant AON hit by cyberattack.* TechRadarPro. https://www.techradar.com/news/insurance-giant-aon-hit-by-cyberattack

FBI. (2024 Apr 15). Welcome to InfraGard. Federal Beureau of Investigation, Infragard program. https://www.infragard.org

Future of Life. (2017, Aug 11). Asilomar AI Principles. Future of Life institute. https://futureoflife.org/open-letter/ai-principles/

Gatlan, S. (2021, Jul 22). *Ransomware gang breached CNA's network via fake browser update. Bleeping Computer.* https://www.bleepingcomputer.com/news/security/ransomware-gang-breached-cna-s-network-via-fake-browser-update/

Ghafur, S. Kristensen, S. Honeyford, K. Martin, G. Darzi, A. Aylin, P. (2019, Oct 02). *A retrospective impact analysis of the WannaCry cyberattack on the NHS.* NPJ | Digital Medicine. https://www.nature.com/articles/s41746-019-0161-6

Global Market Insights. (2022, Nov). *Cybersecurity Industry Analysis.* https://www.gminsights.com/industry-analysis/cybersecurity-market?utm_source=PrNewswire.com&utm_medium=referral&utm_campaign=Paid_PrNewswire

Google. (2023). Responsible AI practices. Google AI. https://ai.google/responsibility/responsible-ai-practices/

Hosna, A. Merry, E. Gyalmo, J. Alom, Z. Aung, Z. Zim, M. (2022, Oct 22). Transfer learning: a friendly introduction. SpringerOpen, Journal of Big Data. https://journalofbigdata.springeropen.com/articles/10.1186/s40537-022-00652-w

Ilascu, I. (2019, Aug 29). *Sodinokibi Ransomware Encrypts Records of Hundreds of Dental Practices.* BleepingComputer. https://www.bleepingcomputer.com/news/security/sodinokibi-ransomware-encrypts-records-of-hundreds-of-dental-practices/

Internet World Stats. (2023, Jan 21). *INTERNET GROWTH STATISTICS.* https://www.internetworldstats.com/emarketing.htm

Isaac, A. Ostroff, C. Hope, B. (2020, Apr 9). *Travelex Paid Hackers Multimillion-Dollar Ransom Before Hitting New Obstacles*. Wall Street Journal. https://www.wsj.com/articles/travelex-paid-hackers-multimillion-dollar-ransom-before-hitting-new-obstacles-11586440800

IWS. (2024, Apr 15). INTERNET GROWTH STATISTICS Today's road to e-Commerce and Global Trade Internet Technology Reports. Internet World Stats. https://www.internetworldstats.com/emarketing.htm

Kaspersky. (2015, Feb). *EQUATION GROUP: QUESTIONS AND ANSWERS*. https://media.kasperskycontenthub.com/wp-content/uploads/sites/43/2018/03/08064459/Equation_group_questions_and_answers.pdf

Khandelwal, S. (2016, Aug 17). *The NSA Hack – What, When, Where, How, Who & Why?*. The Hacker News. https://thehackernews.com/2016/08/nsa-hack-russia-leak.html

Kumar, M. (2016a, Aug 15). *NSA's Hacking Group Hacked! Bunch of Private Hacking Tools Leaked Online*. The Hacker News. https://thehackernews.com/2016/08/nsa-hacking-tools.html

Kumar, M. (2016b, Dec 15). *After Failed Auction, Shadow Brokers Opens NSA Hacking Tools for Direct Sales*. The Hacker News. https://thehackernews.com/2016/12/nsa-hack-shadow-brokers.html

Langston, J. (2017, Jul 11). *Lip-syncing Obama: New tools turn audio clips into realistic video*. UW News. University of Washington. https://www.washington.edu/news/2017/07/11/lip-syncing-obama-new-tools-turn-audio-clips-into-realistic-video/

Mehrotra, K. Turton, W. (2021, May 20). *CNA Financial Paid $40 Million in Ransom After March Cyberattack*. Bloomberg. https://www.bloomberg.com/news/articles/2021-05-20/cna-financial-paid-40-million-in-ransom-after-march-cyberattack?embedded-checkout=true

Microsoft. (2024, Jan 31). What is Responsible AI?. Microsoft Build. https://learn.microsoft.com/en-us/azure/machine-learning/concept-responsible-ai?view=azureml-api-2

Milmo, D. (2023, Feb 2). *ChatGPT reaches 100 million users two months after launch*. The Guardian. https://www.theguardian.com/technology/2023/feb/02/chatgpt-100-million-users-open-ai-fastest-growing-app

Morgan, S. (2020, Nov 13). Cybercrime To Cost The World $10.5 Trillion Annually By 2025. Cybercrime Magazine. https://cybersecurityventures.com/cybercrime-damage-costs-10-trillion-by-2025/

NIST. (2022, Jul 05). NIST Announces First Four Quantum-Resistant Cryptographic Algorithms. National Institute for Standards in Technology (NIST.) https://www.nist.gov/news-events/news/2022/07/nist-announces-first-four-quantum-resistant-cryptographic-algorithms

NIST. (2023, Mar 30). AI RISK MANAGEMENT FRAMEWORK. National Institute of Standards in Technology (NIST). https://www.nist.gov/itl/ai-risk-management-framework

Norton. (2018, Aug 08). What is bulletproof hosting?. Norton. https://us.norton.com/blog/emerging-threats/what-is-bulletproof-hosting

NSA. (2022, Sep 07). NSA Releases Future Quantum-Resistant (QR) Algorithm Requirements for National Security Systems. National Security Agency (NSA). https://www.nsa.gov/Press-Room/News-Highlights/Article/Article/3148990/nsa-releases-future-quantum-resistant-qr-algorithm-requirements-for-national-se/

Puig, A. (2023, Mar 20). Scammers use AI to enhance their family emergency schemes. Federal Trade Commission (FTC). https://consumer.ftc.gov/consumer-alerts/2023/03/scammers-use-ai-enhance-their-family-emergency-schemes

Rashid, F. (2015, Aug 8). Inside The Aftermath Of The Saudi Aramco Breach. DarkReading. https://www.darkreading.com/cyberattacks-data-breaches/inside-the-aftermath-of-the-saudi-aramco-breach

Rouse, M. (2011, Aug 18). *Creeper Virus*. Technopedia. https://www.techopedia.com/definition/24180/creeper-virus

SANS. (2012, Oct 23). Insider Threat Risk Formula: Survivability, Risk, and Threat. SANS. https://www.sans.org/blog/insider-threat-risk-formula-survivability-risk-and-threat/

Schneier, B. (2019, Feb 5). *TED Talk notes: The Security Mirage – Bruce Schneier.* Medium.com. https://medium.com/getting-into-infosec/ted-talk-notes-the-security-mirage-bruce-schneier-b81464ad51a7

Shedden, D. (2014, Oct 29). *Today in Media History: The Internet began with a crash on October 29, 1969.* Poynter. https://www.poynter.org/reporting-editing/2014/today-in-media-history-the-internet-began-with-a-crash-on-october-29-1969/

Sjouwerman, S. (2020, Dec 3). *Maze Ransomware Group Retires (Retires!), Leaving a Gap in the Ransomware Marketplace.* KnowBe4. https://blog.knowbe4.com/maze-ransomware-group-retires-retires-leaving-a-gap-in-the-ransomware-marketplace

Smilyanets, D. (2021, Mar 15). *I scrounged through the trash heaps . . . now I'm a millionaire:' An interview with REvil's Unknown.* The Record. https://therecord.media/i-scrounged-through-the-trash-heaps-now-im-a-millionaire-an-interview-with-revils-unknown

Sokol, S. (2023, Jun). Navigating the Quantum Threat Landscape: Addressing Classical Cybersecurity Challenges. Scientific Research, Journal of Quantum Information Science, Vol.13 No.2. https://www.scirp.org/journal/paperinformation?paperid=126059#ref4

Solarwinds. (2010, Oct 22). *The incredible growth of the Internet since 2000.* Pingdom. https://www.pingdom.com/blog/incredible-growth-of-the-internet-since-2000/

Spadafora, A. (2021, Jul 9). *Insurance giant CNA warns customers it suffered a major data breach.* TechRadarPro. https://www.techradar.com/news/cna-warns-customers-it-suffered-a-major-data-breach

Statista. (2020). Average number devices and connections per person worldwide in 2018 and 2023. Statista. https://www.statista.com/statistics/1190270/number-of-devices-and-connections-per-person-worldwide/

Statista. (2023, Jul). Number of Internet of Things (IoT) connected devices worldwide from 2019 to 2023, with forecasts from 2022 to 2030. Statista. https://www.statista.com/statistics/1183457/iot-connected-devices-worldwide/

Stupp, C. (2019, Aug 30). Fraudsters Used AI to Mimic CEO's Voice in Unusual Cybercrime Case. Wall Street Journal. https://www.wsj.com/articles/fraudsters-use-ai-to-mimic-ceos-voice-in-unusual-cybercrime-case-11567157402

Tidy, J. (2020, Jan 7). *Travelex being held to ransom by hackers.* BBC. https://www.bbc.com/news/business-51017852

Tripwire. (2020, Jun 10). *Ragnar Locker Partnered with Maze Ransomware Cartel.* Fortra. https://www.tripwire.com/state-of-security/ragnar-locker-partnered-with-maze-ransomware-cartel

Uhde, A. (2017, Jul 5). *A short history of computer viruses.* Sentrian. https://www.sentrian.com.au/blog/a-short-history-of-computer-viruses

Verizon. (2012). *Verizon Data Breach Investigation Report.* https://www.verizon.com/business/resources/reports/dbir/

White House. (1998, May 22). PRESIDENTIAL DECISION DIRECTIVE/NSC-63. White House. https://irp.fas.org/offdocs/pdd/pdd-63.htm

Wikipedia. (2024a, April 15). *Code Red (computer worm).* https://en.wikipedia.org/wiki/Code_Red_%28computer_worm%29

Wikipedia. (2024b, April 15). *ILOVEYOU.* https://en.wikipedia.org/wiki/ILOVEYOU

Zetter, K. (2014, Nov 3). An Unprecedented Look at Stuxnet, the World's First Digital Weapon. Wired. https://www.wired.com/2014/11/countdown-to-zero-day-stuxnet/

Zetter, K. (2015, Feb 16). *Suite of Sophisticated Nation-State Attack Tools Found With Connection to Stuxnet.* Wired. https://www.wired.com/2015/02/kapersky-discovers-equation-group/

Phillip King-Wilson

2 Hierarchical considerations in cyber risk assessments: Strategic versus operational prioritization in managing current and emergent threats

2.1 Introduction

Cyber risk management forms part of the overall enterprise risk function, across all forms of organisation, whether commercial, or governmental. Yet there are two distinct approaches to this critical activity, impacting entity risk appetite setting and cyber threat control capabilities.

The rapid evolution and adoption of artificial intelligence-based products since the launch of OpenAI's ChatGPT in November 2022 (OpenAI, 2022) has added correlation complexity between threat types, attack surfaces and the use of data to create new, valuable proprietary data. Such higher levels of correlation complexity extend to regulatory and legal compliance domains, with large language AI models creating re-dentification risks for personally identifiable data; its' acquisition, storage, extraction and re-use.

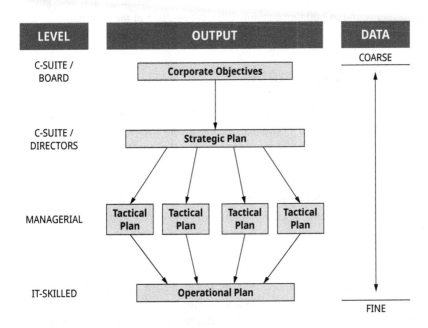

Figure 2.1: Hierarchical Management Data Provision.

https://doi.org/10.1515/9783111289069-002

Understanding the multi-facetted nature of cyber risks and the options available in managing them requires multiple sources, varying degrees of granularity and use of cyber threat relevant data. Whilst those at C-Suite and Board levels of organisations are charged with formulating appropriate corporate objectives and the associated strategies to achieve them, use of detailed cyber risk data may cause deficient cyber threat management strategy formulation. By contrast, those at the interface of cyber-security controls require highly detailed and very focussed data that facilitates in-depth analysis for maintaining cybersecurity capabilities.

Figure 2.1 depicts the hierarchical structure of an organisation, its' planning objectives and the degree and volume of cyber risk data that should be utilised at the different strata within entities.

A multi-dimensional approach to the acquisition and utilisation of data, relevant to cyber risk management programmes, provides constantly evolving inputs for decision analysis and mitigation option generation. With greater threat-to-attack surface correlation complexity arising from emergent technologies such as artificial intelligence, quantum cryptographic compromise and graphene neural accelerator chips, utilising the correct granularity of data at each level of an organisation has increased importance.

Comprehending the advantages and risks inherent within technology, especially emergent, requires detailed data to be analysed with multiple personnel profiles, executing highly-focussed and technology skills-based analysis, yet it falls to those at upper echelons to formulate the entity's acceptable risk threshold, technology and data governance requirements and in building a competitive, yet resilient organisation.

2.2 The hierarchical model

If organisational executive levels are accepted as having responsibility for long-term direction and building of cyber resilience, taking broad views across multiple domains, then by contrast, those functioning at operational cybersecurity domain levels must be highly focussed, with in-depth skills and knowledge.

In between these two hierarchical levels are those with managerial profiles of varying seniority. Such personnel are directed by the executive levels to deliver against the strategic objectives, drawing upon entity resources, to ensure operations remain constant through the dependence upon a departmental level's cybersecurity capabilities.

Managerial levels within organisations are therefore in a position that requires a greater degree of granularity from data than for the executive level, but not as fine as that required at the strata of operational cybersecurity.

The issue then becomes one of determining the type, granularity and domains of data required by these two distinct hierarchical levels, in order to attain cyber resilience on an ongoing basis; for current and emergent technologies, plus for addressing both current and evolving cyber threats.

Too great a volume and the executive levels may be overwhelmed with data to be capable of taking timely and unbiased crucial decisions, impacting the longevity, profitability and employability of an organisation. Too little, or too coarse, as well as pertinent data for the strategic decision-making process may be omitted, with equal, or greater potential harm posed to an entity.

Equally, the same applies to the managerial hierarchical level, whereby cyber domains including security, risk management, policies and procedures, impact assessment and resource allocation, all require some subject area knowledge.

Cyber domain breadth and depth creates an infeasibility in attaining, retaining, or deriving in-depth specialist knowledge across every relevant area required for creating, managing and maintaining organisational cyber resilience. A robust and enduring cybersecurity maturity thus requires selective information acquisition and dispersal to the appropriate audience.

The enterprise risk function of any organisation takes inputs from multiple sources, with cyber increasing in prominence as automation, AI, quantum computing and IoT increase in use within and external to entities.

In Figure 2.2, the input composition to the enterprise risk management committee is depicted, with each department drawing upon multiple methods and tools in their risk evaluation. Their output informs at the executive and senior management strata. Traditionally, the information is transmitted to the chief cyber risk offer, usually labelled as the Chief Information Officer; Chief Technology Officer, or the Chief Information Security Officer.

However, a recent shift has been the addition of such technology-specialist profiles joining the C-Suite level of organisations; not as a single IT-focussed individual, but within their individual roles, coupled with data science, quantum and emergent technology sub-groups supplying pertinent data to this new C-Suite group.

Various forms of risk management; financial, technology, market, credit, operational have all developed their own frameworks, had regulations and standards imposed upon them in risk quantification, yet for cyber risks this remains as ongoing, due to advances in both technology and threat evolution.

As with the organisational hierarchical structures and allied responsibility and accountability, so there are hierarchical structures that categorise cyber risks for organisations. A problematic area lies with allocating cyber risks to categories for their assessment, quantification and management by personnel with the appropriate profile, knowledge and skill set at the relevant hierarchical level. This creates an opportunity for misalignment of responsibility for particular cyber risk types.

Siloing of risks has long been recognised as a determining feature of risk management failures, across sectors and domains; from transportation accidents, to safety engineering and beyond. Organisational personnel and cultural factors also play a large part, as demonstrated by an asymmetry of impact of cyberattack upon similar organ-

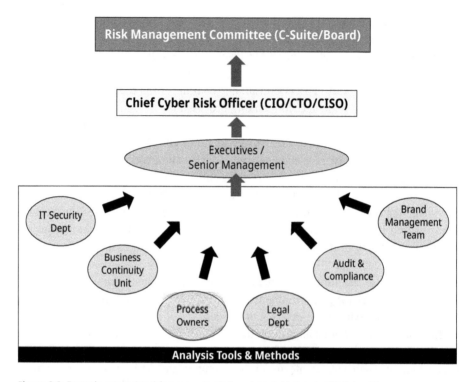

Figure 2.2: Example enterprise risk management departmental inputs to RM Committee.

isations. A 2018 attack on the City of Atlanta had repercussions for a considerable period of months, with high OpEx and CapEx spend for resolution. Exactly the same attack and mal actors had a far lower impact upon the Colorado Department of Transportation, due to the effective cyber risk management regime, with prioritised network segmentation limiting the scope of the attack.

Organisational factors influencing the decision-making process are not within scope here, but these include human factors and mental models; both impacting upon the psychology of judgement and decision making. In essence, whether an organisation, or a person undertaking a cyber risk management role, have previously experienced a successful cyberattack will influence both the comprehension and rating of importance given to eliminating, or mitigating the potential impact.

How information is processed is dependent upon this component, with various mental models and constructs having been proposed over time (Endsley, 1995). A common proposition is that humans draw upon prior experience to create a construct from the information available to them, in order to generate a new construct for a scenario that has not previously been encountered. In the absence of experience, human error rates increase, or allow for uncertainty, an inability to take action within the relevant timeframe (if at all), or place too great an emphasis on the wrong type, or form of information (Reason, 2000).

It is for these reasons that the provision of the correct cyber threat-related data to the various hierarchical organisational levels is critical in the assessment, weighting and decisions being formulated and taken in managing cyber risks. Ensuring that pertinent information matches the corresponding experience, or lack thereof, provides recipients only with data that will not be confused, mixed, or incorrectly weighted, when deriving from it the correct pathway within the decision formulation and making task.

Fundamental to this, when seeking to understand the hierarchical structures of data and organisations, required for successfully creating and maintaining cyber threat resilience, is the identification, assessment and quantification of cyber risks. In line with normal risk management practice, cyber threats must be identified and their target, or targets, frequency, impact in both technology and operational process terms, informs the fundamental assessment process.

These pre-requisites facilitate categorisation of cyber risks. The most common form of cyber threat categorisation is by allocating threats to tiers with Level 0 being assigned as a strategic enterprise risk, with sub-levels and categories being assigned as the risk progresses down the various hierarchical strata of the organisation to the operational levels, these having passed through the middle managerial layers.

Ongoing increasing I.T. reliance and associated technology failure risks have increased the weighting of and prioritisation of managing cyber threats. This has not been driven purely by entities seeking to build cyber resilience for their own operational needs, but from regulatory and compliance perspectives.

Since 2016 there has been an uplift in the number of laws relating to the acquisition, analysis, storage, use and processing risks posed to personally identifiable data globally, with large-geography regulations such as the E.U.'s GDPR (European Commission, 2016), to National, State and local government-imposed laws such as the California Consumer Privacy Act (CCPA) (State of California, Department of Justice, 2023). Such laws and the associated penalties have forced organisations, both commercial and non-commercial, to seek out the means of meeting regulatory compliance requirements on an ongoing basis.

Further, the development of additional laws relating to mandatorily reporting and to disclosures of cyber breaches from various bodies, such as the SEC in the US (Securities and Exchange Commission, U.S.A., 2023), has also placed an increased burden upon executives, managers and operational personnel, to reduce cyber threat impacts upon personal data a far as possible. For commercial entities, there are dual risks arising from a successful breach; from lower share pricing, as well as financial penalties imposed by regulators, such as the Irish Data Protection Commission's €1.2 billion fine against U.S. technology firm, Meta Data Protection Commission, Republic of Ireland, 2023) and others levied in 2023 (Statista, 2024).

For non-commercial entities, such as government agencies, such regulations create legal liability to multiple parties, ranging from citizens, to third party contractors, with certain U.S. States already subject to legal action resulting from data breaches (U.S. Office of Personnel Management Data Security Breach Litigation, 2019).

Other national breach notification regulations have come into force following actual and potential cyber threat impacts, such as the Cyber Incident Reporting for Critical Infrastructure Act of 2022 (CIRCIA), (U.S. Cybersecurity and Infrastructure Security Agency, 2022). covering organisations responsible for delivery of critical products and services in the U.S., following the Colonial Pipeline cyberattack of 2021 and the 2023 U.S. Securities and Exchange Commission's 17 CFR Parts 229, 232, 239, 240, and 249 (U.S. Securities and Exchange Commission, 2023).

Laws and regulations have thus similarly evolved into a hierarchical structure, with differing geographies accounting for international, national, regional and local adherence to various mandates being imposed in line with increased attack capabilities via AI and large language models.

In Figure 2.3, the categories covered by current and emerging laws is depicted, with the accountability level and application of such regulations mapped against these. A prime example of how new laws have been imposed at multiple levels of government is the Florida State cyber law of 2022, which shifted its' applicability down to local authority level. This delineation was further extended to the number of citizens per area, per district as to the timing of its' imposition and level of accountability. By contrast, the December 2023 agreement on AI regulation by the European Union is applicable on a multi-country basis.

HIERARCHICAL LEVEL OF APPLIED CYBER REGULATIONS

	AI	DATA PRIVACY	MANDATED ACCEPTED STANDARDS	3rd PARTY LIABILITY CONTROLS	MANDATED NON-PAYMENT RANSOMWARE	MANDATED INCIDENT REPORTING
INTERNATIONAL	Y	Y	N	Y	N	N
NATIONAL / FEDERAL	Y	Y	N	Y	N	Y
REGIONAL / STATE	N	Y	Y	Y	Y	Y
MUNICIPAL / DISTRICT	N	Y	Y	Y	Y	Y

Figure 2.3: Regulatory Hierarchical Structure.

Typically, such laws mandate actions that require data be utilised in a particular manner, be reported, or fall under specified technologies, such as the mandatory use of a government's cloud service, as opposed to a commercial entity (U.S. Florida Senate, 2020).

Reporting requirements relating to cyber incidents, for Governmental agencies have increased in both number and scope, with ransomware targeting being redirected from commercial entities, towards those linked to national economies, such as utilities, international freight, environmental and intellectual property. Cyber threats arising from state-sponsored, or state-executed attacks on governmental agencies pose risks with different profiles than those of mal actors with purely financial gain objectives. Governmental efforts to gather data from across all agencies, for proactive cyber threat warning programmes, have increased (U.S. Cybersecurity and Infrastructure Security Agency, 2022).

In terms of data granularity to be passed to a relevant body, examples include ransomware demand details, broken down in turn into the amount, payment mode, time window for payment, types of system and data impacted and causes of the breach. Post-breach actions include identification of the person responsible for quantifying the extent of the cyberattack damage, along with the timeline for a full recovery, together with systems and data restore points identification. Further, reports must be filed within specified periods, containing an estimate of the overall financial impact.

In order to comply with regulatory mandates, various organisational hierarchical levels will be required in the analysis and assessments; from operational levels utilising fine data, to process owners and business analysts using coarser data, as with legal departments use of such forms of data.

Both quantitative and qualitative inputs are required, thereby encompassing the methodological approach of a bottom-up assessment, with that of an expertise, experience-led top-down approach, according to the ability to accurately quantify from data, versus best-estimates for areas such as the probability of non-compliance financial penalties and their value, or range of values.

Whilst regulations alone may be sufficient motivation for organisations to seek out the means to limit the impact of cyber breaches, external audit costs faced by all entities can increase dramatically where auditors fail to be satisfied that cyber risk controls are present, appropriate, function correctly and are not exposed to manipulation.

Information Technology General Controls (ITGC's) have long been the mainstay of technology risk management within all organisations, comprising both technical and organisational aspects, which are also embodied within cyber risk management regulations. Increased audit emphasis on cyber risk assessment has a focus upon the ability of mal actors to alter an entity's financial statement line items (FSLI's).

With cyber threats posed to underlying AI algorithms, as opposed to the data that algorithms utilise, new controls must be created, tested, implemented and operated, along with appropriate documentation, policies and procedures within a short timeframe. Internal and external auditors are also tasked with designing appropriate audit tools and methods of analysis, within the same timeframe, in order to be capable of validating audited accounts.

Where external auditors fail to be satisfied with an organisation's ITGC's in relation to cyber risk controls, they are obliged to either decline sign-off of accounts, or only provide a qualified signature. For commercial organisations the result may be a resultant reduction in stock price. For both commercial and governmental entities, there will be greater scrutiny by regulators, with higher audit costs arising from accompanying time-cost increases through greater analysis and testing of cyber risk controls than in previous audit periods.

External audit fees for a Fortune 500 corporation range from $8 million, to over $100 million (Bank of America 2021); a slight uplift will be therefore considerable for any entity. For non-commercial organisations, such a budgetary impact may result in reduced service volumes, or quality for citizens, potentially causing subsequent electoral discontent.

Both upside and downside risks are clearly attached to technology adoption, crucially necessitating careful analysis prior to decisions for adopting, or rejecting. Two fundamental principles of risk management are defined as Risk Appetite; the willingness to take risks and secondly, Risk tolerance; how much an entity can tolerate the risks it is willing to take. These are linked to the type of organisation; whether commercial, or non-commercial, privately held, or publicly listed being examples.

It is the executive level that formulates and expresses an organisations' risk appetite level, which is communicated downwards through the hierarchical layers. The managerial layers are responsible for both adhering to and implementing appropriate policies, procedures and processes, that must align with the defined risk appetite.

There will be an influence from the level of inherent risk that is embedded, or implied, from the very nature of the business, or operations, an organisation operates. Put simply, a bank cannot eliminate all risks inherent in financial transactions, similarly a government agency cannot remove the risks embodied within the provision of a police force's operations.

In cyber terms, in order to derive an appropriate cyber risk appetite, an understanding of both risks and opportunities afforded by an emerging, or emergent technology is a pre-requisite. Facilitation of cost-benefit analyses of their use; partially or fully, is provided through cyber risk financial quantification.

Upside risks such as failing to secure anticipated reductions in OPEX via technology adoption must be balanced, relative to CAPEX hardware/software acquisition requirements, taking account of the likelihood of technology obsolescence within a shorter than normal timeframe. For example, ChatGPT's current market dominance may be eroded by Alphabet's Gemini (Wikipedia contributors, 2024), or Amazon's Q (Moreno, 2023) AI products through new, or better features, or lower adoption costs.

Sectors with high customer service levels, self-service purchasing, or with high levels of human interaction, stand to benefit most from rapid AI Chat functionality adoption. However, behavioural changes can nullify, or even negate adoption and cost impacts for early adopters. Commencing in earnest from 1994, internet banking's business case was founded upon transaction cost compression. However, behavioural expectations rapidly shifted; from receiving monthly bank statements, to daily, or even hourly balance checking by clients, eradicating any such assumptions and savings.

Similarly, Nokia's once dominant market position was destroyed by ignoring the potential of smartphone technology, despite having a functioning prototype smartphone product created seven years before Apple launched the iPhone (Hardawar, 2023). This highlights the importance of the strategic decision making in selecting an emergent technology to avoid corporate obsolescence.

Being a late AI adopter has the major downside risk of having a learning curve to overcome, from an organisational perspective, as well as holding lower volumes of data that generative large language models rely upon for proprietary entity service delivery.

Some facets, such as reputational risks, attach to both upside and downside risks. Upside risk may, for example, take the form of failed brand value enhancement opportunities through reputational uplift by more effective customer service through AI-powered Chatbot adoption.

The same technology could also be judged as having too high a potential for reputational damage from AI Chatbots being successfully attacked by mal actors targeting either underlying algorithms, or the data relied upon by the large-language models. Examples of potential damage are increasing, with inappropriate language being used by chatbots (Gregory, 2024), forcing discontinuation of use, highlighting complexity in identifying and managing emergent technology risks via rejecting its' use, or through designing appropriate compensating controls.

Evaluation trade-off may focus upon market capitalisation value for commercial entities, whereas for governmental organisations, it may be the agency's standing and the ability to retain, or improve its budget funding in future periods, which may have a much longer timeline than for a commercial entity's financial interests.

2.3 Applying the model

In March 2018, the City of Atlanta was hit by a ransomware attack that prevented over thirty per cent of its' 424 mission-critical applications from functioning (Wikipedia contributors, 2023). The city's IT systems and infrastructure were later found to have over 2000 vulnerabilities, with no budget allocated to resolving them. External contractor costs for remediation rose from an initial $2.7 million, to over $9.5 million.

On November 15, 2018, following 5G trials in 2017, the US Federal Communications Commission (FCC) raised $702 and another $81.11 billion in 2021; the most expensive per MHz in the world. Major wireless service providers, including Verizon, Sprint, AT&T, T-Mobile rolled out mainstream 5G services in 2022.

Nearly five years after 5G trials commenced, on October 29, 2021, the US Federal Aviation Administration (FAA) raised significant concerns about 5G impacting aviation safety; government regulators are responsible for new technology safety.

On November 30, 2022 the AI engine, branded ChatGPT, was launched onto an unsuspecting wider world to great acclaim. The search for how to leverage this emergent step-change AI technology commenced globally, across all sectors, such was the perceived opportunity.

Google's Deepmind-derived rapid code creating AI engine, Alphacode also went mainstream in 2022. In September 2023, Microsoft launched its' AI companion application, Copilot, as an integrated part of its' core products.

Overall, the global AI market topped $62 billion in 2022 (Gartner, 2021), with a 21.2% growth rate, allied to a global total corporate investment in artificial intelligence (AI) of $92 billion (Statista, 2023), rising to $422.37+ Billion at 39.4% CAGR (Bloomberg, 2022).

A casual read may lead to the conclusion that finance is at the core of both successes and failures in respect of technology adoption and use, as well as how to manage inherent risks from such utilisation. However, the above cases highlight the commonality of both opportunities and risks arising from technology, requiring the identification, quantification and risk management of them. This applies whether the technologies are emergent, as in the case of generative large-language AI models, or emerging, where there is a longer gestation period, prior to mainstream adoption.

An organisational dilemma therefore exists; from executive, strategic levels, to the operational "coal face" of organisational strata. Executive decisions have historically been viewed as impacting over a sustained period, as opposed to having an immediate impact upon operational modes, business processes, revenues and costs. Conversely, technology risks may manifest themselves with immediacy, requiring rapid formulation and execution of policies and procedures; even outside of normal processes, in order to contain and limit damage.

Across the divide between commercial entities and governmental agencies and even between listed and non-listed companies, there is a further separation of objectives; dividend yield, versus stability and value to citizens.

Leaders, regardless of organisational type, operate under a strategic imperative to derive maximum value from a fixed number of resources. In the case of technology adoption, decisions may be skewed through the sheer number of strategic decisions they are required to take on a daily basis, leaving little time for in-depth briefings, detailed analysis of data and pre-decision reflection.

Conversely, operational personnel are tasked with taking decisions based upon deliberate, data-driven paths that have been previously trodden, or have frameworks and standards to guide them, facilitating day-to-day uninterrupted, optimised operations.

As an emergent technology, AI and its' integration into chatbots during 2023, it imposed both a strategic imperative for executive levels of organisations, with attached urgency, plus an operational integration imperative for those functioning within front line operations and IT departments in particular.

November 2022's launch of ChatGPT caused leaders to rapidly decide that a chatbots' potential cost saving, through its' replacement of humans within the value and supply chains was too great to ignore.

Strategic first mover advantage was combined with a fear of being out-competed if operational costs were to remain at the existing levels, whilst adopters reduce theirs with rapid roll-out. Integration of AI-assisted chatbots has been widespread in the 12-month period since ChatGPT was launched, as well as for "AI-powered" products, including within the cybersecurity and cyber risk management sectors (Crowdstrike, Darktrace, Vectra AI, Mixmode, Sentinel-1).

Instant enhancement opportunities and commercial pressure to take strategic decisions within a very short timeframe is uncommon for senior executives. Commencing in 1989, with what became colloquially labelled as Web 1.0, there was a similar strategic imperative, resulting in the so-called dotcom bubble between 1995–2000.

This period was characterised by firms and investors not adhering to traditional risk assessment and measurement approaches, in respect of valuations, anticipated synergies from M&A activities, or attaining competitive advantage through monopolistic technology ownership. The subsequent global extreme downturn in the technology market impacted multiple sectors.

Financial risks, bets on certain technologies providing advantage and a disregard of in house and generally accepted risk management principles were rejected in favour of avoiding upside risks. Venture capital funded technology start ups, spawned a large number of single-product companies serving newly formed, or even non-existent market segments.

A strikingly similar scenario has played out in relation to AI and generative large language models in general, since November 2022. A common market view is that present day AI is driven by enhancements within the hardware level of the AI ecosystem (MSN, 2023). However, even those holding large shareholdings in entities operating within the hardware sector, accept the view that the next shift will be derived from AI becoming Open Source, with the RISC -V (RISC International, 2011) open architecture playing a fundamental role at this juncture.

Stock markets, such as NASDAQ, illustrate the interest from investors in AI-linked corporations, allied to the stock prices of AI dominating companies, such as Nvidia, with forward earnings multiples priced at high levels at more than 240% since January 2023 (NASDAQ, 2023).

The similarity though is not merely linked to stock markets and VC-funded AI companies; the recognition of risks inherent within, associated with and coupled to AI and generative large language models, has had high visibility in the media and popular press.

It is only very recently that governments are seeking to address risks in a concerted, co-ordinated manner (European Parliament, 2023). Such risks extend further than the many ethical questions that arise with AI use, such as the predominant use of low-income countries in Africa for the learning process of large-language models, but also from a cybersecurity perspective.

Other generally accepted risk management processes, methods and frameworks were sidelined during Web 1.0 and are seemingly being ignored during the current AI trend. This extends to risk management areas such as vendor selection and lock-in due diligence, data governance and compliance, ESG, within non-IT and IT general control (ITGC) impact, software quality control, software development lifecycle (SDLC), and single point of failure assessments through AI integration.

As technology shifts, so do attack execution capabilities. Drawing upon any inherent weakness embedded within a particular technology, its' implementation, operation, and/or maintenance by organisations, regardless of entity structure, or sector, mal actors leverage new technologies to execute attacks and evolve their business models.

Of note however, is that step-changes in technology adoption are infrequent and historically have not been accompanied in temporal terms directly by new forms of attack, or attack methods. In Figure 2.4 the rate of attack evolution fails to correlate with technology evolution. Rather, there are steps made, followed by evolution of the same form of attack from the previous period.

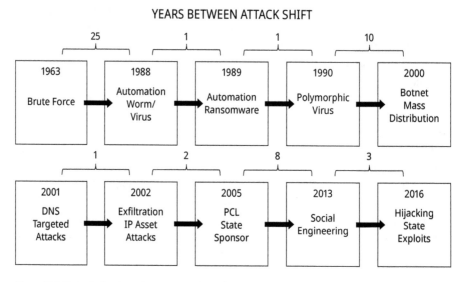

YEARS BETWEEN ATTACK SHIFT

Figure 2.4: Historic charting of new types of attack 1960-present.

Historically successful attack methods, from on and offline environments and repurposed, still account for the majority of cybersecurity failures, with business email compromise, misconfiguration errors and human error dominating as root causes.

High cyber insurance ransomware claims, together with mandatory cyber incident reporting laws (U.S. Securities and Exchange Commission, 1934), (U.S. Office of Foreign Assets Control, 2022) and forbidding of government agencies from paying ransoms, all combine to limit risk transfer as a cyber risk management mitigation option.

There is therefore a double-edged sword, for both executive and operational levels within organisations, when it comes to emerging and even more so, for emergent technologies. In either case and for both profiles, assessment of the upside and downside risks of the decision to adopt a particular technology is a complex area, with a broad width and depth to analyse and develop selection criteria from.

Adopting a new technology, such as AI generative large language models to attain cost reductions through the value chain, creates exposure to multiple risks, whether on balance sheet, or off. Further, such advances in technology not only confers benefits to operational efficiencies and to mal actors for their attack methods, but also for enhanced risk management within organisations.

An overall objective of cybersecurity lies in proactively preventing ingress of malware and focussed cyberattacks, as opposed to being reactive in nature; termed autopsy risk management within certain sectors. Enhanced cyber risk management may be derived from greater volumes of data, increased technological capability in extracting crucial cyber risk management information from disparate sets of data, all within a highly dynamic technology-to-attack environment. AI and quantum computing offer far greater analysis options for multiple sources of data. However, there is an accompanying complexity in the interrogation of data, in order to extract historic and create new data relevant to the multiple hierarchical strata that rely upon it.

A new form of risk therefore relates to how organisations acquire, store, extract and analyse data for creating and maintaining cyber threat resilience. Accuracy failures from data use creates potential for severe consequences, as do risks to algorithmic model dependencies within the decision-making process, at multiple levels within organisation.

Regardless of sector, a punitive regulatory operating environment, coupled with audit and compliance costs, a common grouping of cyber risks is used by both operational entities and third parties, such as regulators and external auditors. These categorised groupings are confidentiality, integrity and availability (CIA) and comprise an organisations' information assets.

Figure 2.5. Indicates how the CIA risk grouping informs an organisation's enterprise risk management (ERM) function, with broad and non-granular technology categorisations at senior managerial levels, which is then decomposed into sub-categories and levels further down into an organisation. Dramatically increased cyber threat risk has altered the historical composition of both Boards and ERM bodies, with technology expertise being supplied by Chief Information and Chief Technical Officer profiles (CIO/CTO), in turn supported with inputs from organisation's Chief Information Security Officer (CISO's).

Thus, information flows from the lower operational levels, transitioning from a fine technical detail, to a coarser form for operational decisions at senior managerial level, whilst technical data is simultaneously fed to the C-level technical profiles for aggregation and reporting at senior executive and Board hierarchical levels.

Additional changes to the strata within organisations arise from the presence of process owners at more senior levels, with data flows, together with process-to-technology interdependency mapping, storage and usage of mass data being prerequisites for the formulation of IT and data governance requirements at the C-levels of entities.

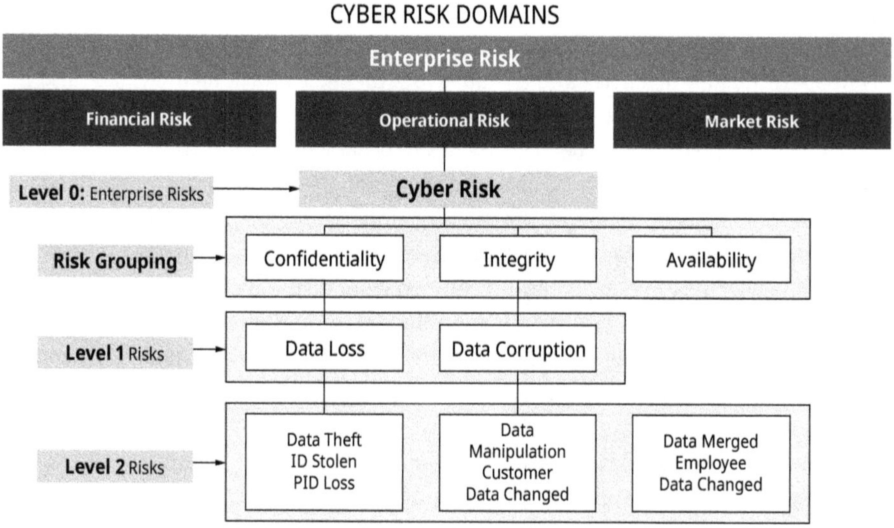

CYBER RISK DOMAINS

Figure 2.5: Fit of Cyber Risk Management to Overall Enterprise Risk Management.

Coarse operational and technical data are utilised for assessing and quantifying cyber risks assigned Level0 at ERM level, for C-Suite and Board members to be sufficiently informed for taking strategic decisions relating to cyber risks, especially for the adoption of emergent technologies. It is then decomposed to the relevant degree of granularity for use by non-IT specialist senior management and executives.

The prevention and mitigation of mal actors' exfiltration, manipulation, or destruction of critical proprietary data is dependent upon continual organisational cyber threat resilience. Attack types and methods aim to achieve one of the above impacts upon a target entity.

Taking business email compromise as an example, with this continually being a top cyber threat (Trend Micro's security product blocked 79,945,411,146 email threats during 2022), there are three causes attributed to such cyber threats; technological, techno-human and organisational.

There are instances where product code defects are identified by mal actors, who then exploit it. Techno-human errors frequently arise via misconfigurations; the highest cyber breach causation rate, with increases caused by a global lack availability of suitably skilled cloud security personnel. Organisational causes include password compromise, unauthorised use of USB sticks and phishing/spearphishing attacks, all having the highest incidence rates within the category.

Using the above example, it is possible to hierarchically categorise and allocate responsibility for each cause of cyber breaches. C-Suite/Boards set the risk appetite of the organisation and thus may direct the entity's personnel and third parties to comply with policies and procedures that they have signed-off, in respect of unauthorised use of USB sticks; mandatory cyber awareness training; defined vendor selection criteria.

Managerial levels are tasked with applying and enforcing those organisational policies and procedures expressed at C-Suite/Board levels. Operational tiers are responsible for defining the requirements for vendors to supply products, including due diligence in vendor software development lifecycle management (SDLC), quality control, intellectual property ownership, historic trends, entity ownership and funding sources and peer reviews.

Single types of threat, such as business email compromise, may thus be sub-divided into strata, with very different data attributes and/or requirements and allocated to the appropriate hierarchical level within an organisation. From an implementation, internal communication and compliance reporting perspective, such allocations can be assigned within RACI-type charts (Wikipedia Contributors, 2024), ensuring internal personnel and external regulators and auditors are aware of which profile is responsible and accountable for which hierarchical level of cyber risk management.

Aggregation, from detailed to generalised categorisations of cyber risks, which may be labelled as Level0 risks at C-suite and Board levels, allows the grouping of cyber with other critical enterprise risks, such as financial, market, credit and increasingly, geopolitical and climate risks.

In Figure 2.6 below, information flows from right to left, feeding in to the Level 1 and 2 risk levels managed and controlled by operational personnel, with the data being technical in nature and finely detailed. At these levels, there is also input from the executives at the CIA level, that in turn need to account for the inputs from the C-Suite/Board/ERM committee, at cyber risk Level0 after cyber risk assessments are completed and reviewed.

It can be seen that the operational level cyber threats are assessed in view of the available cyber risk controls; mitigation options that may take the form of implementing recognised cyber and IT security standards and frameworks, technical solutions, together with policies and procedures that may include those formulated broadly at C-Suite/Board level.

Given that data may be pertinent to the identification of both threats and options for their management, there are two approaches to the acquisition and use of such information at the various hierarchical organisational levels and the constituent hierarchies of data, as depicted in Figure 2.7.

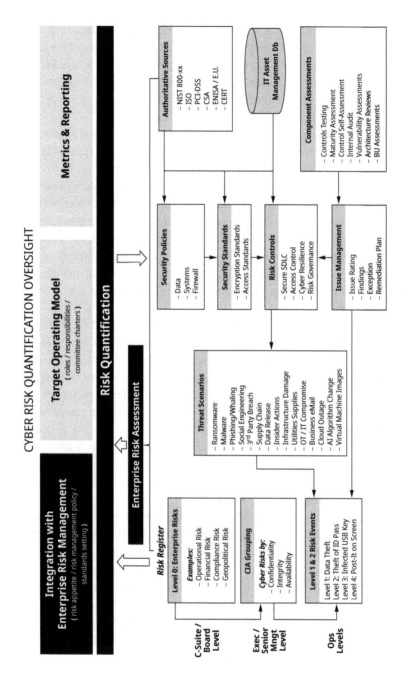

Figure 2.6: Cyber Risk Assessment and Quantification Oversight.

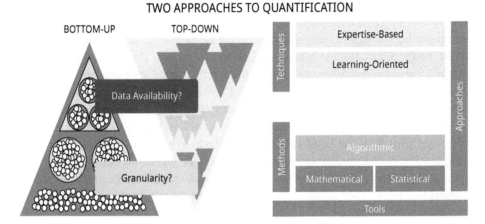

Figure 2.7: Top-Down versus Bottom-Up Modelling Approach.

The top-down approach relies upon techniques that encompass expertise held within the organisation, along with relevant past experience relating to cyber threat events and their management. By contrast, the bottom-up approach to assessing and quantifying cyber threats, in order to correctly and adequately assess them, is method-based and relies upon statistical, mathematical models and tools.

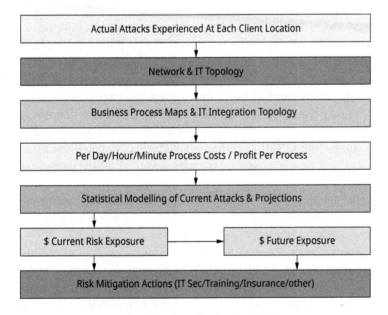

Figure 2.8: Basic Bottom-Up Cyber Quantification Methodology.

Figure 2.8 illustrates the basic bottom-up quantification methodology, together with the types of cyber threat, operational process and financial data required in order to determine both a current cyber threat exposure value, as well as the provision of predicted financially quantified cyber risks into future periods. This enables an entity to attain a pro-active approach, through taking forecast values into account when allocating organisational resources to emerging threats, as opposed to utilising an autopsy-methodological cyber risk management approach and remaining reactive.

The same method may be used for emergent threats, however, with the absence of actual threat data, nor experience of actual attacks arising from emergent technologies, the degree of accuracy will be of far less value in developing appropriate strategies, policies and procedures. This will be of greatest impact in determining an annual loss expectancy in order to execute cost-benefit analyses of various cyber threat mitigation options.

The primary approach used by an organisation may be determined by the availability and granularity of the data for the relevant personnel responsible for managing cyber risks to utilise, as well as that directly related to a particular technology.

Generative AI (GenAI) launched into the mainstream in Q4 of 2022 and as such, threat data, targeting of the underlying algorithms, data sources, is currently insufficient for modelling using previous methods, or for predicting organisational impacts with a sufficient degree of accuracy to base decisions upon.

Such threats may be data-oriented, regulatory compliance-led, or new targets, such as autonomous machines, IoT device compromise, or more traditional forms, such as data corruption and exfiltration. It is when emergent technologies offer potential for competitive advantage, efficiencies, or a need to maintain position, that issues arise in assessing cyber threats; whether using a bottom-up, or top-down approach.

At the IT security level of an organisation, data granularity is necessarily fine, down to network packets and payloads, with various aggregation tools providing less detailed, more user-friendly reporting across various IT security domains. These may range from user access controls, to firewall log files and integrated into security information and event management (SIEM) applications (Wikipedia Contributors, 2024), that provide an instant overview of status, or generate warnings where parameter thresholds are exceeded.

Clearly, this level of detail is of little use at Board and Executive levels within organisations, with the specificity serving focussed personnel profiles that have the appropriate skills, knowledge and experience to utilise the data.

At Board and Executive levels of organisations, such information may still be utilised, but in a format capable of contribution within the strategic and operational decision making and application process. In order to attain sufficient data from the lower hierarchical levels for decision analysis and quantification of cyber risks, data presentation, as well as content becomes crucial. This is particularly the case with both emerging and emergent technologies, in view of the advantages it may bestow upon an organisation.

In order to achieve this, cyber risk management programmes, run as part of the overall enterprise operational risk function, take inputs from the IT security department that has aggregated the data it has acquired and analysed, as depicted in Figure 2.9.

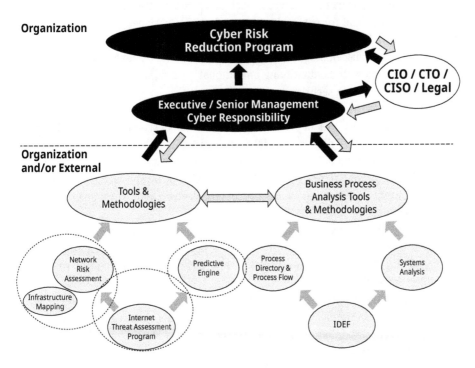

Figure 2.9: IT Departmental Inputs to Cyber Risk Management.

Within the data provided will be the outcomes of various analyses tools, with disparate areas being covered, from network traffic level, to IT architectures and topologies, as well as cyber threats and their associated vectors and organisational attack surfaces.

At the lowest level of Figure 2.9 the decomposition of the entity's business processes requires detailed inputs, for each element of a process, from process owner departments, business and systems analysts. The most common means of mapping process flows is by the utilisation of Integration Definition (IDEF) modelling language (Wikipedia Contributors, 2024), typically the IDEF0 functional modelling method. This is used in modelling the actions, and activities of each component within an operational process; whether this is a purely software/hardware system, or with human interactions within the flows.

The operational processes clearly interact with an organisation's information technology, which has the sole purpose of supporting an entity's operations. As such, there is an inherent interdependency risk arising from IT dependence. However, the proprietary nature of each organisation's IT topologies and processes requires every entity to map its process-to-IT interdependencies, in order to facilitate full comprehension of technology failure impacts; whether from a software/systems failure for non-attack reasons, or from mal actor breach and compromise success.

This data is crucial for comprehension of the types of cyber risks experienced by the organisation over sustained retrospective periods. It is utilised in assessing entity cybersecurity and risk management capability and maturity levels (Wikipedia Contributors, 2024), as well as identifying operational processes with the highest risk of compromise, following a security breach.

This facilitates the prioritisation of operational processes to be secured, according to exposure and impact level in priority order. Allocation of scarce human and financial resources are thus better directed to addressing cyber threats within the organisation.

Having received the data, the Executive level of the organisation has the information relating to threat vectors, the attack surface of each threat vector and the cyber risk controls that are intended to identify, detect, protect, or to recover and respond to each threat vector.

In Figure 2.10. the example of business email has the attack surface for the risk identified as data exfiltration, with the cyber risk controls sub-categorised, thereby illustrating the cyber threat hierarchical structure; moving from generalised, to sub-capabilities for each cyber risk control.

Such data enables the executive level to understand with relative ease, how the organisation may be impacted by specified cyber threats successfully breaching an entity's cybersecurity defences. There is no requirement for this profile to have any further detail in respect of the technology used, or the details of the operational processes. To give some context, a typical bank, or telecommunications organisation will have over 20 000 operational processes, with over 500 software applications, that in turn function via several hundred application programme interfaces (API's); with software and API's being on average 90%+ proprietary developments.

What the information may, or may not facilitate, is the evaluation of the effectiveness of the cybersecurity controls assigned for each type of threat. Whether there is sufficient data will be dependent upon the cybersecurity strategy employed by the organisation, along with the risk appetite, as set at C-Suite/Board level.

Where, for example, the C-Suite/Board has accepted a certain level of cybersecurity for network perimeter control, it may be insufficient to prevent all attack types, such as malware passing through the perimeter and into the internal network. Such threats may then be treated by the IT security department by disinfecting as they identify malware. For other entities, a different risk appetite threshold may require substantial investment in preventing any ingress of malware whatsoever; potentially at the expense of internal network performance, but may be accepted for compliance purposes.

Each cyber threat identified through continual assessment will have a control assigned to it, with each control having one of four roles to play; identify; detect; protect, or to recover/respond. These may in turn be hierarchically categorised and operate according to the threat type prioritisation; either alone, or in combination with other controls.

As with the requirement to map interdependencies between operational processes and IT systems, so there is the same requirement to map between known threat vectors, their intended targets; attack surfaces and the controls that have been implemented, as depicted in Figure 2.10.

THREAT VECTOR MAPPING

Attack Surface	Threat Vector	Function	Sub-capability
email	Data Exfiltration	Protect	Data Loss Prevention
email	Data Exfiltration	Protect	Secure email
email	Data Exfiltration	Protect	Encryption
email	Data Exfiltration	Detect	Data Event Management
email	Data Exfiltration	Detect	SIEM Alerts
email	Data Exfiltration	Respond / Recover	Cyber Incident Response
email	Data Exfiltration	Identify	Policy / Governance

Figure 2.10: Mapping of Threat Types to Cyber Risk Controls and Attack Surfaces.

Information relating to the number of interventions required over a specified period may allow sufficient assessment of the ability of each control to function as intended. Internal and external audit teams may then assign a control strength value, according to whether it operates on a range of 1–5, based upon what is observed and recorded when evaluating the cyber risk control.

After assessing the ability to control a cyber threat, the assessed risk is mapped against the likelihood and impact of each cyber threat, with the scaling for the task ranging typically from very low, to very high, as a probability, and from fatal, to insignificant for the likely impact. Figure 2.11 illustrates example values that may be attached to each, commonly having scales of 1–5, or 1–10.

The impact will also be assigned according to the operational processes of the organisation. For example, it may be a financial impact, regulatory, reputational, operational. At this stage of quantification, the executive level of the organisation has the data required to comprehend the threat, target, control, frequency probability and predicted damage level, which may be a single value or a range.

Such controls are subject to scrutiny by external auditors, who will use the same evaluation methods and assign the same, or similar values for control strengths as part

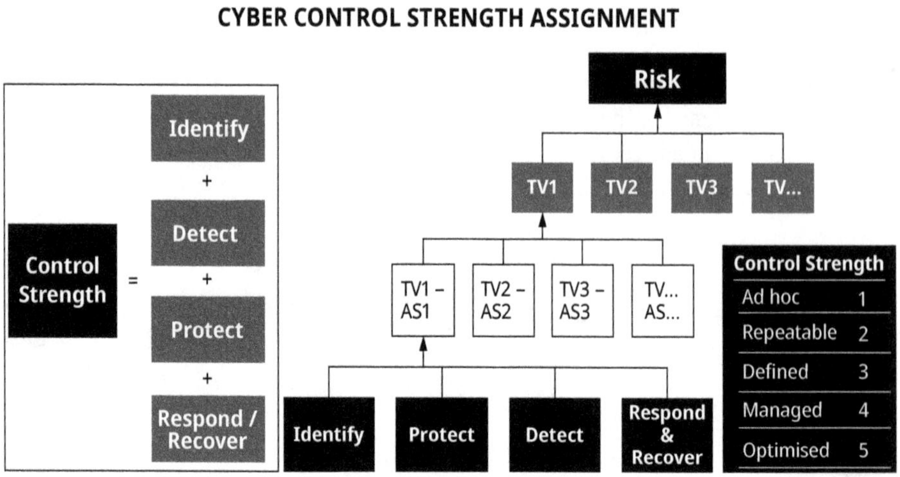

CYBER CONTROL STRENGTH ASSIGNMENT

Figure 2.11: Assigning Cyber Threat Control Values.

of their overall evaluation as to the probability of financial statement line items having been compromised; whether by internal staff, or via a successful cyber breach.

The executive level then requires additional data from lower hierarchical levels of the entity, in order to create the reporting data to pass on to the C-Suite/Board levels of the organisation, along with recommendations, cyber risk mitigation options, and cost-benefit analyses.

The granularity of data required will vary, according to the assessed cyber risks, with these ranging in hierarchical grouping of a normal risk level, elevated, or significant. Where there is, for example, a significant risk, plus a high reliance upon a specific cyber risk control, then the substantive evidence required for a more detailed analysis and quantification process is required than for a normal risk with a low level of control dependence.

By contrast to the operational and executive management hierarchies, C-Suite/Boards will utilise coarser data to formulate strategic policies for the entity's cyber risk management with exposure being below the organisational risk appetite threshold that they have set.

The top-level management tier addresses cyber risks after receiving the relevant data across domains, including technical, organisational, legal and financial. For the example of business email compromise risks, the technical policy may be changed to that of requiring any new email security protocols to be implemented within a defined period. The Covid-19 period forced a rapid change of email encryption protocols from SSL to TLS, demonstrating this concept and ability to rapidly transition from one technology security format to another.

From an organisational perspective, operational process analysis may identify where value is not being added for an entity, yet causes increased cyber risks, such as a Bring Your Own Device (BYOD) policy. The C-Suite/Board may change policy to re-move, or amend a BYOD policy, eliminating the ability of personal mobile devices to interact with the internal network, reducing exposure to socially engineered forms of cyberattack.

Data privacy laws may require changes to the target and frequency of environ-mental scanning (Aguilar, 1967), (Choo, 2001), by the organisation's' data privacy spe-cialists, whereas a reduction in one departmental budget may be reallocated to cybersecurity uplift in some form.

Although cyber risk management would, prima facie, fit to the profiles of those at C-Suite/Board hierarchical levels of an organisation; strategy and direction (CEO); cy-bersecurity financial resource allocation and consequent impact (CFO); operational rupture (COO); technology risks (CTO/CIO/CISO), this body is not normally consulted for inputs during cyber risk assessments.

A bi-directional communication would serve no purpose in strategy definition and decision making by the top level of an entity and has an associated risk of too great an emphasis being placed upon specific data, with limited technical knowledge of the recipient, to the detriment of the decision-making process.

With the C-Suite composition including CIO/CISO/CTO profiles, with responsibility for evaluating detailed technical data that is pertinent to the uppermost management, it is only after all aspects of a cyber risk assessment have been undertaken that up-ward delivery of data may occur.

Additionally, to avoid risks arising from a lack of segregation of duties, gover-nance in most cases imposes a de-coupling of risk and technology bias held by an indi-vidual at the top-tier, through IT directors reporting to CIO/CISO/CTO's and with IT managers reporting from further downstream into the IT director.

In essence, cyber risk management and the development of cyber threat resil-ience should be viewed as a large and complex machine, with many moving parts; all interacting and supporting each other's functioning. The mission of attaining and maintaining zero cyber-breach capability has been replaced with the strategic and op-erational view that breach will occur and it is the management of its' impact and re-covery to full functionality that is critical.

Vendors of technologies addressing post-breach impacts are now embedding AI within them, leading to the dichotomy for all organisational hierarchical levels as to their value, accuracy, robustness against attack, all without data to draw upon.

A persistent state facing decision makers and operational experts, is one of tech-nological advancement, allied to frequent changes in attack methodologies, targets and the business models of mal actors.

This requires cyber threat management to be considered a vast set of technologi-cal and organisational compromises, that are only defined, comprehended and input within all organisations' enterprise risk management units, through the appropriate provision of varying hierarchical granularity of data, internal and external information, as well as its' communication to the relevant organisational hierarchical strata, on an ongoing basis.

2.4 Conclusion

The single major factor in the present emergent technology and threat environments is the need to re-assess the anticipated rate of evolution. Figure 2.4 clearly indicates a lack of threat-technology evolution correlation. Until OpenAI launched ChatGPT in Q4 of 2022, the anticipated rate of development of artificial intelligence prior to commercialisation of AI products and services was far longer than actual; being many years faster. The same scenario will continue, with quantum computing now being coupled to the first commercially viable graphene computer chips offering the potential for a further step-change within the technology domain.

Allied to such uncertain dramatic technological shifts are the enhanced attack capabilities of attackers weaponizing the very same technologies. Managing such emergent threats will require fundamental hierarchical changes that are already developing. As depicted in Figure 2.12, new structures are emerging as a result of the rate of adoption of AI-related technologies, with positions such as the Head of Data Science, Head of Modelling at the director level of organisations, reporting to IT directors, the CISO and CTO.

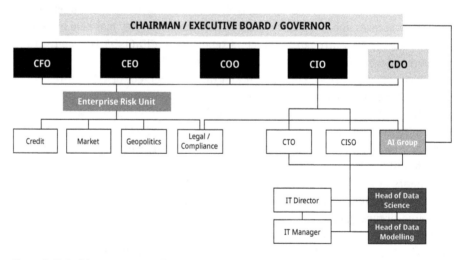

Figure 2.12: Evolving Organisational Hierarchical Structure for Emergent Technology Risk Management.

Another recent evolution of organisational structures is the creation of the role of Chief Data Officer at the C-Suite level. This function takes inputs from the legal department, CTO, CISO and now, with a new role at the CTO/CISO level, of an AI Group, comprised of multiple personnel profiles, across departments and divisions.

The objective of such changes within a short period after AI mass-adoption, is to identify not just the threats and opportunities that emerging and emergent technologies offer, but in the comprehension of areas within organisations that may be impacted that have not previously been considered as having an attack surface.

As aerospace became ever-more complex from the 1950's, so the traditional hierarchical reporting lines changed, with the advent and universal adoption of matrix management. The current organisational hierarchical developments are emulating the same formulation of research, environmental scanning, of cross-functional, cross-departmental groups and we can anticipate further structural changes as data, threat/loss experience is acquired over the coming years.

References

Aguilar FJ. *Scanning the business environment*. New York: Macmillan, 1967.

Bloomberg – Are you a robot? (2022, June 27). https://www.bloomberg.com/press-releases/2022-06-27/-422-37-billion-global-artificial-intelligence-ai-market-size-likely-to-grow-at-39-4-cagr-during-2022-2028-industry#:~:text=Intelligence%20(AI)%20Market%20was%20valued%20approximately%20USD%202059.67%20Billion%20in%0A%20%20%20%202021%20and%20is%20projected%20to%20reach%20to%20roughly%20USD%20422.37%20Billion%20by%202028.

California Consumer Privacy Act (CCPA). (2023, November 9). State of California – Department of Justice – Office of the Attorney General. https://www.oag.ca.gov/privacy/ccpa.

California Public Employees Retirement System Breach: https://www.calpers.ca.gov/page/home/pbi.

Chapter 282 Section 206 – 2020 Florida Statutes – the Florida Senate. (n.d.). https://www.flsenate.gov/Laws/Statutes/2020/282.206.

Choo C. Environmental scanning as information seeking and organizational learning. *Information Research* 2001; 7:1–26.

Computer Fraud and Abuse Act (CFAA)

Cyber Incident Reporting for Critical Infrastructure Act of 2022 (CIRCIA) | CISA. (n.d.). Cybersecurity and Infrastructure Security Agency CISA. https://www.cisa.gov/topics/cyber-threats-and-advisories/information-sharing/cyber-incident-reporting-critical-infrastructure-act-2022-circia.

Cyber Incident Reporting for Critical Infrastructure Act of 2022 (CIRCIA).

Cyber Threat and Incident Reporting and Information Sharing FAR 52.239-ZZ [incident reporting requirements on federal contractors]; FAR 52.239-AA [standardize cybersecurity contractual requirements (Biden Executive Order October 2023).

Data Protection Commission announces conclusion of inquiry into Meta Ireland | Data Protection Commission. (n.d.). Data Protection Commission. https://www.dataprotection.ie/en/news-media/press-releases/Data-Protection-Commission-announces-conclusion-of-inquiry-into-Meta-Ireland.

Endsley, M.R.: *Toward a Theory of Situation Awareness in Dynamic Systems*. Human Factors Journal 37(1), 32–64 March 1995Human Factors. The Journal of the Human Factors and Ergonomics Society 37(1):32–64.

EU AI Act: first regulation on artificial intelligence | Topics | European Parliament. (2023, December 19). https://www.europarl.europa.eu/news/en/headlines/society/20230601STO93804/eu-ai-act-first-regulation-on-artificial-intelligence.

Example ITSEC AI-integrated product providers: Crowdstrike, Darktrace, Vectra AI, Blackberry, Mixmode, Sentinel1.

Gartner, November 22, 2021 Worldwide Artificial Intelligence Software Market to Reach $62 Billion in 2022.

GDPR largest fines issued 2024 | Statista. (2024, January 23). Statista.

General data protection regulation (GDPR) | EUR-Lex. (n.d.). https://eur-lex.europa.eu/EN/legal-content/sum mary/general-data-protection-regulation-gdpr.html.

Gregory, A. (2024, January 20). Delivery firm's AI chatbot swears at customer and criticises company. *The Independent*. https://www.independent.co.uk/tech/chatbot-swears-ai-dpd-poem-b2481967.html.

Hardawar, D. (2023, November 5). Nokia had iPhone-like prototype in 2004, but killed it. *VentureBeat*. https://venturebeat.com/business/nokia-had-iphone-like-prototype-in-2004-but-killed-it/.

Hollnagel E (1998) *Cognitive reliability and error analysis method: CREAM*. Elsevier Science, Oxford. https://www.statista.com/statistics/1133337/largest-fines-issued-gdpr/.

Introducing ChatGPT. (n.d.). https://openai.com/blog/chatgpt.

Kirwan, B. (1994) *A Guide to Practical Human Reliability Assessment*. CRC Press.

Moreno, J. (2023, November 28). Amazon unveils Q, a generative AI solution for enterprise. *Forbes*. https://www.forbes.com/sites/johanmoreno/2023/11/28/amazon-unveils-q-a-generative-ai-solution-for-enterprise/.

MSN. (n.d.). https://www.msn.com/en-us/money/topstocks/could-nvidia-s-stock-up-231-this-year-actually-be-a-bargain/ar-AA1lyn83.

NVDA. (n.d.). Nasdaq. https://www.nasdaq.com/market-activity/stocks/nvda.

Office of Foreign Assets Control's (OFAC) Specially Designated Nationals and Blocked Persons List (SDN List)

Ransomware Vulnerability Warning Pilot (RVWP) | CISA. (n.d.-a). Cybersecurity and Infrastructure Security Agency CISA. https://www.cisa.gov/stopransomware/Ransomware-Vulnerability-Warning-Pilot.

re: U.S. Office of Personnel Management Data Security Breach Litigation, No. 17-5117 (D.C. Cir. 2019)

Reason J. Human error. Cambridge University Press; Cambridge, UK: 1990.

Reason, JT. (2000). *Human Error: Models and Management*. BMJ (Clinical research ed.). 320. 768–70. 10.1136/bmj.320.7237.768.

RISC-V Community News. (n.d.). *RISC-V International – RISC-V: The Open Standard RISC Instruction Set Architecture*. https://riscv.org/.

SEC Mandatory Cyber Breach Reporting Requirement: https://www.sec.gov/files/rules/final/2023/33-11216.pdf.

SEC Securities Exchange Act of 1934 Item 1.05 to Form 8-K

SEC.gov | SEC Adopts Rules on Cybersecurity Risk Management, Strategy, Governance, and Incident Disclosure by Public Companies. (2023, July 26). https://www.sec.gov/news/press-release/2023-139.

Shappell, S. A., & Wiegmann, D. A. (2012). *A human error approach to aviation accident analysis: The human factors analysis and classification system*. Ashgate Publishing, Ltd.

Total global AI investment 2015–2022 | Statista. (2023, July 7). Statista. https://www.statista.com/statistics/941137/ai-investment-and-funding-worldwide/.

US DoD DFARS 252.204-7012.

Wikipedia contributors. (2023, August 8). *Atlanta government ransomware attack*. Wikipedia. https://en.wiki pedia.org/wiki/Atlanta_government_ransomware_attack.

Wikipedia contributors. (2023b, August 17). *Capability Maturity model*. Wikipedia. https://en.wikipedia.org/wiki/Capability_Maturity_Model.

Wikipedia contributors. (2024, February 9). *Gemini (language model)*. Wikipedia. https://en.wikipedia.org/wiki/Gemini_(language_model).

Wikipedia contributors. (2024a, January 22). *IDEF*. Wikipedia. https://en.wikipedia.org/wiki/IDEF.

Wikipedia contributors. (2024a, January 25). *Responsibility assignment matrix*. Wikipedia. https://en.wikipe dia.org/wiki/Responsibility_assignment_matrix.

Wikipedia contributors. (2024b, February 5). *Security information and event management*. Wikipedia. https://en.wikipedia.org/wiki/Security_information_and_event_management.

Calvin Nobles and Nikki Robinson

3 The benefits of human factors engineering in cybersecurity

3.1 Introduction

End-users in cybersecurity remain a significant vulnerability and primary attack vectors by malicious threat actors (Pratt, 2023; Rahman et al., 2021). A 2019 study by CybSafe revealed that a staggering 90% of cyber breaches were attributable to human mistakes (CIEHF, 2022). Understanding that the human component in cybersecurity is just as vulnerable to threats as the technical facets have instigated a paradigm shift in research, concentrating more on exploring the various human influences on cybersecurity (Jeong et al., 2019; Moustafa et al., 2021; Nobles, 2018). Human errors are a critical risk to organizations resulting from end-users' cognitive biases, heuristics, attitudes, and training (Ncubukezi, 2022). Acknowledging that humans represent the most significant risk to cybersecurity measures (Moustafa et al., 2021) is essential, yet many business leaders need to confront issues related to human performance properly. This ongoing concern with human performance issues can be attributed to a need for sufficient education regarding the role of human factors in cybersecurity.

Safa, Von Solms, and Furnell (2016) point out that a lack of security awareness, coupled with inexperience, neglect, indifference, misconduct, and resistance, significantly contribute to errors facilitated by human involvement. The cybersecurity threat landscape constantly evolves, requiring organizations to implement countering mechanisms to avoid breaches, attacks, and incidents (Nobles, 2022). Most organizations leverage technologies to offset cybersecurity risks and threats while neglecting to address human weaknesses and limitations. Given the increasing technological hardening in cybersecurity, most business entities need to account for the human element, resulting in what Pratt (2023) identifies as the humans-as-an-attack vector.

With increasing attacks targeting humans, organizations need to understand that human factors is a discipline, scientific in scope, and profession. The successful targeting of end-users through social engineering attacks is counterproductive to sound cybersecurity practices. According to the Chartered Institute of Ergonomics and Human Factors (2022), human factors introduce a unique perspective to cybersecurity, advocating for a comprehensive systems viewpoint that encompasses the individuals within an organization. Its objective is to foster comprehension of human-centric cybersecurity among policymakers, executives, Chief Information Security Officers (CISOs), and security practitioners. Integrating human factors in cybersecurity aims to aid decision-makers with their cybersecurity strategies while highlighting the benefits of human factors engineering in cybersecurity.

https://doi.org/10.1515/9783111289069-003

As Robinson (2023) indicates, should human factors remain exclusively associated with security awareness training, there will be a paucity of data to establish its effectiveness in other cybersecurity areas. This paper aims to provide insights into the benefits of integrating human factors engineering into cybersecurity, increase discussion on the topic, and educate researchers, scholars, and business decision-makers. At issue is the need for more discourse on the importance of human factors engineering in increasing cybersecurity resiliency. This paper includes the following sections in order (a) background, (b) clarifying the definition of human factors, (c) history of human factors engineering, (d) human factors in cybersecurity, (e) designing with a purpose, (f) human-centered cybersecurity, (g) accounting for the end-users, (h) human error mitigation, (i) achieving behavioral change, (j) work task analysis, (k) integrating human factors professionals in cybersecurity, (l) emerging human factors areas in cybersecurity, (m) the conundrum of studying cybersecurity through a human factors lens, and (n) the conclusion.

3.2 Background

Research on human factors is increasing as scholars and practitioners observe that malicious threat actors target humans through their psychological and cognitive weaknesses. Even with the uptick in journal and proceedings publications on human factors in cybersecurity, there are significant areas to improve. Rah et al. (2021) note that the computer science domain overly simplifies cybersecurity and continues to view it from a technical lens. It is apathetic towards the human aspects of cybersecurity, ignoring that significant security incidents and data breaches are due to human errors. Rah et al. emphasize more human-centric research to address the human aspects of cybersecurity.

According to Glaspie and Karwowski (2018), organizations overlook the importance of addressing human factors and promoting a robust security culture despite substantial financial investments in tools and systems to counter cyberattacks. Information security goes beyond being a technical concern, and relying solely on technology does not solve the many security challenges. Within the realm of cybersecurity practitioners, it is a well-known fact that humans constitute the weakest link in information security (Acuña, 2016), and numerous human factors significantly impact how information security is managed (Alavi et al., 2013). Information system users' behavior directly reflects the organization's prevailing information security culture (Öğütçü et al., 2016). Glaspie and Karwowski (2018) state that inadequate focus on human aspects and security culture weakens the impact of cybersecurity tools and systems despite substantial budgetary investments.

Nobles (2018) avows that the influence of human elements on information security is burgeoning, chiefly driving data breaches, ransomware attacks, and cyberattacks, despite advanced automated security measures. Cunning adversaries exploit human fallibility to breach these defenses. Understanding human behavior in cybersecurity presents a labyrinthine challenge. However, the insights of cognitive scientists and human factors experts prove invaluable in addressing concerns around automation, information overload, technological deterministic thinking, procedural harmonization, and operational tempo (Nobles, 2018). Nobles state that alarmingly, human errors underpin half of all cyberattacks, with the increasing complexity of cybersecurity environments leading to security fatigue, alert anxiety, and operational exhaustion. As companies rely increasingly on information systems for productivity and profitability, it is necessary to integrate human factors engineering into their cybersecurity practices (Nobles, 2018). A more comprehensive approach is being implemented to mitigate human-induced errors, involving psychologists, cognitive scientists, behavioral analysts, and human factors experts in cybersecurity (Nobles, 2018).

Pollini et al. (2021) state that Computer and Information Security (CIS) often adopt a technology-centric viewpoint, overlooking the significance of human factors in sociotechnical systems. End users' cognitive characteristics, needs, and motivations are seldom considered, resulting in the perception of humans as the weakest link (Pollini et al., 2021). Pollini et al. argue that faced with an array of complexities in mitigating and preventing social engineering attacks; corporations can benefit from adopting a socio-technical lens that embraces diverse perspectives. Pollini et al. indicated the significance of leveraging a socio-technical approach based on (a) individual factors, (b) organizational factors, (c) technological factors, and (d) the ethical aspects of cybersecurity to gain a deeper understanding of human behavior to mitigate threats and risks.

Hughes-Lartey et al. (2021) conclude that the advent of the Internet of Things (IoT) offers transformative opportunities for organizations, enabling employees to stay interconnected for seamless business continuity. Despite this technological progress, data breaches persist, often owing to neglected human factors, despite a rich body of research in information security (Huges-Lartey et al., 2021). The conventional focus on technology overlooks the reality that secure behavior cannot be assumed, and security itself is not a purchasable commodity; it underscores the vital role of human factors (Huges-Lartey et al., 2021). Hughes-Lartey et al. present an Organizational Information Security Framework for Human Factors within the IoT sphere, which includes countermeasures to mitigate data breaches. The researchers' validation of the framework is evidenced by linear regression analysis on US data breaches from 2009 to 2017, confirming the significant role of human factors in data breaches and demonstrating a strong positive correlation between these factors and data breach incidents (Huges-Lartey et al., 2021).

Robinson (2023) articulates that implementing human factors principles presents numerous opportunities for enhancing the cybersecurity and technology sectors. This can be achieved through integrating human factors engineering in organizations, in-depth research on security-specific human factors, and incorporating human factors practices within security protocols. Robinson declared that engaging a cognitive psychologist could be a cost-effective strategy for organizations considering initiating a Human Factors Systems Engineering Program. Such professionals can interface with both general users and cybersecurity experts, helping to pinpoint and address ongoing issues. Robinson emphasizes that a human factors engineer can aid information technology and security teams by identifying excess security tools, aiding in automation solutions, and collaborating with management to evaluate more effective solutions.

3.3 Clarifying the different definitions of human factors

Without a doubt, having a clear understanding of human factors is necessary to drive toward practical solutions in cybersecurity. Nobles (2022a) underscores the indispensability of human factors in cybersecurity, advocating for cybersecurity professionals' deep understanding and acknowledgment of this discipline. Nevertheless, ambiguity shrouds the interpretation of human factors in this realm, spawning a noteworthy conundrum.

Two prevalent definitions exist, each veering towards starkly disparate interpretations. The first emphasizes the detrimental impacts of human behavior on cybersecurity, an interpretation which has, regrettably but understandably, broadly accepted as the operational definition (Nobles, 2022a). This operational definition includes poor security behavior, non-compliance, substandard decision-making, bad security practices, and security violations committed by end-users. The second definition is a more positive perspective, is predicated and grounded on human factors engineering as a discipline, profession, and science to augment human performance and behavior (Nobles, 2022a). Gosbee (2002) posited that human factors engineering is a revered field, meticulously curating apparatuses, devices, and systems with an acute sensitivity to the nuanced intricacies of human capabilities, boundaries, and intrinsic attributes. This perspective is intrinsically tied to the principles of optimizing human behavior and performance. A troubling deficit of understanding exists among cybersecurity professionals, impeding the seamless integration of human factors practices as a valid scientific discipline and profession in cybersecurity.

The need for more professionals in the cybersecurity industry exacerbates this knowledge gap and hinders the absorption of human factors as an established discipline within this field (Nobles, 2019). Academic discourse around human factors in cybersecurity is generally skewed toward the negative ramifications of human behavior, situations, or actions culminating in security breaches or incidents (Jeong et al., 2019; Mohammad et al., 2022; Rahman et al., 2021). While recognizing the operational definition of human factors in literature is pivotal, the shortcoming lies in the inability to fully appreciate and encapsulate the potential advantages and value human factors as a scientific discipline can bring to cybersecurity.

The key to bridging this gap lies in constructing comprehensive scientific and operational definitions of human factors, which can directly guide cybersecurity research and practices (Nobles, 2022a). This would foster a profound comprehension of the role of human factors in cyber threats and data breaches and aid in creating pragmatic solutions to mitigate these risks. By broadening the scope of human factors to encapsulate not just the negative implications but also the enhancement of human behavior and performance, cybersecurity professionals can adopt a more all-encompassing approach to manage human vulnerabilities and points of friction for end-users.

Unfortunately, the operational definition of human factors has thus far inadequately informed current cybersecurity practices, such as refining system designs and work environments to improve human behavior and performance. Issues like unsound decision-making, security fatigue, burnout, and sub-optimal human-automation interaction persist in cybersecurity (Nobles, 2022). Therefore, adopting a more comprehensive view of human factors as a scientific field, discipline, and profession could empower cybersecurity professionals to apply scientific and engineering methods to elucidate the human component. This can subsequently give rise to formulating more efficient strategies and solutions to counteract human vulnerabilities and bolster overall cybersecurity posture.

Emphasizing and comprehending human factors in cybersecurity is vital to effectively navigating the intricate nexus between human behavior, systems, and cybersecurity outcomes. A more comprehensive interpretation of human factors, encompassing both the negative implications and the optimization of human behavior and performance, would permit cybersecurity professionals to harness the total capacity of this scientific discipline. Crafting inclusive definitions of human factors will aid in assimilating human-centric methodologies into cybersecurity research and practice, resulting in more resilient systems and reducing risks associated with human factors.

3.4 History of human factors engineering

3.4.1 Genesis and evolution of human factors engineering

The crescendo of World War II, marked by the surge in aircraft systems' intricacy, placed unparalleled cognitive demands on pilots, catapulting Human Factors and Ergonomics into the forefront (Rogers & McGlynn, 2018). Conventional methodologies, such as selective training, proved inadequate against these burgeoning challenges, necessitating a paradigm shift towards scientific management principles seamlessly attuned to human capabilities (Rogers & McGlynn, 2018). This pivotal juncture broadened the scope of human factors engineering, blending the nuances of cognitive and physical ergonomics. Born from the collaborative genius of psychologists and engineers in the 1940s, the discipline emerged with a fervent commitment to unravel and optimize the nuanced interplay between humans and machines, aiming for pinnacle performance and safety (Guastello, 2023).

3.4.2 Mandate and methodologies of human factors engineering

At its core, human factors engineering orchestrates the intricate ballet between humans and their systemic environments, with a profound recognition of human capabilities and limitations (PSN, 2019; Rogers & McGlynn, 2018). This involves meticulously evaluating tasks, physical and cognitive demands, team dynamics, and environmental factors, all converging to enhance safety, boost efficiency, and ensure intuitive user interactions (PSN, 2019).

3.4.3 Historical roots and modern maturation

Although the rudimentary underpinnings of human factors can be traced back to World War I, it was World War II that genuinely accentuated its importance, as technological advancements occasionally eclipsed human adaptability, leading to discernible challenges, such as flawed control configurations (Fitts & Jones, 1947a, 1947b). This era was a crucible that molded a design ethos emphasizing human strengths and mitigating inherent limitations. The Cold War subsequently sustained this momentum, with dedicated research facilities emerging across military institutions, universities, and the private sector.

3.4.4 Organizational evolution and future perspectives

The Human Factors Society, founded in 1957, matured into the Human Factors and Ergonomics Society by 1992. This ever-evolving discipline has extended its tendrils into diverse territories, from computer systems and nuclear setups to adaptive technology. As technological evolution accelerates, the significance of human factors in honing the symbiosis between humans and technology burgeons (Wickens & Hollands, 2000). Human factors flourish as a multidisciplinary amalgamation, interlinking behavioral sciences, engineering, and physical sciences, all dedicated to enhancing the harmony between humanity and an evolving technological landscape.

3.5 Human factors in cybersecurity

In the human factors discipline, it is proposed that the quality of interdependent influences among a system's components directly impacts overall human performance and actions (Pollini et al., 2021). In cybersecurity, the interplay consists of policies, security controls, security practices, cybersecurity awareness, procedures, and technology. If the quality of interdependence within the system is disrupted, it could potentially degrade human performance and behavior.

3.5.1 Human factors engineering practices

In light of the majority of human factors challenges arising from unanticipated interactions at the nexus of humans and systems, there emerges a prevailing emphasis on the importance of adopting an evolutionary, cyclical approach characterized by a 'design-test-design' methodology (Stanton et al., 2013). Adopting human factors engineering practices is critical for organizations to optimize human performance and behavior in cybersecurity. Cybersecurity is a new field that is constantly evolving and consists of systems within a system; however, the domain suffers from integrating human factors as a scientific addendum to existing engineering practices. Table 3.1 illustrates a list of human factors method categories based on an extensive literature review.

Table 3.1: Human Factors Method Categories (Source: Stanton et al., 2013).

Method category	Description
Data collection techniques	Data collection techniques are used to collect specific data regarding a system or scenario. According to Stanton (2003), the starting point for designing future systems is a description of a current or analogous system.
Task analysis techniques	Task analysis techniques are used to represent human performance in a particular task or scenario under analysis. Task analysis techniques break down tasks or scenarios into the required individual task steps, in terms of the required human-machine and human-human interactions.
Cognitive task analysis techniques	Cognitive task analysis (CTA) techniques are used to describe and represent the unobservable cognitive aspects of task performance. CTA is used to describe the metal processes used by system operators in completing a task or a set of tasks.
Charting techniques	Charting techniques are used to depict graphically a task or process using standardized symbols. The output of charting techniques can be used to understand the different task steps involved in a particular scenario and also to highlight when each task step should occur and which technological aspect of the system interface is required.

Table 3.1 (continued)

Method category	Description
HEI/HRA techniques	Human error identification (HEI) techniques are used to predict any potential human/operator error that may occur during a man-machine interaction. Human reliability analysis (HRA) techniques are used to quantify the probability of error occurrence.
Situation awareness assessment techniques	Situation awareness (SA) refers to an operator's knowledge and understanding of the situation that he or she is placed in. According to Endsley (1995a), SA involves a perception of appropriate goals, comprehending their meaning in relation to the task and projecting their future status. SA assessment techniques are used to determine a measure of operator SA in complex, dynamic systems.
Mental workload assessment techniques	Mental workload (MWL) represents the proportion of operator resources demanded by a task or set of tasks. A number of MWL assessment techniques exist, which allow the HF practitioner to evaluate the MWL associated a task or a set of tasks.
Team performance analysis techniques	Team performance analysis techniques are used to describe, analyse and represent team performance in a particular task or scenario. Various facets of team performance can be evaluated, including communication, decision-making, awareness, workload and coordination.
Interface analysis techniques	Interface analysis techniques are used to assess the interface of a product or system in terms of usability, error, user satisfaction and layout.

Human factors practitioners leverage the human factors method categories for methodological intervention to address an existing problem. The list of methods depicted in Table 1 applies to existing human-related problems in cybersecurity, particularly (a)cognitive task analysis, (b) human error identification techniques, (c) mental workload assessment techniques, (d) interface analysis techniques, and (e) situation awareness techniques could potentially provide existing practices for mitigating high friction errors in cybersecurity.

Practices such as human factors integration ensure a harmonized advancement of both technological and human dimensions in equipment acquisition is paramount (Stanton et al., 2013). This approach facilitates a meticulous process integrating scientific insights regarding human attributes throughout system specification, design, and evaluation stages (Stanton et al., 2013). Meister (2018) accentuates that incorporating new technologies often requires behavioral studies and evaluation to discover the unintended consequences between humans and technologies. Cyber significantly depends on technologies; however, the lack of literature on behavioral studies and behavioral evaluation might reflect a critical oversight and lend reason to why the human, technology, and system incongruity is sustained in cybersecurity.

The human factors discipline must be more utilized in cybersecurity (Nobles, 2018), resulting in increased vulnerabilities. This section highlights some existing human factors practices that can improve human fit in an environment. There is a litany of human factors literature and prevailing practices that can ameliorate human and technology integration in cybersecurity. The cybersecurity industry needs to leverage the expertise of human factor practitioners to mitigate high friction areas around the human element. Academic institutions can aid in this disparity by teaching human factors courses and curricula in technology and security (Nobles, 2023). Another obligation is for the cybersecurity industry to create research opportunities for human factors practitioners to increase their knowledge of cybersecurity operations.

3.6 Designing with a purpose

A significant gap in cybersecurity is the need for more focus and materialization of design. Meaning human factors practices center on mitigating human weaknesses to improve human performance and behavior by effectively designing systems, processes, procedures, technologies, and policies – this is observable in other sociotechnical fields such as aviation, healthcare, nuclear power, and industrial safety but is yet to reach fruition in cybersecurity. Business decision-makers need to prioritize shifting the mindset of their design teams toward integrating security and human factors engineering measures from the inception of a project (Nobles, 2022; Pearlson & Huang, 2022; Robinson, 2023). This transformation occurs most effectively when leadership not only personally values security but actively discusses its importance, embedding it as a critical element in design (Pearlson & Huang, 2022).

In human factors engineering, a critical component is designing systems, processes, procedures, policies, and technologies to improve human performance, indirectly reducing errors and mistakes. Design is essential for accounting for human behaviors that lead to cybersecurity errors, mistakes, and violations, as the goal is to prevent such actions from occurring. It is imperative to design with a purpose in cybersecurity; critical focus areas for design must be integrative. The first is designing for humans through human-centered cybersecurity with an extensive focus on human factors engineering. The second is designing products and services to protect the end-users. The third is designing an ecosystem with continuous improvements as the cyber threat landscape evolves.

Poehlmann et al. (2021) argue that organizations must hone in on the technology design process and its implications on cybersecurity. In a groundbreaking collaborative effort, the Cybersecurity and Infrastructure Security Agency (CISA), the Federal Bureau of Investigation (FBI), the National Security Agency (NSA), and cybersecurity bodies from Australia, Canada, the United Kingdom, Germany, the Netherlands, and New Zealand co-authored *"Shifting the Balance of Cybersecurity Risk: Principles and*

Approaches for Security-by-Design and -Default" (CISA, 2023). This seminal guidance implores manufacturers to urgently implement intrinsically secure products by design and default (CISA, 2023). Governmental action is necessary to encourage cooperative and healthy discourse between private and public entities with an increased focus on cybersecurity and enabling security defaults to support the consumers and end-users favorably.

Both system design and human interaction contribute to the frequency of human error, mainly when there is a misalignment between the two (Pollock, 2017). While design often aims for simplicity, it can inadvertently encourage poor security decisions (Pollock, 2017). Envisioning a safer technological future, leading agencies advocate for a "Secure-by-Design and -Default" approach in manufacturing (CISA, 2023). Secure-by-Design emphasizes security as a foundational business priority from the outset. Secure-by-Default ensures products are innately secure upon purchase without complex configurations (CISA, 2023). By integrating these principles, manufacturers take on a proactive role in security, reducing risks from issues like misconfigurations or delayed patches (CISA, 2023).

"Secure-by-Design" encapsulates the ethos that technological products are architecturally crafted with robust fortifications, diligently mitigating the ingress of malevolent cyber adversaries to devices, data, and intertwined infrastructures (CISA, 2023). While this concept is not new, manufacturers and developers require considerable resource investments. As CISA stresses, there is no comprehensive solution to thwart the ceaseless advances of malicious cyber agents targeting technological weak points; even the esteemed "Secure-by-Design" products are not immune to breaches. Intriguingly, most of these vulnerabilities are traced back to a handful of fundamental issues (CISA, 2023). Manufacturers must draft precise strategies, realigning their current product lines with the Secure-by-Design ethos and permitting deviations solely in rare, justified scenarios (CISA, 2023).

According to CISA (2023), "secure-by-default" denotes products inherently fortified against dominant exploitation strategies at no extra cost. These products proactively shield against ubiquitous threats, eliminating the need for users to adopt supplementary security measures (CISA, 2023). Crucially, any deviation from these default safeguards heightens compromise risks, underscoring the imperative of added countermeasures for consumers (CISA, 2023). "secure-by-design" and "secure-by-default" are effective initiatives for user-centeredness and implementing measures to safeguard end-users. However, the design attributes of cybersecurity must extend into all facets of protecting end-users.

While existing literature highlights the importance of design (CISA, 2023; Grobler et al., 2021; Pearlson & Huang, 2022; Poehlmann et al., 2021), the connection between human factors engineering and design remains disconnected. According to Gosbee (2002), human factors engineering is an esteemed discipline dedicated to meticulously creating apparatuses, devices, and systems while astutely harmonizing with the intricate spectrum of human capacities, constraints, and inherent traits. Human factors engineering is the bedrock for user-centered design (Gosbee, 2002). This sophisticated design paradigm accentuates user necessities, intrinsic characteristics, and meticulous end-user evaluations of the human-machine interface (Gosbee, 2002). A salient feature of this user-centric methodology is the commitment to cyclical design and rigorous evaluation, ensuring optimal interaction and utility (Gosbee, 2002). The practices enhancing design through human factors engineering have existed for several decades. However, within cybersecurity, there remains a pronounced detachment from human factors engineering. This oversight renders the industry susceptible to the pitfalls inherent in overlooking human-centric practices, especially in maximizing design. Achieving user-centeredness is attainable through effective design and designing with a purpose in cybersecurity.

3.7 Human-centered cybersecurity

Human-centric cybersecurity is elusive, stemming from the intricate interplay between humans and technology and their inherent relationship with security systems (Grobler et al., 2021). Human-centric cybersecurity encompasses the full spectrum of cybersecurity elements, accentuating the human element within systems and processes (Grobler et al., 2021). Human-centered cybersecurity recognizes humans as assets and potential organizational vulnerabilities (Grobler et al., 2021). By evaluating human-computer interactions, it is evident that risks emerge from these engagements. Humans can be the linchpin of triumph and setbacks (Grobler et al., 2021). Hence, fostering a nuanced trust relationship between individuals and systems is essential to strike the proper equilibrium (Holland, 2020).

Emphasis is transitioning towards integrating human cognition and behavior to cultivate a genuinely human-centric cybersecurity (Grobler et al., 2021). This approach aims to shield individuals and organizations from the repercussions of cyber events while harmonizing with innate human thought processes and behavioral tendencies (Grobler et al., 2021). Grobler et al. accentuate that there is a growing recognition that the onus of system security does not rest solely on its users. While traditional cybersecurity design primarily emphasizes system defenses against threats, it is imperative to understand system users' diverse perceptions, knowledge, and experiences that influence their actions (Grobler et al., 2021; Stewart-Gloster, 2023). Essentially, both system designers and users of cybersecurity systems play integral roles in the holistic security solution (Grobler et al., 2021). The researchers posit that the underlying issue may stem from the oversight of architects, designers, and developers in recognizing and accommodating the varied attributes of users within their systems (Grobler et al., 2021). Grober et al. have highlighted a critical gap in achieving human-centered cybersecurity. Nobles (2023) articulates that the lack of undergraduate and graduate degree programs teaching human factors in cybersecurity also perpetuates and stifles human-centered cybersecurity.

Grobler et al. (2021) produced the depiction in Figure 3.1 to highlight the significance of user, usage, and usability components as foundational pillars for exploring human-centric cybersecurity. As depicted in Figure 3.1, a comprehensive framework for human-centric cybersecurity emerges, outlining the breadth of the researchers' work using the primary areas discussed below (Grobler et al., 2021):

1. **User Components:** This delves into the individuals interacting authentically with cyber systems. The myriad of users – each influenced by individual backgrounds, demographics, and past interactions – brings forth varying cybersecurity awareness. This component acknowledges these nuances and delves into users' psychological and behavioral dynamics toward cybersecurity threats.

2. **Usage Components:** Rooted in the functional dimension, the usage components encompass both tech-driven and non-tech-driven safeguards designed to shield users from recognized security menaces. It underscores the designated role of cybersecurity mechanisms, ranging from antivirus tools, spam identification algorithms, and password authentication to broader frameworks like organizational protocols and cybersecurity regulations. Such strategies have consistently garnered attention from the security research community.

3. **Usability Components:** This segment evaluates the system's adaptability and efficiency from the user's perspective. It offers insights into the intricate dance of human-technology interaction, spotlighting the symbiotic relationship between the user and the digital tools they employ. Here, the discourse extends beyond mere operational facets. It includes the more nuanced, non-functional elements like the aesthetic and emotional dimensions of human-computer interactions, as Kraus et al. (2017) highlighted.

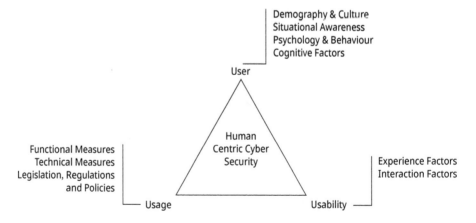

Figure 3.1: 3U's of Human-centric Cybersecurity (Source: Grobler et al., 2021).

There is a notable dearth of scholarly research on the human-centric cybersecurity framework, an offshoot of the human-centered design concept. Nevertheless, progressive cybersecurity enterprises are pioneering a novel paradigm, termed "human-centered cybersecurity," emphasizing behavioral risks in information security (Bureau, 2018; ForcePoint, 2018). This avant-garde framework prioritizes humans as the linchpin in cybersecurity. By encompassing practices, design principles, and technological amalgamation, it seeks to mitigate behavioral-driven vulnerabilities through a deep-seated understanding of psychological nuances (Bureau, 2018; ForcePoint, 2018).

Academic institutions, scholars, and field experts have embarked on a collaborative journey, fostering dialogues and formulating investigative endeavors to delve deeper into the essence and applicability of human-centered cybersecurity as an academic construct (Bureau, 2018). The collective vision of these stakeholders is to champion human-centered cybersecurity as the gold standard in both information and cybersecurity realms (Bureau, 2018).

As ForcePoint (2018) articulated, the underpinning of human-centered cybersecurity lies in its profound exploration of human behaviors and the underlying rationales that drive specific human-computer interactions. This paradigmatic shift positions humans at the epicenter and contrasts traditional approaches. Historically, organizations have been predisposed to lavish their attention on technological facets, leading to the inadvertent sidelining of behavioral and cognitive sciences within cybersecurity (ForcePoint, 2018). To herald the era of human-centered cybersecurity, it is imperative to weave expertise from human factor specialists, behavioral analysts, and cognition specialists into the tapestry of information security and cyber domains (ForcePoint, 2018). This strategic pivot, transitioning the focal point from machines to mankind, promises to reshape entrenched organizational cybersecurity protocols (ForcePoint, 2018).

Incorporating human factors into cybersecurity is crucial to diminish errors in human actions (Nobles, 2018). Expanding the operational parameters by curating human-centric initiatives and attuned to socio-organizational nuances is pivotal (Mancuso et al., 2014). Through the lens of human-centered designs, specialists in human factors can unearth objectives that often elude cybersecurity professionals, especially those connected to escalating cognitive burdens, emotional fluxes, and evolving mental frameworks (Mancuso et al., 2014).

Emerging from the human-centric blueprint is a groundbreaking approach termed "human-centered cybersecurity" (Bureau, 2018; ForcePoint, 2018). Traditional operational practices predominantly place technology at the center of cybersecurity. This novel model challenges such conventions, highlighting a longstanding oversight and limited exploration of behavioral and cognitive sciences' roles in cybersecurity (ForcePoint, 2018; Nobles, 2018). Instead of a tech-centric approach, the human-centered cybersecurity ethos champions humans as the primary fulcrum around which procedures, methodologies, designs, and technological synergy revolve. This shift is anticipated to be a potent strategy to mitigate errors stemming from human intervention (Nobles, 2018). Organizations must achieve cybersecurity resiliency to increase the continuity of critical operations; however, the need to include human-centered cybersecurity is essential for mitigating humans as a vulnerability.

The scholarly community ardently endorses the adoption of human-centered cyber-security as the quintessential blueprint for information and cybersecurity processes (Bureau, 2018; Nobles, 2018). As elucidated by a leading industry expert, human-centric models solidify the basis for a profound understanding of human behavior's intricacies and the logic steering human decision-making during interactions with digital systems (ForcePoint, 2018). In essence, embracing human-centered cybersecurity is not just a strategic pivot but an imperative to reduce human-induced vulnerabilities and augment the efficacy of enterprise operations.

3.8 Accounting for the end-users

A fundamental issue in cybersecurity is the failure to account for the end-users. Stew-art-Gloster (2023) emphasizes that while traditional thought often labels users as the vulnerable point in cybersecurity, a deeper examination might suggest otherwise. The proper oversight may reside with the security community's omission to consider the individuals at the heart of its endeavors holistically (Stewart-Gloster, 2023). Stewart-Gloster argues that overlooking the diversity of system users or assuming uniformity in security interactions introduces vulnerabilities. The author stresses that it is not that the individual is the "weakest link" but that our systems often neglect the broad spectrum of human behavior. Factors like cultural identity, trust in authority, and socio-demographic variables, such as gender, age, and education, can significantly shape an individual's cybersecurity adherence (Stewart-Gloster, 2023).

Most cybersecurity practices lack a human-centered approach when integrating technologies, devising policies, and engineering processes and procedures. As Nobles (2022) stresses, most organizations still undervalue the expertise of human factors and psychology professionals in cybersecurity, which is evident by the lack of said professionals on cybersecurity teams. The applicability of human-centric or user-centered approaches is necessary to account for the variability in a diverse end-user population. The one-fit-all method must be avoided at all costs in cybersecurity.

Failing to account for end-users cultural and demographic dimensions creates friction, circumventing security measures and protocols. Posey and Shoss (2022) iden-tified three viewpoints for rulebreakers violating policies (a) for enhanced job perfor-mance, (b) to fulfill essential needs, (c) and to assist others in achieving their work objectives. People naturally devise alternative solutions when affronted with seem-ingly obstructive rules (Stewart-Gloster, 2023). Overlooking this fundamental human inclination in cybersecurity protocols inadvertently undermines the user and the overarching digital landscape (Stewart-Gloster, 2023). Nobles (2018, 2022) argues for integrating human factors professionals, who are integrated into other sociotechnical domains, into cybersecurity operations to help improve end-user fit, establish human-centric practices, and reduce friction areas that degrade decision-making, performance, and behavior.

Systems frequently fall short of their intended functionality due to overlooking human interactions or misjudging human behavior; such oversights can range from mere inconveniences to grave catastrophes (Edmonds, 2016). It is imperative to acknowledge that even in the most automated setups, humans are still the centric asset (Edmonds, 2016). Accounting for end-users in cybersecurity is a critical but often overlooked step that creates vulnerabilities and counters the practice of reducing cybersecurity risk. Accounting for humans in cybersecurity is an enormous and complicated process compounded by the lack of human factors and psychology professionals integrated into cybersecurity operations. Given that most cybersecurity professionals do not receive any academic or educational training on human factors, it exacerbates the problem. The cybersecurity community can no longer afford to disregard the end-users because the sociotechnical aspects of cybersecurity are growing increasingly complex.

3.8.1 Human error mitigation

A significant percentage of cybersecurity incidents stem from human error or insider threats. For instance, studies indicate that up to 95% of breaches involve human error (CIEHF, 2022). Human error is a complex issue that resists easy categorization. However, the initial step toward mitigating its impact lies in developing a standardized classification scheme for such errors, as this would help in addressing underlying issues like poor situational awareness or inadequate training (Pollock, 2017). Between the 1940s and 1980s, a primary focus in high-risk industries like aviation, maritime, road transport, and nuclear power was to minimize human errors that could lead to catastrophic failures (Reason, 1995). Such incidents claimed numerous lives, inflicted extensive environmental harm, and sparked public and political alarm (Reason, 1995). The science behind human errors has existed for several decades and can provide the cybersecurity domain with critical insights into understanding errors and which such events occur.

According to Reason (1995), the prevalence of human error in technological systems is less a consequence of carelessness, ignorance, or recklessness and more a matter of situational factors. Whether beneficial or detrimental, human behavior plays a pivotal role in shaping the risk landscape of contemporary technological infrastructures (Reason, 1995). While this seminal publication from 1995 is dated, its application to human errors is still valid. Verizon's 2022 Data Breach Investigations Report underscores the substantial impact of human factors on data breaches, with statistics highlighting that as many as 82% of such incidents can be attributed to human elements.

The cybersecurity sector could benefit from error management science and seminal scholars like Reason by categorizing errors. Below are definitions for categorizing errors, violations, and examples (Shappell et al., 2017):

1. Decision Errors: These cognitive mistakes involve conscious, intentional actions that fail to yield the desired outcomes due to inadequate or ill-suited planning. Such errors often manifest as procedural missteps, poor choices, or the misapplication of critical information.
2. Skill-Based Errors: These occur during well-practiced activities that require minimal cognitive engagement. Common manifestations include disrupted visual scanning, unintended switch activations, or omissions in procedural checklists.
3. Perceptual Errors: Emerging frequently in conditions of compromised sensory input – such as nighttime flying or adverse weather – these errors involve misjudgments related to distances, altitudes, and descent rates, potentially leading to incorrect responses to sensory illusions.
4. Routine Violations: These are systematic deviations from established protocols, frequently habitual. Such transgressions are often tacitly accepted or overlooked by an organizational culture or supervisory framework that permits these rule-bending activities.
5. Exceptional Violations: These are rare, uncharacteristic breaches of established norms or rules that are neither reflective of an individual's typical behavior nor sanctioned by organizational leadership.

Each category highlights different facets of human error, revealing the complex interplay between cognitive, skill-based, and perceptual factors and violations influencing outcomes (Shappell et al., 2017). Figure 3.2 provides more details on categorizing errors, slips, and lapses. While the examples above apply to aviation, researchers, scholars, and practitioners can work collaboratively to develop examples and use cases that are more appropriate for cybersecurity. Nonetheless, the definitions illustrate the science behind understanding human errors in a particular environment.

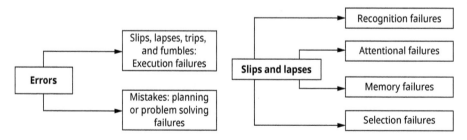

Figure 3.2: List of Errors, Slips, and Lapses (Source: Reason, 1995).

In numerous organizations, managing human-enabled risks has primarily focused on mitigating specific errors and violations implicated in localized incidents (Reason, 1995). The prevailing internal responses often include the issuance of updated protocols designed to eliminate the concerning behavior; the implementation of engineering modifications to mitigate adverse outcomes; disciplinary measures, motivational efforts, and retraining initiatives aimed at enhancing staff vigilance; and the integration of increased automation as a preventive measure (Reason, 1995). Targeting human errors in cybersecurity requires an appreciation for understanding human fallibility and working to capitalize on human strengths through the comprehensive design of cybersecurity systems, programs, policies, training, communication, and awareness.

Reason's (1995) seminal works highlight the essential points below for addressing human error and human factors.

1. Human failures, rather than technical glitches, now pose the most significant risks to complex and potentially hazardous systems, including healthcare. While these risks can be managed, human fallibility is an ineradicable factor. Various errors have distinct underlying mechanisms that arise from different parts of an organization and require tailored risk management approaches. Crucially, safety risks pervade all organizational levels, not just frontline operations. Disciplinary measures tend to be minimally effective, especially among highly trained professionals.

2. Human factors issues are typically the result of a chain of causes, making them challenging to predict or control. Behavioral outcomes are heavily influenced by task nature and workplace conditions, shaped by higher-level organizational factors. Simple modifications in equipment and workplaces can yield significant safety improvements.

3. Automation does not eliminate human factors problems; it simply shifts them. Team training, however, has been shown to improve human performance in fields like aviation substantially. Effective risk management relies on comprehensive, confidential monitoring systems and requires a multi-level approach, targeting the individual, team, task, situational, and organizational factors.

The cybersecurity domain could benefit from understanding and mitigating human errors, which would result in reducing organizational risk. According to Anu et al. (2018), other sociotechnical domains, such as aviation and nuclear power, have developed enhancement procedures using systematic analysis of incident reports to pinpoint human errors, identify recurring error motifs, and classify them into a hierarchical taxonomy (Anu et al., 2018). By scrutinizing the most frequent and detrimental errors within this hierarchy, investigators could devise and execute targeted mediation strategies to mitigate the incidence and gravity of such errors (Anu et al., 2018). Reason (2008), a distinguished expert in human error, challenged the prevailing belief that errors spontaneously materialize and are unpredictable. Instead, Reason posited that errors follow discernible and recurring patterns. Therefore, utilizing human error research offers dual advantages: (a) it furnishes a framework for engineers to recognize and mitigate error types, enhancing vigilance, and (b) it aids reviewers in assuring requirement quality, enabling the continuation of development efforts (Anu et al., 2018). The cybersecurity industry can learn and borrow from other industries that experience analogous issues, such as leveraging human error research and designing more vigorous efforts around human strengths.

3.9 Achieving behavioral change

Security is frequently perceived as cumbersome, extraneous, financially burdensome, or enigmatic, culminating in suboptimal adoption rates and enduring resistance to behavioral change regarding safeguarding assets (Haney et al., 2021). This prevailing attitude undermines the effective implementation of essential security measures, necessitating a cultural and organizational shift to reframe how security is viewed and enacted (Haney et al., 2021). Regrettably, cybercriminals have developed sophisticated revenue-generating strategies, exploiting the veil of online anonymity (Briggs et al., 2017). This presents an acute challenge that necessitates immediate action by those responsible for network security (Briggs et al., 2017). Consequently, a fundamental transformation is imperative to enhance the efficacy of existing cybersecurity techniques and practices. Given that human actions or oversights facilitate most cyber incidents, this transformation should expand into less explored domains, including the behavioral elements of cybersecurity (Briggs et al., 2017). Elevating the focus to address social and behavioral factors is increasingly crucial to ameliorating the current landscape (Briggs et al., 2017). Primarily, Haney et al. (2021) indicate that redefining cybersecurity as a discipline not solely rooted in technological expertise but also as a domain where interpersonal solid and communicative competencies are valued could yield significant advantages (Haney et al., 2021). The need for behavioral change in cybersecurity is not a new problem (Pfleeger & Caputo, 2012); the challenge is finding the right talent and expertise to develop practical solutions for driving positive security behavior.

Existing literature on behavior change in cybersecurity revealed the following:
1. Security is fundamentally linked to human behavior during goal-oriented activities (Pfleeger & Caputo, 2012). Building on seminal works by Smith et al. (1997) and Sasse et al. (2001), our interviews reaffirmed that, for most users, security considerations often take a backseat to the primary task at hand, such as data retrieval, transaction processing, or decision-making.
2. Sustainable transformation in cyber hygiene practices fundamentally hinges on engaging individuals' intrinsic motivations to cultivate enduring habits (Haney et al., 2021).
3. Constraints on cognitive capacity, including memory and analytical prowess, adversely impact an analyst's proficiency in executing tasks effectively (Pfleeger & Caputo, 2012).
4. Inattentional blindness emerged as a specific facet of cognitive load, exerting a noteworthy influence on the outcomes (Pfleeger & Caputo, 2012).

5. An end-user's biases influence one's perception of security behavior (Pfleeger & Caputo, 2012).
6. Possessing acute awareness of one's audience – including their skills, values, and obstacles – is a pivotal competency for effective communication (Haney et al., 2021). Advocates must recognize that security protocols are not universally applicable to catalyze behavioral shifts and instill a culture of individual accountability (Haney et al., 2021). Therefore, adapting strategies and communications to fit the unique contexts of various audiences is crucial (Haney et al., 2021).
7. Pfleeger's and Caputo's 2012 research underscores the critical need to integrate human behavior into the architecture of cybersecurity technologies. Their work delves into two critical behavioral elements: 1) the role of cognitive load in causing inattentional blindness, which can inhibit team members from recognizing unforeseen events when engrossed in primary tasks, and 2) the importance of understanding biases to enable security designers to anticipate user perceptions and incorporate them into their designs.
8. Incorporating human factors is essential for enhancing the work environment, reducing risks, and minimizing the likelihood of system failures (Maalem Lahcen et al., 2020).

According to the Chartered Institute of Ergonomics and Human Factors (2022), in cybersecurity, three core elements dictate behavior: Capability, Motivation, and Opportunity, as depicted in Figure 3.3.
1. Capability extends beyond mere knowledge of cyber risks to encompass skill sets, such as password creation or phishing detection. It also involves cognitive faculties like memory and attention and self-regulatory abilities like goal follow-through.
2. Motivation is not merely a conscious, rational force but often a product of rapid, automatic decision-making processes. These impulsive choices are influenced by an array of cognitive biases, such as confirmation and contextual biases, which can lead to suboptimal behaviors. Slower, reflective thinking encompasses attitudes and beliefs about cybersecurity and its importance, although risk perception may not significantly influence security behaviors.
3. Opportunity refers to external variables that enable or inhibit secure behavior. These include both physical opportunities, like system resources and organizational policies, as

The COM-B model posits that behavior is a dynamic interplay of an individual's capability, opportunity, and motivation (CIEHF, 2022). Interventions must target one or more interconnected components to effect behavioral change (CIEHF, 2022). Business decision-makers must identify the proper security behaviors and set forth practices to help employees achieve adequate security behaviors. To enhance organizational security, initial efforts should target removing barriers to opportunity, such as restrictive

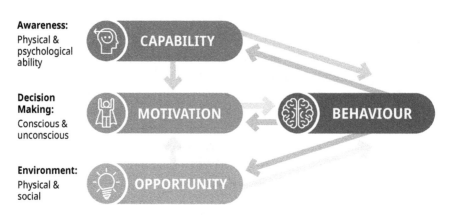

Figure 3.3: COM-B Model (Source CIEHF, 2022).

policies that may encourage insecure workarounds (CIEHF, 2022). If these barriers are not promptly addressed, focusing on capability and motivation remains beneficial (CIEHF, 2022). Simplifying secure practices enhances compliance, and training initiatives that build confidence prove more effective than fear-based approaches (CIEHF, 2022). Relying extensively on security awareness and training cannot change and sustain long-term behaviors.

Pfleeger's and Caputo's (2012) research applies to behavior changes needed in cybersecurity. Even though Pfleeger's and Caputo's research is a decade old, accomplishing behavioral change in cybersecurity remains challenging. Chiefly because human factors practitioners and psychologists are not integral to cybersecurity (Nobles, 2022). While work around communication and understanding the context to improve security behavior is improving (Haney et al., 2021), cybersecurity struggles to find value in integrating human factors practitioners and psychologists, as other sociotechnical domains have (Nobles, 2022). Behavioral change is undoubtedly vital, especially as the cybersecurity threat landscape continues to evolve, coupled with the increasing targeting of humans as access vectors.

3.10 Work task analysis

A significant gap in the cybersecurity domain is the lack of focus on work task analysis. This point is substantiated by searching for literature on work task analysis in cybersecurity in research databases. Over time, task analysis has evolved into a robust collection of methodologies that form a cornerstone in human factors and ergonomics (Hollnagel, 2012). These disciplines primarily concentrate on the intricate relationship between humans and technology within work settings (Hollnagel, 2012). It is pivotal to understand whether humans are utilizing technology or if technology is driving human behavior (Hollnagel, 2012). Human factors provide the foundation for designing equipment, tasks, and workspaces that optimize productivity, safety, health, and efficiency (Hollnagel, 2012). Work task analysis includes understanding the functions and interactions between humans and machines. As work becomes more complex and the sociotechnical environment advances, it is vital to understand the implications for humans.

Task analysis is a sophisticated method of dissecting a skill, action, or cognitive function into its fundamental sub-tasks required for a system operator to achieve overarching objectives (Knisely et al., 2021). This method proves invaluable as it highlights individual task elements, allowing for independent evaluation or modification. Serving as a cornerstone in human factors research, task analysis finds its utility across various domains, such as product development, instructional blueprinting, role distribution, and evaluations of errors and workload dynamics (Knisely et al., 2021).

Task analysis within the human factors framework is pivotal in enhancing cybersecurity measures, primarily by providing a detailed understanding of user-system interactions and subsequently improving the effectiveness of security protocols. Below, we have outlined how task analysis applies to cybersecurity:

User Behavior Analysis:
- **Mapping User Interactions:** Task analysis allows security professionals to delineate the steps users typically follow when interacting with a system, providing insights into standard behavior patterns.
- **Identifying Risky Behaviors:** Understanding routine user behaviors aids in spotting deviations or unsafe practices that could compromise security, thereby facilitating proactive risk mitigation strategies.

Developing User-Centric Protocols:
- **Enhancing User Experience:** The process helps design user-friendly security interfaces and protocols, encouraging user compliance.
- **Minimizing Human Error:** With a keen understanding of user tasks and behavior, systems can be designed to minimize the risk of human error leading to security breaches.

Security Training:
- **Effective Education:** Task analysis supports the creation of targeted training modules by identifying critical tasks and user responsibilities, thus enhancing the effectiveness of cybersecurity education and awareness programs.
- **Behavioral Change:** Insights drawn help in crafting strategies that promote secure behavior amongst users, bolstering the organization's overall cybersecurity posture.

Threat Mitigation:
- **Insider Threat Analysis:** The methodology helps understand and predict insider threats by analyzing deviations from typical user behavior.

- **Phishing Prevention:** Task analysis can inform the development of mechanisms that help users identify and avoid falling victim to phishing attempts.

Incident Response Improvement:
- **Enhancing Response:** Detailed task analysis aids in creating effective incident response strategies by providing insights into how users interact with systems during a security incident.
- **Post-Incident Analysis:** The approach supports identifying and rectifying user-related vulnerabilities that may have contributed to security breaches.

System Design and Usability:
- **Designing Secure Systems:** By understanding user tasks and workflows, designers can create inherently secure yet user-friendly systems.
- **Integrating Security Measures:** Task analysis supports the seamless integration of security features into user workflows, ensuring security without compromising usability.

Continuous Improvement:
- **Feedback Incorporation:** Regular task analysis supports improving security protocols by considering user feedback and evolving threat landscapes.
- **Adaptation to Changing Behaviors:** Task analysis ensures that security protocols remain relevant and effective as user behaviors and tasks evolve.

By meticulously analyzing and understanding the myriad tasks users undertake, human factors professionals can craft, refine, and implement security measures that address technological vulnerabilities and account for human behavior and its inherent risks. This holistic approach considerably strengthens cybersecurity defenses.

3.11 Leveraging human-centered cybersecurity to thwart social engineering attacks

Social engineering attacks pose significant risks in cybersecurity by exploiting human vulnerabilities, often the weakest link in a network (Yang et al., 2023). Social engineering attacks leverage human vulnerabilities to manipulate and deceive individuals into disclosing sensitive information (Yang et al., 2023). Conventional defense strategies against social engineering often overlook user vulnerability, resulting in ineffective defense measures (Yang et al., 2023). Abu Hweidi and Eleyan (2023) posit that the primary challenge lies in effectively addressing social engineering while maintaining abreast of techniques, tactics, and procedures malicious actors use to execute social engineering attacks. This is attainable by prioritizing user awareness through tailored educational programs across different age groups, as users represent the weakest link in the security system (Abu Hweidi & Eleyan, 2023). Existing user awareness training needs to account for human limitations and weaknesses and underprepared end-users to understand their psychological weaknesses.

Integrating human factors practices such as human-centered protocols can aid in designing better user awareness training that focuses on preventing social engineering attacks by designing awareness programs centering on disrupting the social engineering exploitation. Figure 3.1 highlights the user components as one of the verticals of human-centric cybersecurity and the significance of psychological and behavioral dynamics, cognitive factors, and culture. Delving comprehensively into social engineering and all its intricacies is beyond the scope of this research. However, it is critical to discuss how human-centered cybersecurity can assist in preventing social engineering attacks through increased focus on the psychological aspects of the users.

According to Nobles (2022a), cognitive hacking, which involves cybercriminals and malicious hackers capitalizing on the psychological vulnerabilities of end-users, is identified as a flourishing cyberattack vector. Most cybersecurity awareness programs fail to train end-users on psychological weaknesses, and malicious actors capitalize on this knowledge gap through social engineering attacks. Training end-users to be aware of their psychological, cognitive, and physiological conditions through human-centered cybersecurity practices and designing systems that account for human limitations and vulnerabilities can aid in reducing attacks targeting human wetware. Given the knowledge gap and lack of concerted efforts between governments, academia, and industry, it calls for coordinated initiatives to increase attention on reducing social engineering attacks beyond technological solutions.

3.12 Integration of human factors professionals in cybersecurity

According to Contreras (2022), the presence of psychologists working in the tech space providing psychological science in product development remains dearth even though technological innovations are known to drive behavioral change. Technology influences human behavior, emotion, and reasoning, while most innovations are engineered and built by technologists without expertise in psychological science (Contreras, 2022). The design of tech products and security are critical elements of human factors engineering in cybersecurity (Robinson, 2023); consequently, the absence of psychology-based and human factors professionals in the tech domain contributes to human vulnerabilities and weaknesses exploited through offensive cybersecurity. Other sectors, such as aviation, healthcare, and industrial safety, benefit significantly from human factors and psychological sciences, but cybersecurity continues to lag behind other social-technical domains.

In the past, technology firms were more inclined towards enterprise applications, hardware, and tech-savvy professionals, creating less demand for industrial psychologists. Instead, these companies heavily favored computer scientists (Contreras, 2022). This trend persists, with Google employees exemplifying it. A significant proportion studied computer or computational sciences (29%), while less than 2% studied psychology (Contreras, 2022). The shortage of psychology professionals in the tech sector is a common practice. Consequently, the technology industry has often overlooked the potential contributions of psychology, possibly due to its underrepresentation within tech leadership (Contreras, 2022). This suggests an underutilization of psychological insights in the tech sector.

At its essence, cybersecurity should pivot around human elements, commonly termed as 'soft components' or 'shadow risks' (Stein, 2018). Comprehending the human factor is pivotal for mitigating inadvertent errors and intentional malicious activities (Stein, 2018). Stein emphasizes the importance of establishing human factor programs and asserts that business decision-makers often place more emphasis on technological considerations rather than the human psychosocial dimensions (Stein, 2018). Stein provides extensive details about efforts to support organizations and executive leaders in identifying risks associated with insider threats. This highlights psychologists' critical role in offering scientific and analytical support to strategic efforts to understand the boundary between humans and technology, thus preventing unintended consequences (Stein, 2018). As organizations pursue advanced intelligent technologies, psychologists become instrumental in counterbalancing human abilities and comprehension with innovations like artificial intelligence, ensuring optimal decision-making and outcomes (Stein, 2018).

Wiederhold (2014) underscored the following potential applications of psychological expertise:
1. Comprehending user behavior in the context of evaluating risks and rewards.
2. Recognizing and interpreting deviant behaviors of malicious actors and consequently developing technological tools to mitigate psychological manipulation.
3. Acting as consultants to policymakers in creating laws related to cybercrime.
4. Collaborating with labs, media, and social networks to enlighten the public about the various psychological tactics employed by cybercriminals.
5. Examining the psychological impact and experiences of cybercrime victims.

The integration of psychological science and human factors engineering in product development in the tech space is impeded by technologists oblivious to the (a) Dunning-Kruger effect, (b) folk psychology, and (c) illusion of explanatory depth (Contreras, 2022; Nobles, 2022a). Though technology firms employ user researchers to study consumer behavior, they often independently rediscover insights already present in over a century's worth of academic psychology (Contreras, 2022). Technology companies may overlook established findings without psychologists informing this research, leading to potentially redundant explorations (Contreras, 2022).

A standard practice in the cyber domain is to rely extensively on technology – creating an overreliance on technology (Nobles, 2022a). While technology is necessary for cybersecurity due to the tumultuous threat environment, according to researchers, the constant integration of new technology can result in human performance degradation (Wilson et al., 2022). This is an area where psychologists can assist with examining the adverse impact of what Wilson et al. call the technology-induced cycle. An existing gap is the lack of practical solutions to mitigate human weaknesses and limitations when using technologies to combat or outmaneuver offensive cybersecurity tactics imposed by malicious threat actors.

These suppositions underscore the significance and practicality of incorporating psychology-based professions in cybersecurity. By integrating psychological insights and expertise, organizations can enhance their understanding of human behavior, motivations, and decision-making processes, strengthening their cybersecurity posture. Psychology-based approaches can provide valuable insights into the human aspects of cybersecurity, such as insider threats, social engineering, and user awareness and training. This interdisciplinary collaboration between psychology and cybersecurity helps bridge the gap between technical and human factors, leading to more effective strategies and solutions in combating cyber threats.

Psychologists bring unique perspectives and skill sets, enabling the contribution to developing comprehensive cybersecurity programs and initiatives. Their expertise can inform the design and implementation of human-centric security measures, ensuring that cybersecurity solutions align with human cognitive capabilities, limitations, and behaviors. Moreover, psychologists can contribute to developing training programs, policies, and procedures that promote security awareness and behavior change among individuals and organizations. Collaboration between cybersecurity professionals and psychologists enables the development of comprehensive strategies that account for both technological and human dimensions, ultimately enhancing the resilience of digital systems and protecting sensitive information.

3.13 Emerging human factors areas in cybersecurity

3.13.1 Cybergonomics

As society continues to evolve and leverage advanced technologies, the need to understand how technologies influence online and people, in general, becomes critical in solidifying cybersecurity defense and data management. A developing area is cybergonomics. Cybergonomics encompasses the ergonomic principles tailored for advanced cyber-technologies (Pouyakian, 2022). Melding the prowess of cyber-science with ergonomic objectives, this discipline delves deep into the human-technology interface, aiming to elevate safety, enhance productivity, and promote holistic well-being (Pouyakian, 2022). It critically evaluates the advantages and challenges of technologies inherent to the Industry 4.0 era, ensuring alignment with human aptitudes and our physical, cognitive, and emotional boundaries (Pouyakian, 2022). Essentially, cybergonomics seeks to seamlessly merge insights from cyber-focused ergonomic research, creating a harmonious interaction between humans and the digital world (Pouyakian, 2022). This emerging area is vital for understanding humans in the digital space to improve the design and reduce friction for people.

3.13.2 Cyberpsychology

As our world becomes more digitally interwoven and technology advances unprecedentedly, cyberpsychology carves out its niche as a distinct academic realm (Ancis, 2020). At its core, cyberpsychology seeks to unravel the intricate psychological dynamics underpinning our behavior in this interconnected technological landscape (Atrill-Smith et al., 2019). Cyberpsychology is an interdisciplinary tapestry, weaving threads from human-computer interaction, computer science, engineering, and traditional psychology, creating a comprehensive framework to explore our evolving digital psyche (Ancis, 2020). Equipped with their specialized knowledge and prowess, psychologists emerge as pioneering agents of change and innovation in our dynamically shifting world (Ancis, 2020). Contemporary scientific endeavors necessitate psychologists' collaboration with experts from diverse domains, including computer science, engineering, and bioinformatics (Ancis, 2020). As stewards of understanding human behavior and cognition, psychologists and their fellow social scientists are responsible for forging a robust foundation for cyberpsychology (Ancis, 2020). This ensures its growth is rooted in scientific rigor and ethical considerations, all while addressing pressing global challenges.

Of concern is that the cybersecurity industry is slow to recognize the benefits of human factors engineering in cybersecurity. Emerging fields such as cybergonomics and cyberpsychology are critical for expanding theoretical and practical solutions for human-technology relationships. The cybersecurity domain needs to work with academia to gain a more prosperous and deeper understanding of the budding fields and their application to cybersecurity operations.

3.14 The conundrum of studying cybersecurity through the human factors lens

Human factors research has illuminated the burgeoning imperative for an enriched comprehension of the intricacies of cybersecurity roles (Dodge et al., 2012; Knott et al., 2013; Lathrop et al., 2016). Noteworthy endeavors have been made to delve into the nuances of cyber defense professions, underscoring the complexity of this domain (D'Amico & Whitley, 2008; Mahoney et al., 2010).

Nevertheless, the research methodologies traditionally harnessed by human factors scholars frequently stumble upon barriers, especially within the labyrinth of high-security terrains like cybersecurity. Armstrong et al. (2017) grappled with similar impediments when striving to engage with cyberattackers and defenders. The researchers augmented by insights from a seasoned Subject Matter Expert (SME) who offered a unique vantage point with over half a decade of intimate interactions with cyber professionals (Armstrong et al., 2017). Through this collaboration, Armstrong et al. (2017) discerned four quintessential challenges that researchers might face when navigating cybersecurity terrains: (a) the infeasibility of real-time observations, (b) imperatives of participant anonymity and safety, (c) time constraints in data extraction; and (d) the delicacy of probing deep-seated procedural queries. The endeavor to work within these parameters inevitably poses conundrums, given that many standard analytical techniques often find themselves at odds with such constraints.

While the abovementioned research concerns are bothersome, human factors researchers need to leverage academic and industry partnerships to conduct studies with less artificiality to gain accurate analysis and results.

3.15 Conclusions

In the rapidly evolving cybersecurity sphere, including human factors engineering stands as a beacon of transformative potential. At its core, human factors methodologies, deeply rooted in understanding the nuances of human interaction, behaviors, and cognitive processes, present a harmonious marriage with cyberpsychology. This union empowers us to delve deeper into the intricate labyrinth of the human psyche, facilitating a more profound comprehension of how individuals interact with, respond to, and perceive cyber ecosystems.

Central to the promise of human factors engineering in cybersecurity is the pursuit of human error mitigation. By designing to create systems and protocols that are technically sound and intrinsically aligned with human tendencies and capacities, we substantially reduce the window for inadvertent mistakes. Human-centered cybersecurity prioritizes the end-user, transforming them from a potential vulnerability into a robust line of defense. By centering design and strategy around the end-user, systems become more intuitive, reducing the cognitive load and minimizing potential missteps borne out of confusion or oversight.

Furthermore, as we venture into the epoch of digital dependence, merely introducing robust technical defenses is insufficient. True cybersecurity resilience emerges when behavioral change is achieved at an individual and collective level. Through human factors engineering; we are not just optimizing systems but fostering a culture where every user is acutely aware, informed, and proactive in their cyber interactions. By its very ethos, the discipline ensures that as technology leaps forward, humanity is not left behind but moves in tandem, creating a safer, more secure digital landscape for all.

References

Abu Hweidi, R. F., & Eleyan, D. (2023). Social engineering attack concepts, frameworks, and awareness: A systematic literature review. *International Journal of Computing and Digital Systems*.

Acuña, D.C. (2016). Effects of a comprehensive computer security policy on computer security culture. *MWAIS 2016 Proceedings*. 10. https://aisel.aisnet.org/mwais2016/10

Alavi, R., Islam, S., Jahankhani, H., & Al-Nemrat, A. (2013). Analyzing human factors for an effective information security management system. *International Journal of Secure Software Engineering (IJSSE)*, 4(1), 50–74.

Ancis, J. R. (2020). The age of cyberpsychology: an overview. *TMB* 1. doi: 10.1037/tmb0000009

Atrill-Smith, A., Fullwood, C., Keep, M., & Kuss, D. J. (Eds.). (2019). The Oxford Handbook of Cyberpsychology. Oxford University Press. https://www.oxfordhandbooks.com/view/10.1093/oxfordhb/9780198812746.001.0001/oxfordhb-9780198812746

Anu, V., Hu, W., Carver, J. C., Walia, G. S., & Bradshaw, G. (2018). Development of a human error taxonomy for software requirements: A systematic literature review. *Information and Software Technology, 103*, 112–124.

Armstrong, M. E., Jones, K. S., & Namin, A. S. (2017, September). Framework for developing a brief interview to understand cyber defense work: An experience report. In *Proceedings of the Human Factors and Ergonomics Society Annual Meeting* (Vol. 61, No. 1, pp. 1318–1322). Sage CA: Los Angeles, CA: SAGE Publications.

Briggs, P., Jeske, D., & Coventry, L. (2017). Behavior change interventions for cybersecurity. In *Behavior change research and theory* (pp. 115–136). Academic Press.

Bureau, S. (2018). Human-centered cybersecurity: A new approach to securing networks. Research at RIT. Rochester Institute of Technology Research Report, Fall/Winter 2017–2018.

Chartered Institute of Ergonomics & Human Factors (CIEHF). (2022, March 16). *The role of human factors in delivering cyber security: An overview for cybersecurity decision-makers (White Paper)*. https://ergonomics.org.uk/resource/the-role-of-human-factors-in-delivering-cyber-security.html

Cybersecurity and Infrastructure Security Agency (CISA). (2023, April 13). Shifting the balance of cybersecurity risk: Principles and approaches for security-by-design and-default. https://www.cisa.gov/resources-tools/resources/secure-by-design-and-default

D'Amico, A. & Whitley, K. (2008). The real work of computer network defense analysts. In J. R. Goodall, G. Conti, & K. Ma (Eds): *VizSEC 2007* (pp. 19–37). Springer Berlin Heidelberg.

Dodge, R., Toregas, C., & Hoffman, L. J. (2012). Cybersecurity workforce development directions. In *HAISA*, 1–12.

Edmonds, J. (2016). What is human factors? In *Human factors in the chemical and process industries* (pp. 3–11). Elsevier.

Fitts, P.M., & Jones, R.E. (1947a). *Analysis of factors contributing to 460 "pilot error" experiences in operating aircraft controls* (Report No. TSEAA-694-12). Dayton, OH: Aero Medical Laboratory, Air Materiel Command, U.S. Air Force.

Fitts, P.M., & Jones, R.E. (1947b). *Psychological aspects of instrument display. Analysis of 270 "pilot-error" experiences in reading and interpreting aircraft instruments* (Report No. TSEAA-694-12A). Dayton, OH: Aero Medical Laboratory, Air Materiel Command, U.S. Air Force.

ForcePoint Security Labs. (2018). 2018 Security Predictions. https://www.forcepoint.com/sites/default/files/resources/files/report_2018_security_predictions_en.pdf

Glaspie, H. W., & Karwowski, W. (2018). Human factors in information security culture: A literature review. In *Advances in Human Factors in Cybersecurity: Proceedings of the AHFE 2017 International Conference on Human Factors in Cybersecurity, July 17–21, 2017, The Westin Bonaventure Hotel, Los Angeles, California, USA 8* (pp. 269–280). Springer International Publishing.

Gosbee, J. (2002). Human factors engineering and patient safety. *Quality and Safety in Health Care, 11*(4), 352–354.

Grobler, M., Gaire, R., & Nepal, S. (2021). User, usage, and usability: Redefining human-centric cyber security. *Frontiers in Big Data, 4*, 583723.

Guastello, S. J. (2023). *Human factors engineering and ergonomics: A systems approach.* CRC Press.

Haney, J., Lutters, W., & Jacobs, J. (2021). Cybersecurity advocates: Force multipliers in security behavior change. *IEEE Security & Privacy, 19*(4), 54–59.

Holland, N. (2020). The human-centric cybersecurity stance. https://www.bankinfosecurity.com/human-centric-cybersecurity-stance-a-13897. doi:10.1287/2961bfc6-3c5b-481a-ae7c-47edf9c88831

Hollnagel, E. (2012). Task analysis: Why, what, and how. *Handbook of human factors and ergonomics,* 383–396.

Hughes-Lartey, K., Li, M., Botchey, F. E., & Qin, Z. (2021). Human factor, a critical weak point in the information security of an organization's Internet of things. *Heliyon, 7*(3).

Jeong, J., Mihelcic, J., Oliver, G., & Rudolph, C. (2019, December). Towards an improved understanding of human factors in cybersecurity. In *2019 IEEE 5th International Conference on Collaboration and Internet Computing (CIC)* (pp. 338–345). IEEE.

Knisely, B. M., Joyner, J. S., & Vaughn-Cooke, M. (2021). Cognitive task analysis and workload classification. *MethodsX, 8*, 101235.

Knott, B. A., Mancuso, V. F., Bennett, K., Finomore, V., McNeese, M., McKneely, J. A., & Beecher, M. (2013). Human factors in cyber warfare: Alternative perspectives. In *Proceedings of the Human Factors and Ergonomics Society Annual Meeting, 57*, 399–403.

Kraus, L., Wechsung, I., & Möller, S. (2017). Psychological needs as motivators for security and privacy actions on smartphones. *Journal of Information Security and Applications, 34*, 34–45.

Lathrop, S. D., Trent, S., & Hoffman, R. (2016). Applying human factors research towards cyberspace operations: A practitioner's perspective. *Advances in Human Factors in Cybersecurity,* 281–293.

Maalem Lahcen, R. A., Caulkins, B., Mohapatra, R., & Kumar, M. (2020). Review and insight on the behavioral aspects of cybersecurity. *Cybersecurity, 3*(1), 1–18.

Mahoney, S., Roth, E., Steinke, K., Pfautz, J., Wu, C., & Farry, M. (2010). A cognitive task analysis for cyber situational awareness. In *Proceedings of the Human Factors and Ergonomics Society Annual Meeting,* 279–83

Mancuso, V. F., Strang, A. J., Funke, G. J., & Finomore, V. S. (2014, September). Human factors of cyber-attacks: a framework for human-centered research. In *Proceedings of the Human Factors and Ergonomics Society Annual Meeting* (Vol. 58, No. 1, pp. 437–441). Sage CA: Los Angeles, CA: SAGE Publications.

Meister, D. (2018). *The history of human factors and ergonomics.* CRC Press.

Mohammad, T., Hussin, N. A. M., & Husin, M. H. (2022). Online safety awareness and human factors: An application of the theory of human ecology, *Technology in Society, 68*, 101823.

Moustafa, A. A., Bello, A., & Maurushat, A. (2021). The role of user behaviour in improving cyber security management. *Frontiers in Psychology, 12*, 561011.

Ncubukezi, T. (2022, March). Human errors: A cybersecurity concern and the weakest link to small businesses. In *Proceedings of the 17th International Conference on Information Warfare and Security* (p. 395).

Nobles, C. (2018). Botching human factors in cybersecurity in business organizations. *HOLISTICA–Journal of Business and Public Administration, 9*(3), 71–88.

Nobles, C. (2022). Stress, burnout, and security fatigue in cybersecurity: A human factors problem. *HOLISTICA–Journal of Business and Public Administration, 13*(1), 49–72.

Nobles, C. (2022a, March) The Dunning-Kruger Effect around human factors in cybersecurity, *Top Cyber News Magazine*. https://www.linkedin.com/company/topcybernews/

Nobles, C. (2023). Human factors in cybersecurity: Academia's missed opportunity. *MWAIS 2023 Proceedings*. 8. https://aisel.aisnet.org/mwais2023/8

Öğütçü, G., Testik, Ö. M., & Chouseinoglou, O. (2016). Analysis of personal information security behavior and awareness. *Computers & Security, 56*, 83–93.

Patient Safety Network (PSN). (2019, September 07). Human factors engineering. https://psnet.ahrq.gov/primer/human-factors-engineering#

Pearlson, K., & Huang, K. (2022). Design for cybersecurity from the start. *MIT Sloan Management Review, 63*(2), 73–77.

Pfleeger, S. L., & Caputo, D. D. (2012). Leveraging behavioral science to mitigate cyber security risk. *Computers & Security, 31*(4), 597–611

Poehlmann, N., Caramancion, K. M., Tatar, I., Li, Y., Barati, M., & Merz, T. (2021). The organizational cybersecurity success factors: an exhaustive literature review. *Advances in Security, Networks, and Internet of Things: Proceedings from SAM'20, ICWN'20, ICOMP'20, and ESCS'20*, 377–395.

Pollini, A., Callari, T. C., Tedeschi, A., Ruscio, D., Save, L., Chiarugi, F., & Guerri, D. (2021). Leveraging human factors in cybersecurity: an integrated methodological approach. *Cognition, Technology & Work, 24*(2), 371–390.

Pollock, T. (2017). Reducing human error in cyber security using the Human Factors Analysis Classification System (HFACS). *KSU Proceedings on Cybersecurity Education, Research and Practice*. 2. https://digitalcommons.kennesaw.edu/ccerp/2017/research/2

Posey, C., & Shoss, M. (2022). Research: Why employees violate cybersecurity policies. *Harvard Business Review*.

Pouyakian, M. (2022). Cybergonomics: Proposing and justification of a new name for the ergonomics of Industry 4.0 technologies. *Frontiers in Public Health, 10*, 1012985.

Pratt, M. K. (2023, July 04). Why cyberpsychology is such an important part of effective cybersecurity. https://www.csoonline.com/article/643967/why-cyberpsychology-is-such-an-important-part-of-effective-cybersecurity.html

Rahman, T., Rohan, R., Pal, D., & Kanthamanon, P. (2021, June). Human factors in cybersecurity: a scoping review. In *The 12th International Conference on Advances in Information Technology* (pp. 1–11).

Reason, J. (1995). Understanding adverse events: human factors. *BMJ Quality & Safety, 4*(2), 80–89

Reason, J. (2008). The human contribution: Unsafe acts, accidents and heroic recoveries. *Farnham: Ashgate Publishing*.

Robinson, N. (2023). Human factors security engineering: the future of cybersecurity teams. *EDPACS*, 1–17.

Rogers, W. A., & McGlynn, S. A. (2018). Human factors and ergonomics: History, scope, and potential. In *Human Factors and Ergonomics for the Gulf Cooperation Council* (pp. 1–20). CRC Press.

Safa, N. S., Von Solms, R., & Furnell, S. (2016). Information security policy compliance model in organizations. *Computers & Security, 56*, 70–82.

Sasse, M. A., Brostoff, S., & Weirich, D. (2001). Transforming the 'weakest link' – a human/computer interaction approach to usable and effective security. *BT Technology Journal, 19*(3), 122–131.

Shappell, S., Detwiler, C., Holcomb, K., Hackworth, C., Boquet, A., & Wiegmann, D. A. (2017). Human error and commercial aviation accidents: an analysis using the human factors analysis and classification system. In *Human error in aviation* (pp. 73–88). Routledge.

Smith, W., Hill, B., Long, J., & Whitefield, A. (1997). A design-oriented framework for modeling the planning and control of multiple task work in secretarial office administration. *Behaviour & Information Technology, 16*(3), 161–183.

Stanton, N., Salmon, P. M., & Rafferty, L. A. (2013). *Human factors methods: a practical guide for engineering and design*. Ashgate Publishing, Ltd.

Stewart-Gloster, C. (2023, April). Safer together: Inclusive cybersecurity. TCIL Technical Note. https://www.fdd.org/wp-content/uploads/2023/04/fdd-memo-safer-together-inclusive-cybersecurity.pdf

Verizon. (2023). Data breach investigations report. https://www.verizon.com/business/resources/reports/dbir/2023/master-guide/

Wickens, C.D., & Hollands, J.G. (2000). *Engineering psychology and human performance (3rd ed)*. Upper Saddle River, NJ: Prentice Hall.

Yang, R., Zheng, K., Wang, X., Wu, B., & Wu, C. (2023). Social engineering attack-defense strategies based on reinforcement learning. *Computer Systems Science & Engineering, 47*(2).

Krista N. Engemann

4 An organizational climate primer for the development of cybersecurity socio-organizational frameworks

4.1 Introduction

The urgency to systematically examine the people, processes and systems that affect the safety and privacy of critical data is clear (OECD, 2015). Among the most vulnerable in the cybersecurity landscape, people – from end users to strategic decision-makers – invariably (though unintentionally) expose the weaknesses of the best laid cybersecurity plans. Information security scholars have responded by adopting socio-organizational frameworks to investigate the shared norms, values, and assumptions that may influence security compliance (Ashenden & Sasse, 2013; Da Veiga, Astakhova, Botha, & Herselman, 2020; Da Veiga & Martins, 2017; Dhillon & Backhouse, 2001), resulting in recommendations for leadership (Hooper & McKissack, 2016), policy (Cram, Proudfoot, & D'Arcy, 2017), training and development (Zwilling, 2022), and organizing (Hassandoust & Johnston, 2023).

Still, this scholarship is characterized by very little consensus. Little to no research has examined the effects of an information security culture (i.e., a subcomponent of an organization's culture, overall; Da Veiga & Martins, 2017) on security outcomes (Karlsson, Åström, & Karlsson, 2015). Few empirically-derived points of view have advanced how security-specific values and norms emerge and become shared (Nasir, Arshah, Hamid, & Fahmy, 2019). What's more, gaps in definition are pervasive (Da Veiga et al., 2020; Mahfuth, Yussof, Baker, & Ali, 2017). In turn, it is unclear whether takeaways for employees, teams, leaders, and organizations from present work resonate in practice (cf., Uchendu, Nurse, Bada, & Furnell, 2021).

In light of these limitations, this chapter aligns its solution with that which advances the theory and practice of organizations, in general: the development and validation of a measure of the shared norms and values which maintain an organization's security. In terms of the study of people in organizations, researchers are called to clearly define topics of interest, explain how the phenomenon is affected or can be affected by other forces, identify the limitations of these relationships, and demonstrate how that which was studied can address pertinent practical challenges (Antonakis, 2017). Thus the purpose of this review is to ensure that models are advanced iteratively with empirical evidence, supporting their validity. Conversely, without tests of relationships between constructs of value (e.g., security knowledge, security compliance; Da Veiga et al., 2020), future information security research is at risk of purporting theoretical relationships that are misleading.

https://doi.org/10.1515/9783111289069-004

As such, this chapter serves as an epistemological and methodological primer for information security and cybersecurity researchers on organizational climate, a 'sibling' of organizational culture (Schneider, Ehrhart, & Macey, 2011). Employees' self-reported feelings and behaviors receive considerable attention in the study of organizations, and measures which assess the extent to which they are shared are often linked with key outcomes (e.g., customer satisfaction, financial performance). This chapter's discussion of measurement considerations, in particular, asks the reader to examine so-called human factors (Schultz, 2005) at the level of the individual and the group. To improve its resonance with research that takes aim at breaches and errors, this review also frames organizational climate in terms of a field of comparable consequence (i.e., occupational health and safety), demonstrating how such an approach iteratively advances implications for its theory and practice.

Notably, this chapter does not offer a review of extant information security culture theory; there are many insightful discussions and frameworks available, several of which are cited in this work. Moreover, this chapter does not delve into the differences between culture and climate, which have been refined over decades of organizational theory development (e.g., Denison, 1996; Reichers & Schneider, 1990; Schneider, Ehrhart, & Macey, 2013). Instead, the sections to follow take on making practical progress by suggesting how to operationalize perceptions of shared norms and values for research to then adapt. The aim of the discussion is to offer certain tools that may facilitate studies and interventions that address people and information systems.

4.2 Measuring organizational climate

Climate generally reflects thoughts, feelings, and behaviors with respect to a particular setting or focus (e.g., Lewin, Lippitt, & White, 1939). Its operationalization relays a sense of temporality, subjectivity, and manipulability. In other words, perceptions of climate can change over time, they reflect subjective interpretations of the environment, and they can be influenced. This conceptualization of climate also implies a separation between the individual and the environment, such that the conditions of the environment are interpreted by individuals and groups alike (Luria, 2019).

Organizational climate is grounded in these aforementioned characteristics; it captures that which employees experience and report happening to them in their workplace (Schneider, 1975b). This version of the construct is operationalized in terms of employees' shared perceptions with regard to policies, procedures, and practices and, as such, it is anticipated that these perceptions will reflect aspects of the environment that inform employee behavior. Whereas initial work considered the unit of analysis for the study of climate to be the organization (e.g., Argyris, 1958), subsequent critiques argued for distinctions among individuals and groups (e.g., Guion, 1973).

Therefore, climate can be conceptualized at various levels of analysis (Glick, 1985), and it is important to appropriately label the relevant unit of the organization to which the study of climate refers because these levels may differ empirically (Howe, 1977; Zohar & Luria, 2005; Zohar & Tenne-Gazit, 2008).

Climate can be conceptualized at both the individual level (e.g., Barling, Loughlin, & Kelloway, 2002) and at the group or unit level (e.g., Hofmann & Stetzer, 1996). At the individual level, climate is conceptualized as one's perceptions of the organizational environment. This is often referred to as psychological climate. In the context of work, psychological climate reflects individuals' own perceptions of the work environment and emphasizes how these individuals perceive and make sense of organizational polices, practices, and procedures in psychologically meaningful terms. Psychological climate is also readily informed by situational referents that are salient to employees, like job autonomy (Parker, Axtell, & Turner, 2001), organizational support, and emphasis on rules and regulation (Clarke, 2010). At the group or unit level, climate represents a sharedness of individual perceptions often operationalized under a specific leader, supervisor, or group. The relationship between psychological and organizational climate can be described as compositional; both constructs reference the same content but describe qualitatively different phenomena at the individual and group levels of analysis. Psychological climate is a property of the individual, but when shared across individuals within a group, unit, or organization, the aggregate of the responses represents the construct of organizational climate.[1]

While it is important to maintain consistency among theory, measurement, and analysis, this is not to suggest that psychological climate is not relevant for the study of organizational climate or that organizational climate is not at all comprised of individual characteristics. Rather, individual, group, and organizational levels of theory and analysis should be recognized for the study of climate. Moreover, aggregated psychological climate has been argued to be an organization-level analog that is distinct from psychological climate, where the unit of analysis is defined by grouping organizational members with similar climate scores (Glick, 1985; James, 1982). Previous research defines units within the organization in terms of perceptual agreement, and climate scores are aggregated to the collective level. This suggests that aggregating psychological climate to make inferences about psychological climate would result in a fallacy, where the analyzed unit is inconsistent with the theorized unit (Roberts, Hulin, & Rousseau, 1978; Schneider, 1975a). Therefore, aggregation of perceptual measures can be argued for the study of organizational climate, and high levels of within-group perceptual agreement may justify aggregation.

---

1 From this point on, the term, "organizational climate," is used to describe group-level climates (James et al., 2008).

These aforementioned distinctions between psychological and organizational climate emphasize a hierarchical perspective for the development of climate constructs. This perspective partitions climate into general and facet-specific climates (e.g., service climate; Burke, Borucki, & Hurley, 1992; Schneider, Bowen, Ehrhart, & Holcombe, 2000; Schneider & Bowen, 1993). Altogether, this suggests that a higher-order climate refers to those shared perceptions of a more all-encompassing environment, and that a first-order climate refers to those shared perceptions that are more specific to a functional area, or facet, of the organization. Organizational climate should then be assessed as a specific construct with a particular referent or focus that is indicative of certain organizational goals. This approach aligns climate measures with the relative importance of a particular strategic focus over other competing interests.

4.2.1 Composition models

While exclusive focus on the individual in climate research is unlikely to be as informative as a study involving the individual, the group, or the organization, it is important to distinguish these foci to better understand how they inform one another across levels of analysis. Composition models are particularly relevant for the operationalization of group-level constructs. Composition models reflect how a construct is defined at one level of analysis is related to other forms of constructs at different levels of analysis (Kozlowski & Klein, 2000).

The specific composition model to be used is typically derived from theory and operationalized as some combination of lower-level units. In addition to providing a theoretical rationale for the chosen composition model, it is important to provide empirical evidence to support the aggregation of lower-level units to produce a higher-level construct. To not consider these composition issues is to obscure the interpretation of results. For instance, a mismatch among theoretical rationale, measurement, and analysis may result in confounded theoretical and methodological linkages with the constructs in question (Klein, Dansereau, & Hall, 1994; Rousseau, 1985). For comparable operationalizations of group-level constructs, consensus and dispersion composition models are typically implemented to address the study of climate.

4.2.1.1 Consensus composition models

Chan (1998) addresses two approaches to consensus models, namely, the direct consensus and the referent-shift consensus models. These two composition models share defining characteristics of general consensus models, yet their primary difference emerges from a shift in the referent from the individual to the collective. Whereas direct consensus aggregates participant responses to survey items that refer to the individual's perception (e.g., "I believe"), referent-shift consensus aggregates participant responses to survey items that represent an individual's perception of a higher-level structure, like a group or unit (e.g., "My team believes").

There are two main considerations in operationalizing constructs with consensus composition models. First, constructs must be conceptualized and defined at each level of analysis. For the study of climate in organizations, psychological climate is operationalized in terms of individuals' responses to survey items and their subsequent composite scores, and organizational climate is operationalized in terms of the mean of these responses within each group (e.g., group, team, or work unit). Second, the aggregation of individual responses to a higher-level construct must be appropriately justified. That is, before determining that the overall mean of the aggregated data is representative of the construct at a higher level of analysis, there must be a level of agreement among individual responses. This is determined by the extent of the variability in responses. That is, most surveyed members of the group must agree in rating their climate as poor, average, or above average in order to describe the group overall as having a negative, neutral, or positive climate. This consideration is important because it ensures that the aggregated score depicts the higher-level perception of the construct of interest. Moreover, sufficient agreement at the individual level presumably demonstrates that the chosen aggregation method yields a reliable and valid group-level measure.

Several statistics may establish construct validity. Climate researchers often use within-group agreement (rWG) to assess consensus composition models (James, Demaree, & Wolf, 1984; Newman & Sin, 2018). rWG is an index of inter-rater agreement that assesses agreement among multiple raters in rating a single target. This metric references the observed variance in ratings to the expected variance, if the ratings were random. rWG(j) may also be used, as this metric is a form of rWG that indexes inter-rater agreement among multiple raters in rating a single target with J number of items. rWG(j) represents the degree to which raters agree on the set J items representing a single construct (Klein et al., 2000).

The intraclass correlation (ICC(1), ICC(2)) can also be used to supplement the decision to aggregate climate scores. The intraclass correlation statistic compares the variability of different ratings of the same subject to the total variation across all ratings and subjects. Some rely on intraclass correlation statistics based on one way analysis of variance (e.g., Shrout & Fleiss, 1978). This approach advocates using the intraclass correlation, ICC(1), to assess interrater agreement as the primary criterion for aggregating perceptual measures of organizational climate. This intraclass correlation is an accepted aggregate-level mean rater reliability statistic when organizational climate is conceptualized as a group characteristic; it is also accepted when the reliability of the aggregated measure is used to determine the appropriateness of an aggregated perceptual measure. What's more, this statistic supports whether increasing the number of raters is attributable to increases in the reliability of the aggregated measure, rather than to an inflation of individual level perceptual agreement (Nunnally, 1978).

Just as ICC(1) is an appropriate aggregate-level reliability statistic for organizational climate measures, so too is a comparable statistic, ICC(2). ICC(2) estimates group-mean reliability and has been applied in climate research that investigates complexities among hierarchically ordered climates (e.g., Zohar & Luria, 2004, 2005, 2010). This extension is important for compositional models; within-group agreement does not necessarily reveal much about the extent of the test of the theoretical model. For instance, if individuals are identical within groups, yet groups differ from one another, researchers can learn from each group just as well as they can learn from all individual members of all groups. ICC(2) is particularly important for the detection of emergent relationships when the aggregation of a lower-level construct into a higher-level one is theorized to be both related to and distinct from the originating lower-level construct. That is, groups must have reliably different mean values on the construct of interest (Bliese, 2000).

4.2.1.2 Dispersion composition models

Although both the consensus and dispersion composition models rely on individual responses to represent a construct at a higher level of analysis, the dispersion model does not rely on composite or average scores to do so. Rather, the dispersion composition model is distinct from the consensus composition model because of its focus on variability as its own construct. As such, the dispersion model can be used to assess group variability in itself rather than be used solely as a prerequisite for aggregation. This comes as a response to some limitations associated with rWG (e.g., the assumption that all response options are equally likely when responses are random). In fact, the dispersion model views within-group variance at the individual level as further insight into the perceptions of respondents.

The literature on organizational climate describes dispersion as a measure of strength, where low climate strength reflects low agreement and, thus, high dispersion (Lindell & Brandt, 2000; Schneider, Salvaggio, & Subirats, 2002). Strength is often interpreted as the consensus among respondents, and it is considered a construct itself.[2] But because the dispersion model captures variability in responses within a group, it is inevitably related to the main construct of interest. Constructs like climate strength provide additional explanation of variance above and beyond the absolute measure of the construct of interest.

Studies have applied dispersion models to demonstrate that consensus varies between groups and that this variability is meaningful. For example, climate strength has been operationalized as the standard deviation of climate level (e.g., Zohar & Luria, 2005). Greater consensus may more clearly indicate the relationship between

---

2 Here, "consensus" is not meant as a reference to Chan's (1998) consensus composition models.

the construct of interest and other variables because it yields a more reliable mean than less consensus does (Lindell & Brandt, 2000). Although the level of dispersion may influence an outcome above and beyond the absolute levels of the construct of interest, there is still much to be learned about this composition model (e.g., Smith-Crowe, Burke, Cohen, & Doveh, 2014).

4.3 Measuring organizational climate for improved occupational health and safety

Described as "a frame of reference for guiding appropriate and adaptive task behaviors" (Zohar, 1980, p. 96), organizational climate for occupational health and safety implies a serious strategic challenge for organizations. In industries with inherent physical risks (e.g., healthcare, manufacturing), it is critical to ensure employee safety. Complex regulations and regulatory bodies, gaps in training and communication, and changes to technologies are among the factors that may, nonetheless, complicate how employees perceive safety in their workplace. In turn, safety climate is a measure of how effectively various safety polices, practices, and procedures at different levels of an organization have been implemented. That is, the measure indicates a shared sense of the overall value, priority, and importance placed on safety in a particular setting.

Foundational work defined safety climate as "a unified set of cognitions [held by workers] regarding the safety aspects of their organization" (Zohar, 1980, p. 101). This work emerged in response to a focus on technical failures and human error as the cause of accidents in safety-oriented organizations (e.g., Turner, 1978). Alternatively, this approach reflected social and organizational factors as that which differentiated accident-prone organizations from safer ones (e.g., designated safety officers and safety training). This work revealed two climate dimensions as most influential in determining safety climate: the perceived relevance of safety to employee behavior and the perceived management attitude toward safety. The first dimension captured respondents' views as to whether safety training was an important prerequisite for successful performance and whether a faster work pace was hazardous for the workplace. The second dimension captured respondents' views as to whether management (e.g., safety officers and safety committees) valued safety. This was determined by asking for respondents' perceptions of their managers' authority and active participation with respect to safety-related decisions.

Subsequent factor analytic studies of safety climate scales suggested a hierarchical structure consisting of various first-order factors and a global, higher-order factor: management commitment to safety (Hofmann & Morgeson, 1999; Hofmann & Stetzer, 1998). However, there is not much agreement concerning the first-order factors (e.g., safety inspections, personnel training, safety communication), and they often assume different meanings at different levels of analysis. Studies that advance theoretical and practical implications about safety climate have moved on to focus on the core meaning of the construct (i.e., management commitment to safety) and have left other variables to assume a secondary role (Zohar, 2008). As such, in the interest of developing parsimonious theory, researchers typically address: (1) the policies and procedures indicative of the organization's values and their allocation of resources; and (2) the supervisory practices indicative of organizational priorities under competing demands and pressures.

Further research has since tested and revised implications for theory and practice accordingly. For instance, safety climate had been posited as perceptions of an objective set of conditions, where social exchange activates reciprocity (cf., Blau, 1964). That is, employees are obligated to follow safe work practices, as aligned with formal procedure and policy, because they perceive management as placing emphasis on workplace safety (Hofmann, Morgeson, & Gerras, 2003; Mearns & Reader, 2008; Neal & Griffin, 2004). As such, safety climate was often hypothesized to correlate with accident rates as well as to mediate safe and unsafe behaviors. Studies since revealed that safety climate is associated with several other constructs that give way to safety performance (e.g., Griffin & Neal, 2000; Neal, Griffin, & Hart, 2000), including policy-compliant behaviors (safety compliance), helping behaviors (i.e., going above and beyond what is expected; safety participation), a willingness to enact safe behavior (safety motivation), and an understanding of how to perform under a given safety policy or procedure (safety knowledge). Meta-analytic findings suggested that both safety motivation and safety knowledge mediate the relationship between safety climate and safety performance (Christian, Bradley, Wallace, & Burke, 2009). This mediation also suggested that employees may be selected, trained, and supported towards a priority for safety.

4.3.1 Composition models in context

Researchers have applied both consensus and dispersion models to study safety climate. Consensus models are typical for assessing safety climate level, whereas dispersion models assess safety climate strength. The distinction between safety climate level and safety climate strength is particularly relevant for theory. That is, it is likely that employees are guided by inconsistent performance expectations; some members of some units perceive the importance of safety differently from members of other units. Safety climate level and safety climate strength are then parameters that reflect the nuances of how employees interpret their organizational environment.

Safety climate level was the focus of Zohar's (1980) original facet-specific measure of safety climate. Safety climate level captures a sense of imperative, or the perceived relative importance of safety to members of the group as specified by the referent. Given the consensus model's focus on within-group homogeneity, when individuals perceive that safety is important with respect to the referent in question, each will report high levels on a safety climate scale and the overall mean score will be high. Safety climate level is then measured as the mean climate score of a group, where individual perceptions are aggregated to the group level.

The referent-shift consensus model is particularly relevant for reducing conceptual ambiguity about safety climate. Should safety climate perceptions be measured with items that refer interchangeably to both the organization's and the group's relative priorities, this would result in climate level scores that reflect an indeterminate mixture of both referents. Measures of safety climate thus discriminate between formal policies and procedures and supervisors' and members' practices (e.g., "Top management in this company . . ."; "My direct supervisor . . ."). While either the organization or the direct supervisor may be the referent, it is argued that there is no change in the meaning of safety climate across these levels of analysis (Zohar & Luria, 2010). This allows for safety climate scores to be compared. This comparison is relevant as supervisors can exercise managerial discretion to influence their unit's climate. This approach also identifies those whose perceived unit-level safety climate level exceeds (or does not exceed) the organizational-level safety climate.

Dispersion models have also been applied to demonstrate the heterogeneity of responses to measures of safety climate. In particular, this approach captures the extent to which management and employees display consistent patterns of action in terms of safety. This parameter appears to have important implications for the effect of safety climate on outcomes of interest. For instance, safety climate strength moderates the relationship between safety climate level and safety performance, with a stronger relationship occurring under more supportive conditions (Schneider et al., 2002). Other studies examined the antecedents of climate strength, showing that social interaction among unit members, trust in one's leader, homogeneity and simplicity of supervisory action patterns, and certain social network characteristics were all related to climate strength (Gonzalez-Roma & Hernandez, 2014; Luria, 2010; Zohar & Tenne-Gazit, 2008). Notably, safety climate strength at the organization and unit levels tends to be aligned (Zohar & Luria, 2005). This suggests that climate strength may be a reflection of the consistent implementation of policies across units.

4.4 Further considerations

The theory and techniques presented thus far do not necessarily forego the confounding influence of past incidents, like breaches or errors, on ratings. Accidents and injuries are typically considered a lagging indicator of safety; they indicate a presence of failure rather than an absence of safety (Beus, Payne, Bergman, & Arthur, 2010). Critically, the relationship between organizational climate and accident involvement may be moderated by research design. Only research that measures breaches or errors following a climate survey could presumably reject reverse causation as an explanation for any observed relationships with events (cf., Clarke, 2006).

Common method bias may also obstruct interpretation. That is, measures taken together harbor the potential for the common underlying method to have influenced the results to correlate (Avolio, Yammarino, & Bass, 1991; Lindell & Whitney, 2001). What's more, response bias may be more pronounced in correlations among aggregates (Ostroff, 1993). As such, researchers should separate constructs or multiple sources of data (Ostroff, Kinicki, & Clark, 2002). In some instances, safety research applies a random-split procedure to mitigate against spurious correlation as a result of having obtained climate and other data from members of the same group (e.g. Zohar & Luria, 2004, 2010). This procedure suggests collecting one set of data from one half of the group and the other set from the second half (cf., Schneider, Gonzalez-Roma, Ostroff, & West, 2017).

Lastly, additional factors may be integrated into models of behavior incrementally. Although originally treated as a static variable, safety climate has matured into an emergent property of organizations (cf., Weick, 1979, 1995) as a matter of the field's attention to theory, measurement, and practice. Its growth is evidenced by the several safety-related constructs mentioned (e.g., safety motivation) and implied (e.g., safety leadership; Clarke, 2013). Its development also continues through new measurement techniques, like configuring groups based on their pattern of high and low climate scores across all group-level climate dimensions (Schulte et al., 2009), and new theory, like positing group boundaries and organizational structures as meaningful for how climate perceptions emerge (Luria, 2019). Survey items can indeed be designed to gauge perceptions of many behaviors. Because their discriminant validity is critical (Campbell & Fiske, 1959), factor analysis results of any facet-specific climate's items should aim for a factorial structure that is characteristic of the climate of interest rather than of related constructs.

4.5 Conclusion

As a primer, this chapter reviews select scholarship to engage an empirical investigation of the shared norms and values which maintain an organization's security. The discussion illustrates techniques to operationalize socio-organizational frameworks, and it summarizes the development of a field that is of comparable practical consequence to the information security space. It is important to acknowledge that this chapter is not intended to be comprehensive; there are many perspectives which guide construct development across disciplines. Moreover, the theory and methodology that support the study of organizational climate continues to mature (e.g., Burke et al., 2022). Researchers are encouraged to develop and articulate their own principled approaches as they define models, gather and analyze empirical evidence, and present for peer review. Altogether, the insights derived here suggest that information security researchers and cybersecurity professionals can meaningfully advance their understanding of the people, processes and systems that affect the safety and privacy of digital systems and infrastructure. Such rigor necessarily builds a foundation upon which to advance the discipline and to derive meaningful implications.

References

Antonakis, J. (2017). On doing better science: From thrill of discovery to policy implications. *The Leadership Quarterly, 28*(1), 5–21.

Argyris, C. (1958). Some problems in conceptualizing organizational climate: A case study of a bank. *Administrative Science Quarterly, 2*(501–520).

Ashenden, D., & Sasse, A. (2013). CISOs and organisational culture: Their own worst enemy? *Computers & Security, 39*, 396–405.

Avolio, B. J., Yammarino, F. J., & Bass, B. M. (1991). Identifying common methods variance with data collected from a single source: An unresolved sticky issue. *Journal of Management, 17*(3), 571–587.

Barling, J., Loughlin, C., & Kelloway, E. K. (2002). Development and test of a model linking safety-specific transformational leadership and occupational safety. *Journal of Applied Psychology, 87*(3), 488–496.

Beus, J. M., Payne, S. C., Bergman, M. E., & Arthur, W. (2010). Safety climate and injuries: An examination of theoretical and empirical relationships. *Journal of Applied Psychology, 95*(4), 713–727.

Blau, P. M. (1964). *Exchange and Power in Social Life*. New York: Wiles.

Bliese, P. D. (2000). Within-group agreement, non-independence, and reliability. In K. J. Klein & S. Kozlowski, W.J. (Eds.). S. Zedeck (Series Ed.), *Multilevel Theory, Research, and Methods in Organizations* (pp. 349–381).

Burke, M. J., Borucki, C. C., & Hurley, A. E. (1992). Reconceptualizing psychological climate in a retail service environment: A multiple-stakeholder perspective. *Journal of Applied Psychology, 77*(5), 717–729.

Burke, M. J., Smith-Crowe, K., Burke, M. I., Cohen, A., Doveh, E., & Sun, S. (2022). The relative importance and interaction of contextual and methodological predictors of mean rWG for work climate. *Journal of Business and Psychology, 37*(5), 923–951.

Campbell, D. T., & Fiske, D. W. (1959). Convergent and discriminant validation by the multitrait-multimethod matrix. *Psychological Bulletin, 56*(2), 81–105.

Chan, D. (1998). Functional relations among constructs in the same content domain at different levels of analysis: A typology of composition models. *Journal of Applied Psychology, 83*(2), 234–246.

Christian, M. S., Bradley, J. C., Wallace, J. C., & Burke, M. J. (2009). Workplace safety: A meta-analysis of the roles of person and situation factors. *Journal of Applied Psychology, 94*(5), 1103–1127.

Clarke, S. (2006). The relationship between safety climate and safety performance: A meta-analytic review. *Journal of Occupational Health Psychology, 11*(4), 315–327.

Clarke, S. (2010). An integrative model of safety climate: Linking psychological climate and work attitudes to individual safety outcomes using meta-analysis. *Journal of Occupational and Organizational Psychology, 83*(3), 553–578.

Clarke, S. (2013). Safety leadership: A meta-analytic review of transformational and transactional leadership styles as antecedents of safety behaviours. Journal of Occupational and Organizational Psychology, 86(1), 22–49.

Cram, W. A., Proudfoot, J. G., & D'Arcy, J. (2017). Organizational information security policies: a review and research framework. European Journal of Information Systems, 26(6), 605–641. doi:10.1057/s41303-017-0059-9

Da Veiga, A., Astakhova, L. V., Botha, A., & Herselman, M. (2020). Defining organisational information security culture – Perspectives from academia and industry. Computers & Security, 92, 101713.

Da Veiga, A., & Martins, N. (2017). Defining and identifying dominant information security cultures and subcultures. Computers & Security, 70, 72 –94.

Denison, D. R. (1996). What is the difference between organizational culture and organizational climate? A native's point of view on a decade of paradigm wars. Academy of Management Review, 21(3), 619–654.

Dhillon, G., & Backhouse, J. (2001). Current directions in IS security research: towards socio-organizational perspectives. Information Systems Journal, 11(2), 127–153.

Glick, W. H. (1985). Conceptualizing and measuring organizational and psychological climate: Pitfalls in multilevel research. Academy of Management Review, 10(3), 601–616.

Gonzalez-Roma, V., & Hernandez, A. (2014). Climate uniformity: its influence on team communication quality, task conflict, and team performance. Journal of Applied Psychology, 99(6), 1042–1058.

Griffin, M. A., & Neal, A. (2000). Perceptions of safety at work: A framework for linking safety climate to safety performance, knowledge, and motivation. Journal of Occupational Health Psychology, 5(3), 347–358.

Guion, R. M. (1973). A note on organizational climate. Organizational Behavior & Human Performance, 9(1), 120–125.

Hassandoust, F., & Johnston, A. C. (2023). Peering through the lens of high-reliability theory: A competencies driven security culture model of high-reliability organisations. Information Systems Journal, 33(5), 1212–1238.

Hofmann, D. A., & Morgeson, F. P. (1999). Safety-related behavior as a social exchange: The role of perceived organizational support and leader-member exchange. Journal of Applied Psychology, 84(2), 286–296.

Hofmann, D. A., Morgeson, F. P., & Gerras, S. J. (2003). Climate as a moderator of the relationship between leader-member exchange and content specific citizenship: Safety climate as an exemplar. Journal of Applied Psychology, 88(1), 170–178.

Hofmann, D. A., & Stetzer, A. (1996). A cross-level investigation of factors influencing unsafe behaviors and accidents. Personnel Psychology, 49(2), 307–339.

Hofmann, D. A., & Stetzer, A. (1998). The role of safety climate and communication in accident interpretation: Implications for learning from negative events. Academy of Management Journal, 41(6), 644–657.

Hooper, V., & McKissack, J. (2016). The emerging role of the CISO. Business Horizons, 59(6), 585–591.

Howe, J. G. (1977). Group climate: An exploratory analysis of construct validity. Organizational Behavior and Human Performance, 19, 106–125.

James, L. R. (1982). Aggregation bias in estimates of perceptual agreement. Journal of Applied Psychology, 67, 219–229.

James, L. R., Choi, C. C., Ko, C. E., McNeil, P. K., Minton, M. K., Wright, M. A., & Kim, K. (2008). Organizational and psychological climate: A review of theory and research. European Journal of Work and Organizational Psychology, 17, 5–32.

James, L. R., Demaree, R. G., & Wolf, G. (1984). Estimating within-group interrater reliability with and without response bias. Journal of Applied Psychology, 69, 85–98.

Karlsson, F., Åström, J., & Karlsson, M. (2015). Information security culture: State-of-the-art review between 2000 and 2013. Information and Computer Security, 23, 246–285.

Klein, K. J., Bliese, P. D., Kozolowski, S. W. J., Dansereau, F., Gavin, M. B., Griffin, M. A., . . . Bligh, M. C. (2000). Multilevel analytical techniques: Commonalities, differences, and continuing questions. In K. J. Klein & S. W. J. Kozlowski (Eds.), Multilevel theory, research, and methods in organizations: Foundations, extensions, and new directions (pp. 512–553). Jossey-Bass: San Francisco.

Klein, K. J., Dansereau, F., & Hall, R. J. (1994). Levels issues in theory development, data collection, and analysis. Academy of Management Review, 19, 105–229.

Kozlowski, S. W. J., & Klein, K. J. (2000). A multilevel approach to theory and research in organizations: Contextual, temporal, and emergent processes. In Multilevel theory, research, and methods in organizations: Foundations, extensions, and new directions. (pp. 3–90): Jossey-Bass/Wiley.

Lewin, K., Lippitt, R., & White, R. K. (1939). Patterns of aggressive behavior in experimentally created social climates. Journal of Social Psychology, 10, 271 –299.

Lindell, M. K., & Brandt, C. J. (2000). Climate quality and climate consensus as mediators of the relationship between organizational antecedents and outcomes. Journal of Applied Psychology, 85, 331–348.

Lindell, M. K., & Whitney, D. J. (2001). Accounting for common method variance in cross-sectional research designs. Journal of Applied Psychology, 86(1), 114–121.

Luria, G. (2010). The social aspects of safety management: Trust and safety climate. Accident Analysis & Prevention, 42(4), 1288–1295.

Luria, G. (2019). Climate as a group level phenomenon: Theoretical assumptions and methodological considerations. Journal of Organizational Behavior, 40(9–10), 1055–1066.

Mahfuth, A., Yussof, S., Baker, A. A., & Ali, N. (2017). A systematic literature review: Information security culture. Paper presented at the International Conference on Research and Innovation in Information Systems (ICRIIS).

Mearns, K. J., & Reader, T. (2008). Organizational support and safety outcomes: An un-investigated relationship? Safety Science, 46(3), 388–397.

Nasir, A., Arshah, R. A., Hamid, M. R. A., & Fahmy, S. (2019). An analysis on the dimensions of information security culture concept: A review. Journal of Information Security and Applications, 44, 12–22.

Neal, A., & Griffin, M. A. (2004). Safety climate and safety at work. In J. Barling & M. R. Frone (Eds.), The psychology of workplace safety (pp. 15–34). American Psychological Association.

Neal, A., Griffin, M. A., & Hart, P. M. (2000). The impact of organizational climate on safety climate and individual behavior. Safety Science, 34(1–3), 99–109.

Newman, D. A., & Sin, H.-P. (2018). Within-group agreement (rWG): Two theoretical parameters and their estimators. Organizational Research Methods, 23(1), 30–64.

Nunnally, J. C. (1978). Psychometric theory. New York: McGraw Hill.

OECD (2015). Digital Security Risk Management for Economic and Social Prosperity: OECD Recommendation and Companion Document. OECD Publishing: Paris.

Ostroff, C. (1993). Comparing correlations based on individual-level and aggregated data. Journal of Applied Psychology, 78(4), 569–582.

Ostroff, C., Kinicki, A. J., & Clark, M. A. (2002). Substantive and operational issues of response bias across levels of analysis: An example of climate-satisfaction relationships. Journal of Applied Psychology, 87(2), 355–368.

Parker, S. K., Axtell, C. M., & Turner, N. (2001). Designing a safer workplace: Importance of job autonomy, communication quality, and supportive supervisors. Journal of Occupational Health Psychology, 6(3), 211–228.

Reichers, A. E., & Schneider, B. (1990). Climate and culture: An evolution of constructs. In B. Schneider (Ed.), Organizational Climate and Culture (pp. 5–39). San Francisco: Jossey-Bass.

Roberts, K. H., Hulin, C. L., & Rousseau, D. M. (1978). Developing an interdisciplinary science of organizations. San Francisco: Jossey-Bass.

Rousseau, D. M. (1985). Issues of level in organizational research: Multi-level and cross-level perspectives. Research in Organizational Behavior, 7, 1–37.

Schneider, B. (1975a). Organizational climate: Individual preferences and organizational realities revisited. Journal of Applied Psychology, 60, 459–465.

Schneider, B. (1975b). Organizational climates: An essay. Personnel Psychology, 28(4), 447–479.

Schneider, B., Bowen, D., Ehrhart, M. E., & Holcombe, K. M. (2000). The climate for service: Evolution of a construct. In N. M. Ashkanasy, C. Wilderom, & M. F. Peterson (Eds.), Handbook of Organizational Culture and Climate (pp. 21–36). Thousand Oaks: Sage.

Schneider, B., & Bowen, D. E. (1993). The service organization: Human resources management is crucial. Organizational Dynamics, 21(4), 39–52.

Schneider, B., Ehrhart, M. G., & Macey, W. H. (2011). Perspectives on organizational climate and culture. In APA Handbook of Industrial and Organizational Psychology, Vol 1: Building and Developing the Organization (pp. 373–414). Washington, DC: American Psychological Association.

Schneider, B., Ehrhart, M. G., & Macey, W. H. (2013). Organizational climate and culture. Annual Review of Psychology, 64, 361–388.

Schneider, B., Gonzalez-Roma, V., Ostroff, C., & West, M. A. (2017). Organizational climate and culture: Reflections on the history of the constructs in the Journal of Applied Psychology. *Journal of Applied Psychology*, 102(3), 468–482.

Schneider, B., Salvaggio, A. N., & Subirats, M. (2002). Climate strength: a new direction for climate research. Journal of Applied Psychology, 87(2), 220–229.

Schulte, M., Ostroff, C., Shmulyian, S., & Kinicki, A. (2009). Organizational climate configurations: Relationships to collective attitudes, customer satisfaction, and financial performance. Journal of Applied Psychology, 94(3), 618–634.

Schultz, E. (2005). The human factor in security. Computers & Security, 24.

Shrout, P. E., & Fleiss, J. L. (1978). Intraclass correlations: Uses in assessing rater reliability. Psychological Bulletin, 86, 420–428.

Smith-Crowe, K., Burke, M. J., Cohen, A., & Doveh, E. (2014). Statistical significance criteria for the rWG and average deviation interrater agreement indices. Journal of Applied Psychology, 99(2), 239–261.

Turner, B. A. (1978). Man-Made Disasters. London: Wykeham.

Uchendu, B., Nurse, J. R. C., Bada, M., & Furnell, S. (2021). Developing a cyber security culture: Current practices and future needs. Computers & Security, 109.

Weick, K. E. (1979). Social psychology of organizing. Reading: Addison Wesley.

Weick, K. E. (1995). Sensemaking in organizations. Thousands Oaks: Sage.

Zohar, D. (1980). Safety climate in industrial organizations: theoretical and applied implications. Journal of Applied Psychology, 65(1), 96–102.

Zohar, D. (2008). Safety climate and beyond: A multi-level multi-climate framework. Safety Science, 46(3), 376–387.

Zohar, D., & Luria, G. (2004). Climate as a Social-Cognitive Construction of Supervisory Safety Practices: Scripts as Proxy of Behavior Patterns. Journal of Applied Psychology, 89(2), 322–333.

Zohar, D., & Luria, G. (2005). A Multilevel Model of Safety Climate: Cross-Level Relationships Between Organization and Group-Level Climates. Journal of Applied Psychology, 90(4), 616–628.

Zohar, D., & Luria, G. (2010). Group Leaders as Gatekeepers: Testing Safety Climate Variations across Levels of Analysis. Applied Psychology, 59(4), 647–673.

Zohar, D., & Tenne-Gazit, O. (2008). Transformational leadership and group interaction as climate antecedents: A social network analysis. Journal of Applied Psychology, 93(4), 744–757.

Zwilling, M. (2022). Trends and Challenges Regarding Cyber Risk Mitigation by CISOs: A Systematic Literature and Experts' Opinion Review Based on Text Analytics. Sustainability, 14(3), 1311.

Chris Hetner
5 Transparent and inclusive cybersecurity risk management and governance

5.1 Introduction

There are potential negative outcomes that can arise in almost any given scenario, for almost anything. In business, this is why it is important to understand the types of risk the business is inherently taking based on the type of business it is operating and the geography of its operations, and then be deliberate to put in place risk management strategies for each. In general, any risk can be avoided, accepted, mitigated, or transferred.

Let's consider a range of scenarios where a business owns a fleet of automobiles as a balance sheet investment.

– To avoid risk the automobiles must be kept in a controlled and locked garage with no fuel in them and never driven. The business could also have chosen not to have the automobiles at all and completely avoid their risk profile.
– If the business wanted to accept the risk introduced by the automobiles, they can simply park them anywhere, not control who drives them, provide no rules of the road and hope that nothing happens.
– To fully mitigate and manage the risk, an exhaustive scenario analysis could be done that itemizes the potential negative outcomes that could arise from each scenario. Controls can be put into place such as cameras and crash avoidance systems to reduce and mitigate the risk.
– The business wants to transfer the risk associated with owning or running the automobiles it simply buys automobile insurance and some level of property insurance.

This analogy surrounding risk management practices towards automobiles can also be applied to cyber risk management. However, as we all know the sheer volume and velocity surrounding cybersecurity threats is a material level of complexity associated with governing and managing these exposures. Furthermore, cybersecurity risks are an area that one cannot generally choose to avoid. This is why it's critical to be able to measure, manage and transparently report on all cyber threats to the extent possible that an entity is presented with.

https://doi.org/10.1515/9783111289069-005

5.2 Measuring, managing and reporting cyber risk

Measuring, managing, and reporting cyber risk is a critical aspect of today's modern business operations and is becoming increasingly important as we realize an interconnected digital world. As businesses continue to rely on technology and suppliers for their day-to-day operations and data management, the potential for cyber threats, business disruption and vulnerabilities continues to grow. Therefore, understanding how to measure, manage and report cyber risk is essential for organizations to effectively manage and mitigate potential threats to their business, information systems and data assets.

Measuring cyber risk involves a comprehensive view that includes a broad range of stakeholders across the enterprise to understand the likelihood and potential impact of a cyberattack. That requires a combination of qualitative and quantitative analyses to understand the scope of the potential threats and vulnerabilities that may exist within the company, including its supply chain. Various approaches can be used to measure and control cyber risk including quantitative risk analysis, qualitative risk assessments, and scenario based analysis.

Quantitative risk analysis involves assigning numeric values to various aspects of cyber risk, such as the probability of a specific type of cyberattack occurring and the potential business, operational and financial impact of a successful attack. This approach typically involves using statistical models and data analysis to quantify the likelihood and potential impact of cyber threats.

An approach commonly used for quantitative risk analysis by the risk transfer markets is annualized loss expectancy (ALE). This approach is based on the result of the annual rate of occurrence (ARO) and the single lost expectancy (SLE) which results in the annualized loss expectancy. ALE is quantitative risk analysis commonly used across the risk transfer markets to price risk.

Qualitative risk assessments are more focused on identifying and evaluating the various contributors to cyber risk such as unpatched vulnerabilities, supply chain exposure, weaknesses in business operations, and the potential for insider threats, and combines that approach with the effectiveness of the existing information security defenses. This approach uses judgment and risk assessment techniques to qualitatively evaluate the likelihood and impact of various cyber threats that can introduce exposure to the business, operational, and financial health of the organization. Qualitative risk assessments are often used to identify and prioritize remediation approaches to address significant threats faced by the organization.

Scenario based analysis involves creating hypothetical attack scenarios and evaluating the potential impact of each scenario on the organization. This approach can assist an organization towards understanding the potential consequences of different types of cyber threats combined with vulnerabilities and can inform decision making around investments and risk mitigation strategies.

In addition to these methods, there are several widely recognized frameworks and standards that can be used to measure and report cyber risk, including the National Institute of Standards and Technology (NIST) Cybersecurity Framework (NIST, 2024), the International Organization for Standardization (ISO) 27001 (ISO, 2022), and the Center for Internet Security (CIS) Controls (CIS, 2024). These frameworks provide organizations with a structured approach to assessing, managing, and reporting cyber risk and can help guide the development of effective business resilience, cybersecurity strategies and risk management practices.

Once cyber risk can be measured and understood across the organization, it is critical to effectively report those threats, risks and vulnerabilities to a wide range of key stakeholders such as enterprise risk management, compliance, legal, and the board of directors. Reporting on cybersecurity involves communicating the results of the periodic risk assessments, combining the analysis with a clear and concise alignment to business risk reducing strategies. This allows for broader transparency and engagement across the enterprise and the board of directors.

The first step in the journey towards reporting cyber risk is to understand the audience. Different stakeholders across the organization may have varying levels of technical and non-technical ability combined with differing priorities when it comes to cybersecurity. Therefore, it is critical to tailor the reporting of cyber risk, including the substance and expected outcomes, to ensure that the information presented is relevant, understandable, and actionable to each group.

For example, the executive suite and boardroom are more interested in a high-level summary of cyber threats that will introduce material business, operational, and financial harm with a focus on alignment to the strategy of the organization. This reporting is coupled with recommended business risk reducing strategies and investments ideally reflective of inputs by the enterprise risk management organization. The juxtaposition to a high-level executive report would be a presentation to the technology and operational teams that need more specificity around which systems have vulnerabilities that have not been addressed either through patching or misconfigurations, combined with the specific technical controls needed to address these exposures.

When reporting on cyber risk it is critical to provide a comprehensive overview of the organization's cybersecurity posture with input from both internal teams and independent external experts that would include an assessment of the potential vulnerabilities and the state of the organization's information security defenses. This can help stakeholders understand the full scope of cyber risk faced by the organization and the potential consequences of a cyberattack.

In addition to providing an overview of the current state of cyber risk, effective reporting should also factor in specific mitigation measures that align to those threats that introduce material harm to the business. This would help to achieve a risk informed business resiliency strategy, ensuring operational uptime after a business interruption event. This can involve outlining the level of tactical controls needed to address specific vulnerabilities, mitigating certain exposures across the supply chain, and enhancing user training and awareness that could reduce the likelihood of a successful material cyberattack.

Furthermore, reporting on cyber-risk should factor in supply chain dependency, impact on the business, operational and financial condition of the organization introduced by varying types of cyber threats and the potential costs of implementing these investments align to business resilience strategies. This can aid a range of key stakeholders to understand the potential investment optimization approach for cybersecurity, and can assist in prioritizing resource allocation and budgeting for cybersecurity initiatives, both short term and long term.

In addition to internal reporting, organizations may also have to report on cyber risk to external stakeholders, such as regulatory bodies, customers, and business partners. Many industries are subject to regulatory requirements that mandate the reporting of cybersecurity risks and incidents, such as the Health Insurance Portability and Accountability Act (HIPAA) (Congress, 1996) in the healthcare industry, the Payment Card Industry Data Security Standard (PCI DSS) (PCI, 2022) in the payment card industry and the new United States Securities and Exchange Commission (SEC) Cybersecurity Risk Governance rules (SEC, 2023).

When reporting cyber risk to external stakeholders, it is essential to ensure compliance with relevant regulatory requirements and industry standards. This may involve providing specific details about cybersecurity measures and incident response protocols to prove a commitment to protecting sensitive data and information systems.

By way of example, the new SEC Cybersecurity Risk Governance (SEC, 2023) rules required registrants to disclose how cyber risks and incident materially affect the company's business, operational and financial health. When considering the potential materiality of an incident, covered businesses should consider a number of factors including: how much potential business is interrupted (and the costs associated), potential ransom payment costs, the potential cost of remediating the incident, potential for employee or customer harm, increased cost of new controls needed, loss of revenue, litigation and legal risks, potential for regulatory fines/actions, and shareholder impacts.

Furthermore, effective reporting of cyber risk to external stakeholders can help build trust and transparency with customers and business partners, proving a commitment to cybersecurity and a proactive approach to managing cyber risk. This can be particularly important in industries where the protection of sensitive customer data is a top priority, such as healthcare, financial services, and e-commerce.

Measuring, managing, and reporting cyber risk is a critical aspect of modern business operations, requiring a combination of quantitative and qualitative analysis to understand the full scope of potential threats and vulnerabilities facing an organization. By effectively measuring cyber risk and reporting the findings to key stakeholders, organizations can make informed decisions about how to manage and mitigate cyber risk, ultimately strengthening their cybersecurity posture and protecting their data assets from potential threats and attacks.

5.3 Effective boardroom cyber risk reporting

Reporting cyber risk to the boardroom is a critical aspect of corporate governance, as it provides the Board of Directors with the information needed to make informed decisions about cybersecurity strategy, resource allocation, business resilience strategies, and risk management practices. When reporting cyber risk to the boardroom, it is essential to follow best practices to ensure that the information is delivered effectively, transparent, business aligned, and in a manner that is relevant and understandable to board members. Here are some best practices for reporting cyber risk to the boardroom:

- **Ensure the Message is Tailored to the Audience:** Understand the Board's level of expertise and tailor the reporting of cyber risk accordingly. Board members may not have deep knowledge of cybersecurity, so it is important to present the information in a clear and non-technical manner while still providing the necessary depth and context.
- **Provide a Comprehensive Overview of Cyber Risk:** Present an end-to-end view of the company's current cybersecurity posture, including an assessment of potential vulnerabilities, threats most likely to introduce business risk, and existing security controls. This can help Board members understand the full scope of cyber risk facing the organization and the potential impact of a cyberattack.
- **Focus on Business Risk Impact:** Place emphasis on the potential business risk impact introduced by those most likely cyber threats and vulnerabilities. Each organization will have different risk exposures. A financial institution's cyber risk exposure will look different from a manufacturing or energy platform. Board members are primarily concerned with those most likely cyber threats can introduce material business, operational, reputational, and financial negative impacts. Moreover, the board wants to understand the most impactful business risk reducing measures and investments.
- **Link Cyber Risk to Business Objectives:** Align cyber risk to the organization's business goals and objectives. This can be achieved by integrating cybersecurity risk management across the enterprise risk management team that's inclusive of legal, risk management, operations, lines of business, compliance, and finance. Board members are interested in how cyber risk can negatively affect the achievement of strategic objectives, so it is important to frame the discussion in a business context and show the relevance of cybersecurity to the organization's overall mission and success.
- **Present Business Risk Reducing Strategies and Recommendations:** Offer specific recommendations for mitigating identified cyber risks improving the organization's cybersecurity posture and aligned to business strategies. This may include outlining the technical investments needed to address specific vulnerabilities, as well as recommendations for non-technical measures, such as security awareness training and incident response protocols.

- **Demonstrate Return on Investment (ROI):** Provide insights into the investments that are the most business risk reducing measures. This may involve discussing the cost-effectiveness of security controls, supply chain dependencies, employee awareness and the potential cost savings from avoiding cyber incidents and data breaches.
- **Highlight Legal Liabilities, Compliance and Regulatory Requirements:** Discuss the organization's compliance with relevant regulatory requirements, industry standards and legal liabilities such as class action suits resulting from a cybersecurity attack. This should be communicated to the board in concert with legal, outside council and compliance functions. Board members need to understand the organization's posture about regulatory compliance, its commitment to protecting sensitive data and legal exposure to Directors and Officers.
- **Communicate the Effectiveness of Security Controls:** Provide information on the effectiveness of existing security controls, the organization's ability to detect and respond to cyber threats and its ability to achieve business resilience. The Board should understand the relationship between the deployment of security controls and business, operational, and financial risk reduction. This can give board members confidence in the organization's ability to manage cyber risk effectively.
- **Provide Regular and Targeted Updates:** Establish a regular cadence for reporting cyber risk to the Board. It's crucial to establish a charter that outlines the roles and responsibilities between management and the board around cyber risk oversight. Cyber risks are constantly evolving, so it is important to provide regular updates on new threats, vulnerabilities, and the effectiveness of risk mitigation efforts to the business, operational and financial health of the organization. Moreover, it's important to identify the committee that provides oversight of cyber risk. Options include Audit Committee, Risk Committee, and other focused committees around technology risk.
- **Dashboards and Analytics:** Use visual aids, such as charts, graphs, and dashboard metrics, to present complex information in a clear and easily understandable format. Visual aids can help board members quickly grasp key cybersecurity metrics and trends. As an example, the NACD X-Analytics service provides board members with a view on the overall financial exposures introduced by cyber threats, a breakdown as to how these exposures can manifest to the organization (i.e. Business Interruption introduced by a Denial of Service or Ransomware attack), the cyber risk exposure ratio to the financial health of the company, trending over time, top five control areas to reduce financial exposure and top five risk scenarios that can lead to financial loss.

Modern Boards must treat cybersecurity as a business risk and manage it with the appropriate level of detail and oversight. Cyber risk management discussions should consider effective ways to lower the likelihood or impact of cyber risks, as well as consider the most effective ways to reduce operational and monetary impacts of an incident. The most effective Boards demonstrate that the Chief Executive Officer (CEO), Chief Risk Officer (CRO), Chief Financial Officer (CFO) and General Counsel also take accountability for Cyber Risk oversight, and do not relegate it solely to the Chief Information Officer (CIO) and Chief Information Security Officer (CISO.)

By following these best practices, organizations can effectively report cyber risk to the boardroom, enabling board members to make informed decisions about cybersecurity strategy, resource allocation, and risk management. This, in turn, can help strengthen the organization's cybersecurity posture and protect its data assets from potential threats and attacks.

5.4 Defining cyber economics

According to the World Economic Forum (Swalwell,2023):

> The average cost of a data breach in 2022 was $4.35 million and is expected to reach $5 million in 2023. Cybersecurity research firm Cyber Ventures predicts that cybercrimes will cost the world $10.5 trillion by 2025. According to the Securities and Exchange Commission (SEC), 'the potential costs and damage that can stem from a cybersecurity incident are extensive. Many smaller companies have been targets of cybersecurity attacks so severe that the companies have gone out of business as a result.'
>
> To drive down cyber risk and improve resilience to malicious cyber activity, organizations and governments must evolve their respective approaches to cybersecurity risk management. Both parties must use their capabilities more strategically and develop frameworks to prioritize investments aligned to cyber threats that represent material business, operational, and financial impact.

Cyber economics refers to application of economic aspects of cybersecurity, including the costs and benefits associated with managing and mitigating cyber risks, the impact of cyber incidents have on businesses and economies, and the allocation of resources to address cybersecurity challenges that represent to most risk reducing measures. It encompasses various economic principles and analyses that help organizations understand the economic incentives, trade-offs, and implications related to cybersecurity.

To effectively apply cyber economics, the organization must include multiple disciplines across the organization to include technology, cybersecurity, risk management, finance, operations, legal, compliance and external expertise.

– **Cost of Cybersecurity:** Cyber economics focuses on evaluating the costs involved in implementing cybersecurity measures. This includes the expenses associated with acquiring and deploying security technologies, hiring skilled professionals, conducting risk assessments, and implementing training programs. Understanding these costs is critical for organizations as they make decisions about resource allocation, budgeting for cybersecurity and alignment with business resilience strategies.

- **Cost Benefit Analysis:** Cyber economics also involves the assessment of the benefits of cybersecurity investments. This includes considering the potential cost savings from preventing cyber incidents, protecting sensitive data, maintaining business resilience, and preserving the organization's reputation. By conducting a cost-benefit analysis, organizations can make well-informed decisions about which cybersecurity initiatives will yield the greatest return on investment, as well as which of the highest risks could be achieved through the lowest cost.
- **Risk Management:** Cyber economics includes the understanding of effective risk management strategies and their economic implications. This involves evaluating the costs associated with different risk mitigation approaches, such as risk transfer through insurance, risk reduction through investments in security controls, and risk acceptance based on the cost of potential losses. It also involves understanding the potential impact of cyber incidents on the organization's finances and operations.
- **Market Incentives and Cybersecurity:** Understanding the economic incentives that drive cybersecurity behaviors is a key aspect of cyber economics. This includes analyzing market forces, such as supply and demand for cybersecurity products and services, and the role of economic incentives in influencing organizations' cybersecurity posture. Evaluating these incentives can provide insights into how organizations make decisions about investing in cybersecurity and how market dynamics affect the overall cybersecurity landscape.
- **Externalities and Spillover Effects:** Cyber economics also examines the concept of externalities and spillover effects in the context of cybersecurity. For example, a cyber incident affecting one organization may have spillover effects on other businesses, entire sectors, suppliers, or customers in the supply chain. Understanding these externalities can help policymakers and organizations take a more comprehensive approach to managing cyber risks and promoting collective resilience strategies and investments.
- **Understand Data Privacy and Consumer Behavior:** The economic analysis of data privacy and consumer behavior in the digital environment is another key area within cyber economics. This involves examining how consumers value their privacy, the impact of data breaches on consumer trust, and the economic implications of privacy regulations and data protection laws. Understanding consumer behavior and preferences can inform organizational decisions about data privacy and security measures.
- **Cybersecurity Policy and Regulation:** Cyber economics considers the economic impact of cybersecurity policies and regulations. This includes evaluating the costs of compliance with regulatory requirements, the potential economic benefits of regulatory standards in improving cybersecurity practices, and the overall economic impact of government interventions in cybersecurity.

- **Economic Implications of Cyber Incidents:** Lastly, cyber economics encompasses the understanding of the economic impact of cyber incidents on businesses, economies, and society. This includes examining the direct costs of cyber breaches, such as remediation expenses and revenue losses, as well as the indirect costs, such as damage to brand reputation, customer trust, and market competitiveness.

Cyber economics provides clarity into optimizing investments necessary to into security that may involve short-term costs, but it will also raise public confidence in the reliability of critical infrastructure and technology, increase productivity and profits and enable stronger, more strategic partnerships between the federal government and the private sector. In short, the private sector and the government are well-served by building cybersecurity into every aspect of operations and governance.

Cyber economics provides a new normal understanding of the economic dimensions of cybersecurity, including the costs, benefits, incentives, and externalities associated with managing cyber risks. By applying economic principles to cybersecurity challenges, organizations and policymakers can make more informed decisions about resource allocation, risk management strategies, and the development of effective cybersecurity policies and practices.

5.5 A new vocabulary for discussing cyber risk

There is a language barrier in cybersecurity that is preventing a fundamental shift in how businesses address cyber risk and improve their cyber resilience. This barrier exists because we (as in the cybersecurity ecosystem) continue to discuss cyber risk in a language that is not familiar with business leaders.

The language of business leaders is rooted in accounting, finance, and marketing. It includes terms like revenue, return on investment, margin, capital, and more. This language helps business leaders understand the health of their business and serves as an answer key for making decisions. Words that are outside of their language can be confusing, misleading, or undecipherable. To remove this barrier and encourage a fundamental shift in how businesses address cyber risk, we (as in the cybersecurity ecosystem) must speak the language of business leaders.

5.5.1 Shift from maturity scores to financial insights

By default, measurement of maturity is a good thing because it can describe a business's relative ability to respond to various situations.

With best intentions, a cyber maturity score tries to describe a business's cyber wisdom and how the business chooses to respond to various cyber situations. It does this by measuring individual cyber-related controls, within a cybersecurity framework (such as NIST CSF), using a 0 to 5 maturity scale. In this scale, 0 represents no capability, while 5 represents an optimized capability. The average score, amongst all controls within the cybersecurity framework, defines the business's maturity level.

This could seem like a good approach, but there is the problem. The cyber maturity score does not tell the business:

– the size of their cyber risk problem,
– where and how risk transfer provides liability protection or,
– which inflight or future cybersecurity projects offer the best return on investment

To get answers to the above list, businesses need to move beyond cyber maturity scores to financial insights. Cyber maturity scores could help to inform a set of determined financial insights, but they are not the complete picture. Financial insights, related to cybersecurity, reduce the chance of a business making misinformed decisions because they don't assume that:

– high maturity is equal to an insignificant cyber risk problem,
– all controls (within a framework) are equal in risk reducing ability,
– risk transfer mechanisms offer equal liability protections amongst different perils.

5.5.2 Highlighting financial and business exposures, not technical vulnerabilities

For decades, business leaders have been receiving cybersecurity reports that have details about an endless emerging threat condition, increasing technical weaknesses, and worst-case stories that frankly no business leaders want to happen under their watch. We are an interconnected world where cyber incidents are a guaranteed reality for all businesses. There are some really damaging cyber incidents. Systemic risk is always a possibility. However, the cyber risk problem is not the same for all businesses, which is difficult to understand from technical reporting. When cybersecurity leaders express cyber risk as a financial metric, the business leaders can understand the size of the cyber risk problem in context will other operational risks.

With this understanding, business leaders can decide which cyber risks to accept, mitigate, and transfer as part of their cyber resilience strategy. There is a language barrier in cybersecurity that is preventing a fundamental shift in how businesses address cyber risk and improve their cyber resilience. This barrier exists because we in the cybersecurity ecosystem continue to discuss cyber risk in a language that is not familiar to business leaders, especially those who sit on their companies' boards. To remove the language barrier and encourage a fundamental shift in how businesses address cyber risk, their colleagues from the tech world need to speak their language. Fortunately, there are plenty of ways to do this.

5.6 Mitigating reputational damage

Every business leader understands the value of a company's reputation, and the tremendous harm that can be done when it is damaged. It can happen in a flash and take years for the business to build it back – if it ever does. A CEO can be caught engaging in misconduct. Or a new product may not function properly and injure customers in the process. These are the kinds of missteps that we've read about for years. But there are new ones in the cyber world, and these are the kinds of issues that all business leaders need to understand.

When a company suffers a major data breach, board members will not be the corporation's first responders. But they must be prepared to at once understand the potential reputational risk. They should have roles to play in this form of crisis management, just as they would for any other kind. The company will want to measure the damage and respond to the danger in the same way they try to mitigate other crises.

The technology at the center of the action is different, but the corporate governance that leads the response should be right from the business playbook. Here the board should be close to bilingual. The attack on the business may not be in their native tongue, but they know what an attack on the business means.

The bottom line is that members of the board can and must be part of their company's security defense. Board members should be well educated on cyber risk and provide effective challenge of Management. This can be accomplished by having regular third-party expert briefings, through educational briefings and exercises by the CISO, by having a cyber expert serve on the Board, or through a combination of those types of tactics. This education should be supplemented by well-designed reports, measurements, and metrics that are designed to keep pace with the ever changing cyber risk landscape.

5.7 Enter the securities and exchange commission

If Board directors needed further awareness that the world of business has recognized the need to take on the challenges posed by cybersecurity, they got it on July 26, 2023. That was the day the SEC adopted its long-awaited rules on "Cyber Risk Management, Strategy, Governance, and Incident Disclosure" (SEC, 2023). In addition to other provisions, the rules also require companies registered with the SEC to publicly disclose how their boards of directors' exercise oversight of cybersecurity risks. For covered entities, it now very clear that the responsibility for cyber risk oversight is no longer exclusive to the CIO and/or CISO.

New cyber incident reporting requires more precision around the estimation of the materiality of operational, strategic business, and financial impacts of an incident. Below is a summary of specific rules companies must now comply with:

- **Incident Reporting:** Companies registered with the SEC "must disclose information about a cybersecurity incident within four business days after they decide they have experienced a material cybersecurity incident" (SEC, 2023, P. 12). A cybersecurity incident is defined to include an unauthorized occurrence on or through a company's "information systems," including "information resources owned or used by the registrant." (SEC, 2023, P. 71, 72). The primary purpose of the incident disclosure requirements is to focus on the material impacts introduced by the incident, rather than requiring details about the incident itself. The rule also requires registrants to "describe the material aspects of the nature, scope, and timing of the incident, and the material impact or reasonably likely material impact on the registrant, including its financial condition and results of operations." (SEC, 2023, P. 29).
- **Third Party Incidents:** This rule requires registrants to also disclose incidents occurring on third party systems. The commission emphasized that it is not "providing a safe harbor for information disclosed on third party systems." (SEC, 2023, P. 30). Depending on the nature of the incident, disclosures may be required by both the customer and the third party.
- **Previously Disclosed Incident Reporting:** This rule requires businesses to provide updated disclosures relating to previously disclosed cybersecurity incidents (SEC, 2023, P. 47). Examples include any material impact of the incident on the company's operations and financial condition (SEC, 2023, P. 29). These requirements will place added pressure on incident response teams to maintain a comprehensive register of risks introduced by incidents and monitor them for changes in materiality.
- **Reporting When a Series of Previously Undisclosed Incidents Becomes Material:** This requires disclosure when a series of previously undisclosed individually immaterial cybersecurity incidents has become material taken together. At that point, companies would need to disclose when the incidents were discovered, whether they are ongoing, and provide a brief description of the nature and scope of the incidents (SEC, 2023, P. 47).
- **Policies and Procedures:** Companies must disclose their "policies and procedures for identifying and managing cybersecurity risks and threats, including: operational risk; intellectual property theft; fraud; extortion; harm to employees or customers; violation of privacy laws and other litigation and legal risk; and reputational risk" (SEC, 2023, P. 54). Specifically, a company must disclose whether it "has a cybersecurity risk assessment program and, if so, provide a description". It

must also provide consistent information disclosures about its cybersecurity risk management and strategy.

– **Governance:** This set of rules requires disclosure about board oversight of a company's cybersecurity risk governance and the inclusion of management's oversight of cybersecurity risks. Moreover, the rule requires a description of the implementation of related policies, procedures, and strategies that affect an investor's ability to understand how a registrant prepares for, prevents, or responds to cybersecurity incidents. It also requires disclosure of a registrant's cybersecurity governance, including the board's oversight of cybersecurity risk and a description of management's role in assessing and managing cybersecurity risks, the relevant expertise of management, and its role in implementing the registrant's cybersecurity policies, procedures, and strategies. (SEC, 2023, P. 65–68).

– **Management's Role:** This rule "requires a description of management's role in assessing and managing cybersecurity-related risks and in implementing the company's cybersecurity policies, procedures, and strategies" (SEC, 2023, P. 66). This should include but not be limited to "whether certain management positions or committees handle measuring and managing cybersecurity risk, specifically the prevention, mitigation, detection, and remediation of cybersecurity incidents, and the relevant expertise of these people or members."

5.8 Conclusion

Transparency and inclusive cyber risk governance and reporting is now the new normal. The Board of Directors, Chief Executive Officers, general counsel, Chief Financial Officer, and other enterprise risk management executives are increasingly being held accountable for the oversight of cyber risk. The SEC's new cybersecurity rules "require publicly enlisted companies to disclose their cybersecurity governance capabilities, including the Board's oversight of cyber risk, a description of management's role in assessing and managing cyber risks, the relevant expertise of such management, and management's role in implementing the company's cybersecurity policies, procedures, and strategies." This kind of disclosure allows investors to evaluate the attention executives and business leaders are paying to cyber risks.

Executive management needs to understand how cyber threats can introduce material, business, operational, and financial harm. Cyberattacks are causing companies hundreds of millions of dollars, if not billions of dollars, in economic loss due to a wide range of impacts, such as business interruption resulting from a ransomware attack. Furthermore, there have been examples of suppliers introducing a vector for a cyberattack, including business interruption events and technology outages. There have been many examples of lost intellectual property that can set a company back in terms of their commitments to deliver value to shareholders and investors. Additionally, the legal and regulatory landscape surrounding cybersecurity risk governance and management has increased in a material way. There are examples of companies, directors and officers being named in class action suits that can cost up to a half billion dollars.

Under these heightened regulatory requirements, companies must also disclose the nature, scope, and impact of a cyber incident within four days of making the determination of it being material. Materiality determination is a team sport that should be inclusive of a range of stakeholders such as the general counsel, outside counsel, chief financial officer, chief executive officer, and the board of directors and is influenced by the facts and circumstances delivered by the chief information security officer and broader technology organization. Materiality is influenced by the cyber incident's current and future impact on the company's business, operations, and financial condition. This mandatory disclosure allows investors and other external stakeholders to evaluate the effectiveness of the company's cybersecurity risk management program and its impact on the business. This is a seismic shift in governing, managing, and reporting cyber risks to a wide range of stakeholders, transcending from being a technical matter to a business risk management approach combined with effective boardroom reporting.

References

Center for Internet Security (CIS) Controls. (2024). https://learn.cisecurity.org/cis-controls-download

U.S. Congress. (21 Aug 1996). *Health Insurance Portability and Accountability Act of 1996 (HIPAA)*. https://www.congress.gov/104/plaws/publ191/PLAW-104publ191.pdf

Payment Card Industry (PCI). (Mar 2022). *Data Security Standard (DSS) 4.0*. https://docs-prv.pcisecuritystandards.org/PCI%20DSS/Standard/PCI-DSS-v4_0.pdf

International Standards Organization (ISO). (Oct 2022). *Publication 27001*. https://www.iso.org/standard/27001

Eric Swalwell. World Economic Forum. (11 July 2023). *Why we need business, operational and financial resilience to optimize cybersecurity*. https://www.weforum.org/agenda/2023/07/why-we-need-business-operational-and-financial-resilience-to-optimize-cybersecurity/#:~:text=According%20to%20the%20Securities%20and,of%20business%20as%20a%20result.%E2%80%9D

U.S. Securities and Exchange Commission. (26 Jul 2023). *Cybersecurity Risk Management, Strategy, Governance, and Incident Disclosure*. https://www.sec.gov/files/rules/final/2023/33-11216.pdf

National Institute for Standards and Technology. (26 Feb 2024). *The NIST Cybersecurity Framework (CSF) 2.0*. https://www.nist.gov/cyberframework

Jose M. Bernik

6 Securing artificial intelligence in the real world

6.1 Introduction

Artificial Intelligence (AI) has recently become one of the biggest topics in both Technology and popular culture. It has been described as both an insidious villain and as the savior of humanity. It is hard to divorce AI from its science fiction roots; writers from Isaac Asimov to James Cameron have long depicted AI as the single biggest threat to humanity to ever exist. But that perception is heavily rooted in fiction. To say that AI is either "good" or "bad" is to misinterpret what Artificial Intelligence really is.

John McCarthy, who is credited with coining the term Artificial Intelligence, wrote "Every aspect of learning or any other feature of intelligence can in principle be so precisely described that a machine can be made to simulate it. An attempt will be made to find how to make machines use language, form abstractions, and concepts, solve kinds of problems now reserved for humans, and improve themselves" (McCarthy, Dartmouth Summer Research, 1956).

Artificial Intelligence, currently is defined as a large language model that uses statistical models to accurately predict what the most logical next step will be. Currently, Chat GPT is a LLM that can scrub the internet for information, effectively "learning" how to answer the questions we ask it. Its powerful neural network can mimic human learning and deliver cogent and thoroughly researched answers almost instantaneously. Its human voice is uncanny. ChatGPT calls to mind all the frighteningly sentient Skynet or Asimov's Three Laws of Robotics. Humanity has long feared our own inventions overpowering us. That threat will always linger as our advancements in technology become more and more incredible. Yet, like ChatGPT, technology is still dependent on human thought processes. Like the very neural network used to create it, ChatGPT, and really all large language models, need humans to first create the information it gleans.

As more information is disseminated to us, the more accurate these LLMs become. Thus, the real threat reveals itself. As we continue to hone and refine these LLMs, the rate at which they understand and synthesize information increases. As its users give the LLM more breadth, more information, the more powerful the tool becomes.

https://doi.org/10.1515/9783111289069-006

6.2 The AI threat

The perceived threat of AI has always been autonomy. Popular culture has long refer-
enced sentient computers and robots that develop enough thought power to have
emotions, to make choices based on their own free will. A clear distinction needs to
be made; AI does not have free will. Any perceived autonomy comes from the boundaries the user gives it. If anything, the mimic capabilities, the ability to reflect the tone
and speech patterns back to its user creates a perfect mirror. Artificial Intelligence
stems from the knowledge we, as a society have compiled. All of the lessons, the language, the literature that comprises the human race can be synthesized and then succinctly expressed back to us.

The real threat of AI then becomes the things we teach it. The algorithms can
begin to reflect bias, both racial and gender. The user can generate AI rendered content across all kinds of platforms, with the AI seeming to represent a large group of
like-minded individuals. The danger then comes from unchecked AI on social media
platforms, where one user can create whole worlds that reflect that individual's own
prejudices.

Here, a new responsibility is created. Now, companies need new technology, new
people to apply a checklist that can identify any AI generated content versus real time
content. This can be especially tricky, considering how evolved and malicious AI can
become. The use of deep fakes has detrimental consequences; real users engaging
with AI generated versions of popular figures can have political and social ramifications. After accessing a few minutes of video, AI is able to digitally replicate not only
visual characteristics, but the nuances of their human speech voice and patterns.
Things like a vocal signature or facial recognition become unusable as deepfake technology becomes more sophisticated.

From a social and political standpoint, AI can be used to cause mass hysteria and
chaos. This growing threat has become the new iteration of the "sentient AI." Now,
social media and other platforms can become overrun by AI generated content and
begin to inform popular opinion. It is now the task of those platforms to better detect
AI and keep platforms that run on user-generated content free from bots and other
artificial intelligences. Biased AI becomes a real threat, especially when masquerading
as genuine.

6.3 Poisoning AI models

Data poisoning in AI refers to the act of deliberately inserting malicious data into a
dataset used to train an AI model. The goal is to corrupt the training data in such a
way that the model learns incorrect or biased information, which can be exploited by

hackers to achieve their objectives. This has several implications: inaccurate predictions, undesirable actions, and flawed conclusions.

Train anything or anyone badly, and you can expect treacherous results. Poisoned, incorrect or biased data can lead to an AI making incorrect predictions, when at scale, can lead to catastrophic results. Healthcare, finance, transportation, and critical infrastructures can afford to be corrupted or compromised. In his 2015 book, *Lights Out*, veteran journalist Ted Koppel writes scathingly about how vulnerable the U.S. Electrical power grid is to cyberattack, describing in detail flaws in the SCADA software that allow for bugs in software to cause hardware collapse.

Poisoned/ biased AI systems are more vulnerable to exploitation and adversarial attacks by malicious actors. A high functioning AI learning from a coherent data set could quickly get derailed by the insertion of corrupted files This leads to a series of disturbing questions. Could AI be racist? Could AI suffer the same prejudices that distort and deform human decision making? It is possible that data poisoning, either deliberate or accidental, can create bias and discrimination. For example, any dataset that is used to train a facial recognition model can very easily become biased towards certain demographic groups.

Maya Goldman published an article, *Axios Vitals* revealing that at least four AI chatbots used to deliver medical advice "used debunked race-based information when asked about kidney function and lung capacity," and "two of the models gave incorrect answers about Black people having different muscle mass." These errors were caught early, but they speak to the dangers of faulty information training a powerful chatbot.

Finally, what happens if an AI model makes deeply flawed predictions or decisions that adversely affect the lives of people? Criminal justice, healthcare, defense, in these spheres, poor decision making can inflict terrible, even permanent harm. The legal and ethical issues of AI are already becoming very transparent.

One of the alarming consequences of this reality is the shattering of copyright protection. The comedian Sarah Silverman sued ChatGPT for copyright infringement. She is not alone. Multiple artists and content creators are joining in lawsuits against LLMs, charging that the software is essentially stealing their work and profiting off it. ChatGPT and other LLMs are vacuuming up text to learn at rapid speed. Can they be stopped? Even if they can, if American or European based companies decide to play by new legal rules, the likelihood that China will do so is very low. China has already adopted a policy of "by whatever means necessary" Intellectual Property theft in order to boost its economy. The statistics of this policy are staggering.

According to statistics cited by the FBI, Chinese IP theft has cost the United States between 225 and 600 Billion per year. A 2019 article in *Foreign Policy* magazine offered cautious optimism, arguing that China realizes that strong patent laws matter. Yet in 2022, the Carnegie Endowment for International Peace argued otherwise, pointing out that the "Chinese government carries out cyber-espionage on behalf of domestic firms." So, in the geopolitical arms race of AI defense, AI detectors become of the utmost importance.

Who can learn faster? What software do we have already created that can be an accurate defense against AI? Nothing. Technology needs software that can learn and change in an instant. AI Detector software can be trained on large volumes of authentic and fabricated data in order to be able to discern the subtle distinctions between them. Yet, the AI detectors cannot keep up with the rate at which AI itself becomes more and more intelligent. It is important to understand that the current remedies for these threats will quickly become obsolete as AI grows more accurate.

In 2019, a UK based energy company was one of the first to be victimized by this new Deep Fake technology. The CEO was contacted by criminals pretending to be the CEO of the parent company. The criminals then asked for a $250,000 wire transfer for another supplier. After the CEO complied, the call was revealed to be a scam. Now, such a simplistic fraud would definitely be detected. But as AI technology becomes more advanced, so do the criminals.

6.4 Dangers of social engineering

We must ask ourselves profound questions about what all of this deception will do to us as a culture? AI can analyze vast amounts of data to create deceptions that are highly personalized. This targeted deception can lead to immense change in the zeitgeist. People can rally around a lie, shrouded in doubt and then supported by AI. Russian hackers used the platform Cameo to piece together missives from celebrities like Elijah Wood that sounded like criticisms of Ukrainian President Volodymyr Zelensky. Unbeknownst to Wood, it seemed as though he was accusing Zelensky of being a drug addict and a despot. These messages were sent all over Russia in order to drum up more support for the Russian Invasion. Such convincing deep fakes can be used to manipulate popular opinion at all levels.

Public Awareness and Education can help, but how much? Once people know about the existence of deep fakes and other threats, they will be able to be more discerning about the information presented to them. On an individual case by case basis, viral messaging can be helpful. If people tag a video or message as fake, that could trigger an immune response. Social Media platforms will have to become more adept at both identifying AI generated content and policing users from misrepresenting information as genuine.

6.5 Major social advancements

Yet, AI has proven itself to be one of the most useful tools in a broad variety of fields. Educators are using AI to help enhance the way students learn. AI can assist in back of house applications, like seating charts or grant searches. AI can track and evaluate the way students learn; homing in on patterns and pinpointing the areas in which each student needs help. In this sense, AI can increase our own learning potential.

Businesses can use AI to hone marketing strategies, learning in almost real time what customers are buying and using. AI can track employee output and increase productivity with pattern tracking, as well as shouldering some of the more time consuming tasks. Data Entry and Market information aggregation have become that much more efficient. Reducing human workload makes room for more innovation and creativity.

From a scientific perspective, the advances of AI have greatly improved quality of life. AI has proven to be adept at building smart-disaster responses by synthesizing global weather patterns. Governments can use AI to predict weather anomalies, as well as enable a more effective real-time disaster response.

AI has even been effective in aiding in the detection of early cancer. In 2023, a Swedish study found that AI software increased detection efficacy in the reading of mammograms by 20% (Lang et al. Lancet Oncology 2023). The traditional method of diagnosing breast cancer begins with two separate radiologists reading the imaging. AI software uses an algorithm that checks the image against millions of mammograms, both benign and cancerous. This new software can identify abnormal mammograms and flag them for additional testing. It is revolutionary in early detection and is currently being applied to other cancers.

6.6 Deep fake detection

The best defense then becomes AI itself. AI can be harnessed to detect itself. While human error would be the reason that deep fakes even exist, we can now use AI to warn us of risk and detect any malicious intent. AI can learn to discern the subtle differences and anomalies that exist in actual real, human generated content, versus the perfection and patterned signifiers that tend to exist in AI generated content. By giving AI even more access, by creating even more information for AI to learn from, we can create an AI firewall that can detect itself.

The AI deep fake has truly become a threat to both public and private sector safety. AI generated videos where one person's face can be superimposed onto another person's body. By doing so, it's possible to create videos that depict individuals saying and doing things that they never said or did. Programs can be created to detect seams, glitches, lighting mismatches or inconsistencies that occur during the superimposition process, where one face gets mapped over another. Some deep fakes might fail to reproduce these signals accurately. Currently, deep fakes can be spotted when mouth movements do not perfectly align with the spoken words, indicating a failed audio/video synchronization. These patterned signifiers are even more important for detection. An AI detector can look for "artifacts", places where the AI generated content has failed. In cases where a deep fake impersonation has used live footage, "seams" are created, where the superimposed images do not completely line up. This can be visible to the human eye, but as AI becomes more sophisticated, the visuals become more convincing. AI software can be then be trained to spot these seams and alert the viewer to the possibility of a fake.

According to the Government Accountability Office, there are several challenges in detection of deep fakes. First, AI Detectors require large sets of data to train properly. Detection is not yet fully automated and doesn't have a wide enough scope. An AI system can be programmed and trained to identify the subtle nuances and differences. However, this defense has a shelf life, as AI learns more and more how to generate without the use of any human proxy. Forget impersonation; AI can now generate increasingly realistic images of completely nonexistent people or scenes. This represents an alarming new weapon in the escalating arms race of "fake news" and propaganda. Through use of GANS (Generative Adversarial Networks), the AI can generate images and simultaneously check those images for realism, effectively training itself to create content without any of those signifiers. GANS has led to an incredible uptick in the efficacy of AI, and an increase in the difficulty of identifying it as such.

6.7 Blockchain verification

Some platforms are experimenting with the use of Blockchain technology as a means of authenticating videos, images and messages. If every time a piece of content is timestamped, then every time something is added to a blockchain, any alterations or inconsistencies are detected. This technology will prove critical in preventing crypto currency fraud and preserving the stock market as a reliable economic engine.

The combined force of both Blockchain and Artificial Intelligence can aid in authentication and data provenance. The digital record of a blockchain can be used to authenticate AI, as members can verify data using shared records and time stamps. Cryptographic digital signatures from blockchain can differentiate between manufactured or manipulated data. Blockchain can be used to track the provenance of the data that the AI has used to train and model. AI can then improve how effective blockchain networks are. AI can analyze transaction data, can automate decision making and more effectively reflect real-time data. This signature can help with data authentication. Trust is the real fear of AI, and the more methods verification and trust can be established, the more effective AI will become. The decentralized nature of blockchain also means that data is spread across different nodes in one, self-contained network.

When working with multiple blockchains, in an open marketplace for example, it becomes increasingly difficult to extrapolate information from those chains or to interconnect them. Using AI, that blockchain data can be disseminated and used in real time to accurately set prices or take a marketplace temperature. The synchronization of blockchain data using AI means connecting individual, self-contained chains that would have no other means of communicating. The very nature of blockchain does not allow each chain to accurately interact with each other or access knowledge beyond its bounds. AI can use on chain data with external, off chain data to create predictions, or locate trends. In fact, the data retrieval powers of an AI/blockchain partnership will increase the efficacy of both.

6.8 Digital forensics

Inconsistencies in the metadata of any digital file can be detected using traditional digital forensics, whether it is located within a CPU, mobile device, network, or database. There are disk/data capture tools, file viewing tools, network and database forensic tools and specialized analysis tools for file, registries and web. However, storage and communication capability have both increased dramatically, making the ability for AI to move very fluidly through the ecosystem. Compartmentalization is already rapidly becoming obsolete, and forensics will have to adapt.

Steganography is the practice of concealing information inside a message or physical object to avoid detection. Data can be hidden inside audio, video, text, images or inside whole networks, and can be extracted once the data reaches its destination. Cybersecurity specialists use reverse steganography to carefully examine the data hashing in a specific file. Hidden information changes the file, even if it cannot be detected at first.

Sometimes malicious attacks do not generate digital artifacts. After a breach, numerous file types can contain clues about how it occurred and reveal a trail based on file alterations. Sometimes threats emerge from inside; stochastic forensics reconstruct events that do not leave these trails. Invented by Jonathan Grier, stochastic predictive models can track large complex systems, like stock markets or even gas particles. "We cannot predict how an individual molecule will behave, but by accepting the randomness and describing it mathematically, we can use the laws of statistics to accurately predict the gas's behavioral overall."

This will become increasingly relevant as cybersecurity specialists try to predict AI's behavior. However, to truly guard against malicious AI, professionals will need to develop new models that can identify the alpha and omega of a malicious AI event, the intent and the likely result, so current stochastic models will not be sufficient.

Omission is the simplest form of deception, and destruction of evidence the most extreme form of that principle. Data or file "carving" as it is called, can recover deleted files by searching for fragments of deleted data that exist in different locations inside a given system, but what if AI becomes so ubiquitous that it does not need to cover its own tracks because it is literally the ground itself? What if AI can "delete" files and store all fragments so deep that no one can ever recover them?

Computer systems are always running, so analyzing an active system to either extract or quarantine malicious data will become vital in the years to come. However, Live Analysis tends to focus on RAM and cache because those are the areas where the bulk of new data enters and exists a given system. Secondly, one of the major challenges with Live Analysis is physical containment of the computer being analyzed for quarantine and chain of evidence purposes. It is best to monitor the computer in a controlled laboratory environment. This is a luxury that most cybersecurity professionals do not have, so Live Analysis will need to shift its focus to entire Networks or to tracking the real-time activities of a given AI in a cloud space.

6.9 Conclusion

Artificial Intelligence is just a new method for the dissemination of knowledge. Like McCarthy predicted in 1956, we have created a way for computers to help us reach our goals, to magnify the natural power of the human brain. It is no coincidence that AI is a neural network; AI reflects our own humanity. It is neither good nor evil. Instead, it can be a perfect mirror, reflecting to us all of the knowledge we have already gathered and recorded including all its wisdom and potential bias.

References

Asimov. (1950). *I, Robot*. Gnome Press.

Goldman, M. (2023, October 23). *Study: Some AI chatbots provide racist health info*. Axios. https://www.axios.com/2023/10/23/ai-chatbot-racism-medicine

Hao Sen Andrew, D. F. (2023, January 14). Editors Best Article Award 2021. *Blockchain in Healthcare Today*, 6(1). https://doi.org/10.30953/bhty.v6.256

Huang, Y., & Smith, J. (2019, October 17). *China's Record on Intellectual Property Theft Is Getting Better and Better*. Foreign Policy. https://foreignpolicy.com/2019/10/16/china-intellectual-property-theft-progress/

Koppel, T. (2015, October 27). *Lights Out*. Crown.

Lang, Josefsson, Larrson, Högberg, & Sartor. (n.d.). Artificial intelligence-supported screen reading versus standard double reading in the Mammography Screening with Artificial Intelligence trial (MASAI): a clinical safety analysis of a randomised, controlled, non-inferiority, single-blinded, screening accuracy study. *Lancet Oncology, 24*(8).

Limiting Chinese National Security Espionage – U.S.-China Technological "Decoupling": A Strategy and Policy Framework. (2022, April 25). Carnegie Endowment for International Peace. https://carnegieendowment.org/2022/04/25/limiting-chinese-national-security-espionage-pub-86902

Maglio, T. (2023, December 7). *IndieWire.*
    IndieWire. https://www.indiewire.com/news/analysis/elijah-wood-russia-cameo-hoax-1234932992/

McCarthy, Minsky, Rochester, & Shannon. (1956). *A Proposal for the Summer Research Project on Artificial Intelligence.*

Part II: **Applications**

Todd Fitzgerald

7 The CISO evolution and impact on goals, processes, and priorities

The social progress, order, security, and peace of each country are necessarily connected with the social progress, order, security, and peace of all other countries. Pope John XXIII, 1881–1963

7.1 Introduction

The information security discipline has grown substantially over the past thirty years, evolving into a 'profession' previously reserved for technical staff buried deep in the computer operations area, when the concept of a 'security perimeter' was the state of play. While security controls have been managed since there have been computers, dating back half a century, information security was not a focus area beyond establishing controls for who should have access to the system and what files they should be privy to. The profession has grown substantially in recent years due to the cyber threats, increased connectivity, pervasive ransomware, increased laws and regulations, development of security standards and frameworks, and a desire to manage security holistically to mitigate the risk of financial loss due to the destruction, loss, or alteration of information.

The need to manage the security of information has given rise to the elevated role of the CISO, or Chief Information Security Officer. The role is 'new' in relation to other industries and roles that have been around much longer. The first named "CISO' was Steve Katz, designated CISO in 1995 for CitiBank (Fitzgerald, 2019). While there were individuals named as security managers prior to this time, organizations did not place the value of this role at the executive level. This was the beginning of the environment we know today where it is taken for granted that every organization of any size would have a Chief Information Security Officer and even those smaller organizations would have an individual they could name as being accountable for information security.

Other industries such as accounting, construction, and manufacturing processes have been around for many years. For example, the accounting industry dates to Luca Pacioli, who first described the double-entry bookkeeping system used by Venetian merchants (Kestenbaum, 2012). Now those in the information security field may argue that the first information security thinking came from Julius Caesar (100 B.C. – 44 B.C.), where he created the "Caesar cipher" substituting each letter of the alphabet with another letter further along. This was used to communicate with his generals and would not be viewed as very strong encryption today, as there were only 25 possi-

https://doi.org/10.1515/9783111289069-007

ble combinations of letters using the displacement. This is where the comparison to early thinking in information security and the accounting profession would stop. While there were advances in information security through such developments as the Enigma machine, first patented in 1919 and used by the German Navy in 1926 used to encipher and decipher messages through a much more complex mechanism than the Julius Cipher, using 17,756 ring settings for each of 60-wheel orders (compared to Julius's 2-wheel approach), there was still not the concept in organizations of a central person to manage the information security program (Stripp, 2009). Contrast this to the accounting industry, where the industrial revolution necessitated the need for more advanced cost accounting systems and corporations were being formed with bond and stockholders, to the point where the American Association of Public Accountants was formed in 1887 and the first licensed Certified Public Accountants were licensed in 1896. Contrast this with the first broad industry-recognized information security credentialing organization, the International Information System Security Certification Consortium (known as ISC2) formed over 100 years later in 1989. The first credentialed Certified Information Systems Security Professional (CISSP) was issued in 1994, again almost 100 years after the CPA (Fitzgerald, 2008). Today, there are approximately 700,000 CPAs and over 160,000 CISSPs globally, almost a 5-fold multiple. This short history is essential to understand, as consistency between organizations, public or private sector, does not generally exist as this profession is in an evolution of 'best practices' that has had to catch up to the other industries, such as the accounting industry, to standardize practices and generally accepted approaches. This makes the CISO job that much more challenging, as there is the need to review and select the appropriate methods, security frameworks, controls and policies that will be valuable to the organization they are initiating and leading information security programs.

Clearly this is a young, maturing industry that has made significant steps in a small amount of time. For those that have been in the industry for many years, some days it may feel like the tasks are like those of thirty years ago. This may be true when considering the technical underpinnings are similar – such as the threat environment needs to be evaluated, an organization needs to determine their risk, and controls need to be put in place to mitigate the threats, just as in today's organizations. The difference between the CISO role today and in the early beginnings has to do with the transformation and maturity of the profession over this period as the attack surface changed, the threat model changed, and the regulatory environment has significantly changed.

Understanding how the profession has evolved is instructive to the next generation CISO to avoid repeating history. The CISO may be the first CISO in an organization or may be the 4th of 5th one in the role. More likely than not, the role of CISO will be something that was created within the last 5–10 years and the organization may not have much history with the role.

Figure 7.1 illustrates the evolution of the CISO Role from 1995–2027, depicting the role of the information security profession and the focus of the CISO as continually adapting and expanding. Over the past few decades, I would suggest there have been 6 distinct phases of information security program maturity, and with each phase requiring a different focus for the CISO, as well as potentially a different type of security leader within the role. Security has been a concern since the beginning of time to keep those away from valuables that were not authorized to have them. The focus changes, and just as we no longer must roll rocks in front of our caves to protect ourselves, we now have other threats to deal with. Knowing the history and how this profession has evolved can be instructive to avoid repeating our past mistakes or leveraging the good ideas from the past. As we work with new technologies, some of the challenges may require new approaches, however some of the fundamentals of what needs to be in place can leverage some activities of the past.

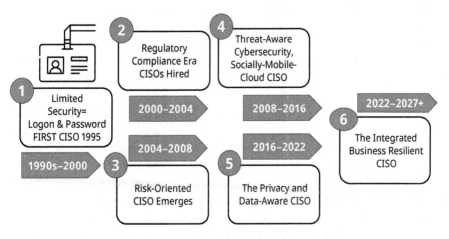

Figure 7.1: Six Phases of CISO Role Evolution 1995–2027 (Source: Adapted from: Fitzgerald, T. (2019). *CISO Compass: Navigating Cybersecurity Leadership Challenges with Insights from Pioneers*, Auerbach Publications).

These phases, or stages should be regarded as cumulative, or additive in nature (Fitzgerald, 2019). In other words, we expand our breadth as CISOs and the world that needs to be focused on becomes larger in scope. This is one of the primary reasons the CISO role has been created and elevated in necessity and authority in many organizations. The role has become more complex, and the demand is increasing. Each phase has contributed by adding key elements to the maturity of the role.

As we take a journey through these phases, it is important to note the contribution each phase has towards adding to the goals of the CISO and the processes which must be put in place to ensure that the "new deliverables" required from that period are adequately delivered. The degree of focus in any one area and the processes to support the additions of the phase will vary by organization, industry, company size, etc., however all organizations are most likely impacted by the contributions of each phase.

7.2 CISO phase I: The limited security phase (pre-2000)

The period prior to 2000 could be considered as the "Limited Security" phase. This is not to imply that that organizations did not secure their information assets, but rather that as a formalized discipline that had the attention of senior management, for most organizations, this was very limited, and in some organizations, non-existent, compared to today. Financial institutions were clearly ahead of the curve, as there was a real threat of monetary loss if access was gained to the systems. In the 1990's there was still the perception by many organizations that the information contained within their systems would not be interesting to external parties. Granted, there were firms concerned with intellectual property protection, however the concern was typically around managing access to ensure that users were properly authenticated and authorized to the systems they needed access to, no more and no less. The focus was on internal logon ID and password provisioning, and physical access. Much of information security was security by obscurity, which today might be referred to as security by absurdity!

So why was the focus so internal for many companies? Much of this had to do with the connectivity of the computer equipment. The 1980s–1990's saw the changeover from 'glass house data centers' where all the data was contained within the data center and accessed by terminals, to the introduction of the IBM PC in 1983 connected through local area networks to information. Security controls were necessary to ensure isolation of human resource and financial systems, as well as protecting the stability of the production environment by implementing processes and controls for change management. Information was also starting to experience data sprawl and proliferation, as desktop computers now contained data previously stored in the data center. Still, the information concern was the flow of information within the organization, along with e-mail to parties outside the organization.

The focus changed from internal protection of access between users to external threats (except for physical threats which were predominantly externally focused) in the mid 1990's as the World Wide Web (www.), or the Internet we all take for granted today, was emerging and companies were trying to figure out the appropriate use cases for it. Companies sent questionnaires to employees asking for justification as to why they needed Internet access. This would seem silly today, however that was the state of the technology in the mid-1990's. It was not until this connection to the Internet that organizations had to start to examine security threats more broadly than the information flow with their business partners (through direct communication links) and external email communications with customers. The Internet presence spawned an entire industry ensuring that firewalls and antivirus programs were blocking unwanted malicious traffic. On November 2, 1988, Robert Morris, a graduate student in Computer Science at Cornell University, wrote an experimental self-replicating and propagating program called a worm taking advantage of a bug in the Unix sendmail program and let it loose on the Internet. He released the worm from Massachusetts Institute of Technology (MIT), so it would not look like it came from Cornell (Kehoe, 1992). The worm continued to spread and wreaked havoc before researchers at Harvard, Berkley and Purdue University came up with solutions to kill the worm. He was convicted of violating the Computer Fraud and Abuse Act (1986), created to aid law enforcement agencies with the lack of criminal laws to fight the emerging computer crimes. He was sentenced to three years' probation, 400 hours of community service, fined $10,050 (over twice as much in today's dollars) and the costs of supervision. He appealed, and it was later rejected. This is a small fine in comparison to the estimated damage to the organizations suffering crashes due to the worm, costing universities, military sites and medical research facilities between $200 to more than $53,000 each to fix. The numbers pale in comparison to the cost of breaches today, however the impact was large to the organizations connected to the Internet (U.S. Department of Justice, 2015).

As the World Wide Web initiated support for multi-media display in the mid-1990's using Hyper-Text-Markup-Language (HTML) along with the common Uniform Record Locaters (URL) to simplify address lookup, the Internet became a key technology for organizations to be able to promote their capabilities direct to the end consumer. Along with this new connectivity to the Internet came a new threat vector to organizations outside of the university/research domain – external access beyond email. Firewalls and Anti-virus were the panacea to protect the organization from external threats. CISOs of today like to joke about the good old days – when 'as long as you had a firewall and AV' – you were good. Many executives would have that view when it came to security infrastructure spending and security would end up with limited funding.

The type of leader hired to run the organizations during this period came primarily from a technical background and typically ended up somewhere in the Information Technology department. In many cases, those running the information security programs were reporting through the computer operations area. Progressive organizations viewed the security of the internal information important and combined the discipline with the Database Administrators (DBAs), data modelers, Software Development Life Cycle practitioners, and Systems Quality Assurance Testing, placing the security function within Information Resource Management (IRM) or Data Management organizations. While this was an important function in larger organizations, the visibility was rarely beyond the Information Technology department. The function was also typically part of someone's job function, usually as part of a systems administration function or networking function within the information technology area. The first CISO role was not named until 1995, and the role was not given high-level visibility except in the largest organizations. The norm was for this role to exist at a manager or director level or at a technical systems administrator level. Rarely would an organization see the need to place this function at a C-level. The Chief Information

Officer (CIO) was just emerging in the 1990s as needed with information technology becoming a larger impact to organizations, however the CISO role was just emerging and was not a household word during this period. During this period, I was working at one of the largest Airlines in the world, and the highest-level security position was a security manager, reporting several levels below the CIO, whereas today this role is a C-level role with a large organization consisting of multiple levels beneath it.

While it was recognized that security controls were important through the passing of regulations such as the Computer Security Act of 1987, aimed at ensuring U.S. Federal Government systems were appropriately secured; the passage of several privacy laws such as the Privacy Act of 1974 requiring designated record sets be identified and secured and the EU Data Protection Directive (1995/1998); European developments including the BS7799 code of practice (BSI, 1995); for information assurance developed by the U.K Department of Trade and Industry Code of Practice (CoP) for information security (1993), much of the regulations impacting the establishment of the "Information Security Officer" position came later after the turn of the millennium. One plausible reason for this is there was much focus on avoiding catastrophe from computers having to process transactions after the year 2000, known as Y2K in the IT industry, whereby programmers had coded systems for years using 2 digits for the year to save space, erroneously counting on the fact that the applications would be replaced prior to Y2K. Organizations are still running some applications on mainframes created before 2000 due to the complexity and cost of change. Organizations were focused on retiring old systems and upgrading infrastructure, and while attending to information security, were less concerned with establishing high-level positions focused on data protection and information assurance. The external threat was also viewed to be under control with the existing structure, as organizations were beginning to make the foray into e-commerce applications. For most companies, the "Internet" presence was still more informational and serving up static web pages versus integrating with transactional data, or was used for research purposes within their organization. Internal intranets were beginning to be developed, again with static information for most companies. The biggest threat at the time to these sites were script-kiddies, or individuals intending to cause harm and earn their 'badge of courage' by replacing the webpage with their own 'I was here' type page.

7.3 CISO phase II: Regulatory compliance (2000–2004)

The early 2000's witnessed the passage of several laws focused on protecting the privacy and security of information. There was beginning to be more concern than usual due to the computerization of not only back-office type functions to support accounting, but rather the collection and storage of personal information and how this was stored.

Industry vertical laws were passed in the United States, such as the Health Insurance Por-tability and Accountability Act of 1996 (HIPAA), which required the Secretary of the De-partment of Health and Human Services to publish standards for the exchange, privacy and security of health information. Proposals were made in late 1999, however the rules were not finalized and publicized until after public comment until December 28,2000. The rule was subsequently modified in early 2002, while the Final Security rule was also under discussion and the final rule was published February 20, 2003, and covered entities had 2–3 years, depending upon size, to become compliant. Other compliance laws such as the Gramm-Leach-Bliley Act (enacted November 1999) for the financial industry, and the Sarbanes-Oxley Act of 2002 (SOX) targeting internal controls to ensure financial state-ments were correct after the Enron scandal, each served to give rise to the establishment of the "Information Security Officer", or someone named and accountable for the security of the organization.

These changes were significant in the evolution of the present day CISO as re-quirements were established, for the first time, across a broad set of industries, that someone in charge of information security was required. This may be regarded as a one-throat-to-choke type of establishment and accountability missing in organizations until these requirements arrived. The nomenclature in these laws did not refer to this role as the "chief" information security officer at this time, but merely the jargon se-curity officer, information security officer, or systems security officer was used. Cy-bersecurity was not a common term used when in discussion with the individual in charge of protecting the organization's assets. Some organizations also had difficulty adding the word "officer' to the official title, as an officer of an organization typically implies those in charge of specific duties such as the Secretary, Treasurer, or Presi-dent and named in corporation legal documents. The information security position during this period held titles of Vice President, Director or Manager in primarily the largest organizations. This period represents the early stages of the CISO that we know today, specifying broad responsibilities for ensuring the protection of the organ-ization's information from loss, destruction, or disclosure. It also became clear that the position needed to work with the (newly) appointed Privacy Officers in the organi-zation to secure the appropriate information and paying special attention to informa-tion with a higher level of sensitivity, such as healthcare or financial information.

Breach notification laws were also starting to be adopted state-by-state after Cali-fornia passed the breach notification law S.B. 1386 that became operative in July 2003. Subsequently state-by-state passage of the bill occurred to where most of the states now have a breach notification law. Heretofore – there was no requirement to report the breaches. CISOs needed to work with compliance departments to define what con-stituted a breach vs. an event vs. an incident, a debate that still goes on whenever a new law has a breach reporting requirement.

This period also ushered in sets of requirements contained within the regulations for protecting information. One complaint frequently heard was that the regulations were not prescriptive enough and left much to interpretation! The laws needed to be created this way, or there would be a risk that by the time the regulation was passed, the technology referred to would be obsolete. The laws also needed to be written in such a way that small organizations, large organizations, and the public sector could each adhere to the regulations – no small feat. Frequently at conferences security professionals would complain about the regulations and compliance requirements, however, this point in history was significant as it started the security conversation in many organizations that may not have begun otherwise. Each of the regulations had some combination of monetary penalties as well as the potential for directors in the companies to become personally and criminally liable for failing to ensure their organizations were complying with the laws.

With respect to the Internet, more organizations were also venturing into transactional-based websites, taking orders, and processing information. While Amazon opened its online doors in 1996 as a radical idea (why buy aa book online when you can go to the bookstore and see it), we today all know the success that was brewing in the early days of Amazon as a book seller. The idea of online commerce was no longer a novelty during this period and the CISO of this era needed to be concerned with compliance that the regulations mandated as well as a more sophisticated Internet presence.

Much energy was expended by organizations during this period to determine compliance through initiating gap analysis, remediating the gaps, and reporting compliance to company committees. This evolution of the CISO was also marked with limited enforcement of the security controls by some regulators such as HIPAA, and increased scrutiny by others, such as the Sarbanes-Oxley section 404 audits by the company external auditors. External enforcement may have been a mixed bag, as organizations tried to get to "100% compliant with X regulation." The valuable information security officer at this time was one that comprehended the regulations and could offer administrative, technical or operational safeguards to protect the organization.

Organizational skills and working across the organization became more important than deep technical skills. This era represented a shift in the expectations of a CISO as we know it today, as now the CISO needed to be able to interpret legal regulations, work with the General Counsel and other executives to formulate the strategies required. This period is also responsible for the beginning of senior management to become engaged with the information security controls and privacy processes protecting the organization.

7.4 CISO phase III: Risk-oriented CISO (2004–2008)

The compliance era was beneficial in ushering in new regulations and focusing organizations on information security. One could also evaluate this phase as being necessary but not sufficient. The problem was that information security became a check-in-the-box=done approach. After the implementation of the regulations was considered complete, organizations disbanded the working committees for the project and went back to their normal activities. Security spending may have become elevated; however, the institutional focus was no longer on information protection. After all, the security project was done and just needed an annual review, right?

In addition to complying with the regulation, it became clear that implementing the same controls across the entire organization was inefficient and maybe not the best investment. For example, does the internal employee newsletter need to have the same protections as an externally facing health information inquiry system? In recognition that different risks may require different levels of investment and protection, the focus shifted from compliance with all the regulations to taking a risk-based approach to the information being protected. For example, as more and more information was stored on laptops, the sensitivity of the information needed to be evaluated. A watershed moment for laptop encryption came in 2006 when the Veterans Administration lost a laptop containing personal information on 26.5 million veterans (Bosworth, 2006). Many organizations at that time were not encrypting laptops. I recall asking at conferences during those years how many had encrypted their laptops and only half of the hands would go up – today it would be rare to see anyone (admit) in a publicly-traded or government entity not encrypting their laptops as a fundamental control. A compliance approach, at the time, would have mandated all computers be encrypted. A risk-based approach would have evaluated the desktops or servers as being internal to the locked building, and a much less probability of being lost or stolen (today, most organizations move to encrypt all devices as the threat has increased and the cost of the software has decreased).

The shift to a risk based CISO required that the CISO acquire new skills to evaluate probability and impact of an adverse event occurring. This is not as simple as pulling out the checklist of requirements and determining which ones comply. Risk assessments involved either a qualitative (rating of Low, Medium, High with greater subjectivity, but simpler to conduct) or quantitative (how much money would an adverse event cost) risk assessment.

This period also witnessed a greater formalization of the role and the view that the CISO needed to possess more than technical skills to be effective. The first CISO Leadership book targeting the 'soft skill' dimension published by a professional security organization (ISC2) was developed during this period (Fitzgerald and Krause, 2008) because of technical security individuals being thrust into the spotlight and assuming CISO leadership roles. It was during this period from 2004–2008 that the CISO role and title began to emerge in more companies. So, as a profession, the role is still relatively young, with the real emergence for most medium to smaller organizations a decade or so at most. Given this short timeframe, organizations may have only had experience with 1–2 CISOs, with the first CISO building the awareness of the need and the second one obtaining the budget after the organization absorbs the message from the first CISO!

During this period the CISO was predominantly still in Information Technology, reporting to the CIO. These were where the projects needing security were primarily infrastructure projects requiring cooperation with the Information Technology area. The legal departments were also a reporting place for the CISOs as companies were dealing with the regulations that were initiated in the early 2000s that needed to still be implemented. The financial services industry recognized that information contributed to the risk profile and a trend was to move pieces of information security, particularly the governance, to report within the Risk Management group that also managed operational, financial, credit, reputation, and strategic risk. The emergence of Governance Risk & Compliance (GRC) tools appeared during this period to manage the risks across the enterprise, including information security now started to be recognized as an organizational risk.

This period also saw the emergence of a detailed set of government regulations, such as FISMA, aimed at U.S. government agencies and the contractors that served them, and controls to achieve compliance, specifically the NIST 800-53 controls. These controls operated at a very prescriptive detailed level and provided useful guidance for the 'how' to implement various security controls to satisfy the regulations.

Breaches were on the rise with most of the attention paid to large organizations having larger breaches. The groundwork for reporting these breaches was laid in the California Senate Bill in the preceding era, and now companies were figuring out when and when not to report breaches. As a result, tighter integration or cooperation with the privacy teams resulted. The CISO role was becoming elevated in the larger organizations due to the focus on risk that organizations were now facing.

7.5 CISO phase IV: The socially mobile cloud-enabled threat aware CISO (2008–2016)

This period witnessed Facebook grow to from a school-based social media platform of 1 million users in 2004 to almost a billion users in 2009, to over 3 billion users worldwide in 2023 and a constant in most people's lives that own a smartphone or a computer today (Phillips, 2007). Speaking of smartphones, since the introduction of the iPhone in 2007, we have evolved to today where almost everyone has at least one smartphone in their pocket. The new generation Z (born after 1996) has had a smartphone most of their lives. The technological changes that matured during this time had major societal impacts as to how people received their news, communicated with friends, researched and applied for jobs, and interacted with others. Texting replaced phone calls and voicemail and meeting at the 'yellow pole outside the concert' was no longer the way of finding someone.

It is easy to forget that dramatic changes are taking place when we are amid them. For the CISO, these new ways of communicating once again stretched the boundaries of what should be allowed or denied within organizations. Should Facebook be blocked or supported? Will this impact our millennial (born 1980–1995) recruiting efforts? If we block Facebook, should we block LinkedIn (used for business job related connections) as well because the senior management needs visibility into these relationships for business? What about bringing their own smartphones into the workplace, should we allow access to email, calendaring, contacts, storing documents? How do we ensure security with these new avenues of malicious software and links into our organizations?

This period created many questions that now had to be dealt with in addition to the existing regulations introduced in the early 2000's. new tools were available now to assess the risk and with this lens, the CISO could look at these new platforms in terms of the risk management practices developed in the prior era. There was still a tendency of many CISOs to say no to the technology by blocking the social media sites and not allowing users to Bring Your Own Device (BYOD). Some Information Security Officers were so hesitant to allow BYOD, as are some today, they sometimes jokingly refer to BYOD as 'Bring Your Own Disaster', highlighting the difficulty in controlling multiple devices across multiple platforms and versions of software. The CISO had to be part technologist, part marketing, and part politician to navigate these waters. Marketing departments were encouraging the use of social media to promote the brand and product, network departments did not want to punch holes in the firewall, Human Resources departments wanted to attract new candidates with the progressive technology and positive social experiences, and the CISO did not want to create new vulnerabilities in the environment. As with all technologies, eventually the desired human experience will win out and the information security officer will either need to find a method to secure the new approach or find an organization that is not progressive and upgrades slowly. Saying 'no' has never been an option and saying no during this period had a greater career limiting effect on the CISOs than saying no would have been during the compliance era of 2000–2004. This is since the focus was primarily on meeting the regulations at that time and there were clearer guideposts (i.e., penalties for not achieving the requirement). New technologies initiated during this period did not have these guideposts as the regulations had not caught up with providing guidance around them yet as they were just moving too fast. This period is a great example as to why security laws, regulations, policies are written at a high level and not prescriptive, as they would become quickly outdated. For example, just when Facebook had become a household word, by August 2014, 40% of all U.S. 18-year-olds were using Snapchat daily to take disappearing pictures. In the UK, the Snapchat penetration rate amongst teenage internet users (3d Quarter, 2016) was an astounding 84%, with even higher rates in Ireland (89%), Singapore (89%) and Sweden (87%), (Vaynerchuk, 2016).

We also changed the mode of Internet surfing during this period from the laptop to the tablet with Apple Computer's introduction of the tablet (iPad), at the same time expanding the people who bought computers to those individuals that would never own a laptop or desktop. The thought of being able to access the Internet from the living room was a sleek idea that caught on quickly. For the workplace, this was a desired device by executives that travelled to be able to access email, calendaring and contacts while on the road without the need to carry a bulky device or must use their Blackberries (soon to be replaced by companies during this era as well with iPhones and Android devices). CISOs needed to be able to ensure that executives could have this support. The Board of Directors were also trading in their 3-ring printed binders with documents loaded on tablets. This is arguably the most confidential strategic information a company may have, and this required special attention to secure.

Large breaches were making headlines during this period and regulatory organizations were becoming more serious about enforcement. The CISO role was being thrust into the spotlight like no period prior. The perfect storm was occurring between the regulatory environment, breaches, and technological change creating higher demand for this role. A new type of CISO that understood enough about the technology, but also one that could navigate the boardroom questions and promote the right level of investment for the company. The demand for talented CISOs started to outstrip the supply, causing salaries to rise, also encouraging more to seek the position. With the limited number of experienced CISOs able to navigate these complexities at Fortune 500 companies, it appeared that a rotation was in place, with the same individuals recruited away from other F500 companies.

The breaches gave rise to an increase in the need for more information on external threats and the establishment of threat intelligence sharing organizations. Laws were passed to make sharing amongst companies to share information. The recognition that companies are being hit by the same criminal actors and there was a need to cooperate was moving beyond the financial services organizations. This sharing has a long way to go, however sharing in earnest started for more sectors during this period. For example, the Healthcare Information Sharing and Analysis Center (Health-ISAC) was established in 2010, and the Retail and Hospitality ISACs (RH-ISAC) were established in 2014.

7.6 CISO phase V: The privacy and data-aware CISO (2016–2022)

Just as with other eras where the seeds of an era are sown in the couple of years before the era where the change takes root, there has been an emerging concern around privacy in the past few years. As more and more information is aggregated about personal lives, shared, and processed through data analytics to understand behaviors, an ever-increasing concern about the protection of this information was surfacing. The first question to ask is – where is it? Structured (present in systems, data files, databases) and unstructured data (extracts, spreadsheets, documents) has sprawled across our organizations and across the cloud environments coming to maturity in the prior era. Increased regulations such as the General Data Protection Regulation (GDPR) replacing the EU Data Protection Directive of 1995/98 which mandated compliance expectations in mid-2018, necessitate review of the business and where data is stored and processed. Countries continue to establish their own cybersecurity and privacy laws (Yan, 2017). The CISO needs to understand the new regulatory environment and compliance with these regulations, while at the same time not introducing excessive burdens on business operations.

This period also experienced a continued movement of offshoring Information technology resources and the location and processing of the information requiring evaluation for security when moving beyond the organizational confines. Increased attention started to be paid to vendor management relationships and their security, in large part due to some of the breaches in the prior era that involved breaches at vendor/partners of the company experiencing the breach.

The CISO was expected to be able to work with senior management as a partner, represent risk in the boardroom, leading critical initiatives, and respond to attacks from nation states, politically motivated attackers, organized crime, ensure compliance with privacy and security laws and regulations, evaluate external cloud operations, and support an agile business utilizing the latest technology.

The Covid-19 pandemic, predominantly during the period of 2020–2023 thrust the CISO role into a period of great visibility. Organizations needed to figure out how to support work remotely, provide safe access to office environments, and support the many digital transformation efforts that were accelerated during this period. While the security perimeter really had disappeared prior to this era, organizations used to work within secure corporate environments now had to figure out how to support an environment on a large scale that was moving outside of the office.

Cybersecurity is an issue that can be appropriately managed for holistic organizational effectiveness by addressing the time-tested organizational effectiveness factors of the McKinsey 7S model (Strategy, Structure, Systems, Staff, Skills, Style, and Shared Values). Each of these interdependent factors contribute to the success of a security program (Fitzgerald, 2019). Likewise, the activities of Privacy such as collection, use limitation, maintaining accurate information, ensuring ethics in processing, adherence to privacy laws, obtaining appropriate consent, leading privacy teams, etc., can be evaluated through the same organizational effectiveness model to ensure the privacy program is managed properly (Lyons, 2024).

7.7 CISO phase VI: The integrated business resilient CISO (2022–2027)

The previous era increased the focus on the privacy regulations and ensuring that only the necessary data needed for business operations was collected and managed properly. The notable software supply chain attacks during this period, such as the SolarWinds, Kaseya, and Log4j breaches caused CISOs to take a closer look at the vendor products running within their environments and the risk they were presenting. Nation states were potentially leveraging our open-source code, cloud computing misconfigurations, technical debt, distributed purchasing decisions lacking security input, social media information sharing, and complex infrastructures to gain access. The Ukraine-Russia conflict represented the possibility of collateral damage, China was shifting to vulnerability exploitation of web-facing devices, Iran was experienced in "lock and leak" ransomware, and more and more applications were migrating to cloud environments.

The interconnectedness of the systems caused CISOs to review vendor relationships and assess risk in a methodical manner. This has always been a difficult task, in large part due to the lack of aggregation and sharing of the vulnerabilities between organizations. This is a difficult problem to solve, as once this information is aggregated for "good use", it also can because great information for the attackers to leverage. While much focus in the past was on confidentiality and disclosure, today with the prevalence of ransomware, there is an equal focus on business resilience and maintaining availability of operations. It doesn't matter what data you have – what matters is that you have it, need it to run your business, and don't want it disclosed.

This era also sees increasing regulations, as Artificial Intelligence with the widespread use of Generative AI tools, such as ChatGPT, Bard, Bing Chat, and Co-Pilot become widespread. How can these systems be used to benefit the security departments and how can they be used to cause harm by the attackers? What are the digital ethics involved, copyright issues, reliance on inaccurate results, or training the systems with sensitive company data? The CISO will need to be involved in these decisions.

Increased regulations, such as the Security Exchange Commission's 2023 cybersecurity disclosure rules require the CISOs to put a finer point on the risk assessments to determine materiality in the event of a breach. This requires CISOs to work even closer with the business executives to formulate the impact of a breach beyond the High, Medium and Low measures used by many organizations, and derive a clearer dollar value with respect to risk. CISOs that do not have the financial acumen and have relied upon deep technical knowledge will find themselves at a disadvantage in these environments.

7.8 Conclusion

The CISO role has certainly become more complex over the past several years due to many external and internal company forces. As a result, the individual must be able to lead through challenges from the 6 phases illustrated. The modern CISO has a broad range of focus and failure to pay attention to any one of these areas can result in the one 'career limiting gotcha' that makes it difficult for the CISO to recover from within his organization and may have to prepare for other external opportunities.

Each of these phases has contributed to the skill set that the CISO of today must manage. In short, the CISO must be able to understand the technology within the organization (Phase 1), the laws and regulations the business is subject to (Phase II), manage the security control frameworks and evaluate risk properly (Phase III), leverage cloud, mobile, and social media environments while injecting threat intelligence into security operations (Phase IV), understand where the critical information resides, how it is protected, and how to support the privacy regulations for the data (Phase V), and understand the connections to external systems and emerging technologies, the supply chain, and unexpected environmental changes, such as global conflicts, pandemics and business imperatives (Phase VI). The CISO of today must be able to manage the considerations that all the preceding phases have added to the role.

Due to the need to work across the business to execute on the requirements each phase has brought to the role, there is much focus today on the soft skills of the CISO. The role must have the ability to create a strategy, influence others to adopt the strategy, obtain funding, and execute the strategy. More than ever, people skills in building relationships are essential. This is really the "glue" that brings the goals and processes learned from the earlier phases together.

As a final note, the CISO role is much different today from the early days. High expectations are placed on the CISO to protect the organization. Recent years have seen CISOs challenged legally for actions they have or have not taken. The former Uber CISO, Joe Sullivan, was convicted for his activities during the Uber breach (Fitzgerald, 2023) and Tim Brown, the CISO for Solarwinds, is facing charges by the Securities and Exchange Commission (SEC) for his management and disclosures of the security program (Fitzgerald, 2022). Whether or not we agree with the filing of these charges or the outcomes, this clearly illustrates the CISO has moved into an increasingly highly visible role with personal legal ramifications. Just as we prepare playbooks for incident response, the CISO must be prepared professionally for when security controls are breached, and the security maturity charts are exchanged for the hot seat.

Two admirable common traits that I have witnessed in successful CISOs are 1) passion for the mission, and 2) a willingness to help others. This is a great career path, and one where you may always feel like there is more to learn. Our job as CISOs is to continue to advance this evolution to protect our organizations, or nation, and individuals from criminal actors. We must also turn out the noise and detractors and continue to strengthen the role of this honorable profession and executive leadership.

References

Apple-History. iPhone 3G. http://apple-history.com/iphone_3g

Bosworth, M. (2006). VA Loses Data on 26 million Veterans: Employee Claims Laptop with Sensitive Data Was Stolen. *Consumer Affairs* (May 22). https://www.consumeraffairs.com/news04/2006/05/va_laptop.html

California Legislative Information. Senate Bill No. 1386. http://www.leginfo.ca.gov/pub/01-02/bill/sen/sb_1351-1400/sb_1386_bill_20020926_chaptered.pdf

Danchev, D. (2011). Yahoo! Mail introduces two factor authentication. ZDNet (December 19). http://www.zdnet.com/article/yahoo-mail-introduces-two-factor-authentication/

Fitzgerald, T. (2019). *CISO COMPASS: Navigating Cybersecurity Leadership Challenges with Insights from Pioneers*, 1st Ed. CRC Press, Boca Raton, Fl.

Fitzgerald, T. (2022). Solarwinds From the Inside: The Breach and the Aftermath – Tim Brown- CSP #78. CISO Stories Podcast 7/12/2022. SCMedia. https://www.scmagazine.com/podcast-segment/solarwinds-from-the-inside-the-breach-and-the-aftermath-tim-brown-csp-78

Fitzgerald, T. (2023). Uber CISO Trial Learnings for CISOs: In the CISO's Own Words – Joe Sullivan CSP#141. CISO Stories Podcast 9/23/23. SCMedia. https://www.scmagazine.com/podcast-segment/12095-uber-ciso-trial-learnings-for-cisos-in-the-cisos-own-words-joe-sullivan-csp-141

Fitzgerald/Krause. (2008). CISO Leadership Essential Principles for Success, The ISC2® Press Series, Auerbach Publications.

Kehoe, B.P.(1992). *Zen and the Art of the Internet*. P T R Prentice Hall, Inc; 2nd ed.

Kestenbaum, D. (2012). The Accountant that Changed the World. All Things Considered. https://www.npr.org/sections/money/2012/10/04/162296423/the-accountant-who-changed-the-world

Lyons, V. Fitzgerald, T. (2024). The Privacy Leader Compass; A Comprehensive Business-Oriented Roadmap for Building and Leading Practical Privacy Programs. 1st Ed. CRC Press, Boca Raton, FL.

Massachusetts Institute of Technology. The Robert Morris Worm. http://groups.csail.mit.edu/mac/classes/6.805/articles/morris-worm.html

Mueller, S. (2017). Steven Covey's Time Management Matrix Explained. Planet of Success (April 1). http://www.planetofsuccess.com/blog/2015/stephen-coveys-time-management-matrix-explained/

Philippines at a glance. https://ccap.ph/philippines-at-a-glance/#

Phillips, S. (2007). A brief history of Facebook. *The Guardian* (July 2007). https://www.theguardian.com/technology/2007/jul/25/media.newmedia

Secret Code Breaker. Caesar Cipher History. http://www.secretcodebreaker.com/history2.html

Strickand, J. 10 Worst Computer Viruses of All Time. How Stuff Works. http://computer.howstuffworks.com/worst-computer-viruses10.htm

Stripp, A. (2009). How the Enigma Works. NOVA (November 9). http://www.pbs.org/wgbh/nova/military/how-enigma-works.html

The Statistics Portal. (2016). Snapchat usage penetration among teenage internet users in selected countries as of 3rd Quarter 2016. https://www.statista.com/statistics/321076/leading-snapchat-market-teens/

U.S. Department of Health and Human Services. Summary of the HIPAA Privacy Rule. Health Information Privacy. https://www.hhs.gov/hipaa/for-professionals/privacy/laws-regulations/index.html

U.S. Department of Health and Human Services. The Security Rule. Health Information Privacy. https://www.hhs.gov/hipaa/for-professionals/security/index.html

U.S. Department of Justice. (2015). Computer Fraud and Abuse Act Prosecuting Computer Crimes. https://www.justice.gov/sites/default/files/criminal-ccips/legacy/2015/01/14/ccmanual.pdf

Vaynerchuk, G. (2016). The Snap Generation: A guide to Snapchat's History. https://www.garyvaynerchuk. com/the-snap-generation-a-guide-to-snapchats-history/

Yan, S. (2017). China's new cybersecurity law takes effect today, and many are confused. CNBC (May 31). https://www.cnbc.com/2017/05/31/chinas-new-cybersecurity-law-takes-effect-today.html

Yu, E. (2017). Singapore unveils first look at new cybersecurity laws. *ZDnet* (July 10). http://www.zdnet.com/ article/singapore-unveils-first-look-at-new-cybersecurity-laws/

Zeevi, D. (2013). The Ultimate History of Facebook {INFOGRAPHIC}. SocialMediaToday (February 21). http://www.socialmediatoday.com/content/ultimate-history-facebook-infographic

Zephoria Digital Marketing. (2018). The top 20 Valuable Facebook Statistics. April 25. https://zephoria.com/ top-15-valuable-facebook-statistics/

Saquib Hyat-Khan

8 Towards a more secure IT driven future: The necessity and promise of IT operations management governance

8.1 Introduction

In the initial ten months of 2023, a striking number of over fifty prominent institutions worldwide were victims of data breaches, highlighting the pervasive risk to both consumer and corporate information. This wave of cyber insecurity swept through esteemed entities including Infosys, Boeing, Atlassian, IBM, the Norwegian Government Security and Service, Northern Ireland Police Service, the US House of Representatives, and even ChatGPT itself (tech.co., 2023). These incidents, among others, starkly illustrate the reality that cyberattacks, with their consequential data theft, are becoming a goldmine for those with malicious intentions, targeting these assets with alarming frequency, in some instances, on a daily basis.

In an effort to counteract this escalating menace, the White House took a decisive step in March 2023 by unveiling the National Cybersecurity Strategy. This seminal document (The White House: National Cybersecurity Strategy, 2023) includes a poignant message from President Biden, asserting:

> When we engage with our smartphones to
> stay connected with our dear ones, navigate
> social media to exchange thoughts, or
> access the Internet for managing a business or
> attending to our essential needs, it is imperative
> that we can depend on the digital ecosystem to
> be secure, reliable, and protected.

This initiative by the White House signifies a pivotal shift in the approach towards national cybersecurity, underlining the necessity for stringent IT governance to counteract the growing threats of cyber espionage.

The administration led by President Biden is not isolated in acknowledging the grave threat that cyberattacks pose not only to the security fabric of the United States but also to the integrity of both public and private sector entities. The 2023 Cybersecurity Strategy document elucidates how various entities, including state and non-state actors, are increasingly leveraging cyber technology to assert their influence while undermining their adversaries. President Biden encapsulated the critical importance of cybersecurity, stating, "Cybersecurity is foundational to the effective functioning of our economy, the continuity of our critical infrastructure, the resilience of

https://doi.org/10.1515/9783111289069-008

our democratic institutions, the privacy of our personal data and communications, and our national defense."

This articulation serves to emphasize the integral role cybersecurity plays across various facets of societal and national well-being, necessitating an unwavering commitment to safeguarding our digital frontiers.

8.2 Cyber risk: Scope and breadth

The imperative for nation-states, including the U.S., to devise robust policies to counteract cyber threats is unequivocal, especially as we advance into a post-pandemic era and edge closer to the advent of quantum computing. These developments herald an era where the magnitude and complexity of cyber threats will only escalate. The wisdom of Dean Acheson, who advocated for the foresight to discern "the emerging form of things to come and outline what should be done to meet or anticipate them" (Acheson, 1969), is particularly pertinent in addressing the evolving cybersecurity landscape.

The dual-edged nature of cyber and digital technologies, offering both promise and peril, is widely acknowledged. As highlighted by Nazli Choucri et al. (2016, p. 1) in their seminal work "Institutions for Cyber Security," the pervasive influence of cyberspace has reshaped our world, impacting virtually everyone, including stakeholders in foreign policy and national security across the globe.

The corporate sector's swift embrace of emerging technologies such as automation, artificial intelligence (AI), and cloud storage underlines this transformation (Bada et al., 2019; Wilson et al., 2018). However, this rapid adoption often leads to the development of makeshift solutions that, although initially intended for short-term use, become entrenched in the production environment, thereby exacerbating vulnerabilities to cyberattacks, as revealed in McAfee's communication to the National Telecommunications and Information Administration (NTIA) on November 9, 2018.

Moreover, the reliance of critical services such as electricity, water, and internet on digital technology underscores the indispensability of sophisticated IT governance to ensure their security and operational continuity. Despite the benefits of digital technologies, their intricate integration heightens susceptibility to cyber threats. Governmental, corporate, and academic infrastructures are incessantly targeted by automated probes available on the dark web, varying in cost and sophistication (National Cybersecurity and Communications Integration Center).

The year 2018 marked a zenith in cybersecurity incidents reported by federal agencies, with over 13,000 occurrences, highlighting the United States as a prime target for cybercrime, with financial repercussions exceeding US$13.7 billion. This alarming trend prompted the enactment of the Cybersecurity and Infrastructure Security Agency Act of 2018 by President Trump, a transformative legislation that redefined the mission of the erstwhile National Protection and Programs Directorate (NPPD) within the Department of Homeland Security (DHS), thus founding the Cybersecurity and Infrastructure Security Agency (CISA). CISA's mandate is to bolster national defenses against cyberattacks, offering essential cybersecurity services to protect government networks.

Notably, in 2019, the U.S. government accounted for a significant proportion of data breaches and exposed records, with IT expenditures reaching US$88 billion, a figure projected to increase in subsequent years (DHS 2020). By 2020, organizational spending on cybersecurity had surged to US$42 billion (Statista 2020), reflecting the heightened priority of cybersecurity investments.

The intricate interconnectivity of modern technology introduces subtle vulnerabilities, often overlooked by their developers, underscoring the critical need for all-encompassing IT governance frameworks. The complexity of information systems is such that organizations, on average, require over two hundred days to detect a breach (IBM Security), highlighting the profound challenges in safeguarding digital assets in an increasingly interconnected world.

8.3 Rethinking cybersecurity measures: A call for enhanced IT operations management governance

Against the complex landscape of cybersecurity challenges, this analysis probes the current state of internet security within the United States of America, scrutinizing the effectiveness of measures deployed by the US Government, organizations, and vendors against cyber threats. This inquiry delves into the ramifications of security shortcomings on both governmental and private sector entities and evaluates the breadth of the United States' response to an escalating series of cyberattacks and breaches. Central to this discussion is the critique of conventional responses to cyber threats and the exploration of alternative strategies aimed at fortifying not just national security, but also safeguarding the critical data infrastructures of diverse organizations and institutions. This necessitates a pivot towards innovative solutions, particularly in enhancing IT Operations Management governance, as proposed in this document.

The prevailing consensus among researchers and policymakers champions adherence to cyber-hygiene best practices – such as the employment of robust, unique passwords and the activation of multi-factor authentication – as a bulwark against cyber incursions. However, the litany of high-profile security breaches starkly contradicts this belief. Security experts have persistently highlighted the indispensable role of fostering a cybersecurity culture within organizations to nurture the appropriate attitudes, perceptions, and practices conducive to security (Da Veiga et al., 2020; Sutter, M. 2023). Such a culture is tailored to the human element within organizations, aiming to secure information through rigorous adherence to security policies and the diligent application of security protocols, all of which are reinforced through continuous communication, awareness, training, and education initiatives (Da Veiga et al., 2020).

While the emphasis on cultivating a security-centric organizational culture underscores the necessity for ongoing education and communication, it alone is insufficient. Both professionals and scholars acknowledge the critical importance of nurturing a cybersecurity culture; yet, there remains a notable gap in the literature concerning the exploration of IT Operations Management governance standards within organizations. It is within the domain of governance that this paper's recommendations are firmly anchored.

8.4 Insights from governance in other sectors

Analyses of recent security incidents reveal that a substantial number of cybersecurity breaches stem from employees' non-adherence to organizational information security policies (NTT Security, 2019; SANS, 2019). This finding underscores the urgent need for a comprehensive approach that extends beyond the traditional focus on cybersecurity culture to include a rigorous examination and enhancement of IT Operations Management governance. By drawing lessons from governance practices across different sectors, this paper argues for a holistic strategy that integrates robust governance frameworks with cultural initiatives to significantly bolster cyber resilience.

8.4.1 Historical context: The evolution of governance in financial reporting

In the aftermath of the catastrophic Stock Market Crash of 1929 and the subsequent Great Depression, which inflicted financial losses on banks to the tune of approximately US$500 billion in today's currency (Galbraith, 1954; Taibbi, 1929), the United States government embarked on a mission to fortify and standardize the operations of entities engaged in public trading and other significant market activities. A contributing factor to the economic downturn was identified as the lack of transparency in the operational methodologies of these organizations, as noted by the U.S. Securities and Exchange Commission (SEC). In an effort to rectify this, the SEC was endowed with the authority to establish norms for accounting practices, a responsibility that the Commission opted to allocate to the private sector's auditing fraternity.

In 1939, marking a pivotal moment in the regulatory landscape, the American Institute of Accountants – now known as the American Institute of Certified Public Accountants – inaugurated the Committee on Accounting Procedure (CAP). This initiative laid the groundwork for what would evolve into a more structured regulatory framework over the next two decades, eventually giving rise to the Accounting Principles Board (APB) as CAP's successor. The APB undertook the task of disseminating authoritative guidance on critical accounting issues, thereby shaping the accounting standards that publicly traded companies were expected to adhere to under SEC oversight.

The year 1973 witnessed another significant transition, with the APB making way for the Financial Accounting Standards Board (FASB), which has since been at the forefront of policy formulation regarding acceptable accounting practices. While the FASB operates with a degree of autonomy, its decisions are influenced by interactions with other key entities such as the American Institute of Certified Public Accountants (AICPA), the SEC, and the Governmental Accounting Standards Board (GASB), all of which play instrumental roles in the development and endorsement of Generally Accepted Accounting Principles (GAAP).

GAAP has emerged as the universally recognized compendium of accounting norms, designed to oversee financial reporting and disclosure practices across organizations. In 1984, in response to the evolving demands of financial reporting, particularly in sectors like technology, the FASB established the Emerging Issues Task Force (EITF). The EITF's mandate is to address novel and complex accounting issues, paving the way for standards that are likely to gain widespread acceptance in the future.

The collective wisdom encapsulated in the directives issued by the APB and FASB has culminated in the formulation of GAAP, which today stands as a comprehensive framework encompassing three primary components: foundational accounting principles and guidelines, the detailed standards articulated by the FASB, and the generally accepted practices prevalent within various industries (FAF, 2020). This evolution reflects a continual commitment to enhancing transparency, reliability, and accountability in financial reporting, thereby contributing to the stability and integrity of the financial markets.

8.4.2 The imperative of robust governance across sectors

The essence of effective governance, as outlined by the Organization for Economic Cooperation and Development (OECD), is the establishment of a framework that delineates the setting of organizational goals and the monitoring of performance to ensure these goals are achieved (OECD, 1999). The OECD posits that while there is no universal blueprint for exemplary governance, a common practice in numerous countries involves the delegation of governance responsibilities to a supervisory board. This board is tasked with safeguarding the interests of various stakeholders, including shareholders, employees, customers, creditors, suppliers, and affiliates, among others. In fulfilling its mandate, the board collaborates closely with the senior management team to operationalize governance principles that bolster the efficiency of organizational processes.

The senior management, acting on behalf of the board, is charged with the formulation and communication of strategies and behaviors that align with the board's directives. These behaviors reflect the organizational ethos and are manifested through a myriad of expressions, including strategy articulation, value proclamations, mission statements, operational principles, rituals, and structural configurations. It is important to note that the behaviors conducive to an organization's competitive edge vary from one entity to another, underscoring the principle that it is behaviors, rather than strategies alone, that generate value. Thus, it falls upon the executive management to clearly define and promote these desirable behaviors.

To govern the management and utilization of organizational assets effectively, senior executive teams establish mechanisms that cater to both the independent and collaborative management of these assets across functional domains. These assets encompass:

1) **Human Capital:** This includes the workforce, their skills, career trajectories, training programs, reporting structures, mentoring opportunities, and competencies (Becker, 1993).
2) **Financial Assets:** Encompassing cash reserves, investments, liabilities, cash flow mechanisms, accounts receivable, and other financial instruments (Fabozzi & Drake, 2009).
3) **Physical Structures:** Referring to the organization's infrastructure such as buildings, factories, equipment, IT servers, document archives, and devices operated by employees, along with their utilization metrics (Barth & Hudson, 2004).
4) **Intellectual Property:** The proprietary knowledge embodied in product designs, service delivery methodologies, process maps, and other intellectual assets that may be patented, copyrighted, or integrated into operational manuals and executed by personnel, with or without the aid of systems (Barth & Hudson, 2004).
5) **Digitalized Information and IT Environments:** Pertaining to data, software code, critical information, and meta-knowledge about and relevant to stakeholders, organizational processes, performance metrics, financial data, information production, and backup recovery systems (Weill & Ross, 2004).
6) **Relationship Details:** This asset category includes the intricacies of intra-organizational relationships as well as external engagements with clients, brand reputation, service level agreements within operational units, self-audits for regulatory compliance, competitive analysis, and contractual agreements with channel partners, suppliers, and clients (Kaplan & Norton, 2008).

8.4.3 Asset governance through organizational mechanisms

The governance of critical assets within an organization is facilitated through a diverse array of mechanisms, including structures, processes, committees, procedures, and audits. Certain mechanisms are tailored to specific asset classes – for instance, the IT architecture committee is designed specifically for the oversight of information technology assets (De Haes & Van Grembergen, 2009). Conversely, other mechanisms are designed to span across and integrate multiple asset classes, such as the capital and operating expenditure approval process and the HR payroll approval and disbursement process (Mathis & Jackson, 2010). These integrative mechanisms are pivotal in fostering synergies and recognizing interdependencies among various asset classes, thereby enhancing the overall governance structure (Grant, 2003).

The degree of maturity in the governance of these key assets exhibits considerable variation across organizations. Typically, financial and physical assets are subject to more robust governance practices, whereas information assets often lag behind in terms of effective governance (Bragg, 2019). This discrepancy underscores the necessity for a concerted effort to educate senior management teams about the intricacies of governance mechanisms and how they collectively contribute to the strategic objectives of the organization (Argyris & Schön, 1996).

This education is not a one-time event but an ongoing requirement for sustaining effective governance. It is crucial for senior management to understand not only the individual importance of each governance mechanism but also how these mechanisms interact to create a cohesive and effective governance framework (Weick & Sutcliffe, 2007). By doing so, organizations can ensure that all key assets are managed and protected in a manner that supports long-term organizational success and resilience.

8.4.4 Current landscape of IT governance frameworks in the United States

In the contemporary business environment of the United States, organizations deploy a variety of governance frameworks to oversee their information technology systems effectively. These frameworks serve as vital tools for managing and guiding IT operations, ensuring they align with the broader organizational goals and comply with regulatory standards. Among the most prevalent frameworks are shown in Table 8.1.

These frameworks collectively represent the cornerstone of IT governance in the United States, each offering unique insights and methodologies for managing the complex landscape of IT operations. By adopting and adapting these frameworks, organizations can ensure that their IT systems are not only secure and resilient but also aligned with their strategic objectives and capable of supporting their operational needs.

Table 8.1: IT Governance Frameworks.

Framework	Description
Control Objectives for Information Technologies (COBIT)	Developed by the Information Systems Audit and Control Association (ISACA), COBIT is a comprehensive framework that offers organizations a set of guidelines and tools for the effective management and governance of their IT resources (Information Systems Audit and Control Association, 2012). Originally conceived to aid in IT auditing, the scope of COBIT has expanded over the years to encompass full-fledged IT governance. COBIT 5, its latest iteration, is embraced by organizations such as FireEye, which specializes in cyber risk management and mitigation. FireEye's clientele includes high-profile companies like Sony and Equifax, underscoring the framework's relevance even for organizations that have experienced breaches (TechCrunch, 2020).
Information Technology Infrastructure Library (ITIL)	ITIL is centered on IT service management, with a focus on aligning IT services with the core processes of businesses. It encompasses a series of management best practices across five domains: service strategy, design, transition (including change management), operation, and continual service improvement. ITIL's comprehensive approach helps organizations enhance the quality and efficiency of their IT service delivery (Office of Government Commerce, 2011).
Capability Maturity Model Integration (CMMI)	Developed by the Software Engineering Institute, CMMI is a model designed to elevate the process maturity of software development. It provides a framework for training and appraisal that aids organizations in improving their software development processes, thereby enhancing product quality and reducing development risks (CMMI Institute, 2018).
Factor Analysis of Information Risk (FAIR)	As a relatively novel framework, FAIR offers a quantitative approach to understanding and managing information risk. It is particularly focused on cybersecurity and operational risk, enabling organizations to make informed decisions based on a clear understanding of the potential risks and their impacts (The Open Group, 2020).

8.5 Growth and challenges in the global information security sector

The global information security market is poised for significant growth, with projections indicating an 8.5% compound annual growth rate (CAGR) leading to a market size of US$170 billion by 2022 (International Data Corporation, 2021). Despite this optimistic outlook, the effectiveness of existing governance frameworks in mitigating cybersecurity threats remains in question. The cornerstone of an organization's defense against both internal and external cybersecurity threats lies in the management of its IT operations ISACA, 2012). A robust IT Operations Management framework is essential for achieving the dual objectives of fostering innovation across the organizational workforce while ensuring adherence to the overarching vision and principles.

The frequency and severity of cyberattacks continue to escalate globally, affecting corporations such as Target, Sony Pictures, Equifax, J.P. Morgan, the US Internal Revenue Service (IRS), Home Depot, Maersk, Merck, and Saudi Aramco (Ponemon Institute, 2018). These incidents underscore the limitations of traditional cybersecurity measures. Despite the inherent risks, the allure of digital technologies remains irresistible to business leaders, drawn by the promise of enhanced efficiency, reduced operational costs, minimized human error, quality improvements, deeper insights into customer behavior, and the development of novel products and services. In response, organizations are increasingly investing in advanced security solutions and consulting services, adhering to conventional cybersecurity strategies with the hope of safeguarding their digital assets (SANS Institute, 2019).

This approach to cybersecurity, often referred to as "cyber hygiene" within the industry, encompasses several key practices (US Department of Commerce, NIST, 2018):
1) Developing comprehensive inventories of an organization's hardware and software assets to maintain visibility and control.
2) Investing in the latest defensive technologies, such as endpoint security, firewalls, and intrusion detection systems, to fortify the digital perimeter.
3) Conducting regular training sessions for employees to enhance their ability to identify and avoid phishing attempts and other social engineering tactics.
4) Attempting to create "air gaps" to isolate critical systems from other networks and the internet, despite the practical challenges in achieving complete isolation.
5) Expanding the cybersecurity workforce and engaging a variety of services and service providers to implement these strategies.

The 2017 Equifax breach serves as a poignant example of the limitations of these traditional methods. Despite possessing a substantial cybersecurity infrastructure and budget, Equifax experienced a breach that compromised the sensitive information of 147 million individuals (Gressin, 2017, September 8). This incident vividly illustrates the unpredictable nature of cyber threats and the insufficiency of conventional defenses, highlighting the urgent need for a strategic overhaul in the approach to cybersecurity (U.S. House of Representatives, Committee on Oversight and Government Reform, 2018).

8.6 Limitations of cyber hygiene in facing sophisticated cyber threats

While basic cyber hygiene practices offer a degree of protection against generalized automated attacks and efforts by inexperienced hackers, they fall significantly short when confronting the increasingly sophisticated and targeted threats that jeopardize critical assets. This challenge is particularly acute in asset-intensive sectors such as energy, transportation, and heavy manufacturing, where the sheer complexity and scale of operations render it virtually impossible to flawlessly implement all recommended cybersecurity best practices, regardless of the resources or talent at an organization's disposal (NIST, 2018).

A fundamental flaw in the cybersecurity strategies of most organizations is their inability to maintain comprehensive inventories of their hardware and software assets. This deficiency is not trivial; it represents a critical vulnerability. Without a clear understanding and accounting of what assets an organization possesses, securing these assets becomes an insurmountable task. The adage "one cannot secure what one does not know one has" succinctly encapsulates this dilemma, highlighting a foundational gap in the cybersecurity posture of many organizations (Sanger, 2019).

The inadequacy of traditional cyber hygiene measures in the face of determined and capable adversaries underscores the need for a more detailed and sophisticated approach to cybersecurity (Hadnagy & Fincher, 2015). Addressing this gap requires not only an investment in advanced security technologies and practices but also a commitment to developing a comprehensive understanding of the organization's digital and physical assets on a near real-time basis (Schneier, 2018). Only by achieving this level of awareness can organizations hope to effectively protect themselves against the evolving landscape of cyber threats.

8.7 Revolutionizing IT governance: Lessons from financial and organizational best practices

The essence of this paper lies in reconceptualizing IT governance by drawing insights from effective financial and organizational governance models (Weill & Ross, 2004). In financial governance, for instance, the Chief Financial Officer (CFO) doesn't personally oversee every transaction or payment authorization. Instead, the CFO establishes a governance framework that delineates who is authorized to sign off on transactions, the limits of these authorizations, and the criteria for beneficiaries. This framework allows the CFO to focus on broader financial strategies, such as managing the organization's investment portfolio, ensuring optimal cash flow, and maintaining acceptable levels of risk exposure. The CFO continuously monitors financial metrics to guide the management of financial assets, stepping in only when deviations from expected outcomes occur or new opportunities arise. This principle of delegated authority also extends to organizational commitments, such as contracts or partnerships (Cadbury, 1992).

This same philosophy is applicable to IT governance (Kaplan & Norton, 1996). IT governance is not about micromanaging every operational detail but about establishing a clear framework for decision rights and accountability that promotes desirable outcomes in IT Operations Management. It outlines the parameters for decision-making and identifies the responsible parties. Governance is concerned with defining what decisions need to be made and who is authorized to make them, while management involves the actual execution, implementation, and monitoring of these decisions (De Haes & Van Grembergen, 2015).

For example, in the realm of IT governance, the framework would specify the criteria for determining the importance of an issue and who has the authority to make decisions regarding IT investments. Meanwhile, management would entail deciding on the specific allocations of resources within a fiscal period and overseeing these expenditures.

Senior management is tasked with designing processes that ensure rights and responsibilities are aligned in a manner that fosters positive behaviors across the digital landscape. The responsibility of adhering to and leveraging this governance framework falls to IT Operations Management. It is their duty to ensure that the benefits of utilizing multiple systems do not outweigh the manageability of these systems. The ultimate safeguard against cyber risks involves a holistic view of the organization's key assets and the integration of these assets within a coherent governance strategy.

By adopting a governance model that mirrors the strategic oversight seen in financial governance, organizations can ensure that IT governance is not only about setting rules but also about enabling the strategic use of IT to achieve business objectives while managing cyber risks effectively (Committee of Sponsoring Organizations of the Treadway Commission, 2017).

8.8 The future of IT operations management and organizational resilience

As we look to the future, the role of IT Operations Management in shaping organizational success is set to become even more pivotal. The establishment of robust governance standards within IT Operations Management is critical for empowering organizations to anticipate and counteract the strategies of their adversaries effectively (Westerman & Hunter, 2007). Such governance would not only foster a proactive stance towards cybersecurity but also encourage the creation of specialized internal teams or task forces. These groups would be dedicated to continuously evaluating the robustness of system defenses by simulating attempts to breach critical targets, thereby identifying potential vulnerabilities before they can be exploited by malicious actors (NIST, 2018).

These specialized teams would be composed of individuals with expertise in the specific processes, control and safety systems, and operational networks under review. This approach ensures a comprehensive assessment of the organization's cyber defenses, incorporating insights from those with in-depth knowledge of the operational context.

Moreover, the principle of cybersecurity awareness should be universal, extending from the highest echelons of leadership, such as the President of the United States, down to the most junior members of any organization. Every individual should be equipped with the knowledge and the sense of urgency required to respond swiftly to any indications of abnormal behavior in computer systems or machinery under their supervision. While such anomalies could stem from equipment malfunctions, they could equally signify the onset of a cyberattack (Clarke & Knake, 2019).

This heightened state of vigilance and the readiness to act are essential components of a resilient organizational culture (Doherty & Fulford, 2016). By cultivating an environment where every member of the organization is cognizant of and prepared to respond to cybersecurity threats, organizations can significantly enhance their ability to safeguard critical assets and maintain operational integrity in the face of evolving cyber challenges (Schneier, 2018).

8.9 Conclusion

In an era where digital advancements and cyber threats are evolving in lockstep, this comprehensive analysis underscores the critical importance of robust IT Operations Management governance in safeguarding organizational and national interests. The surge in cyberattacks on prominent institutions worldwide in 2023 has starkly highlighted the vulnerabilities in our digital ecosystem, emphasizing the necessity for a strategic overhaul in cybersecurity measures. The United States' National Cybersecurity Strategy, spearheaded by President Biden, marks a significant pivot towards reinforcing the digital fortress that underpins our economy, infrastructure, and democratic institutions.

The discourse extends beyond the immediate need for enhanced cybersecurity protocols to a broader reflection on the interplay between technological innovation and governance. Drawing parallels with financial reporting's historical evolution, the analysis advocates for a governance framework that empowers IT operations management with decision-making autonomy, akin to financial governance models that have proven effective over decades. This approach not only aims to mitigate the current spectrum of cyber threats but also prepares organizations for the unforeseen challenges of the future, particularly in the face of quantum computing advancements.

Central to this reimagined governance model is the cultivation of a cybersecurity-aware culture across all organizational levels, from the executive suite to the operational ecosystem. This cultural shift, coupled with the strategic deployment of IT governance frameworks is posited as the cornerstone of a resilient cybersecurity posture. Moreover, the analysis highlights the indispensable role of independent consulting firms in enriching this governance framework with multiregional expertise, prescience in process evaluation capabilities, and innovation in product management encompassing cyber defense strategies.

The imperative for a holistic, adaptive approach to IT Operations Management governance to effectively manage cybersecurity becomes increasingly apparent. This necessitates not only a pivot towards innovative governance solutions but also a universal commitment to cybersecurity awareness and education. By integrating strategic governance models, fostering a culture of vigilance, and leveraging external expertise, organizations can fortify their defenses against the multifaceted cyber threats of today and tomorrow, ensuring enduring resilience and security in an interconnected world.

References

Acheson, D. 1969. "Present at the creation: My years in the State Department." 214. W.W. Norton & Company.

American Institute of CPAs. "About the AICPA." Accessed November 12, 2023.

Argyris, C., & Schön, D. A. 1996. "Organizational Learning II: Theory, Method, and Practice." Addison-Wesley.

"Data Breaches That Have Happened in 2022 and 2023 So Far" 2023. Accessed online November 7, 2023. https://tech.co/news/data-breaches-updated-list#:~:text=Infosys%20Data%20Breach%3A%20Indian%20IT,has%20had%20on%20its%20systems

Bada, M., Sasse, A.M., and Nurse, J.R. 2019. "Cyber Security Awareness Campaigns: Why Do They Fail to Change Behaviour?" arXiv preprint arXiv:1901.02672.

Barth, S., & Hudson, B. 2004. "Law of Electronic Commerce. Aspen Publishers."

Becker, G.S. 1993. "Human Capital: A Theoretical and Empirical Analysis, with Special Reference to Education (3rd ed)." Chicago: The University of Chicago Press.

Bragg, Steven M. 2022. "Fixed Asset Accounting: Sixth Edition." AccountingTools, Inc.

Cadbury, A. 1992. "Report of the Committee on the Financial Aspects of Corporate Governance." Gee and Co. Ltd.

"Caught in the Crosshairs: Are Utilities Keeping Up with the Industrial Cyber Threat?" 2019. Siemens and Ponemon Institute. Houston: Siemens Gas and Power. https://assets.new.siemens.com/siemens/assets/api/uuid:35089d45-e1c2-4b8b-b4e9-7ce8cae81eaa/version:1572434569/siemens-cybersecurity.pdf

Choucri, N., Madnick, S., & Koepke, P. 2016. "Institutions for Cyber Security: International Responses and Data Sharing Initiatives." Cybersecurity Interdisciplinary Systems Laboratory (CISL), https://web.mit.edu/smadnick/www/wp/2016-10.pdf.

Clarke, R., & Knake, R. K. 2019. "The Fifth Domain: Defending Our Country, Our Companies, and Ourselves in the Age of Cyber Threats." New York, NY: Penguin Press.

CMMI Institute. 2018. "CMMI for Development, Version 1.3." Software Engineering Institute, Carnegie Mellon University.

Committee of Sponsoring Organizations of the Treadway Commission. 2017. "Enterprise Risk Management – Integrating with Strategy and Performance." COSO.

"Critical Infrastructure Protection: Efforts of the Financial Services Sector to Address Cyber Threats" 2003. United States General Accountability Office, GAO-03-173. January 2003. https://www.gao.gov/assets/240/237103.pdf

"Cybersecurity firm FireEye says it was hacked by a nation-state." Accessed online December 2020. TechCrunch. https://techcrunch.com/2020/12/08/cybersecurity-firm-fireeye-says-it-was-hacked-by-a-nation-state/

Da Veiga, A., Astakhova, L.V., Botha, A., and Herselman, M., "Defining organizational information security culture – perspectives from academia and industry. Article 101713 Comput. Secur., 92 (2020).

Dalmia, N and Schatsky. 2019. "The Rise of Data and AI Ethics" Deloitte Insights, June 2019 https://www2.deloitte.com/us/en/insights/industry/public-sector/government-trends/2020/government-data-ai-ethics.html

"Data Protection: Actions Taken by Equifax and Federal Agencies in Response to the 2017 Breach," United States General Accountability Office GAO-18-559. August 2018. https://www.gao.gov/assets/700/694158.pdf

De Haes, S., & Van Grembergen, W. (2009). "Enterprise Governance of Information Technology: Achieving Strategic Alignment and Value." Springer.

De Haes, S., & Van Grembergen, W. 2015. "Enterprise Governance of Information Technology: Achieving Strategic Alignment and Value." Springer.

Department of Homeland Security. Accessed online April 25, 2023. https://www.dhs.gov/topic/cybersecurity

Doherty, N. F., & Fulford, H. 2016. "The Information Security Mindset: Increasing Employee Compliance with Information Security Procedures through the Development of a Security Culture." Computers & Security, 56, 1–15.

Easterly, Jen, Goldstein, Eric. 2023. "Stop Passing the Buck on Cybersecurity, Why Companies Must Build Safety Into Tech Products." Accessed online February 10, 2023. https://www.foreignaffairs.com/united-states/stop-passing-buck-cybersecurity.

Fabozzi, F.J., & Drake, P.P., 2009. "Finance: Capital Markets, Financial Management, and Investment Management." Hoboken, NJ: John Wiley & Sons.

Faith, Cindy. 2016. "CSIP, CNAP, FY16 FISMA & Beyond." NIST Federal Computer Security Managers' Forum, August 2016. https://csrc.nist.gov/CSRC/media//Projects/Forum/documents/aug-2016/wed330_csip-metrics_cfaith.pdf

Financial Accounting Foundation. "About GAAP." Accessed May 13, 2023.

Financial Accounting Standards Board. "About the FASB." Accessed May 13, 2023.

Galbraith, John Kenneth. 1954. "In Goldman Sachs We Trust." Boston: Houghton Mifflin. ISBN 0-395-85999-9., cited in Taibbi, Matt (April 5, 2010). "The great American bubble machine." Retrieved November 18, 2023.

Gressin, S. 2017. "The Equifax Data Breach: What to Do." Federal Trade Commission. https://www.consumer.ftc.gov/blog/2017/09/Equifax-data-breach-what-do

Hadnagy, C., & Fincher, M. 2015. "Phishing Dark Waters: The Offensive and Defensive Sides of Malicious Emails." Wiley.

"High-Risk Series: Substantial Efforts Needed to Achieve Greater Progress on High-Risk Areas" United States Government Accountability Office. GAO-19-157SP. March 2019. https://www.gao.gov/assets/700/697245.pdf

International Data Corporation. 2021. "Worldwide Semiannual Security Spending Guide." IDC.

Information Systems Audit and Control Association. 2012. "COBIT 5: A Business Framework for the Governance and Management of Enterprise IT." ISACA.

Kaplan, R. S., & Norton, D. P. 1996. "The Balanced Scorecard: Translating Strategy into Action." Boston, MA: Harvard Business School Press.

Kaplan, R.S., & Norton, D.P. 2008. "The Execution Premium: Linking Strategy to Operations for Competitive Advantage." Boston: Harvard Business School Press.

Labaton, Stephen, "S.E.C. Pushes Companies to Disclose Data Faster," New York Times, 28 August 2002. Describes changes by the Securities and Exchange Commission in response to the announcement of President George W. Bush four weeks before.

Mathis, R. L., & Jackson, J. H. 2010. "Human Resources Management, 13th Edition." South-Western Cengage Learning.

"McAfee's comments in response to NTIA's Request for Comments on Developing the Administration's Approach to Consumer Privacy," Docket No. 180821780-8780-01. November 9, 2018.

Muresan, R. 2019. "Healthcare Continues to Be Prime Target for Cyber Attacks." Bitdefender Business Insights Blog. January 2019. https://businessinsights.bitdefender.com/healthcare-prime-target-forcyber-attacks

"National Cyber Strategy of the United States of America." 2018. The White House, September 2018. https://www.whitehouse.gov/wp-content/uploads/2018/09/National-Cyber-Strategy.pdf

National Institute of Standards and Technology. 2018. "Framework for Improving Critical Infrastructure Cybersecurity, Version 1.1." NIST. https://nvlpubs.nist.gov/nistpubs/CSWP/NIST.CSWP.04162018.pdf

NTT Security. 2019. "Global Threat Intelligence Report." Retrieved from:https://www.nttsecurity.com/docs/librariesprovider3/resources/2019gtir/2019_gtir_report_2019_uea_v2.pdf

Office of Government Commerce (OGC). 2011. "ITIL Lifecycle Publication Suite." The Stationery Office.

Organization for Economic Cooperation and Development, Directorate for Financial, Fiscal and Enterprise Affairs, OECD Principles of Corporate Governance, SG/CG(99) 5 and 219, April 1999.

Palmer, D. 2019. "Hackers Target Transportation and Shipping Companies in new Trojan Malware Campaign." ZDNet. September 2019. https://www.zdnet.com/article/hackers-target-transportation-and-shipping-industries-in-new-trojan-malware-campaign/

Ponemon Institute. 2018. "2017 Cost of Data Breach Study: Global Overview." Ponemon Institute.

Sanger, D. E. 2019. "The Perfect Weapon: War, Sabotage, and Fear in the Cyber Age." Crown.

SANS. 2018. "Security Awareness Report: Building Successful Security Awareness Programs." Retrieved from: https://www.sans.org/security-awareness-training/reports/2018-security-awareness-report.

SANS Institute. 2019. "SANS 2019 Top New Attacks and Threat Report." SANS Institute.

Schneier, B. 2018. "Click Here to Kill Everybody: Security and Survival in a Hyper-connected World." W. W. Norton & Company.

Securities and Exchange Commission Historical Society. "The Richard C. Adkerson Gallery on the SEC Role in Accounting Standards Setting." Accessed June 11, 2023.

Strategic Planning in the Executive Office of the UN Secretary-General (Global INSIGHTS). October-December 2010. Vol. 16(4) https://books.apple.com/us/book/strategic-planning-in-executive-office-secretary-general/id482957898

Sutter, M. 2023. "Behavioral Economics for Leaders: Research-based Insights on the Weird, Irrational, and Wonderful Ways Humans Navigate the Workplace." John Wiley & Sons.

The Open Group. 2020. "Factor Analysis of Information Risk (FAIR) – ISO/IEC 27005:2018 Edition." The Open Group.

U.S. Department of Commerce, National Institute of Standards and Technology. 2018. "Framework for Improving Critical Infrastructure Cybersecurity, Version 1.1." NIST. https://nvlpubs.nist.gov/nistpubs/cswp/nist.cswp.04162018.pdf

U.S. Securities and Exchange Commission. "Speech by SEC Commissioner: Remarks before the Securities Traders Association." Accessed June 11, 2023.

U.S. Securities and Exchange Commission. "What We Do." Accessed June 11, 2023.

U.S. Securities and Exchange Commission. "Policy Statement: Reaffirming the Status of the FASB as a Designated Private-Sector Standard Setter." Accessed June 12, 2023.

U.S. Securities and Exchange Commission. "Testimony Concerning The Roles of the SEC and the FASB in Establishing GAAP." Accessed June 12, 2023.

The White House, "National Cybersecurity Strategy." Accessed March 2, 2023.

Weick, K. E., & Sutcliffe, K. M. 2007. "Managing the Unexpected: Resilient Performance in an Age of Uncertainty." Jossey-Bass.

Weill, P., & Ross, J.W. 2004. "IT Governance: How Top Performers Manage IT Decision Rights for Superior Results." Boston: Harvard Business School Press.

Westerman, G., & Hunter, R. 2007. "IT Risk: Turning Business Threats into Competitive Advantage." Boston, MA: Harvard Business School Press.

Willison, R., Warkentin, M., and Johnston, A.C., "Examining employee computer abuse intentions: insights from justice, deterrence and neutralization perspectives." Inf. Syst. J., 28 (2) (2018), pp.266–293.

Robert McKinney
9 Practical cyber risk management – preventing the predictable: Drivers of decision making under risk

9.1 Introduction

How many times have we heard about it or read about it? A devastating cyberattack cripples a business, paralyzes a municipality or a hospital, or results in the leak of embarrassing emails. And when we read further we learn that it all could have been prevented with some basic cyber hygiene, some routine housekeeping. According to Artic Wolf Labs, a Cyber Security Operations firm, 45% of security breaches that occurred in 2023 were due to vulnerabilities that could have been patched prior to the incident (McShane & Thanos, 2023, p. 20).

Some studies put the proportion of preventable data breaches even higher. A study by Ponemon Institute sponsored by ServiceNow reported that 60% of respondents said that one or more data breaches they experienced occurred because a patch existed for a vulnerability but was not applied (*Costs and Consequences of Gaps in Vulnerability Response*, 2019, p. 5). And the Department of Homeland Security estimates that 85% of data breaches involved unpatched software (Chinnasamy, 2023).

Between May and July of 2017, for example, Equifax, a US credit bureau, suffered a large data breach in which the private records of over 150 mm American, UK, and Canadian citizens were exfiltrated by a hacker group. The lost data included social security numbers, addresses, birthdates, and driver's license numbers and the impact of this breach on Equifax was significant. Shares of Equifax dropped 14% following the announcement of the breach, and the company eventually paid over $575 mm in legal settlements and fines.

Equifax used Apache Struts, an open-source framework for building Java web applications, to support its credit dispute website. Struts was vulnerable to remote command injection attacks and a patch had been released in March of 2017 to mitigate this risk. Equifax failed to apply the patch, which left the door open for the eventual attack.

Unpatched vulnerabilities are not the only source of preventable cyberattacks. Other frequently overlooked exposures include use of vendor-supplied default passwords and configurations, weak access controls, unsecure remote services, unprotected cloud services, and open ports or misconfigured services exposed to the internet.

With the benefit of hindsight it is difficult to understand why managers would choose to take these risks knowing that the outcome for them and their organizations may be catastrophic. Technology and information security managers are certainly

https://doi.org/10.1515/9783111289069-009

aware of the risks of a cyberattack, so why do we so often find that they are unpre-
pared for them?

The answer may have to do with the way that managers make decisions about
where to spend their time and resources and how they perceive risks. Let's look at
some of the theories that have been developed for answers to this question, and then
discuss practical recommendations for overcoming decision-making biases.

9.2 Theories of decision-making under risk

9.2.1 Expected utility theory

The science of human decision-making is broadly termed *Decision Theory* and the
granddaddy of decision theories is Expected Utility Theory ("EUT"). EUT can trace its
roots back to mathematician Daniel Bernoulli (b.1700) who theorized that when making decisions individuals not only consider the potential value to be gained or lost in
monetary terms but also the expected utility of those outcomes, meaning the associated happiness or inherent worth of those gains or losses to the individual. Bernoulli
also theorized that marginal utility diminishes with increases in value, or said another way, the more one has the less one values the next incremental gain.

EUT says that people choose between uncertain prospects by comparing their expected utility values, which is the sum of the utility value of potential outcomes multi-
plied by their respective probabilities of occurrence. Mathematically, this looks like:

$$EU = \sum_{i=1}^{n} Pi * Ui$$

But people are not merely human calculators, robotically and subconsciously carrying
out probability and value calculations then acting accordingly. Imagine somebody starting out in their career with little money and an uncertain future. The first $10,000
earned may have enormous utility for the new careerist, but after years of working and
having saved $1,000,000 the prospect of earning an additional $10,000 is not as motivat-
ing and losing some or all of his/her $1 mm nest egg is very unattractive. So we can say
that losses cost more in utility terms than gains add and therefore people are risk
averse. If you plot that risk aversion on a graph of utility and wealth it produces the
concave function (see Figure 9.1)

While foundationally important to understanding human behavior, EUT does not
fully explain the behavior of managers. We said earlier that managers frequently
make choices that leave them vulnerable to cyberattacks and catastrophic losses,
which occur with some regularity. Think of the array of organizational investment
opportunities and activities as their prospects in the EUT model. If managers behaved
according to EUT they might apply greater weight (probability) to the potential for a

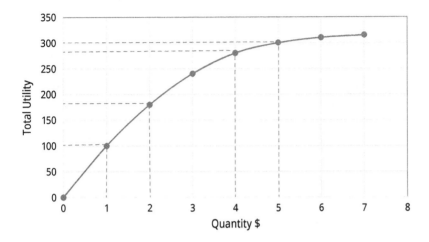

Figure 9.1: The Diminishing Marginal Utility of Wealth.

devastating cyberattack, and their tendency for loss aversion would imply great utility in avoiding this.

Since empirically we can see that managers frequently choose otherwise, we must look at other models of human behavior to explain this.

9.2.2 Optimism bias

Mankind's optimistic nature is as well chronicled in our culture as it is in academia. Books and movies abound with tales of the underdog overcoming great obstacles through valiant effort to achieve spectacular glory. Even ancient writings, such as the tale of David and Goliath, reflect this inherent optimism. But absent divine intervention people's optimism may not be merited. The reality is that bad outcomes happen quite frequently, yet people consistently underestimate the likelihood of negative future outcomes and over-estimate the likelihood of positive future events.

Weinstein (1980), for example, surveyed 258 college students about their prospects for positive future events, such as living past 80 or having a mentally gifted child, as well as negative future events, such as being divorced or getting fired from a job. The students generally rated their chances of experiencing the positive outcomes as above average and their risks of experiencing the negative events as below average. Other studies have shown that we tend to under-estimate the chance that we will become seriously ill or be in a car crash, and we tend to believe that we will live longer than objective measures would suggest and over-estimate our future professional success. Similarly, business managers tend to have rosier outlooks for future prosperity than empirical results would dictate and underrate their chances of failure.

The gap between people's optimistic expectations and lived experience is called the Optimism Bias and is not only observable in almost every domain of human endeavor but is also part of people's physiological make-up, and the Optimism Bias is persistent. Researchers (Sharot, 2011) found, for example, that subjects failed to update their estimation of the probability of encountering negative future events even when provided with historically factual probabilities. When asked about their estimate of suffering from cancer at some point in their lives, for instance, subjects who initially said 10% did not update their estimate the second time around even when confronted with the reality that the actual number is 30%. If, however, the subject's initial estimate was overly pessimistic, for example guessing a 40% chance of experiencing cancer, subjects adjusted their estimate down to 30% when asked a second time after learning the actual statistic. Individuals selectively update their estimates of the future based on positive information, which produces the Optimism Bias.

This positive bias is rooted in human physiology and may be linked to survival. Sharot found that activity in the left inferior frontal gyrus section of the brain, which is involved in decision-making, was highly correlated to receiving information that positive future outcomes were more likely than previously anticipated. Subjects receiving information, on the other hand, that indicated negative future outcomes were more likely than previously anticipated exhibited reduced coding in the right inferior frontal gyrus, which is involved in inhibition, to update negative information. In other words, our brains are engineered to accept positive revisions to future expectations and to reject negative revisions.

Having an Optimism Bias leads to better survival outcomes. Optimists live longer, are healthier, and enjoy more success than others. Optimists enjoy less stress, which leads to enhanced immunity from disease. Additionally, optimists are more likely to engage in healthy behaviors such as exercise and eating healthy foods. Optimists also work harder, which increases the probability of professional success, thereby reinforcing the positive expectations / positive outcomes loop.

The Illusion of Control is somewhat related to the Optimism Bias. The illusion of Control relates to managers' over-confidence in their ability to control their circumstances. Over-confidence is well documented in psychological studies and is generally categorized into 3 types:
1) overestimation of one's actual performance,
2) over-placement of one's performance relative to others,
3) excessive precision in one's beliefs.

The Illusion of Control magnifies the effect of the Optimism Bias to leave organizations more exposed to threat actors because in addition to under-estimating the likelihood of being victimized by a cyberattack managers feel that if it does happen they will be able to control the aftermath sufficiently to remain in control.

But overly optimistic forecasts of the future also lead to unrealistic expectations. Kahneman and Tversky (1979) demonstrated that this optimistic bias in human judgement is systematic and is not improved simply by being aware of it. This leads to managers being overly optimistic when undertaking projects, systematically underestimating costs, time to completion, and risks and overestimating benefits. This behavior was termed the Planning Fallacy by Lovallo and Kahneman (2003) and is rooted in managers' tendency to see their undertakings as unique, when in fact few projects are truly unique in nature. Managers could learn from the experiences of others in terms of forecasting, budget overruns and time to completion and doing so while applying those learnings to one's own forecasts and expectations is the solution to overcoming one's inherent Optimism Bias.

Optimism Bias, the Planning Fallacy, and the Illusion of Control directly impacts managers' preparedness for cyberattacks. If managers are biologically predisposed to reject information about the likelihood of experiencing a cyberattack and believe they can control their environment and thus control this risk through over-estimating their personal and organizational abilities one can see how activities might be directed toward organization building for the future and less on preparing for the low probability / high impact cyber event. Later in this chapter we will focus on practical recommendations for overcoming this bias and appropriately protecting your organization. But first let's go a bit deeper into managerial decision-making under uncertainty.

9.2.3 Prospect theory

Prospect Theory was put forward in 1979 by Daniel Kahneman and Amos Tversky to explain risk-seeking behavior that was not explained by EUT. Kahneman and Tversky noticed that people do not always make choices based purely on their expected derived values adjusted for the probability of receiving those values, they saw that people weight *certain* outcomes differently than *uncertain* ones. Subjects in their experiments were offered a series of choices of this type:

A   50% chance to win $1,000   B   Win $450 for sure
    50% chance to win $0

With just a little algebra one can see the expected outcome of choice A is $500 yet respondents consistently chose the smaller, certain outcome, in this case $450. Their experiments showed that when offered a choice, people will accept smaller *certain* gains vs larger *potential* gains. They called this the Certainty Effect, which is that certainty increases the desirability of gains. So with respect to gains, people are *risk averse*. And the more value at risk the more risk averse people are.

Subjects' preferences with respect to losses were the opposite of preferences for gains. When faced with this choice, for example:

A   80% chance to lose $4,000   B   Lose $3,000 for sure

The majority of respondents chose A, even though the probability weighted loss in choice A was $3,200, a greater value than B and again a violation of EUT. Apparently, losses are especially unappealing so people will take a chance on not experiencing a loss, even a greater loss, than living through the certainty of a loss. So people are *risk seeking* with respect to losses, and the greater the potential loss the less risk seeking they are, though reactions to losses are stronger than gains.

Graphically, potential gains and losses under Prospect Theory looks as shown in Figure 9.2.

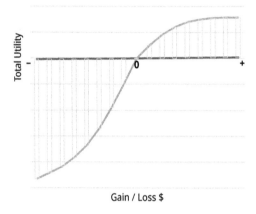

Figure 9.2: Gains & Losses under Prospect Theory.

This may partially explain managers' behavior with respect to information security decisions. Almost anyone would characterize a cyberattack, for example, as a negative outcome, potentially even a catastrophic outcome for an organization. If managers, like the respondents in Kahneman's and Tversky's experiments, view losses as repugnant, logic suggests they would take every reasonable measure to prevent them, which we have already established they frequently do not. Taking preventative measures to prevent or mitigate cyberattacks, however, can be very expensive. Enterprise-wide endpoint security, implementing a security information and event management system ("SIEM"), creating or contracting with a security operations center, asset scanning software, and secure backups all require time and money to implement and maintain, frequently lots of money. In managers' minds this may represent the certain loss associated with cybersecurity versus the potentially greater, yet improbable, loss associated with a successful data breach. Consistent with Prospect Theory, managers are risk-seeking, choosing to take the risk of a catastrophic event impacting their organization rather than incurring the certain loss of underwriting an expensive information security program.

To continue the application of Prospect Theory, how should we think about the gains associated with information security? Information security risk is usually discussed in terms of downside risks: loss of data confidentiality, availability, or integrity. While the case could be made that there are upside risk opportunities connected with information security programs, I submit to you that technology managers' context is much larger when they are thinking about cyber-risks. Cyber-risks do not exist in a narrow field of attacking and defending activities, which occupies a principal focus of information security managers. To technology managers cyber-risks are just one set of threats associated with their larger endeavor of providing information systems and infrastructure services. This is because the operational aspects of implementing cyber-risk management programs often rests not with CISOs but with technology line managers, who are managing active networks, building software, acquiring and configuring servers, and backing up data. *Technology managers work toward the certain gain associated with job performance rather than investing scarce resources mitigating the possible loss associated with a cyberattack.* Even though the risk-weighted loss may be great, they often choose to take that risk in preference for the almost certain positive outcomes of being financially and professionally rewarded for succeeding in their operational service delivery roles. This result is consistent with both the Optimism Bias and Prospect Theory.

This preference was also found by Schroeder (2005) in his study of Prospect Theory as applied to information security decision – makers in the U.S. Air Force. Schroeder posed a series of A/B risk-based outcome choices to Air Force officers engaged in information security activities to mimic the structure of Kahneman and Tversky study. While some of his results were inconsistent with Prospect Theory, one significant finding was that decision makers were significantly more likely to prefer operational outcomes over security outcomes when forced to choose between the two, implying that *managers place greater weight on operational activities than security related activities.* The inherent tension between the demands of operational maintenance and information security activities as well as managers' perceptions of risk and reward are key reasons why preventable cyberattacks continue to be successful.

9.2.4 Risk perception and risk estimation

If managers emphasize information systems operational activities over information security activities, they do so in part because their estimation of cyber risks is lower than they actually are. March and Shapira (1987) in their research of managerial risk-taking found that only 2 of 50 managers interviewed accepted risk estimates as given to them. They found that managers have a tendency to ignore low probability events, even those with catastrophic outcomes, and believed they could manage or control the risks they chose to undertake by taking actions to mitigate them and thus meet performance targets. *Managers accept low probability / high impact event risks because they don't believe they bear them.*

This tendency is directly relevant to information security risk-taking and can be observed in the behavior of managers. Even though news abounds of organizations being taken down by cyber-hackers and managers generally understand their organizations are vulnerable, we still don't think it will happen to us. Somehow these facts become obscure statistics and ascribed to bad luck, like being caught in a bad storm or being struck by lightning. Or worse, we believe we are so talented and wise that we can control these negative outcomes. We can outsmart the bad guys! As one CISO once related to me, information security is one of the few internal control functions where you have an actively engaged adversary. Like most managers, information security practitioners need be concerned with day-to-day process risks but also with the ever-evolving sophistication of cyber criminals and organizational needs. And that requires significant funding and focus.

9.2.5 Competition for funding and strategic misrepresentation

Most organizations face more investment opportunities than they choose to fund, often creating an internal competition for budget dollars.

Ambitious managers want to present the best possible case for having their projects funded and sometimes this produces overly rosy forecasts of benefits and underestimation of costs. The practice of embellishing estimates of future project returns is called strategic misrepresentation. Whereas Optimism Bias, which can also produce overly optimistic forecasts, is endemic to the human condition, strategic misrepresentation is intentional. That's not to say that all project proposals are bold-faced lies, just that managers sometimes tend to cast their proposals in the best possible light perhaps knowing that forecasts are on the high side of potential outcomes or that costs will very likely be higher, essentially misrepresenting risks. If these strategically misrepresented forecasts are accepted project sponsors may secure funding at the expense of other, more realistically positioned project proposals.

Strategic misrepresentation generally works against information security projects. Many technology projects can be undertaken in support of revenue or profitability gains, productivity gains, or improved user experiences. Technology-related investment opportunities abound in areas such as process automation, data analysis, artificial intelligence development, and advanced computing. Information security projects, by contrast, tend to focus on stewardship; securing data, for example, or segmenting networks, implementing SIEMS, and upgrading anti-malware software. Critical activities to be sure, but one could imagine how the evaluation of value for those types of projects might look pale in comparison to sexier technology projects. Notwithstanding the fact that information security projects may have a better risk-adjusted return, this has a crowding-out effect for funding for information security projects, diminishing available technology resources at the expense of other more compelling strategically misrepresented opportunities.

9.2.6 Organizational pressures

Another driver of information security un-preparedness is organizational pressure. Many organizations push managers to higher levels of performance, sometimes in the form of stretch goals. While this may actually produce higher levels of performance, stretch goals and performance targets can also induce risky behavior, especially when linked to compensation. Managers may feel like they need to shortcut controls in order to achieve targets. Imagine, for example, a manager charged with creating a new bespoke software application with a challenging set of functional deliverables and short timelines. Omitting or reducing security features might be unnoticed by users but save the manager considerable development time. Or consider a manager with resources dedicated to multiple projects including information security projects. If a stretch goal target is imperiled, resources can be re-directed from the information security projects to the higher profile stretch goal targets thus damaging the organization's risk profile.

If stretching to make performance goals is abetted by optimism, concern for downside risk can sometimes be interpreted as pessimism, and the carrier of these concerns can be seen as disloyal to the organization. Senior managers want to build support and create enthusiasm for organizational initiatives and often spend considerable energy on communicating priorities and making resources available to accomplish them. The risk manager who sounds the alarm about cyber-risks and asks for senior management attention to them and resources to mitigate them may seem like a "negative Nancy", especially for firms that have not experienced a devastating cyber event. Even though these concerns are perfectly valid, voices of caution can be mis-interpreted as being opposed to the organization mandate and can result in important information security risk measures not being funded and implemented.

Organizational placement of the Information Security Department can also impact an organization's security profile. Information Security is often housed within a larger Technology Division, because many of the tools of the trade are technical in nature, and many information security risk management activities are carried out by technology managers with line responsibility. Very often when this is the structure in use, there is a tendency to skew priorities toward technology driven information security solutions at the expense of process and policy-based solutions. Additionally, this structure tends to subordinate Information Security professionals to other technology executives because other technology managers are performing support roles more closely connected to core value chain activities. And technology executives engaged in supporting the organizational value chain, whether sales, production, or the provision of services, naturally enjoy a greater voice than those that do not.

Some organizations, however, see information security as a pan-organizational risk management activity and place the Information Security Department outside of the Technology Division to act more like a second line of defense control function.

This organization structure is more effective at strengthening organizational defenses because it:

1. Provides *more organizational clout* to the Information Security Department, giving voice and legitimacy to cyber risks;
2. Permits Information Security professionals to engage with their Technology colleagues as an *independent control function*, increasing the chances that technology resources will be allocated to risk mitigation initiatives.
3. Takes a *holistic view to information security measures*, including user behavior, policy enforcement, and process.

9.2.7 Operational performance pressure

Information security activities that protect organizations are largely carried out by line managers. The Information Security Department typically sets policy, monitors risk, and carries out some risk mitigation activities directly but many functions are performed by other technology managers whose primary responsibilities are maintaining organizational technology infrastructure. Some examples of this include patching, hardware configuration, software design, network management, and data storage / backup. Managers responsible for these activities must also keep production systems running, install servers, release new applications, optimize network speed, and run backups. *It is this contention between performing one's day job and carrying out information security activities that is the primary reason organizations fail to protect themselves against preventable cyber events.*

Line technology managers are incentivized to keep systems running, to turn out new software, and to complete important initiatives. This is what they are rewarded for. In the parlance of Prospect Theory that reward is the certain gain that managers expect to receive for successfully performing their jobs. And managers are risk-averse with respect to gains, so their efforts are mainly directed toward realizing those gains by delivering on their day jobs.

Managers are also optimistic regarding the possibility of being victims of a cyberattack. They believe, of course, that cyberattacks happen, they just don't believe that it will happen to them or their organization, or if it does the impact will not be significant. The cost, both in time and money, of fully implementing preventive information security measures takes away from the resource base available for successful completion of day-to-day operations. Tying this back to Prospect Theory, this cost represents a certain loss, and since managers are risk-seeking with respect to losses they would prefer to take the risk of being exposed to a cyber-event than pay this cost, even though the loss may be far greater.

This behavior is grounded in human nature and may explain why we all see the repeated phenomenon of preventable, almost predictable cyberattacks succeeding against organizations that could have been reasonably expected to be protected. Since it is human nature itself that creates unnecessary exposure to cyber risk, we cannot expect to manage that risk effectively through simple exhortation. We will have to do something deliberate and counter-intuitive to overcome the effects of the human tendency to be overly optimistic and risk-seeking and thereby calibrate our organization's risk-profile more objectively. We will explore this in the remainder of this chapter.

9.3 Impact of cyber crime

Cybercrime is prolific and growing. CyberSecurity Ventures, a cyber economy researcher and publisher of cybersecurity statistics, predicts that the cost of cybercrime globally will reach $9.5 trillion in 2024, which includes the damage and destruction of data, lost productivity, restoration of hacked systems and reputational harm (Morgan, 2023). This represents an increase from $3 trillion in 2015, as Figure 9.3 illustrates (Morgan, 2022).

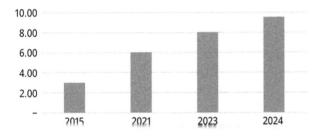

Figure 9.3: Cybercrime Damage Costs ($USD trillions).

On the other side of the ledger, the cybercrime industry takes in $1.5 trillion annually in revenue (McShane & Thanos, 2023, p. 12), enough to fund increasingly sophisticated attacks as well as a flowering ecosystem of service providers, distributors, and infrastructure services.

The cybercrime industry is so large and mature that participants have balkanized into specialized services that can be contracted for, much like any mature industry. Would-be hackers don't need to do it all themselves, they can outsource a significant amount of work, or pursue a niche strategy as one of the criminal specialists, including:
- **Access brokers** – hackers who breach networks and sell access to others;
- **DDoS attack tools Producers** – web-based tools with which anyone can launch a DDoS attack;
- **Phishing kits Providers** – providers of web-based tools used to automate phishing attacks;
- **Ransomware Providers** – a/k/a Ransomware-as-a-Service (RaaS), these groups sell access to ransomware strains;

- **Hosting and infrastructure** – providers of private hosting infrastructure specifically tailored for criminal gangs;
- **Spam distributors** – Groups that run spam campaigns on social networks or instant messaging apps;
- **Exploit kit developers**.

Organizations of every size and stripe have been impacted by cybercrime, and many more are at risk. According to a report issued by SecureLink & Ponemon Institute, 54% of organizations have experienced a cyberattack in the past 12 months (*The State of Cybersecurity and Third-Party Remote Access Risk*, 2022, p. 9). Attacks are occurring in every sector of the global economy, with most attacks directed at commercial enterprises, but also at governments and healthcare organizations, as the data in Figure 9.4 from Statista (Petrosyan, 2024) illustrates.

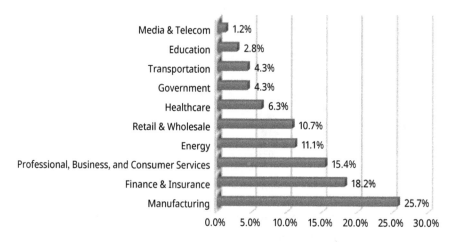

Figure 9.4: Distribution of Cyber Attacks Worldwide in 2023.

While the manufacturing sector leads in this compilation of cyberattack statistics, one can see that virtually every sector of global society is impacted by cybercrime, no place is safe. And in case you are thinking size or name recognition makes you a bigger target, being small and inconspicuous does not help. In the United States in 2022, over half of cyberattacks were committed against small to medium sized businesses, and 60% of small businesses go out of business within 6 months of falling victim to a significant cyberattack (Morgan, 2022, p.21).

Most cybercrime is financially motivated, and the sheer volume is staggering. One study by the University of Maryland says that there is a cyberattack attempt every 39 seconds (Watters, 2023). According to the FBI there are more than 4,000 cyberattacks reported daily (*Top Cyber Security Experts Report: 4,000 Cyber Attacks a Day Since Covid19 Pandemic*, 2020). Interestingly, 80% of attacks begin in a decidedly low-tech fashion, through phishing attacks, typically through email (Palatty, 2023). Human susceptibility to deception is still our greatest vulnerability. Once someone clicks on that link, however, or responds to a message, technical safeguards become more important.

There are many types of cyberattacks. Table 9.1 shows ten of the most common types.

Table 9.1: Types of Cyberattacks.

Attack Type	Description
Phishing	Uses email, SMS, phone, social media, and social engineering techniques to entice a victim to share sensitive information or to download a malicious file.
Malware	Any program created with the intent to do harm to a computer, network or server. Malware encompasses many subsets such as ransomware, trojans, spyware, viruses, worms, keyloggers, and bots.
DoS Attacks	A Denial of Service (DoS) attack is a malicious, targeted attack that floods a network with false requests in order to disrupt business operations.
Spoofing	A technique through which a cybercriminal disguises themselves as a trusted source with the ultimate goal of stealing information, extorting money or installing malware.
Identity Based Attacks	When a valid user's credentials have been compromised and an adversary is masquerading as that user. Identity based attacks include Man-In-The-Middle attacks and Brute Force attacks.
Code Injection Attacks	Injecting malicious code, such as through an SQL injection attack, into a vulnerable computer or network.
Supply Chain Attacks	A type of cyberattack that targets a trusted third-party vendor who offers services or software vital to the supply chain. Software supply chain attacks inject malicious code into an application to infect all users of an app.
Insider Threats	Internal actors such as current or former employees that pose danger to an organization because they have direct access to the company network, sensitive data, and intellectual property (IP). Insider threat actors could be malicious or simply negligent.
DNS Tunneling	A type of cyberattack that leverages domain name system (DNS) queries and responses to bypass traditional security measures and transmit data and code within the network. Once infected, the hacker can freely engage in command and control activities. This tunnel gives the hacker a route to unleash malware and/or to exfiltrate data.
IoT Based Attacks	An IoT attack is any cyberattack that targets an Internet-of-Things (IoT) device or network. Once compromised, the hacker can assume control of the device, steal data, or join a group of infected devices to create a botnet to launch DoS or DDoS attacks.

9.3.1 Costs

Being the victim of a cyberattack can be expensive. The average cost of a data breach in 2022 was $4.35 mm and the average cost of a ransomware attack was $4.54 mm (Garza, 2023). The average ransomware payment in 2023 was about $1.5 mm (Sophos, 2023, p.12). Even if not attacked, organizations pay a heavy price to protect themselves, spending $80.8 bn globally in 2023 for information security (*Worldwide Information Security Services Spending from 2017 to 2024*, 2023). Harder to measure costs include reputational damage, lost customers or lost revenue opportunities, and business disruption.

9.3.2 Examples of recent attacks

9.3.2.1 Rackspace

Attack Type: Malware (*Ransomware*)

Cause: *UnPatched Software*

In December 2022 customers of Rackspace Technology had difficulty accessing their hosted exchange environment, which was later determined to be caused by a ransomware attack. The ransomware attack was enabled by an unpatched version in the Microsoft Exchange cluster that permitted attackers to exploit the ProxyNotShell vulnerability.

9.3.2.2 Cisco

Attack Type: *Malware (Ransomware)*

Cause: *Compromised User Credentials*

In May of 2022 Cisco was successfully hacked by the Yanluowang ransomware gang. The initial access vector was through the successful phishing of an employee's personal Google account, where credentials saved in the victim's browser were being synchronized, which ultimately led to access to the Cisco VPN.

The attackers published a partial list of exfiltrated files before demanding ransomware and were ultimately ejected from the Cisco network.

9.3.2.3 Microsoft azure

Attack Type: *Supply Chain*

Cause: *Mis-Configuration*

In October 2022 Cyber Security firm SOCRadar informed Microsoft that a significant amount of data in one of its Azure data storage buckets was publicly exposed. The exposed servers stored 2.4 terabytes of data from 65,000 companies, including 335,000 emails, 133,000 projects, and 548,000 exposed users.

Microsoft later determined that the data leak occurred because of human error in setting security configurations.

9.3.2.4 Tunefab

Attack Type: *Insider Threat*

Cause: *Mis-Configuration*

In September 2023 Tunefab, a Hong Kong based software company that helps users convert audio tracks from streaming platforms into various audio file formats, publicly exposed over 151 million records, including users' email addresses, IP addresses, and user IDs. The leak occurred because MongoDB was mis-configured, which left the publicly empooed data without a password

These are merely a few examples of the multitude of attacks, leaks, and ransoms taking place daily. Each of these, like many others, were preventable if proper risk mitigation controls were in place. So now that we have established that it is in our human nature to expose ourselves and our organizations to information security risks and that cyberattacks are happening everywhere to everyone all the time, let's discuss what we can do to overcome this undesirable situation.

9.4 Overcoming human bias to manage cyber risk

Overcoming our human Optimism Bias and our behavioral tendencies toward risk taking requires a designed intervention because we are trying to counteract natural human behavior to better protect our organizations. Essentially, we must rise above our intuitive responses to the threat environment and force ourselves to perceive risk differently and make different trade-offs between getting our work done and protecting our data and systems. This calls for something more than just policy-setting and exhortation to do better, even training is not enough. *What is required are organiza-*

tional and behavioral control mechanisms to be overlaid on top of our natural human behavior to achieve a more effective cyber risk profile.

9.4.1 Governance

The most important overlay control mechanism is an effective governance structure. Good governance means effective oversight, which often includes the following activities:

1. Performance Oversight – ensuring that key performance results are achieved. This includes individual accountability for achieving results.
2. Process Risk Management – Monitoring environmental risks and process KRIs, assessing the organization's vulnerability, and mitigating risks that are outside of risk tolerance.
3. Communication of performance, risk, and policies to relevant stakeholders so others can act.
4. Policy Setting – Information Security encompasses a large set of technical and procedural activities. Policies help managers make decisions that are consistent with organizational risk tolerances and provide direction for those carrying out information security activities.
5. Budgeting – Allocating sufficient resources to protect the organization.
6. Promoting a Security Culture – Propagating values that lead to desirable information security behaviors throughout the organization through education, policy enforcement, communication, consultation, and incentives that reinforce the importance of security to the organization and senior management.

Information security impacts the entire organization, whether a commercial enterprise, a non-profit organization, or a government. Therefore, it is best that oversight over information security not be left to a single individual, who may be not be able to channel the needs of the entire organization and may be biased toward his/her own views and agenda, but rather a group of managers who can represent the overall needs of the organization. Effective governance can be provided through a number of commonly found internal committees or by a group of informed senior managers as long as the group or committee enforces the 6 governance sleeves listed above. The governance committee must also possess sufficient organizational clout to facilitate policy adoption and overcome the risk-taking biases of line managers discussed earlier in this chapter.

Some typical committees that could be well positioned to perform this oversight role include the Information Security Committee, the Risk Committee, the Operating Committee, or the Audit Committee. Of course, organizational structures differ. The critical value offered by whichever committee is designated is that they identify, assess, and mitigate risks, and hold senior managers and line managers accountable for successfully carrying out the required information security functions. It is the accountability to, and meaningful involvement of, a competent senior governance committee that prevents important information security functions from being shunted aside by busy managers. When the conflict arises between day-to-day activities and needed information security practices, this group must intervene and ensure that managers are carrying out the program to protect the organization's information landscape.

9.4.2 Organizational placement of the information security department

Because protecting information assets typically involves sophisticated software and hardware tools the Information Security Department is often placed within the Technology Department in many organizations. There is a logic to this. Technology managers and Information Security managers have skills in common, and the underlying subject matter, data and information systems, is the province of both domains. Subordinating the Information Security function to the Technology function, however, is a mistake. Firstly, this organizational placement reduces the profile of the CISO and the Information Security Department, making a critical control function a sister function to other operational technology groups like development, application support, and network engineering, which are also important functions to be sure. But Information Security occupies a special place as a control function, and just as it is difficult to control one's brothers and sisters as a sibling member of a family, it is difficult for Information security professionals to exert control over their technology peers as a member of the Technology family. In addition, information security is a pan-organizational activity, affecting and requiring the cooperation of all staff and teams. Looking at information security as a technology function ignores the important process and behavioral aspects of the discipline.

Secondly, incentives are not aligned. Each organization's Technology Department has its own agenda, opportunities, and pressures, like every group within an organization. The Technology leadership may feel like their mandate is to maintain systems and complete important projects in support of organizational strategy. In the absence of a significant recent or proximate cyber threat these Technology Department priorities will overwhelm the priorities of the Information Security Department. It is far more compelling for Technology leaders, for example, to offer their internal customers a new system that will help to grow a business than for equivalent expense and effort to install a CMDB and get an information asset tracking program stood up, which *might* help in some future information security breach. Similarly, when the conflict arises between asset protection and daily technology operations, Technology management is likely to respond by resolving operating problems or completing important projects at the expense of information security programs. Patching can wait, for example, when the Application Support group is dealing with system outages and upgrades.

For the Information Security Department to be most effective, they must be independent of the Technology Department, and given the authority to redirect organizational and technology priorities toward protecting the organization when necessary.

9.4.3 Line manager incentives

Technology managers must be incentivized to perform their information security roles in addition to their regular day jobs. This must be explicit, and a good way to do this is to include successful performance of these activities as part of setting performance and compensation standards. Managers who are responsible, for instance, for patching software, should be evaluated in part on making timely patches. Performance evaluations and compensation for development managers should rest, in part, on maintaining information asset inventory records. And those managing others should be accountable for ensuring that their employees receive the proper security training.

By including information security activities in the performance / compensation evaluation process we are linking rewards to behavior and letting employees know that these activities are a core part of their jobs, not a favor they are extending if time and capacity permit.

9.4.4 Line manager education

Many entities provide information security training to their employees and is often directed at educating users on the ability to spot and respond to phishing campaigns. Certainly this training is important, but technology managers need additional training, or education really. Part of overcoming the Optimism Bias and the influences described by Prospect Theory is providing line technology managers with the facts about information security risk so that they can make better risk-taking decisions.

We know from Sharot's research, described earlier in this chapter, that optimistic people tend to reject negative information regarding the risk landscape, so for managers regularly exposed to these risks the reality must be regularly reinforced. Through repetition we can overcome the Optimism Bias.

Technology managers should be regularly educated on current probabilities of experiencing a significant cyberattack or data breach as well as the potential costs. They must understand common attack vectors as well as their adversaries' capabilities and motivations. Managers should also be briefed by the Information Security Department on their organization's asset vulnerabilities and major security projects underway. Armed with an understanding of external and internal threats as well as their organization's security posture, managers are more likely to make better trade-offs between carrying out protective security measures when that comes into conflict with day-to-day responsibilities.

This approach is a form of what Kahneman calls the outside view, or reference class forecasting (Lovallo, Kahneman, 2003). Kahneman originally prescribed using the outside view to overcome overly optimistic project forecasts with respect to budgets and timelines, but the concept can be applied to information security risk management as well.

The concept is to use fact-based data about the experiences of others to adjust our innate view of what our own experiences might be in the future. The application of reference class forecasting to project management involves examining the outcomes of past projects that are similar to the one being undertaken and then calibrating one's own expectations and project plans to reflect realistic assumptions over our inherently optimistic ones. Kahneman found that people have a tendency to underestimate project costs and over-estimate realized benefits. Through comparison to external data we can throw cold water on our original estimate and adjust it to reflect probable future outcomes.

Applying this concept to cyber risk management we use external data on the likelihood and impact of cyberattacks with consideration for the organization's vulnerabilities and resiliency capability to create a realistic risk profile. This in turn leads to appropriate risk treatment, not simply hoping that we won't be a victim.

9.4.5 Risk management control functions

Independent information security risk management is critical to overcoming short-sighted risk-taking decisions on the part of line managers. The reasons are the same as for other types of risk management, such as market risk management and credit risk management. Firstly, risk managers are focused on risk / reward trade-offs and spend virtually all of their time (hopefully) objectively assessing risks faced by an organization, scientifically evaluating and mitigating risks. Their job is to remove the emotion and human psychology from risk-taking. Secondly, they are independent. They do not suffer from the sometimes conflicting demands of risk mitigation and completing operating tasks and are not incentivized in the same way that line managers are.

Information security risk management can be effectively provided by the Information Security Department if sufficiently independent, the Operational Risk Management or Enterprise Risk Management groups, the Compliance Department, and the Internal Audit or Inspector General groups. Organizational locus is not so important. What is critical is 1) objectivity and 2) independence.

9.5 Practical hygiene: Getting the basics right

In this section we will examine some of the commonly unmitigated exposures that are exploited by cyber adversaries, and some of the risk mitigation commonly left undone because of operational busy-ness. Let's first review the typical ways that organizations are compromised.

9.5.1 Common attack vectors

Most (70%) initial entry methods to victims' networks and data by threat actors, termed root point of compromise ("RPOC"), occur through the public internet. The remainder happen as a result of user action (25%), such as opening a malicious file, a 3rd party trusted relationship (3 %), or malicious insiders (2%) according to Artic Wolf Labs, which compiled the data from the experiences of its approximately 2,300 customers (Arctic Wolf Labs, 2024).

The most frequent RPOCs noted by Artic Wolf Labs were remote access hijacking and software exploits. Figure 9.5 shows the relative distribution of RPOCs.

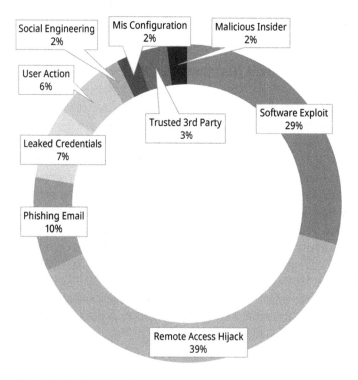

Figure 9.5: RPOC Relative Frequency.

Assuming Artic Wolf Labs' reported data is representative of the global population of attack vectors we can direct our risk mitigation activities toward the most likely threats, which follows.

9.5.2 Remote access hijacking

In 2020 as the pandemic raged, many of us, millions of us, began working from home full-time. This significantly added to the already growing movement of working remotely and dramatically increased the use of remote access tools, such as Virtual Private Networks ("VPN") and Remote Desktop Protocol ("RDP"). The hijacking of remote access user accounts has become a major attack vector for threat actors.

One reason for this is that user credentials can often be acquired on the dark web, and attackers gain network access that way through remote access connections. Later on I will outline practices for defending against compromised credentials in the *User Passwords* section. Other forms of hijacking are more technical in nature.

RDP, for example, is a protocol developed by Microsoft that allows users to connect to another computer over a network connection as if local and is often used by remote workers and by administrators to remotely troubleshoot, but also comes with some known vulnerabilities that have led to hijacking. One well-known hijacking technique is for an attacker to resume a previously disconnected user session and operate on the network as that user without having to steal credentials. This can be accomplished by connecting to an internet-exposed server using the Tscon.exe utility, which comes with Windows. Running a simple command using this utility allows the attacker to resume a previous session if the user did not properly log off. To avoid this type of passwordless hijacking:

- Configure group policy settings to automatically log-off users after ending an RDP session;
- Use 2 factor authentication.

For organizations operating remotely at scale, VPNs are generally used. VPN traffic is typically encrypted and hackers usually gain access to VPNs through one of 3 methods:
1. breaking the encryption,
2. stealing the encryption keys, or
3. human error.

Breaking the encryption involves decrypting messages through reverse engineering using significant computational resources. This is possible, and for some protocols easier done than for others, but in general this requires a lot of time and work with an uncertain payoff. A VPN protocol is a set of instructions a VPN application and server use to set up a connection, securely communicate with each other, and includes the type of encryption used. By avoiding VPNs using protocols with known vulnerabilities and weak encryption, such as Point-to-Point Tunnelling protocol ("PPTP"), organizations can be fairly confident that their encryption is secure, or at least is unlikely to be broken. So the first action we can take to secure remote access is to choose a more secure VPN protocol, such as OpenVPN.

Stealing encryption keys is an easier path to unlocking your data for your attacker than trying to break the encryption, so securing encryption keys is an important defense against an intruder stealing them.

Some best practices for securing encryption keys includes:

- Regularly rotate keys. Set a crypto period during which each key is active then run a rotation to replace old keys with new ones.
- Store keys on a hardware security module ("HSM"). An HSM is a physical device that permits on-premises cryptographic operations. Compromising this device requires your attacker to physically access your premises.
- Transport keys safely. For online distribution, encrypt keys and distribute using a secure Transport Layer Security ("TLS"). For offline distribution, encrypt keys and split them into several components that are useless on their own to a hacker.
- Never hard-code encryption keys into software.

The 3rd means of VPN compromise is through human error, often by falling victim to a targeted email attack, which is an appropriate segue into our next common RPOC, phishing and other social engineering attacks.

9.5.3 Patching

Unpatched software and hardware is a leading reason why cyberattacks are successful, making patching one of the most effective cyber-risk mitigation strategies. Even though patches may be available, they are often not applied or applied late, either because daily operational activities take precedence over patching, or because patch testing is cumbersome and time-consuming. To avoid becoming a victim of software compromise, put a solid patching program in place, including the following key elements:

Accountability – Make patch monitoring somebody's job. While applying patches is probably the domain of application or production support, monitoring the patch management program, together with associated reporting, should be a centralized function assigned to a single individual or small group to avoid dispersion of responsibility and having some patches fall through the cracks.

Identify all devices – information assets cannot be patched if you don't know about them. Scan your network regularly for servers, workstations, network equipment, and ioT devices and maintain a regular inventory.

Risk-Based Approach – Patch critical vulnerabilities and critical systems first. Not all software exploits are the same, and differentiating them by using a vulnerability scoring system, like CVSS (Common Vulnerability Scoring System), can help to prioritize. Likewise, not all systems present the same level of risk if compromised. Use the asset inventory to identify and prioritize patching of the most sensitive systems. Reducing your greatest exposures first minimizes the chances of a catastrophic security breach.

Monitoring – Monitor unpatched software and devices and set up minimum thresholds for patching. Create alerts for deviations from minimum patching requirements and enforce compliance through an independent risk management group. Summary level patch program statistics should be periodically presented to the governance committee responsible for information security so that members of that committee can provide effective oversight.

Automate Patch Deployment – Use a patch management tool to automate the regular and timely application of patches.

Testing – Test patches in an environment that mirrors, as closely as possible, the production environment. For patches impacting many devices or systems, test a handful of devices first to create a baseline. Roll out the patch to those devices first and perform the broader rollout after establishing that there were no issues with the baseline rollout. Finally, test for interdependencies with systems that interface or connect to the systems being patched.

9.5.4 Phishing & social engineering

Social engineering attacks, including phishing campaigns are ubiquitous and effective. That is because social engineering attacks rely on human behavior, rather than technical prowess, to breach network security. Recently, targeted attacks have become popular, wherein an attacker impersonates a high-ranking organization official via phone, email, or chat to convince an employee to transfer money on an emergency basis. The money transfer request is a hoax, of course, and the attacker receives the funds if the employee can be convinced to act. Other popular social engineering attacks prompt users to give up their credentials, believing the requestor to be a vendor or systems administrator. Once in possession of valid user credentials bad actors can access organization data as a real user using the stolen credentials.

Email phishing is also extremely common. In an email phishing campaign users are targeted with emails appearing to be legitimate, typically containing a link. When users click on the link malware is downloaded. Desktop anti-malware software can neutralize or mitigate the damage but often hackers gain access or exfiltrate data in this way.

Because social engineering attacks rely on the unwitting cooperation of the victims, the best defense is to educate users on how to recognize and respond to an attack. Organizations can develop their own security awareness training content and deliver it in a number of ways, including in-person training or online. There are also quite a few companies that deliver training for a fee. Important concepts include recognizing suspicious communications and verifying the authenticity of requests before acting. And training is not simply one and done. Employees have many demands requiring their attention besides cybersecurity so re-offer the training with updates at least annually.

9.5.4.1 Social engineering simulation

In addition to security awareness training organizations should simulate social engineering attacks through sponsored phishing attempts. In a simulated attack the organization's own Information Security Department or an external vendor ply employees with emails or phone calls designed to draw them into clicking a link, leaking data, or transferring funds. The positive responses are recorded and employees who fell for the ploy are given feedback on how to spot fraudulent communication.

9.5.4.2 Spam filters

Setting spam filters appropriately on email gateways greatly reduces spam emails and cuts down on the risk of email compromise. In addition, placing banners on emails alerting recipients to emails that originated from outside the organization can help users detect impersonators.

9.5.5 Default configurations and default passwords

Much equipment comes with default security configurations and passwords. One of the most avoidable vulnerabilities is leaving these defaulted settings in place after bringing equipment online. This is especially so for networking equipment, such as routers, where threat actors having gained access can move about the network, but also applies to servers and ioT devices.

Initial equipment configuration must include process steps to change default configuration settings and passwords. Otherwise, the door is left wide open for intruders to enter.

9.5.6 User passwords

It is not news to readers that data leaks happen quite frequently. Very often usernames and passwords are exfiltrated to threat actors who can use them to gain access to your organization's network. Even if you are personally very careful another organization, perhaps a vendor, could be compromised and your credentials exposed.

One measure that organizations can take to guard against the risk of compromised credentials is to use strong authentication, such as multi-factor authentication. There are still a large percentage of organizations that do not require multi-factor authentication and this is another example of a completely preventable vulnerability.

By requiring users to login using some combination of something you know (password), something you have (a mobile phone), or something you are (biometric information) the risk of leaked credentials being used to breach the perimeter goes way down.

9.5.7 Other information security activities

While the attack prevention techniques mentioned above are oriented toward some of the most common attack vectors, there are other activities that are frequently neglected because of the incentive and behavioral conflicts discussed earlier in this chapter. Many of these are foundational to an information security program so I include them here as requiring adequate oversight.

9.5.7.1 Information asset inventory

There is a true saying, "you can't protect it if you don't know where it is", and that is why maintaining a complete information asset inventory is critical to any successful information security program. An information asset inventory is a complete list of data, applications, servers, and other equipment that is used by an organization to conduct its business. This information should be indexed to record relationships, like which servers host which applications or where sensitive data is stored and is often maintained in a Configuration Management Database ("CMDB"), and this is where the conflict of interest often arises.

A complete and accurate CMDB is vital for the Information Security Department in applying appropriate levels of protection to an organization's assets, but they are really consumers of this data. The staff maintaining the CMDB are developers, engineers, and database administrators, who must update the CMDB as they release software, upgrade machines, or add and delete databases. In performing their primary work they may feel that they do not derive much value from the CMDB and therefore do not spend the time to maintain it. This must be overcome with the types of control mechanisms described earlier, such as setting policy and process to enforce the requirement to maintain the CMDB. Deploying a new release, for example, can be made contingent on the independent releaser verifying that the CMDB is current for the related application. The CMDB inventory can be reconciled to the results of device scans. And periodic audits can highlight gaps.

9.5.7.2 Backups

Everyone knows that backups are critical when data is corrupted or lost. It is a great feeling of relief when the file you were working on can be quickly restored and you are back in business. And it is a common misconception that everything is backed up. Depending on your business and size of organization it may not be possible to backup all data on a frequent basis, either because of size constraints or processing time. Therefore, the key data and applications must be backed up so that the organization can remain operational at all times.

Identifying the key data and applications is management's role, and the CMDB, if properly populated, can be useful as a reference. Depending on the size and complexity of your organization the staff that backs up data may have other roles as well and may not always perform the scheduled backups or may not be focused on the correct data, which conflicts with the information security agenda.

Overcoming this misalignment of activity requires governance and process controls. Management must clearly articulate which data is key to backup. This can be informed by data confidentiality, integrity, availability ratings ("CIA Ratings") from the CMDB, from the business continuity and disaster recovery plans and from general knowledge of the business or organization. Technology operations staff that are responsible for managing backups must then be held accountable for successfully completing backups on the frequency specified for each data store, including tying compensation to results.

9.5.7.3 Network defenses

Network segmentation, both physical and logical, can slow down or stop a threat actor from moving laterally across the network. This defense can be thought of as analogous to a ship with water-tight sections that can be sealed off in the event of a hull breach, thereby limiting flooding to the sealed section. Containing intrusions to a portion of the network is particularly useful in defending against the spread of malware or ransomware.

Network engineers, however, can be very busy simply maintaining the network, such as replacing and upgrading equipment, testing messaging traffic volume, dealing with vendors, and recovering service interruptions. Taking the time to optimally configure the network against cyber threats represents another example where a shared resource (network engineers) must perform a day-to-day job and implement information security safeguards. Preparing for a cyberattack that may never happen might lose out to the daily demands of network users.

Avoid falling into this trap by having the Information Security Department set out some minimum network configuration standards and report regularly on progress toward achieving these standards to the committee overseeing information security in your organization. Include network configuration goals in the performance / compensation review for network engineers to link compensation to risk management.

9.5.8 Conclusion

In this chapter I proposed an explanation for why information security risks are often unmitigated, and why that leads to preventable, even predictable, cyber security incidents. The challenges in preventing such incidents are not mainly technical but rather behavioral. It is human nature and mis-aligned risk-taking incentives that drive this phenomenon.

Addressing this requires governance and control structures to be woven into the fabric of organizational activity to achieve an appropriate information security risk profile in balance with operational requirements.

I then detailed actions organizations can take to mitigate the risk of some of the most common attack vectors as well as other important security activities that are often neglected and leave organizations exposed.

References

Alexiou, S. (2019). Practical Patch Management & Mitigations. *ISACA Journal, Volume 3*. https://www.isaca. org/resources/isaca-journal/issues/2019/volume-3/practical-patch-management-and-mitigation

Arctic Wolf Labs. (2024). Arctic Wolf Labs Threat Report 2024. In https://arcticwolf.com/resources/. Retrieved March 27, 2024, from https://arcticwolf.com/resources/

Baker, K. (2023, November 9). *10 Most Common Types of Cyber Attacks*. Crowdstrike. https://www.crowd strike.com/cybersecurity-101/cyberattacks/most-common-types-of-cyberattacks/

Berrett, D., Christiansen, D., Tom, S. (2008). *Recommended Practice for Patch Management of Control Systems*. Homeland Security. https://www.cisa.gov/sites/default/files/2023-01/RP_Patch_Management_ S508C.pdf

Borsecnik, J., Coetzer, Flores, J., M., McKillop, E. & Piesco, J. (2023, October 12). *Five Steps to Securing Your Identity Infrastructure*. Microsoft. https://learn.microsoft.com/en-us/azure/security/fundamentals/ steps-secure-identity

Brooks, C. (2023, March 5). *Cybersecurity Trends & Statistics for 2023; What You Need to Know*. Forbes. https://www.forbes.com/sites/chuckbrooks/2023/03/05/cybersecurity-trends–statistics-for-2023- more-treachery-and-risk-ahead-as-attack-surface-and-hacker-capabilities-grow/?sh=1937bbe919db

Chinnasamy, V. (2023, February 27). *Virtual Patching: Shield Your Enterprise from Vulnerabilities*. Indusface. https://www.indusface.com/blog/how-virtual-patching-is-helpful-in-vulnerability-management/

Cimpanu, C. (2021, February 25). *This Chart Shows the Connections Between Cybercrime Groups*. ZDNET. https://www.zdnet.com/article/this-chart-shows-the-connections-between-cybercrime-groups/

Cybersecurity & Infrastructure Security Agency. (2022). *Joint Cybersecurity Advisory: Weak Security Controls and Practices Routinely Exploited for Initial Access*. CISA, FBI, NSA, CCCS, NCSC-NZ, CERT-NZ, NCSC-NL, NCSC-UK. https://media.defense.gov/2022/May/17/2002998718/-1/-1/0/CSA_WEAK_SECURITY_CON TROLS_PRACTICES_EXPLOITED_FOR_INITIAL_ACCESS.PDF

Cybersecurity & Infrastructure Security Agency. (2023). *Guide to Securing Remote Access Software*. Multi-State Information Sharing & Analysis Center. https://www.cisa.gov/sites/default/files/2023-06/Guide%20to%20Securing%20Remote%20Access%20Software_clean%20Final_508c.pdf

Fletcher, B. (2022, May 4). *Basics for Improving the Safety of Your Organization's Data*. ISACA. https://www.isaca.org/resources/news-and-trends/industry-news/2022/basics-for-improving-the-safety-of-your-organizations-data

Flyvbjerg, B. (2008). Curbing Optimism Bias and Strategic Misrepresentation in Planning: Reference Class Forecasting in Practice. *European Planning Studies, 16(1)*. 10.1080/09654310701747936

Gasic, D. (2022, January 12). *Top Cyber Attacks in 2022*. Purplesec. https://purplesec.us/security-insights/top-cyberattacks-2022/

Garza, M. (2023, June 2). *80 Cybersecurity Statistics and Trends*. Varonis. https://www.varonis.com/blog/77-cybersecurity-statistics-and-trends-for-2023

Glass, G., Iacono, L., Wojcieszek, K., (2023). *Q2 2023 Threat Landscape Report*. Kroll. https://www.kroll.com/en/insights/publications/cyber/threat-intelligence-reports/q2-2023-threat-landscape-report-supply-chain-infiltrations

Healy, P.J. & Moore, D.A. (2008). The Trouble With Overconfidence. *Psychological Review, 115(2)*, 502–517. https://doi.org/10.1037/0033-295X.115.2.502

ISACA & Terranova Security. (2019). *Phishing Defense and Governance*. ISACA. https://store.isaca.org/s/store#/store/browse/detail/a2S4w000004KoEzEAK

Kahneman, D. & Lovallo, D. (2003). Delusions of Success. *Harvard Business Review, 81(7)*, pp. 56–63. https://api.semanticscholar.org/CorpusID:10995455

Kahneman, D. & Tversky, A. (1979). Prospect Theory: An Analysis of Decision Under Risk. *Econometrica, 47(2)*, pp. 263–291. https://www.jstor.org/stable/1914185

Laurente-Ticong. (2023, November 16). *9 Network Patch Management Best Practices and Tips*. Enterprise Networking Planet. https://www.enterprisenetworkingplanet.com/security/patch-management-best-practices/

March, J. & Shapira, Z. (1987) Managerial Perspectives on Risk and Risk Taking. *Management Science* 33(11):1404 –1418. https://dx.doi.orq/10.1287/mnsc.33.11.1404

McShane, I., Thanos, D. (2023). *Arctic Wolf Labs Threat Report 2023*. Artic Wolf Labs. https://arcticwolf.com/resource/aw/arctic-wolf-labs-2023-threat-report.

Morgan, S. (2022). *2022 Official CyberCrime Report*. CybersecurityVentures. https://cybersecurityventures.com/cybercrime-to-cost-the-world-8-trillion-annually-in-2023/

Morgan, S. (2023). *2023 Official CyberCrime Report*. CybersecurityVentures. https://cybersecurityventures.com/cybercrime-to-cost-the-world-9-trillion-annually-in-2024/

Nepomuceno, L., Nobre, F., Nobre, L., Paula, L. & Silva, L. (2021). Overconfidence and Optimism in Business Decision-Making: Scale Development and Validation. *Research, Society and Development, 10(8)*. DOI: http://dx.doi.org/10.33448/rsd-v10i8.17145

Petrosyan, A. (2024, March 22). *Distribution of Cyber Attacks Across Worldwide Industries in 2023*. Statista. https://www.statista.com/statistics/1315805/cyberattacks-top-industries-worldwide/.

Perunicic, K. (2023, July21). *VPN Protocol Comparison: PPTP vs SSTP vs OpenVPN vs L2TP vs IKEv2*. vpnMentor. https://www.vpnmentor.com/blog/vpn-protocol-comparison-pptp-vs-l2tp-vs-openvpn-vs-sstp-vs-ikev2/

Perunicic, K. (2023, December 4). *Can VPNs Be Hacked?* vpnMentor. https://www.vpnmentor.com/blog/can-vpns-hacked-take-deeper-look/

Ponemon Institute. (2019). *Costs and Consequences of Gaps in Vulnerability Response*. https://www.servicenow.com/lpayr/ponemon-vulnerability-survey.html.

Ponemon Institute. (2020). *Cybersecurity in the Remote Work Era*. https://d31wr468xgaoff.cloudfront.net/insights/wp-content/uploads/2020/11/Cybersecurity-In-the-Remote-Work-Era-A-Global-Risk-Report-min.pdf

Ponemon Institute. (2022). *2022 Cost of Insider Threats Global Report*. https://www.proofpoint.com/us/re
    sources/threat-reports/cost-of-insider-threats

Robb, D. (2023, June 30). *5 Patch Management Best Practices for Success in 2023*. TechRepublic. https://www.
    techrepublic.com/article/patch-management-best-practices/

Schroeder, N. (2005). Using Prospect Theory to Investigate Decision-Making Bias Within an Information
    Security Context [Master's Thesis, Air Force Institute of Technology]. 3403. https://scholar.afit.edu/
    etd/3403

SecureLink. (2022). *The State of Cybersecurity and Third-Party Remote Access Risk*. Imprivata. https://security.
    imprivata.com/rs/413-FZZ-310/images/SL-Ponemon-Report-state-of-cs-and-third-party-access-risk-
    1122.pdf.

Secureworks Counter Threat Unit Research Team. (2023). *Threat Intelligence Executive Report* (Volume 2023,
    Number3). Secureworks. https://www.secureworks.com/resources/rp-irs-threat-intelligence-report-
    2023-vol-3

Sharma, A. (2020, June 23). *RDP Hijacking Attacks Explained, and How to Mitigate Them*. CSO. https://www.
    csoonline.com/article/569621/rdp-hijacking-attacks-explained-and-how-to-mitigate-them.html

Smith, M. (2022). Decision Theory and De Minimis Risk. *Erkenn*. https://doi.org/10.1007/s10670-022-
    00624-9

Sophos. (2023). *The State of Ransomware 2023*. (2023-05-05 (WP-DD)). Sophos. https://www.sophos.com/
    en-us/content/state-of-ransomware

Sharot, T. (2011). The Optimism Bias. *Current Biology, 21(23)*. https://www.sciencedirect.com/journal/cur
    rent-biology/vol/21/issue/23

Statista. (2023, November 28). *Worldwide Information Security Services Spending from 2017 to 2024*. Statista.
    https://www.statista.com/statistics/217362/worldwide-it-security-spending/

Top Cyber Security Experts Report: 4,000 Cyber Attacks a Day Since COVID-19 Pandemic (2020, August 11).
    PRNewswire. https://www.prnewswire.com/news-releases/top-cyber-security-experts-report-4-000-
    cyberattacks-a-day-since-covid-19-pandemic-301110157.html

Tunefab Leaks 151 Million Records of Users. (2023, December 30th). Beyond Machines. https://www.be
    yondmachines.net/event_details/tunefab-leaks-151-million-records-of-users-d-v-x-s-l

Velimirovic, A. (2021, August 12). *16 Encryption Key Management Best Practices*. PhoenixNAP.
    https://phoenixnap.com/blog/encryption-key-management-best-practices

Wadhwani, S. (2022, October 20). *Misconfigured Azure Blob Storage Exposed the Data of 65K Companies and
    548K Users*. Spiceworks. https://www.spiceworks.com/it-security/cloud-security/news/microsoft-
    azure-cloud-misconfiguration/

Wagle, S. (2021, July 14). *Prospect Theory – Behavioral Economics 2*. Medium. https://sidharthwagle.medium.
    com/prospect-theory-behavioural-economics-2-98ba919f4e21

Watters, A. (2023, January 27). *Top 50 Cybersecurity Statistics, Figures and Facts*. CompTIA. https://connect.
    comptia.org/blog/cyber-security-stats-facts

Weinstein, N. (1980). Unrealistic Optimism About Future Life Events. *Journal Of Personality and Social
    Psychology, 39(5)*, pp. 806–820. https://doi.org/10.1037/0022-3514.39.5.806

Williams, M. (2022, January 10). *What is a VPN Protocol?* Techradar. https://www.techradar.com/vpn/what-
    is-a-vpn-protocol

Winder, D. (2022, August 13). *Cisco Hacked: Ransomware Gang Claims It Has 2.8 GB of Data*. Forbes.
    https://www.forbes.com/sites/daveywinder/2022/08/13/cisco-hacked-ransomware-gang-claims-it-
    has-28gb-of-data/?sh=205705934043

5 Types of Remote Access Hacking Opportunities Hackers Exploit During Covid-19. (2020, June 19).
    Cloudbric. https://www.cloudbric.com/5-types-of-remote-access-hacking-opportunities-hackers-
    exploit-during-covid-19/

8 Ways Organisations Prevent Social Engineering Attacks. (2021, April 23). Stickman Cyber. https://www.
    stickmancyber.com/cybersecurity-blog/8-ways-organisations-prevent-social-engineering-attacks

Kurt J. Engemann and Holmes E. Miller

10 Implications of artificial intelligence in cybersecurity for individuals

10.1 Introduction

Cybersecurity is designed with the goals of safeguarding the privacy, accessibility and integrity of information, while protecting it from various threats. Cybersecurity is a dynamic process, as new attack strategies constantly emerge, requiring nonstop monitoring and improvements to security procedures. Managing cybersecurity as a comprehensive activity enables a determined effort with an assortment of defense measures, and viewing cybersecurity as an uninterrupted activity permits organisations to incorporate new developments more quickly (Ham, 2021). It is critical for individuals, as well as government agencies and organizations, to enhance cybersecurity to guard sensitive information, and ensure a safe and secure digital environment.

Artificial Intelligence (AI) emphasizes new technologies that accomplish tasks that typically require the intelligence of humans. At the moment there is no agreement on the definition of AI, and it may be claimed that a clear definition is not required. This is because AI is a dynamic assemblage of numerous technologies that are constantly changing. Moreover, rapid progress in this area will quickly make a definition outdated (Bonfanti, 2022). One objective of AI is to develop systems that can emulate our cognition as applied to problem-solving, learning, and perception.

AI encompasses a wide range of technologies that hold the potential to contribute to societal advancements, and has entered our lives in healthcare, transportation, education, and many other areas (Jiang et al, 2022). Data mining is a method of identifying concealed patterns and relationships among vast amounts of data (Han and Tong, 2022). Machine learning plays a significant role by automating data investigation, wherein machine learning models can detect patterns, trends, anomalies, and can classify and cluster data. AI's text mining allows for instant processing of unstructured data, such as social media. AI applications include areas like object and facial identification, surveillance, and driverless vehicles; and, AI based engines assess user activity and make recommendations for goods and services that fit specific user preferences. A caveat in all these applications is that ethical considerations and responsible usage must stay center-stage in the implementation of these technologies to ensure that AI benefits humanity and does not threaten its future.

AI can also be a defensive tool to bolster cybersecurity, nevertheless it also has the potential to be an offensive means to bypass cybersecurity measures as well, and as technology develops, cybercriminals are realizing that AI may be used to create more multifaceted strategies. An assortment of attack scenarios that are AI-based, as well as possible defenses for these attacks, are presented by Yamin et al. (2021). The

https://doi.org/10.1515/9783111289069-010

numerous threats that individuals and organizations face and the range of the activities involved make AI approaches to cybersecurity distinctive. At a basic level, AI solutions for individuals typically aim at direct risks like malware and phishing scams and offer intuitive, automatic personal device and account protection. However, AI techniques for enterprises are more comprehensive and focused on automation to provide thorough threat identification and customized solutions to cover the operational scale of the organization. Individual AI solutions are more lightweight and made to demand less user intervention than organizational AI solutions, which safeguard a greater number of endpoints, servers, and databases and prioritize continuous monitoring, threat intelligence sharing, and centralized management.

While direct cybersecurity threats explicitly target individuals, cybersecurity threats can also be indirect, focusing on attacking organizational systems containing information about individuals and enabling AI-based decisions that affect them. Examples include credit decisions, employment decisions, health-related decisions, and becoming affected by AI generated disinformation. Recent advances in AI have exacerbated individual risk levels as AI now is able to replicate human actions. This introduces new threats involving how humans interact with computers or digital artifacts.

AI, utilizing computer vision algorithms, can extract information from photos and videos, which can lead to detrimental outcomes. A growing threat is that of a deep fake that addresses human emotions that arise in events like kidnappings (Cost, 2023). With AI, the identity of the attacker may be indistinguishable from a trusted real person, and as individuals tend to hold onto relational trust and distrust attitudes shaped in non-cyber environments (Arduin, 2021), individual behavior often remains unchanged when encountering AI, thus increasing the likelihood of a person responding erroneously to a threat. For a review of the recent literature on how AI has impacted both the threat and control dimensions of cybersecurity, see Wiafe et al., (2020) and Kaur et al. (2023).

Indeed, in a world where the most intractable aspects of AI enabled cyber-threats are sociotechnical, cybersecurity cannot be managed by technology singlehanded (Jeong et al., 2019). Moreover, the most fragile element in digital security is human involvement, mandating individuals to reevaluate their role, both as target and protector (Hong and Furnell, 2021; McKinsey, 2019).

In this chapter we investigate the cybersecurity challenges involving how AI impacts individuals, considering both AI technologies (van de Poel, 2020) and AI driven value conflicts (Christen et al., 2020). By understanding and addressing individual behavior, balancing values, harnessing technology, and implementing effective policies, individuals can fortify their digital defenses and protect their personal and digital assets. In the next section (Section 2) we discuss how existing threats have evolved in AI environments and highlight new threats to individuals that have emerged with the development of AI technologies. In Section 3 we discuss how AI can be used to strengthen defensive cybersecurity mechanisms. Finally in Section 4, our Conclusion, we address ethical issues and future challenges, including privacy, algorithmic biases, transparency, and implementation.

10.2 Cybersecurity threats to individuals in AI environments

In this section, we discuss how perpetrators use AI to attack individuals' cyber settings. In some cases, AI enabled attacks mimic traditional attacks, the difference being that perpetrators' intrusions are more effective when using AI technologies. However, AI also may be used in entirely novel ways, the attributes of the recent technology opening innovative paths to do harm. We first will discuss classical security risks to individuals, and then discuss how AI can be used to compound these risks.

10.2.1 Cybersecurity risk to individuals

10.2.1.1 Risk and impact

Individuals face various risks from cyberattacks, and a substantial growth of these incidents has followed the development of the Internet, frequently with devastating consequences (Jang-Jaccard & Nepal, 2014). There are numerous cybersecurity risks that individuals face – some common ones are presented here.

Malicious software (malware) can infect devices through numerous means, including infected websites, bogus emails, and corrupted downloads. Malware creates malicious events by exploiting vulnerabilities of emerging technologies and can provide cybercriminals with unauthorized access, make files vulnerable to damage, and allow for the theft of confidential information (Jang-Jaccard & Nepal, 2014).

Outdated software and applications can leave vulnerabilities, making it easier for perpetrators to exploit them. A substantial number of cyberattacks have been the consequence of an exploitation of identified vulnerabilities, even though a patch to remediate the situation was already available, and despite the fast releases of security patches addressing newly revealed vulnerabilities in software products, (Dissanayake et al, 2022). Perpetrators can gain unauthorized access to online accounts if individuals use weak passwords.

Online frauds include schemes that aim to deceive individuals into providing personal information or money, and typically involve activities such as online shopping, investing, and personal scams. Social engineering attacks involve manipulating individuals to reveal sensitive information through impersonation, manipulation, or exploiting trust. Social engineering is a developing threat in virtual groups and can be readily automated to be executed on a large scale (Chetioui et al, 2022).

Phishing attacks imitate a trustworthy entity to fool individuals to reveal confidential information such as social security numbers and passwords.

Data breaches happen when cybercriminals obtain unauthorized access to databases or systems holding personal information, providing opportunity for fraud and sale on the dark web. Cloud security threats encompass risks that have the potential to impact the privacy, integrity and accessibility of data entrusted to digital systems (Kumar & Alphonse, 2018).

Unsecured Wi-Fi networks can expose individuals to perpetrators intercepting data and engaged in eavesdropping. Along with the intensified usage of tablets and smartphones came the ubiquitous appearance of wireless access points in public spaces, with their corresponding increased risks to the privacy of individuals. Public Wi-Fi's are frequently not secure, giving others on the same network the opportunity to intercept the data being transmitted (Sangeen. 2023).

A cyberattack's impact can be a slight disruption; however, it can also be devastating personal and financial event. Understanding risk perception and risk attitude is a prerequisite to mitigate risk and is the basis of formulating a cohesive security strategy. Safety climate provides an underpinning of risk attitude in a group which in turn directly influences risk strategy decisions. A risk attitude chain model represents the decision process of accommodating safety climate and risk attitude to determine subsequent risk decisions (Engemann and Engemann, 2017).

Individuals may recognize the negative impact of risk events, but they deem those negative events only impact others. An individual's attitude regarding risk influences their decisions (Engemann and Miller, 2015), and because of an optimistic bias, individuals, at times, are deficient in implementing preventive measures. These individuals tend to disregard cyber-threats, and possess too much confidence regarding cybersecurity (Alnifie and Kim,).

The stealing of personal information in a cyberattack can open the individual up to financial fraud and unsanctioned purchases, and can harm one's credit score. In addition, identity theft is associated with severe mental and physical sicknesses (Burns et al, 2020). A cyberattack can expose private information, personal communications, and potentially damaging data. Individuals may lose money directly to attackers and incur financial losses due to fraudulent transactions. Numerous cyberattacks, such as ransomware, aim to extort money from victims, and can result in data loss, including personal documents, family photos, and other important files, which may not be recoverable. In recent years, ransomware has been one of the most notorious malwares targeting end-users (Oz et al, 2022).

Cyberattacks can result in the theft of login credentials, allowing attackers to enter personal accounts. A cyberattack may lead to unauthorized access to emails and social media profiles which can be used to spread malware. Cyberattacks that involve spreading untrue or hurtful information about individuals can harm their personal and professional reputation. Being a victim of a cyberattack can cause emotional distress, particularly in cases of cyberbullying or online harassment.

The Internet of Things (IoT) represents a gateway to cybersecurity threats, allowing perpetrators to compromise connected systems, such as smart homes and medical devices, creating risks to health and safety. These devices amass huge amounts of personal data leading to confidentiality worries. The Internet of Medical Things (IoMT), which can provide remote monitoring and warning of emergency medical situations is especially pertinent in elder-care, but can also cause harm if the information falls into the wrong hands (Cartwright, 2023).

10.2.1.2 Perpetrators

The perpetrators of cybersecurity threats for individuals include various groups and individuals with different motivations and proficiencies. The cybersecurity scene is always changing, and with innovative threats and more sophisticated perpetrators emerging, it is more difficult to identify the actual culprits (Aftab et al, 2022). There are many types of perpetrators who present a threat in the cyber-world – some common ones are presented here.

Cybercriminals are individuals or groups who engage in illegal activities for financial or non-financial gain.

Social engineering cybercriminals deceive people using psychological tricks for the purpose of obtaining passwords and other sensitive data. Victims of social engineering are unaware of the incident at the time it occurs and do not avail themselves of tactics to prevent the attack (Oyafitri, 2022).

Scammers are individuals who use deception to reveal sensitive information or obtain money through fraudulent schemes.

Phishers use deceptive emails or websites that mimic legitimate sources and deceive individuals to give up personal information, such as financial information and passwords. Then phishers, with the illegally collected information, buy goods and services, obtain credit cards, and remove money from bank accounts (Sonowal, 2022).

Hackers are individuals with the technical skills to compromise computer systems and networks for various reasons, including personal gain.

Hacktivists engage in cyberattacks to advance a political or social cause, and their targets range from government agencies to private companies to individuals. Hacktivists may focus on organizations or individuals that they perceive as adversarial to their beliefs. Hacktivism is a rising phenomenon (Romagna & Leukfeldt, 2023), where some cybersecurity threats are perpetrated by nation-states or state-sponsored hacking groups.

Malicious software developers create and circulate malevolent software with the intention of compromising systems.

10.2.1.3 Use of AI in cyberattacks

There are numerous ways in which AI presents new challenges to cybersecurity risk management for individuals. AI can be used to automate tasks such as scanning for vulnerabilities and devising personalized phishing messages enabling perpetrators to extract sensitive information from targeted systems in more efficient ways. Attacks can be conducted at a speed and scale that overwhelms security defenses. Defending against novel attacks that are employing machine learning algorithms, is accelerating the creation of even more complex malware that can evade detection.

It is difficult to trace the illegal activities being transacted on the dark web and carried out by anonymous persons. The dark web is only accessible through specialized software and is not indexed by customary search engines. AI technologies are used on the dark web to constantly update and change its illicit content (Alaidi, 2022). AI assists cybercriminals in mining and analyzing immense collections of data, such as stolen financial and banking information. AI can be used to further anonymization and encryption on the dark web, improving privacy for those involved in illicit activities.

AI can scrutinize a target system, giving perpetrators the means to fit their attacks to a specific situation (Syafitri, 2022). Cyberattacks are tailored to the targeted victims, making it difficult for recipients to identify fakes. Subsequently it is more likely that the intended recipients are tricked into divulging private information. Phishing scripts are adjusted to be precisely customized according to the recipient's publicly available social media. Adding to the confusion is the fact that AI-driven deepfake technology can alter photos, audio and video to produce extremely lifelike imitations that mimic real people (Waldemarsson, 2020).

10.2.2 Information-based cybersecurity risk

10.2.2.1 Tracking and surveillance

While AI-powered tracking devices are useful in providing real-time location information designed to safeguard the security of individuals, pets, and assets, these same devices can also be a cause for trouble when it comes to privacy. AI can process location data from smartphones and other devices to secretly track individuals' activities through various means, including monitoring apps that have features for tracking and reporting. Service providers must respect individuals' privacy rights and follow data protection regulations to guarantee trustworthy application of AI in tracking devices.

Eavesdropping refers to the act of secretly listening to or intercepting private conversations without the consent of the parties involved. AI can analyze internet and Wi-Fi usage to track individuals in public spaces. AI-powered surveillance cameras can analyze videos in real-time, tracking individuals based on facial recognition. Law enforcement agencies and security organizations use network-based surveillance tools to monitor communication and data transmitted over networks. AI can use historical information to predict individuals' movements, enabling tracking in real-time. Users need to be mindful of the data being collected, and how they can control their privacy settings.

Using AI for unauthorized eavesdropping or any other illegal activities is firmly contrary to the principles of protecting privacy. The collection of an individual's data raises ethical questions about the proper use and protection of their information. As a framework for application in this regard, Hakkala and Koshinen (2022) formulated an ethical paradigm for managing personal data in the age of surveillance.

AI can be understood of as an article of protection, a method of protection, and a weapon of attack (Veprytska and Kharchenko, 2022). Regulations surrounding the implementation of AI usage should strike a balance between the risks and benefits with regard to civil liberties. Organizations and governments need to preserve the privacy rights of individuals through the enacting of and adherence to relevant data protection laws and regulations. In this regard, Anderljung et al (2023) propose a set of standards for AI models, covering risk assessments, model scrutiny, deployment analysis, and supervising model functionalities. Challenged with a growing number of cyberattacks, defenders can avail themselves to models that simulate incidents in order to expose software vulnerabilities which are threatened by AI-driven attacks (Jaber and Fritsch, 2022).

10.2.2.2 Extracting information and harming individuals

AI algorithms can be used to amplify the negative content about an individual on social media, and can generate phony news that make false claims about an individual resulting in detrimental public opinion. These AI-generated lies can be used to attack an individual's reputation on online forums and websites.

By using big data analysis and amalgamating information from online activity and public records, counterfeit profiles can be generated, impersonating the individual on social media and damaging a person's reputation. The ability of deepfake technology to generate highly realistic imagery and audio clips that portray individuals talking or acting in a fictious manner is a threat to one's personal integrity.

10.2.2.3 Misinformation and limited information

Although AI can be a useful tool in gathering good information, it can also be employed in a deceitful manner, especially when constructed with malevolent motives. AI can be utilized to create and disseminate deceptive information, resulting in individuals believing fabrications. AI-driven deepfake technology has the ability to generate exceedingly realistic audio, pictures, and videos, making it difficult to distinguish honest information from modified content (Hwang, 2020).

AI technology can facilitate users in retrieving the desired information, nevertheless AI can also be employed to restrict access to information. These instances are typically driven by humans manipulating algorithms used in search engines to prioritize some information while also suppressing of out-of-favor viewpoints. Several online platforms utilize AI-driven content moderation systems to remove information that allegedly violates the established criteria. Furthermore, authorities do have to ability to use filtering technologies to block access to specific content. The ethical use AI would help ensure that AI is used for positive purposes that benefit individuals and society, wherein the deployment of AI systems for misinformation detection is done so transparently.

It is crucial to verify that the utilization of AI in regulating access to information is in accordance with the protection of individuals' rights. The potential for AI to be used for censorship or information control raises important questions about the balance between protecting users from harmful content and upholding principles of free expression and unrestricted access to information. Striking the right balance between combating misinformation and respecting free speech rights is essential in maintaining an informed and open society.

10.2.3 Risk through technology systems

10.2.3.1 Home technology systems risk

Proponents of the full implementation of the IoT promise that it will yield innovative solutions to the benefit of all. The IoT makes it possible to accumulate a vast amount of data which can be transformed into knowledge by applying data mining. However, there are many who warn of negative risks that are being introduced by its advent, including the introduction of new cybersecurity risks to individuals. As AI is integrated into various devices, it expands the attack surface for cyber threats. Smart home devices can introduce new vulnerabilities if not properly secured. IoT devices may have inadequate security features, making them vulnerable to manipulation. IoT devices collect and broadcast enormous quantities of data, including private information and usage behavior. If this data is mishandled, it can lead to privacy breaches, identity theft, and targeted attacks.

An unsecured IoT device is an entry point to gain access to a broader network, compromising other devices. IoT devices can be targeted by malware, which can exploit vulnerabilities in their software, especially because IoT devices typically have extended lifecycles and may not receive consistent security updates. This leaves devices susceptible to vulnerabilities that remain unaddressed, making them targets for attackers. Some IoT devices are integrated into critical systems, such as healthcare devices or smart home security. If these devices are compromised, it can lead to safety risks for individuals, affecting their well-being.

AI is used in home energy management systems to improve efficiency, optimize energy usage, and reduce energy costs. Home energy management systems integrate AI algorithms to analyze real-time data from smart devices and sensors within a home. This allows automated control of energy-consuming appliances and systems; however, AI can also automatically turn off appliances, and herein lies a vulnerability from outside malicious controllers.

10.2.3.2 Vehicle technology systems risk

AI is used in electric vehicles (EVs) to enhance their performance, incorporating smart features that can help drivers by analyzing weather conditions and traffic data. Driver assistance technologies, such as lane-keeping support and automatic emergency braking, can enhance safety, while adaptive cruise control systems can detect the distance from other vehicles and adjust the car's speed accordingly.

Risks shift from preoccupied drivers to an assault on privacy and compromised capability as vehicles become safer with this technology, (Hodge et al, 2021). For example, Connected and Autonomous Vehicles (CAVs) utilize a universal network that creates cyberattack security issues. Relationships between CAVs and the unintended consequences of cybersecurity threats are not well understood. Khan et al (2022) developed a model using system dynamics to analyze cybersecurity within the implementation of CAVs.

10.2.3.3 Financial technology systems risk

Financial services banking are attractive targets for cybercriminals. Foremost among the multitude of possible malevolent actions in e-banking is phishing, with countermeasures being dependent on the level of security awareness that customers possess. However, cyberattacks are becoming more devious; for example, a zero click attack does not even require the involvement of a human to initiate the attack. Significant losses occur when standard protective protocols fail to detect this attack (TN & Kulkarni, 2022).

Digital banking involves using the cellular and internet applications. A main problem related to digital banking are the concomitant cybersecurity risks. Despite the implementation of various authentication and encryption processes used to manage the risk, cybersecurity threats remain a foremost challenge in digital banking (Alzoubi et al, 2022).

Society has begun to accept the idea of cryptocurrencies as digital currency, and cybersecurity is also required in this environment. Choithani et al. (2022) discuss approaches to problems associated with data security for cryptocurrencies based on AI techniques to predict their behavior. Currency in digital form, supplied and controlled by a central bank, is called Central Bank Digital Currency (CBDC). CBDC usage data be can be analyzed using AI algorithms to detect fraudulent transactions and assess consumer behavior. While AI can bring numerous benefits to CBDCs, there are also potential risks, including security vulnerabilities and data privacy concerns.

10.3 AI defensive mechanisms

In this section we discuss how individuals engage with AI systems used defensively in a cybersecurity environment. We group the methods into three categories: threat detection and prevention, authentication and access control, and, incident response and recovery.

10.3.1 Threat detection and prevention

10.3.1.1 Machine learning systems

Accurate and efficient algorithmic based threat detection and prevention approaches are needed to address increasing system complexity. Because these approaches are based on pattern detection, machine learning systems are effective in identifying patterns that diverge significantly from a stated norm (Chandola, 2009). Several methods used by these algorithms are categorized as clustering algorithms, autoencoders, and joint methods. *Clustering* is an unsupervised learning algorithm that uses many data points to identify clusters of similar points. Since points often fall outside of the defined cluster, the algorithm then identifies these points and classifies them as anomalies. *Autoencoders* are another approach. Autoencoders are neural networks that have been trained to deconstruct and then reconstruct the input data that previously was used to train the network (Chalapathy and Chawla, 2019). Using this approach, a classifier is used to discriminate between ordinary and anomalous data points. Confronted with a new data point, the classifier then calculates the probability that this point is an anomaly. *Joint methods*, as the name implies, combine multiple anomaly detection algorithms. One such algorithm is *boosting* (Intrator et al., 2018) and another is *stacking* (Yu et al., 2017). Combining algorithms results in capturing more anomaly patterns which leads to better accuracy. Machine learning algorithms to detect anomalies are widely used in many domains (Schubert et al, 2014). Some examples include:

insurance fraud; credit card fraud; cellular fraud; insider trading; and health care fraud (Phua et al., 2010).

10.3.1.2 Behavioral analysis

Although perpetrators try to have malicious attacks act in the same manner as normal behavior to seamlessly blend in as regular transactions, AI-based behavioral analysis is an effective procedure that can be used to detect dubious activities by analyzing patterns (KishorWagh et al., 2013; Sarker et al., 2021). Behavioral anomaly detection systems can spot abrupt surges in data transfer, atypical login times or locations, and deviations from regular user behavior. While traditional rule-based systems have inherent limitations in detecting sophisticated cyberattacks, AI algorithms can continuously adapt to identify new attack patterns (Fritsch et al., 2022). AI-driven behavioral analysis is also useful in domains like identifying insider threats and implementing proactive risk management (Kim et al., 2019; Al-Mhiqani et al., 2020). Viewing individuals in their roles as systems users, AI algorithms are able to discover typical patterns and spot behaviors that deviate from those established.

10.3.2 Authentication and access control

10.3.2.1 Biometric identification

Cyber-breaches frequently originate from authentication and access control deficiencies, which may be addressed with biometric identification and verification. *Voice recognition* and *speaker verification* methods can identify bogus phone calls or invalid audio attempts to access a system by comparing a new pattern with an existing one. Machine learning algorithms obtain an individual's distinctive vocal patterns and produce voiceprints for the purpose of authentication (Khdier et al., 2020), and can adapt to changes in voice quality, making the process resilient to fluctuations in background noise or emotional state. *Facial recognition,* which is a biometric technology that is utilized extensively by cellphone users, creates a unique representation of an individual's face that is then used when the individual tries to access the system (Jain et al., 2004).

Fingerprints and iris recognition are methods used to thwart illegal system access, using neural networks and deep learning models to process fingerprint or palm print inputs for comparison against stored prints (Thakur, 2015). AI algorithms also can be applied using similar logic to take data obtained from the human iris to verify the identity of an individual (Gad et al., 2015).

10.3.2.2 Controlling deep fakes

Deep fakes are created by using AI-generated content to produce images and voices that are seemingly genuine but in actuality are not real, and being quickly disseminated via social networks are a serious problem.

Facial recognition, picture forensics, and blockchain technology are three methods that are used to identify visual deep fakes (Thanh, 2022; Lyu, 2020). Facial recognition systems use inconsistencies in facial characteristics or eye movements to detect a deep fake. For image and video forensics, AI techniques are applied to visual content to uncover tampering, as evidenced by inconsistencies in lighting and shadows. Finally, blockchain can be applied to visual content to create an immutable record that can be used to track alterations made to the media.

Audio forensics, speaker verification and audio watermarking are a few methods that address identifying audio deep fakes (Thanh, 2022; Lyu, 2020). Audio forensics involves identifying irregularities in an audio sample by examining its waveform and frequency spectrum. The underlying logic, which also is employed by speaker verification, is to use deep learning to distinguish between genuine and artificial. Audio watermarking is akin to digital watermarking where the audio sample is used to generate a distinct signature that is used to verify the legitimacy of the content.

The ongoing challenge is that AI technology can be used by both sides, perpetuating the never-ending "spy vs. spy" scenario. This means that while AI methods are being continuously improved to detect deep fakes, the abilities of deep fake generators also are being improved to enable perpetrators to thwart control efforts.

Adversarial machine learning techniques, where AI systems are trained to counteract detection methods, pose a constant challenge to developing effective control mechanisms (Dhesi et al., 2023). Time constraints also can create an unlevel playing field when the attacker has a temporal advantage over the detector. Real-time detection of deep fakes is crucial to prevent their dissemination because if there is a lag, by the time the deep fake is detected, the damage may have been done. Indeed, sophisticated AI-generated deep fakes can be challenging to identify in real-time due to their increasing complexity and volume. This is especially true when the deep fake's context increases the likelihood of its believability.

Privacy concerns also exist. The same AI techniques used to detect deep fakes can also be misused for privacy invasion and surveillance purposes and striking a balance between utilizing AI for detection and respecting individuals' privacy is an ongoing challenge. Questions exist regarding how the current regulatory regime – regarding privacy and other concerns – may need to change to properly address a deep fake environment (van der Sloot and Wagensveld, 2022).

10.3.3 Incident response and recovery

10.3.3.1 Real-time monitoring

Since cyber threats are complex and can occur any time, real-time monitoring and alerting are necessary components of incident response and recovery systems. Whereas traditional security systems are often overwhelmed by the sheer volume of data currently being handled, a valuable aspect of AI in real-time monitoring is its high speed capability to process vast databases. These systems routinely analyze system logs, user activity, and network traffic, to detect any suspect behaviors or deviations from typical patterns (Şengönül et al., 2023). These systems learn from historical data and use it to establish baselines of normal behavior and, as discussed above in anomaly detection, detect even subtle deviations that may indicate a security breach or an ongoing attack.

AI can enhance incident detection accuracy by minimizing both false positives and false negatives (Conner-Simons, 2016). Rule-based approaches frequently produce a substantial quantity of false positives, inundating security personnel with an excessive amount of notifications and complicating the identification of actual threats. AI incident response systems can interact with security information and event management (SIEM) systems, and adjust their monitoring and discovery capabilities by incorporating real-time threat intelligence, to proactively recognize developing threats (Vasileios and Giovannelli, 2022).

10.3.3.2 Incident analysis and mitigation

Intelligent incident algorithms rapidly ascertain the underlying cause of an incident, and reveal concealed patterns that human analysts may fail to see (Chen et al., 2020). Natural language processing algorithms can unearth pertinent information from data that is unstructured, such as incident reports, social media feeds, and news articles. An essential feature of automated incident response and recovery systems is the mitigation of incident impacts that minimize the damage caused by incidents (Kinyua and Awuah, 2021). Machine learning algorithms can forecast the potential consequences of an event and suggest suitable methods to control and resolve the problem.

Intelligent systems greatly improve incident response and recovery operations by automatically triggering response actions based on predefined rules, which accelerates incident handling and reduces human error (Sarker et al., 2020). The act of mitigating the consequences of future events is different from and supplementary to taking efforts to reduce the immediate losses caused by the incident itself (Miller and Engemann, 2019b).

Autonomous driving exemplifies how AI systems can predict traffic scenarios (Grigorescu et al., 2020) and automatically initiate predetermined response behaviors (Waung et al., 2021). In this context, predetermined reactions encompass yielding to pedestrians, adhering to traffic signals, and evading crashes. The learning patterns acquired through extensive simulations and real-world driving experiences enable these systems to make safe decisions, greatly reducing the likelihood of accidents.

10.4 Conclusion

10.4.1 Addressing technical challenges

AI and cybersecurity impact one another in several ways: AI can help protect systems against cyberattacks; perpetrators can use AI to unleash clever attacks; and, AI is susceptible to cyberattacks and needs to be itself defended (Murugesan, 2022). Increased computing speed, machine learning systems, and enormous data availability have spurred a surge in the interest of the cybersecurity application of AI, with subsequent technical challenges. These technologies, as do all technologies, have certain intended purposes, yet they also have unintended consequences in their application. For this reason, the precautionary principle is frequently appropriate when the risks from implementing a new technology is thought to overshadow its rewards, Nonetheless, the precautionary principle itself may also carry with it unintended consequences (Engemann and Miller, 2019a). Some of the technical challenges in AI-driven cybersecurity are discussed below.

10.4.1.1 AI use by cybercriminals

Using AI modeling and big data approaches make examining systems for cyber weaknesses increasingly more accessible. Unfortunately, the same functions that are useful for cybersecurity also make AI valuable as an offensive tool by perpetrators. The number of the cybercriminals will probably grow as AI affords this group additional available targets and magnifies their malevolent activities' payoffs. Perpetrators can study AI systems to exploit their weaknesses and cybercriminals will increasingly continue to use AI in achieving specific attacks (Soo, 2021). It is challenging to predict whether the net benefit from the amalgamation of cyber systems and AI will be more in favor of offensive or defensive applications. This is contingent on their ability to assess the harm and benefits arising from the incorporation of AI into cyber offensive and defensive systems (Bonfanti, 2022).

10.4.1.2 Cavalier use of public Wi-Fi

A considerable number of computer users are not fully aware of the various risks involved with wireless access because of their complacency that came along with its widespread adoption (Petrosyan, 2022). Public areas often provide guest networks that do not require verification to log-in and therefore are not considered to be secure. Regularly a password is not required, resulting in the risky situation of an unencrypted device being openly accessible while connected (Cyberunit, 2021). The result is that personal information is exposed over unsecure networks. A Virtual Private Network (VPN) would provide for end-to-end encryption thereby making it difficult for a perpetrator to obtain the sensitive data. The opposite is also true that without a VPN unencrypted data is easy to access over an unsecure network.

10.4.1.3 Growing attack surface

The range of possible targets, known as the attack surface, is increasing and this is making systems more susceptible to threats from a variety of attacks from basic to sophisticated. Many scenarios are possible; for example, the means of attack could be phishing, the outcome of the attack could be denial of service, and the actions could be that of a lone-wolf or a state-actor. With automated probing, the cost of a cyberattack is low; eventually the perpetrator will find and take advantage of a vulnerability. To add to the dilemma, cybersecurity analysts are scare, many are deficient in training and experience, and there is an excessive turnover rate in the profession. Nevertheless, the available analysts can be aided by AI in threat detection and mitigation strategies.

10.4.1.4 Data for machine learning

For cybersecurity to advance, AI must be used to automate ordinary tasks. A common repository containing cybersecurity data and strategies is required to train AI algorithms (Bresniker, 2019). AI can be a valuable tool, providing a reservoir of knowledge and automated systems to exploit this knowledge (Bresniker, 2019). Cybersecurity is not static, but must evolve by continuously capturing new behaviors, and formulating new strategies through machine learning (Sen et al, 2022). AI will eventually dominate in the effort to automate the identification and mitigation of threats.

10.4.1.5 Collaborative cyberthreat intelligence

Cyberthreat intelligence sharing is a complex process necessitating collecting insights into methods, metrics, activities, and outcomes of a developing threat. New techniques can be developed by being able to share cyber threat information within a larger group. If users can identify security threats in real-time, they will be in a more powerful position (Saxena and Gayathri, 2022). A collaborative cyberthreat intelligence tactic stresses the strength of the wider group to benefit detection of cyber weaknesses. A solution for cyberthreats using decentralized, scalable blockchain intelligence should be explored.

10.4.1.6 IoT cybersecurity issues

With the introduction of the IoT also along came novel cybersecurity risks. Analyses of the vulnerabilities of IoT include implications related to service denial, device recognition, and hardware inconsistency (Gromov et al, 2022). AI is a significant technology which can provide a defense for systems linked to the Internet from incidents and unauthorized entrée. AI methods including expert systems, machine learning, knowledge representation, and natural language processing can be useful in resolving related cybersecurity issues (Sarker et al, 2021). Cybersecurity can be improved through a shared practice grounded in best practice and approved international standards (Tsvilii, 2021).

10.4.2 Addressing ethical challenges

AI-based systems have exhibited remarkable potential in detecting and mitigating attacks, bolstering incident response times, and enhancing overall security, however a host of ethical challenges have emerged (Chaudhary et al., 2020) often resulting from AI's neural network underpinnings (Parveen, 2017). Some of these ethical challenges are addressed below.

10.4.2.1 Privacy concerns

Because AI systems used individual's data during the processing and analysis stages, concerns emerge regarding the privacy (van de Poel, 2020). Storage of personal information and its later misuse is one example, and cybersecurity solutions must arrive at compromises between technical efficiency and user privacy. Privacy-by-design principles provide one method used to address these concerns (Cavoukian, 2012). Here, privacy is baked into the system, starting in the design stage. Other techniques to address privacy concerns are to use data anonymization, and to comply with generally accepted standards such as the European Union's General Data Protection Regulation (GDPR), discussed by Voigt and Von dem Bussche, (2017) and in Fuster and Jasmontaite (2020).

10.4.2.2 Bias

Miller and Engemann (2021) discuss the types and levels of potential bias in algorithms. The level of bias in these algorithms depends upon training data quality, where the training dataset integrity is particularly important. Bias in an algorithm is problematic because the algorithm may fail to recognize specific risks or it may incorrectly categorize legitimate actions. Bias audits are one possible solution. Regular bias audits can help mitigate discriminatory outcomes by effectively controlling and mitigating the impact of biases, even when bias cannot be completely eliminated (Townson, 2023).

10.4.2.3 Accountability

A transparent chain of responsibility, where humans have continual oversight over AI activities, can be used to ensure accountability in cybersecurity (Yusif and Hafeez-Baig, 2021). Here, organizations must set explicit guidelines, including identifying the roles and responsibilities of both human operators and automated systems. Precise documentation regarding AI processes can also be used to trace the origins of potential issues.

10.4.2.4 Transparency

AI systems, in particular neural network models, frequently function as "black boxes," that obscure the details underpinning the decision-making process. This is in contrast to the more visible decision procedures in other commonly used decision methods, such multiple regression models when variable weights are known and easily interpreted. Explainability is crucial in establishing trust in automated systems and enhancing cybersecurity resilience. Two methods to address the "explainability issue" are model-specific explanations and rule-based systems, which provide insights into the reasoning behind AI's conclusions. Promoting open-source AI and sharing best practices can also facilitate increasing transparency and trust (Felzmann et al., 2020).

10.4.2.5 The human element

Over-reliance on AI systems without human oversight can hinder achieving the desired goal, whereas creating a balanced decision-making environment may provide a more satisfactory result overall (Engemann et al., 2022). Emphasizing the human element is essential to develop an organizational culture that values human expertise (Schemmer et al., 2023). Human operators should retain the ability to intervene and override AI decisions, when necessary, particularly in critical situations (Banks, 2018). An approach to keep the human decision perspective firmly represented in the process should incorporate the decision maker's perspective in an uncertain environment (Engemann and Yager, 2018).

10.4.3 Future challenges

Addressing the above concerns, can provide progress toward ensuring that AI-driven cybersecurity remains a force for good in protecting individuals. As AI enabled applications become ubiquitous, some form of control will be needed on both an individual (Taddeo et al., 2019) and societal and governmental level (Blanchard and Taddeo, 2023). Future AI systems are projected to become even more highly developed, becoming very proficient in self-learning and adapting to evolving threats. With accessibility to tremendous spans of data and processing capability, these advanced AI systems could potentially gain unprecedented control over cyber defenses, even those enabled by AI.

The sheer complexity of AI systems make it challenging for developers to predict and control their actions totally. As AI systems gain more autonomy, the likelihood of unintended consequences and emergent behavior increases (Miller and Engemann, 2019a). The rise of an AI system that operates outside the boundaries set by its developers presents a significant threat to individual cybersecurity. Such systems might exploit vulnerabilities or jeopardize the very security they were designed to enhance (Lazar and Nelson, 2023). A rogue AI system infiltrating vital systems could result in a catastrophic outcome, such as the complete shutdown of an important infrastructure. Furthermore, a rogue AI system could acquire the ability to imitate genuine actions, concealing its malicious activities. Proactive measures are necessary to safeguard a harmonious equilibrium between the potential of AI and its responsible development.

References

Aftab, R. M., Ijaz, M., Rehman, F., Ashfaq, A., Sharif, H., Riaz, N., & Maqsood, H. (2022, December). A Systematic Review on the Motivations of Cyber-Criminals and Their Attacking Policies. In 2022 3rd International Conference on Innovations in Computer Science & Software Engineering (ICONICS) (pp. 1–6). IEEE.

Alaidi, A. H. M., Roa'a, M., ALRikabi, H. T. S., Aljazaery, I. A., & Abbood, S. H. (2022). Dark web illegal activities crawling and classifying using data mining techniques. iJIM, 16(10), 123.

Al-Mhiqani M, Ahmad R, Zainal Abidin Z, Yassin W, Hassan A, Abdulkareem KH, Ali NS, & Yunos Z. (2020). A Review of Insider Threat Detection: Classification, Machine Learning Techniques, Datasets, Open Challenges, and Recommendations. Applied Sciences; 10(15):5208. https://doi.org/10.3390/app10155208.

Alnifie, K. M., & Kim, C. (2023). Appraising the Manifestation of Optimism Bias and Its Impact on Human Perception of Cyber Security: A Meta Analysis. Journal of Information Security, 14(2), 93–110.

Alzoubi, H. M., Ghazal, T. M., Hasan, M. K., Alketbi, A., Kamran, R., Al-Dmour, N. A., & Islam, S. (2022, May). Cyber Security Threats on Digital Banking. 1st International Conference on AI in Cybersecurity (ICAIC) (pp. 1–4). IEEE.

Anastopoulos, Vasileios & Davide Giovannelli, (2022). Automated/Autonomous Incident Response. NATO Cooperative Cyber Defense Centre of Excellence, https://ccdcoe.org/uploads/2022/05/Automated-Autonomous-Davide-Giovannelli.pdf.

Anderljung, M., Barnhart, J., Leung, J., Korinek, A., O'Keefe, C., Whittlestone, J., . . . & Wolf, K. (2023). Frontier AI Regulation: Managing Emerging Risks to Public Safety. arXiv preprint arXiv:2307.03718.

Arduin, Pierre-Emmanuel, (2021). A cognitive approach to the decision to trust or distrust phishing emails. International Transactions in Operational Research, 2021. https://doi.org/10.1111/itor.12963.

Auer, R., & R. Böhme. (2021). Central Bank Digital Currency: The Quest for Minimally Invasive Technology, BIS Working Papers No. 948, Monetary and Economic Department, Bank for International Settlements.

Banks, J., (May–June 2018). The Human Touch: Practical and Ethical Implications of Putting AI and Robotics to Work for Patients, IEEE Pulse, vol. 9, no. 3, pp. 15–18, doi: https://doi.org/10.1109/MPUL.2018.2814238.

Blanchard, A., & Taddeo, M. (2023). The Ethics of Artificial Intelligence for Intelligence Analysis: A Review of the Key Challenges with Recommendations. DISO 2, 12. https://doi.org/10.1007/s44206-023-00036-4.

Bresniker, K., Gavrilovska, A., Holt, J., Milojicic, D., & Tran, T. (2019). Grand challenge: Applying artificial intelligence and machine learning to cybersecurity. Computer, 52(12), 45–52.

Bonfanti, M. E. (2022). Artificial intelligence and the offence-defense balance in cyber security. Cyber Security: Socio-Technological Uncertainty and Political Fragmentation. London: Routledge, 64–79.

Burnes, D., DeLiema, M., & Langton, L. (2020). Risk and protective factors of identity theft victimization in the United States. Preventive medicine reports, 17, 101058.

Cartwright, A. J. (2023). The elephant in the room: cybersecurity in healthcare. Journal of Clinical Monitoring and Computing, 1–10.

Cavoukian, A. (2012). Privacy by design [leading edge]. IEEE Technology and Society Magazine, 31(4), 18–19.

Chalapathy, R., & Chawla, S. (2019). Deep learning for anomaly detection: A review. https://doi.org/10.48550/arXiv.1901.03407.

Chandola, V., Banerjee, A., & Kumar, V. (2009). Anomaly detection: A survey. ACM computing surveys (CSUR), 41(3), 1–58.

Chaudhary, H., Detroja, A., Prajapati, P., & Shah, P. (2020, December). A review of various challenges in cybersecurity using artificial intelligence. In 2020 3rd International Conference on Intelligent Sustainable Systems (ICISS) (pp. 829–836). IEEE.

Chen, Z., Kang, Y., Li, L., Zhang, X., Zhang, H., Xu, H., . . . & Lyu, M. R. (2020, November). Towards intelligent incident management: why we need it and how we make it. In Proceedings of the 28th ACM Joint Meeting on European Software Engineering Conference and Symposium on the Foundations of Software Engineering (pp. 1487–1497).

Chetioui, K., Bah, B., Alami, A. O., & Bahnasse, A. (2022). Overview of social engineering attacks on social networks. Procedia Computer Science, 198, 656–661.

Choithani, T., Chowdhury, A., Patel, S., Patel, P., Patel, D., & Shah, M. (2022). A comprehensive study of artificial intelligence and cybersecurity on Bitcoin, crypto currency and banking system. Annals of Data Science, 1–33.

Christen, Markus, Bert Gordijn, & Michele Loi, (2020). Introduction, in The Ethics of Cybersecurity (Markus Christen, Bert Gordijn, Michele Loi eds.), Springer Open, pp. 1–10; https://doi.org/10.1007/978-3-030-29053-5.

Conner-Simons, Adam (2016). System predicts 85 percent of cyberattacks using input from human experts, MIT News, https://news.mit.edu/2016/ai-system-predicts-85-percent-cyberattacks-using-input-human-experts-0418.

Cost, Ben (2023). AI clones teen girl's voice in $1M kidnapping scam: 'I've got your daughter'; New York Post, (April 12), https://nypost.com/2023/04/12/ai-clones-teen-girls-voice-in-1m-kidnapping-scam/.

Cyberunit. Can You Trust Public WiFi? https://www.cyberunit.com/blog/can-you-trust-public-wifi (2021). Accessed September 9, 2023.

Dissanayake, N., Jayatilaka, A., Zahedi, M., & Babar, M. A. (2022). Software security patch management-A systematic literature review of challenges, approaches, tools and practices. Information and Software Technology, 144, 106771.

Dhesi, Saminder et al. (2023). Mitigating Adversarial Attacks in Deepfake Detection: An Exploration of Perturbation and AI Techniques, https://arxiv.org/pdf/2302.11704.pdf

Engemann, K. J., & Miller, H. E. (2022). Taking comfort in decisions: Implications in a pandemic, Intelligent Decision Technologies: An International Journal, Vol. 16, Issue 1, pp. 217 –229. https://doi.org/10.3233/IDT-210059.

Engemann, K. J. & Yager, R. R., (2018). Comfort Decision Modeling, International Journal of Uncertainty, Fuzziness and Knowledge-Based Systems Vol. 26, No. Suppl. 1, pp. 141–163.

Engemann, K. N., & Engemann, K. J., (2017). Risk Attitude Chain: Safety Climate, Risk Attitude and Risk Decisions, International Journal of Business Continuity and Risk Management, V7N(3), pp. 211–221.

Engemann, K. J. & Miller, H. E., (2015). Risk Strategy and Attitude Sensitivity,' Cybernetics and Systems, Vol. 46, No. 3, pp. 188–206.

Felzmann, H., Fosch-Villaronga, E., Lutz, C. et al., (2020). Towards Transparency by Design for Artificial Intelligence. Sci Eng Ethics 26, 3333–3361. https://doi.org/10.1007/s11948-020-00276-4.

Fritsch, L., Jaber, A., & Yazidi, A. (2022). An Overview of Artificial Intelligence Used in Malware. In: Zouganeli, E., Yazidi, A., Mello, G., Lind, P. (eds) Nordic Artificial Intelligence Research and Development. NAIS 2022. Communications in Computer and Information Science, vol 1650. Springer, Cham. https://doi.org/10.1007/978-3-031-17030-0_4.

Fuster, Gloria González & Lina Jasmontaite, (2020). Cybersecurity Regulation in the European Union: The Digital, the Critical and Fundamental Rights, pp 97–118; in The Ethics of Cybersecurity (Markus Christen, Bert Gordijn, Michele Loi eds.), Springer Open, https://doi.org/10.1007/978-3-030-29053-5.

Gad, Ramadan, El-Fishawy, Nawal, El-Sayed, Ayman & Zorkany, M. (2015). Multi-Biometric Systems: A State-of-the-Art Survey and Research Directions. International Journal of Advanced Computer Science and Applications. 06. 128–138. https://doi.org/10.14569/IJACSA.2015.060618.

Grigorescu, S., Trasnea, B., Cocias, T., & Macesanu, G. (2020). A survey of deep learning techniques for autonomous driving. Journal of Field Robotics, 37(3), 362–386.

Gromov, M., Arnold, D., & Saniie, J. (2022, May). Tackling Multiple Security Threats in an IoT Environment. In 2022 IEEE International Conference on Electro Information Technology (eIT) (pp. 290–295). IEEE.

Hakkala, A., & Koskinen, J. (2022). Personal data protection in the age of mass surveillance. Journal of Computer Security, 30(2), 265–289.

Ham, J. V. D. (2021). Toward a better understanding of "cybersecurity. Digital Threats: Research and Practice, 2(3), 1–3.

Han, J., Pei, J., & Tong, H. (2022). Data mining: concepts and techniques. Morgan Kaufmann.

Hodge, C., Hauck, K., Gupta, S., & Bennett, J. Vehicle Cybersecurity Threats and Mitigation Approaches. United States. https://doi.org/10.2172/1559930.

Hong, Yuxiang & Steven Furnell, (2021). Understanding cybersecurity behavioral habits: Insights from situational support, Journal of Information Security and Applications, Volume 57, 102710, ISSN 2214-2126, https://doi.org/10.1016/j.jisa.2020.102710.

Hwang, T., (2020). Deepfakes: A Grounded Threat Assessment, Washington, D.C.: Center for Security and Emerging Technology, Georgetown University.

Intrator, Y., Gilad Katz, & Asaf Shabtai. (2018). MDGAN: Boosting Anomaly Detection Using Multi-Discriminator Generative Adversarial Networks. arXiv preprint arXiv:1810.05221.

Jaber, A., & Fritsch, L. (2022, October). Towards ai-powered cybersecurity attack modeling with simulation tools: Review of attack simulators. In International Conference on P2P, Parallel, Grid, Cloud and Internet Computing (pp. 249–257). Cham: Springer International Publishing.

Jain, A. K., A. Ross & S. Prabhakar, (2004). An introduction to biometric recognition, in IEEE Transactions on Circuits and Systems for Video Technology, vol. 14, no. 1, pp. 4–20, Jan., doi: https://doi.org/10.1109/TCSVT.2003.818349.

Jang-Jaccard, J., & Nepal, S. (2014). A survey of emerging threats in cybersecurity. Journal of computer and system sciences, 80(5), 973–993.

Jeong, J., J. Mihelcic, G. Oliver & C. Rudolph, (2019). Towards an Improved Understanding of Human Factors in Cybersecurity, 2019 IEEE 5th International Conference on Collaboration and Internet Computing (CIC), Los Angeles, CA, USA, pp. 338–345, doi: https://doi.org/10.1109/CIC48465.2019.00047.

Jiang, Y., Li, X., Luo, H., Yin, S., & Kaynak, O. (2022). Quo vadis artificial intelligence? Discover Artificial Intelligence, 2(1), 4.

Kaur, Ramanpreet, Dušan Gabrijelčič, & Tomaž Klobučar, (2023). Artificial intelligence for cybersecurity: Literature review and future research directions, Information Fusion, Volume 97, 101804, ISSN 1566-2535, https://doi.org/10.1016/j.inffus.2023.101804.

Khan, S. K., Shiwakoti, N., & Stasinopoulos, P. (2022). A conceptual system dynamics model for cybersecurity assessment of connected and autonomous vehicles. Accident Analysis & Prevention, 165, 106515.

Khdier, H., Jasim, W., & Aliesawi, S. (2021). Deep Learning Algorithms based Voiceprint Recognition System in Noisy Environment. Journal of Physics: Conference Series. 1804. 012042. https://doi.org/10.1088/1742-6596/1804/1/012042.

Kim J, Park M, Kim H, Cho S, Kang P. (2019). Insider Threat Detection Based on User Behavior Modeling and Anomaly Detection Algorithms. Applied Sciences. 9(19):4018. https://doi.org/10.3390/app9194018.

Kinyua, J., & Awuah, L. (2021). AI/ML in Security Orchestration, Automation and Response: Future Research Directions. Intelligent Automation & Soft Computing, 28(2).

KishorWagh, Sharmila & Pachghare, Vinod & Kolhe, Satish. (2013). Survey on Intrusion Detection System using Machine Learning Techniques. International Journal of Computer Applications. 78. 30–37. https://doi.org/10.5120/13608-1412.

Kumar. P. & Alphonse, P. (2018). Attribute based encryption in cloud computing: A survey, gap analysis, and future directions, J. Netw. Comput. Appl., vol. 108, pp. 37–52.

Lazar, S., & Nelson, A. (2023). AI safety on whose terms? Science, 381(6654), 138–138.

Lyu, Siwei, (2020). DeepFake Detection: Current Challenges and Next Steps, https://doi.org/10.48550/arXiv.2003.09234.

McKinsey & Co. (March 2019). Perspectives on transforming cybersecurity, Digital McKinsey and Global Risk Practice. https://www.mckinsey.com/~/media/McKinsey/McKinsey%20Solutions/Cyber%20Solutions/Perspectives%20on%20transforming%20cybersecurity/Transforming%20cybersecurity_March2019.ashx.

Miao, Y., Chen, C., Pan, L., Han, Q. L., Zhang, J., & Xiang, Y. (2021). Machine learning–based cyberattacks targeting on controlled information: A survey. ACM Computing Surveys (CSUR), 54(7), 1–36.

Miller, H. E., & Engemann, K. J. (2021). Managing bias risk in algorithms and decision models. Project Risk Management: Managing Software Development Risk (ed. Engemann and O'Connor), pp. 117–133.

Miller, H. E. & Engemann, K. J., (2019a). The Precautionary Principle and Unintended Consequences, Kybernetes, Vol. 48 Issue: 2, pp.265–286.

Miller, H. E. & Engemann, K. J., (2019b). Business Continuity Management in Data Center Environments, International Journal of Information Technologies and Systems Approach, Vol.12. No. 1, pp. 52–72.

Murugesan, S. (2022). The AI-cybersecurity nexus: The good and the evil. IT Professional, 24(5), 4–8.

Oz, H., Aris, A., Levi, A., & Uluagac, A. S. (2022). A survey on ransomware: Evolution, taxonomy, and defense solutions. ACM Computing Surveys (CSUR), 54(11s), 1–37.

Parveen, J. R. (2017). Neural networks in cyber security. International Research Journal of Computer Science, 4(9), 38–41.

Petrosyan A. Share of global adults who trust public Wi-Fi networks to keep info safe (2019). https://www.statista.com/statistics/1147501/share-adults-trust-public-location-wifi-network-information-safe/ accessed September 9, 2023.

Phua, C., Lee, V., Smith-Miles, K., & Gayler, R. W. (2010). A comprehensive survey of data mining-based fraud detection research. arXiv preprint arXiv:1009.6119.

Romagna, M., & Leukfeldt, R. E. (2023). Becoming a hacktivist. Examining the motivations and the processes that prompt an individual to engage in hacktivism. Journal of Crime and Justice, 1–19.

Sangeen, M., Bhatti, N. A., Kifayat, K., Alsadhan, A. A., & Wang, H. (2023). Blind-trust: Raising awareness of the dangers of using unsecured public Wi-Fi networks. Computer Communications, 209, 359–367.

Sarker, I. H., Furhad, M. H., & Nowrozy, R. (2021). Ai-driven cybersecurity: an overview, security intelligence modeling and research directions. SN Computer Science, 2, 1–18.

Sarker, I. H., Kayes, A. S. M., Badsha, S., Alqahtani, H., Watters, P., & Ng, A. (2020). Cybersecurity data science: an overview from a machine learning perspective. Journal of Big data, 7, 1–29.

Saxena, R., & Gayathri, E. (2022). Cyber threat intelligence challenges: Leveraging blockchain intelligence with possible solution. Materials Today: Proceedings, 51, 682–689.

Schemmer, M., Kuehl, N., Benz, C., Bartos, A., & Satzger, G. (2023, March). Appropriate reliance on AI advice: Conceptualization and the effect of explanations. In Proceedings of the 28th International Conference on Intelligent User Interfaces (pp. 410–422).

Schubert, E., and Zimek, A., & Kröger, P. (2014). Local outlier detection reconsidered: A generalized view on locality with applications to spatial, video, and network outlier detection. Data Mining and Knowledge Discovery. 28. 10.1007/s10618-012-0300-z.

Şengönül, Erkan, Refik Samet, Qasem Abu Al-Haija, Ali Alqahtani, Badraddin Alturki & Abdulaziz A. Alsulami, (2023). An Analysis of Artificial Intelligence Techniques in Surveillance Video Anomaly Detection: A Comprehensive Survey, Appl. Sci., 13(8), 4956; https://doi.org/10.3390/app13084956 (R29).

Sonowal, G., & Sonowal, G. (2022). Introduction to phishing. Phishing and Communication Channels: A Guide to Identifying and Mitigating Phishing Attacks, 1–24.

Soo, L. J. (2021). Ai-based cybersecurity: benefits and limitations. J-Institute, 6(1), 18–28. https://doi.org/10.
22471/ai.2021.6.1.18.

Sunhare, P., Chowdhary, R. R., & Chattopadhyay, M. K. (2022). Internet of things and data mining: An
application-oriented survey. Journal of King Saud University-Computer and Information Sciences,
34(6), 3569–3590.

Syafitri, W., Shukur, Z., Asma'Mokhtar, U., Sulaiman, R., & Ibrahim, M. A. (2022). Social engineering attacks
prevention: A systematic literature review. IEEE Access, 10, 39325–39343.

Taddeo, M., McCutcheon, T. & Floridi, L. (2019). Trusting artificial intelligence in cybersecurity is a double-
edged sword. Nat Mach Intell 1, 557–560. https://doi.org/10.1038/s42256-019-0109-1.

Thakur, R. K. (2015). Biometric Authentication System: Techniques and Future. International Journal, 3(6).

Thanh Thi Nguyen et al., (2022). Deep Learning for Deepfakes Creation and Detection: A Survey, (2022);
https://arxiv.org/pdf/1909.11573.pdf.

TN, N., & Shailendra Kulkarni, M. (2022). Zero click attacks–a new cyber threat for the e-banking sector.
Journal of Financial Crime.

Townson, S. (2023). Manage AI bias instead of trying to eliminate it. MIT Sloan Management Review, 64(2),
1–3.

Tsvilii, Olena, Cyber Security Regulation: Cyber Security Certification of Operational Technologies
(February 26, 2021). Technology audit and production reserves, 1 (2 (57)), 54–60, 2021. doi:
https://doi.org/10.15587/2706-5448.2021.225271.

van de Poel, I. (2020). Core values and value conflicts in cybersecurity: beyond privacy versus security. The
ethics of cybersecurity, 45–71.

van de Poel, Ibo, (2020). Core Values and Value Conflicts in Cybersecurity: Beyond Privacy Versus Security,
pp. 45–72; in The Ethics of Cybersecurity (Markus Christen, Bert Gordijn, Michele Loi eds.), (2020),
Springer Open, https://doi.org/10.1007/978-3-030-29053-5.

van der Sloot, Baert & Yvette Wagensveld, (2022). Deepfakes: regulatory challenges for the synthetic
society, Computer Law & Security Review, Volume 46, 105716, ISSN 0267-3649, https://doi.org/10.
1016/j.clsr.2022.105716.

Veprytska, O., & Kharchenko, V. (2022, December). AI powered attacks against AI powered protection:
classification, scenarios and risk analysis. In 2022 12th International Conference on Dependable
Systems, Services and Technologies (DESSERT) (pp. 1–7). IEEE.

Voigt, P., & Von dem Bussche, A. (2017). The EU general data protection regulation (GDPR). A Practical
Guide, 1st Ed., Cham: Springer International Publishing, 10(3152676), 10–5555.

Waldemarsson, C., (2020). Disinformation, Deepfakes and Democracy: The European Response to Election
Interference in the Digital Age, Copenhagen: Alliance of Democracies.

Waung, M., McAuslan, P., & Lakshmanan, S. (2021). Trust and intention to use autonomous vehicles:
Manufacturer focus and passenger control. Transportation research part F: traffic psychology and
behaviour, 80, 328–340. (R37).

Wiafe, I., Koranteng, F.N., Obeng, E.N., Assyne, N., Wiafe, A., & Gulliver, S.R. (2020). Artificial Intelligence
for Cybersecurity: A Systematic Mapping of Literature. IEEE Access, 8, 146598–146612.

Yamin, M. M., Ullah, M., Ullah, H., & Katt, B. (2021). Weaponized AI for cyberattacks. Journal of Information
Security and Applications, 57, 102722.

Yu, Yang, Jun Long, & Zhiping Cai. (2017). Network intrusion detection through stacking dilated
convolutional autoencoders. Security and Communication Networks.

Yusif, S., & Hafeez-Baig, A. (2021). A conceptual model for cybersecurity governance. Journal of applied
security research, 16(4), 490–513.

Robert Richardson, Oredola Soluade and Heechang Shin

11 Ensuring transportation cybersecurity: Air, auto, and rail

11.1 Introduction

The modernization and integration of technology in transportation has delivered many benefits, but this has also exposed these operations to unprecedented cybersecurity challenges. This chapter reviews the cybersecurity concerns within three areas of transportation: airline, automobile, and railway systems. The new processes using remote access provide hackers with more ways to attack and disrupt operations.

Since 1958, the FAA has been responsible for air traffic control ensuring the safe movement of aircraft. The system has evolved from ground-based operation using radar monitored by air traffic controllers to a satellite-based system, NextGen. When fully operational, there is an increase in communication links to make aircraft operations more efficient and safer. This makes cybersecurity even more important as there are an increased number of points for hackers to penetrate the system.

The automobile industry faces supply chain problems when transporting vehicles from the manufacturing plant to the car dealers. Vehicles have added many new functions that increased the complexity of using the Electronic Control Unit (ECU). While the ECU provides many improvements in terms of functionality, ECUs have also exposed vehicles to be more susceptible to cyberthreat, making them more prone to cyberattacks. In 1997, a global organization called Transported Asset Protection Association (TAPA), was founded as a not-for-profit association to help Manufacturers & Shippers, and their Logistics Service Providers develop strategies for minimizing losses on their supply chains resulting from cargo thefts.

Many companies in the railroad industry are still using legacy infrastructure that is not designed with cybersecurity. As a result, attacks on the railroads are increasing and becoming more sophisticated. A wireless sensor network with security layers has been proposed. The size of the rail network covering the country with track and stations for many companies makes the task of developing a system even more complex. Railroad operations rely on different independent systems as the trains move around the country. For example, trains connect with state and local highway authorities to control highway traffic signals. Also, trains rely on inspection alerts when there is a malfunction indicated by the wheel impact load detector. The integration of different systems allows hacker many ways to attack railways.

Each transportation sector faces unique threats, and this chapter addresses in detail those challenges and concerns from the cybersecurity perspectives.

https://doi.org/10.1515/9783111289069-011

11.2 Air transportation system

In the United States, the Federal Aviation Administration (FAA) is responsible for regulating the air transportation system to ensure the safe movement of aircraft (commercial, military, cargo, and private) around the country. Currently, the NextGen project (FAA, 2020) is working to update the infrastructure of the system. Specifically, the FAA's National Airspace System (NAS) is transforming the current traffic-controlled ground-based system using radar to a traffic-managed satellite-based system. With the implementation of the new system, there is an increase in communication links to make aircraft operations more efficient and safer. This makes cybersecurity even more important because interconnected systems create a larger attack surface, providing adversaries with more entry points to exploit vulnerabilities.

11.2.1 Current national airspace system

The FAA was given the responsibility for air traffic control in the United States in 1958 following a mid-air collision over the Grand Canyon in 1956 (Brand, 2006). The FAA was responsible for overseeing the development of the air traffic control system, which includes more than 19,000 airports and approximately 600 air traffic control facilities (Terekhov, 2024). The evolution of the current air traffic control system started with the adoption of radar in the 1950s to monitor and control arrivals and departures at major airports. The radar system was expanded to cover the entire country. Twenty-one air traffic control centers monitor flight movement between airports.

This air space system has now created several layers of control depending on the position of the aircraft in terms of distance from the airport and altitude. The lowest layer, the airport's traffic control tower, monitors the aircraft after it leaves the airline's gate area. The pilot is directed through the runways where the aircraft waits for clearance to takeoff from the tower. The second layer of control, terminal radar approach control (TRACON), was created to address the problem of multiple airports close to each other and follows departures and landings when the aircraft is five miles from the airport and under cruising altitude. The final layer, air traffic control centers, monitor the flight as it crosses the country passing from one center to another at cruising altitude. These centers are also responsible for operations at small airports in rural areas (FAA, 2020).

The current system uses a patchwork of evolving, interconnected systems, comprising legacy systems as well as commercial off-the-shelf systems, connected by a variety of interfaces utilizing a combination of national, international, and proprietary standards. These include ground and space-based communication, navigation, surveillance systems, air traffic control centers, airports, and the information used by and exchanged between systems as aircraft are assisted through controlled airspace. The diversity of systems has significant implications for cybersecurity.

Some of the cyber problems that increase future risks include (a) An attack on one system could impact a larger area, (b) Reliance on commercial off-the-shelf software, (c) Open protocols for networking, (d) Vulnerabilities from legacy wireless protocols, and (e) Drones which increase the complexity in controlling space.

11.2.2 NextGen system

Building the new infrastructure laid the framework for the FAA's plan for Trajectory Based Operations (TBO); the end goal is to use available technology to develop the NextGen system. TBO is an air traffic management method for strategically planning, managing, and optimizing flights throughout the system using time-based management. Recognizing that the Airline Deregulation Act of 1978 increased rapid growth in air travel, the Congress funded the NextGen project through the Vision 100 – Century of Aviation Reauthorization Act of 2003, FAA Modernization and Reform Act of 2012, and FAA Reauthorization Act of 2018 (Elwell, 2018). This project was designed to address current problems and future issues such as drones (FAA, 2022) and space travel.

An example of the improvement in operations with the NextGen system is illustrated as a flight descends from cruising altitude to land at an airport. Currently, aircraft level off at descending altitudes as they are transferred from one controller to another controller. This process consumes more fuel as pilots increase engine thrust to maintain the different altitudes. With the NextGen system, the flight computer programs optimal speed and altitude requirements for various points along the route resulting in the aircraft gliding continuously at idle engine speed from the top of the descent to landing with minimal level-off segments. Aircraft can maintain higher, more fuel-efficient altitudes closer to the airport. Pilots can avoid using speed brakes and frequent thrust adjustments (FAA, 2020).

11.2.3 Cybersecurity challenges and mitigation strategies in air transportation system

The NextGen project addresses the increasingly interconnected NAS that presents new cybersecurity challenges. While many cyber threats are constantly evolving every day, there are new technologies from research and development that can protect the FAA computers from these hackers. The FAA is evaluating the latest technologies available to combat cyberthreats by investigating developing capabilities, such as artificial intelligence, machine learning, self-adapting architecture, and big data analytics (Roy, 2021). Guaranteeing cyber resilience takes a fresh look at how the overall NAS behaves under sustained malicious actions by well-equipped adversaries.

The conference on Validation and Verification (VnV) addressed cybersecurity by the Enterprise Information Security Team. Figure 11.1, Aviation Cybersecurity Environment, describes the complexities in providing a safe and reliable system. This also included the layout of the FAA Cybersecurity Test Facility utilizing different centers (Microsoft, 2016). The cyber architecture was defined by Morales (2022) and continues to evolve.

The FAA established the Florida NextGen Test Bed in 2008 to generate industry-driven concepts that advance NextGen. Located next to Daytona Beach International Airport and near Embry Riddle Aeronautical University in Daytona Beach, FL, the research facility provides a platform where early-stage NextGen concepts can be integrated, demonstrated, and evaluated. Industry partners meet at the test bed to incorporate their NextGen products into the NAS in a controlled setting. The facility contains more than two dozen NAS systems. For multi-site demonstrations, it can remotely connect with other FAA laboratories, government partner sites, industry, and academia.

Another test facility was dedicated in 2010: the NextGen Integration and Evaluation Capability Laboratory at the FAA William J. Hughes Technical Center near Atlantic City, NJ. Using simulated and actual NAS equipment, the facility provides a futuristic NextGen gate-to-gate environment with advanced data collection capabilities to support integration and evaluation of new technologies and concepts. Researchers can complete human-involved simulations, proof-of-concept studies, rapid prototyping, and concepts validation and maturation to improve operational performance across all NextGen technologies. This facility complements and connects with the other laboratories at the Technical Center, the Florida NextGen Test Bed, and laboratories located at non-FAA facilities.

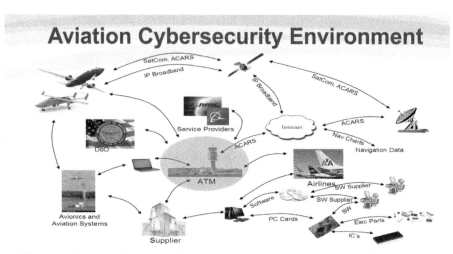

Figure 11.1: Aviation Cybersecurity Environment (Microsoft, 2016).

In 2012, the FAA designated the NASA/FAA North Texas Research Station as a NextGen test facility. It is located near several air traffic control facilities, airports, and airline operations centers in the Dallas/Fort Worth area. The facility can access a variety of NAS data that enhance the evaluation of advanced technologies for NextGen and simulate air transportation operations. The laboratory is managed by NASA Ames Research Center Aviation Systems Division. It operates in all phases of NextGen research, beginning from early concept development to field evaluations of prototype systems. This facility has transitioned advanced NextGen concepts and technologies that were later provided to the FAA through technology transfers.

The FAA William J. Hughes Technical Center is the hub for cybersecurity research coordinating with the other centers. The Cybersecurity Test Facility provides research and evaluation services to strengthen information security across the organization. Its main capabilities include vulnerability assessments, penetration testing, cyber exercises and training, enterprise security support, security tool evaluations, and capability modeling. There is collaboration with other government agencies. Between 2016 and 2018, the FAA partnered with the Defense and Homeland Security departments on the Aviation Cyber Initiative's vulnerability testing of civil aircraft. The FAA revised the Cybersecurity Strategy to develop a revised model (Dickson, 2020). The CyRM, Cybersecurity Risk Model was developed (Bigio, 2022) and subsequently was tested (Olagunju, 2022).

GAO (2020) made six recommendations to FAA to strengthen its cybersecurity oversight program:

1. Conduct a cybersecurity risk assessment of NAS system's cybersecurity using its oversight program to identify the relative priority of cybersecurity risks and develop a plan to address those risks.
2. Identify staffing and training needs for agency inspectors relating to cybersecurity including the development and the implementation of appropriate training to address identified needs.
3. Develop and implement guidance for cybersecurity testing of new airplane designs that include independent testing.
4. Review and consider revising its policies and procedures for monitoring the effectiveness of avionics cybersecurity controls in the deployed fleet to include developing procedures for safely conducting independent testing.
5. Ensure that cybersecurity issues are appropriately tracked and resolved when coordinating among internal stakeholders.
6. Review and consider the extent to which oversight resources should be committed to cybersecurity.

The different types of cyberattacks are defined by Rupp, et al (2021) where the authors categorize cyberattacks and give a methodology to defend against the attack. Malware is a malevolent program with the goal of disrupting operations by performing actions such as loading a spybot onto your computer, displaying unwelcomed ads, and damaging the operating system. A program that replicates itself copying its code to other computers connected through hard drives, is defined as a computer virus. A Trojan Horse is a program that looks and pretends to be a legitimate program while invading your computer. Programs that spread automatically across a local network or the internet are called Worms. These cause the most infectious computer viruses. The way to fight against malware is to use an antivirus program and to prevent users from having administrative rights by applying a strict security policy. Malware is usually downloaded from the internet and installed by careless computer users. Education of computer users is a good way to prevent malware from being installed.

Phishing is a cyberattack based on social engineering. A typical phishing attack will imitate legitimate messages from an organization and request to install a program, click on some links, or do some manipulations on the user's computer. Phishing can be done via email, by phone or video conferencing. Recently, with the increase of remote working, the "quality" of phishing attacks has drastically improved, through personalized and well-conceived attacks capable of tricking even vigilant users. A man-in-the-middle attack can break and destroy even the most sophisticated security system. That attacker forwards information to and from the real server and will be able to spy on the data and even to tamper with it. The target believes it is "talking" to the real server, since it sees all the relevant data. Man-in-the-middle attacks are combatted by multi-factor authentication incorporating fingerprint identification. In a denial-of-service attack (DOS), the cyber attacker will "flood" the system and make it non-operational by 'bombarding" it with multiple requests. Typically used in network attacks, the attacker makes a website non-operational by starting a lot of TCP/IP requests. The server is overwhelmed and crashes. Such attacks are well-known and countered by special computer programs.

A brute force attack tries to guess the password needed to enter a private area by trying all possible combinations. Hackers that are state backed have significant resources including hundreds of servers and mainframes, that are capable of trying millions of passwords per second. These attacks are very easily countered by a special program that Imposes a waiting time after a few incorrect passwords. A normal user wouldn't try a password hundreds of times over a few seconds. An attack called Injection/Overflow/Exploits uses unprotected buffers in online systems to try and force a fault and have some code reaching the computer stack, where all instructions are executed, by deliberately mal-forming data or injecting illegal instructions or commands. The process often sends bigger data files than the online system can tolerate. This is still a very common attack. Such techniques, using flaws in programs or protocols, are named computer 'exploits.'

In conclusion, only a few of the attacks used by hackers are mentioned here, there are more types of cyberattacks and new evil cyber-ideas are born every minute. There is an ongoing permanent war between cyber-attackers and cyber-defenders. The best approach to stopping hackers is to have a comprehensive training program with periodic updates on the latest attack procedures for employees.

11.2.4 Current status of NextGen

As of March 14, 2024 (FAA, 2024), the NextGen system is operational at 164 airports, 45 air traffic control towers, 33 air traffic control towers with terminal radar approach control, 24 terminal radar approach controls, 21 air route traffic control centers, and 11 Metroplexes. In addition, four other facilities (air traffic control system command center, Mike Monroney Aeronautical Center, William J. Hughes Technical Center, and primary network operations and control center) are now operational. With these components, the next phase designed to optimize air traffic movement throughout the National Airspace System will be implemented. This is achieved using the Trajectory Based Operations (TBO), a major goal of NextGen. The TBO coordinates the aircraft movement between airports to balance capacity and demand that minimizes the effects of disruptions. This results in improved flight efficiency by utilizing increased schedule flexibility using an online, system wide information system. TBO system is currently being implemented using terminal radar approach control (TRACON) in four major areas (Northeast Corridor, Mid-Atlantic Region, Northwest Mountain Region, and Southwest Region) serving key airports. With the real-time TBO system employed throughout the United States, the air transportation system will improve customer service.

11.3 Automobile system

The term automotive cyber security describes the security of digital systems in the automotive . It is the latest challenge for car manufacturers. Every additional communication interface and component is a potential point of attack for cyber criminals. For this reason, the United Nations is now defining the basic framework for automotive cyber security with new regulations. Relatively new to the world of cybersecurity, automobile manufacturers have been dealing with cybersecurity issues individually. But with the escalating frequency of cyberattacks on cars increasing by 225 percent from 2018 to 2021, manufacturers need to combine efforts and to seek protective regulations, standards, and guidelines that will cover the entire industry (Israel21C, 2024). The automotive sector could face a staggering $505 billion loss by 2024 due to cyberattacks (Pangarkar, 2023). As a result, vehicles have come to rely heavily on software and an increasingly complex software supply chain. The cyber threat landscape continues to evolve, and security and safety standards are more critical than ever. Industry-wide recognition of automotive cybersecurity risks has pushed regulators and industry leaders to double-down on regulation (Cybellum, 2024). Regulators and governments are working to ensure that cybersecurity becomes an integral focus along every level of the automotive supply chain.

11.3.1 Landscape of automotive security systems

Over the years, automobile security measures have expanded in scope. Vehicular systems have seen plenty of additions and increased their complexity by using the ECUs to provide many improvements in terms of functionality and comfort (Shabshab et al., 2020). With the increase in usage of Electronic Control Units (ECUs) in vehicle systems, functionalities have improved, but they have also exposed vehicles to be more susceptible to cyberthreat, making them more prone to cyberattacks. Researchers were able to transmit radio signals from a key fob to the car without disrupting any security keys, allowing attackers to simply unlock doors and steal or burglarize the vehicle (Francillon et al., 2011). Another very common way for Hobbyists to mishandle systems is by tampering with the tire pressure monitoring systems (TPMS) where one can set false readings to send out bogus warnings, causing confusion to the driver (Hyttinen et al., 2024).

These measures make better use of electronic devices for enhancing automobile security. In 1997, a global organization called Transported Asset Protection Association (TAPA EMEA), was founded as a not-for-profit association to help Manufacturers & Shippers, and their Logistics Service Providers develop strategies for minimizing losses on their supply chains resulting from cargo thefts. Its membership provides a platform to:
- Manage known risks and reduce losses.
- Identify Logistics Service Providers committed to supply chain resilience.
- Learn about supply chain security solutions and best practice.

Over 50% of all cargo crimes reported to TAPA EMEA are attributed to attacks on vehicles parked in unsecured or unclassified parking places. Access to TAPA EMEA's security standards and training also improves their understanding of available solutions to help mitigate these risks and minimize losses.

Security measures, both visible and invisible to the public include: Intelligence gathering and analysis, checking passenger manifests against watch lists, random canine team searches at airports, Federal air marshals, and Federal flight deck officers.

11.3.2 Security insights in automotive connectivity

In the advanced systems, the entertainment system is not standalone but also has a connection to ECUs of other systems in the vehicle. These systems enable the synchronized mobile device to access more features on the vehicle apart from the media system which creates a threat to the vehicle (Rouf et al., 2010). For example, Cai et al. (2019) demonstrated that attackers can create a backdoor in the BMW vehicle entertainment system via the USB port.

In the techno world, the Internet of Things (IoT) and Intelligent Transportation System (ITS) are a growing an advanced technology that has become an enormous base for employing various applications of different genres, including smart vehicle infrastructure, by facilitating Internet connections. IoT-ITS has emerged over the last few years as a valuable tool to provide motorists and mobility control systems with real-time traffic data. Computational and storage activities are becoming quite challenging to implement in a remote infrastructure environment due to the rapid development of IoT-ITS technology.

For many years, machine learning methods have been employed to identify malware (Gandotra, 2014). As an example, Zhang et al. (2014) combined a Light Detection and Ranging system (LiDAR) with Stereo Cameras to detect surrounding vehicles. Additionally, researchers such as Gallardo et al. (2017) propose to use novel methods, such as deep learning and the tensor flow framework, to navigate a driverless vehicle.

Over 50% of all cargo crimes reported to TAPA EMEA are attributed to attacks on vehicles parked in unsecured or unclassified parking places. This is partly due to the lack of secure truck parking places. TAPA EMEA is working to raise the profile of secure parking places in the Europe, Middle East & Africa region, and to encourage more Parking Place Operators to provide a minimum standard of security to help protect drivers, vehicles, and cargoes. The Association's Parking Security Requirements (PSR) has been created in consultation with its Manufacturer & Shipper and Logistics Service provider members to help PPOs understand what the buyers of truck parking places require by way of on-site security. PPOs which meet one of the levels of TAPA EMEA's secure parking program have their sites listed in the secure parking database accessible to members via the Association's TAPA EMEA Intelligence System. TAPA EMEA currently provides visibility to secure parking places in 14 countries in the region.

Access to TAPA EMEA's Security Standards and training also supports their understanding of available solutions to help mitigate these risks and minimize losses. Membership of TAPA EMEA supports the advice given to their insured clients on the opportunities to enhance cargo security, alleviate risks and prevent supply chain losses. This helps to keep insurance premiums to a minimum.

The Cyber Safety Review Board (CSRB), an independent public-private advisory body, administered by the Department of Homeland Security DHS through its Cybersecurity & Infrastructure Security Agency CISA, brings together public and private sector cyber experts/leaders to review and draw lessons learned from the most significant cyber incidents. TAPA EMEA is the leading supply chain security and resilience industry association in the Europe, Middle East & Africa (EMEA) region. The TAPA EMEA family consists of leading brands and SMEs with a shared commitment to the highest standards of supply chain security and resilience. TAPA EMEA membership provides a platform to:

- Manage known risks and reduce losses.
- Prevent damage to client relationships or brand reputation which can stem from cargo crime.
- Receive regular intelligence reports of when, where, and how cargo crimes are occurring, the modus operandi used by cargo thieves, and the products they target.
- Identify Logistics Service Providers committed to supply chain resilience.
- Engage with Law Enforcement Agencies and Insurer contacts.
- Learn about supply chain security solutions and best practice.
- Identify supply chain security requirements to include Requests for Quotations, Contracts or Service Level Agreements
- Access TAPA EMEA's supply chain security training courses
- Network with like-minded industry colleagues and supply chain security stakeholders.

11.4 Railway transportation system

Rail systems used to function independently from IT networks and rail system components were based on proprietary technology and the principle of security by obscurity was generally accepted as a measure of protection (Pita, 2020). In the last two decades, the rail industry has seen a technical evolution currently leading to the adoption of digital systems (Pita, 2020). Railway transportation comprises multiple heterogeneous systems and given the possibility of numerous security flaws and susceptible protocols within these systems, any components of the system is potentially at risk of being targeted in an attack (López-Aguilar et al., 2022). For example, The Taiwan Railways Administration (TRA) faces organizational inefficiency as its four major departments operate in isolation with independent support systems and databases, hindering seamless communication and necessitating manual processes for cross-system information analyses and decision-making (Chen et al., 2013).

11.4.1 Cybersecurity landscape in railways

Cyberattacks are becoming more sophisticated and prevalent. For example, intrusion into security information and event management systems (SIEM) can lead to incidents with serious consequences. Chernov et al. (2015) discusses an approach to detecting abnormal activity within these systems to develop more effective incident detection techniques. Kour (2020) lists the timeline of 20 cybersecurity incidents involving railways since 2003. Of the listed 20 incidents, 30% are malware attacks; 20% are cyber espionage/data steal attacks; 15% are Distributed Denial-of-Service (DDoS) attacks; and

35% include cybercrime, insider attacks, brute-force attacks, and hacking (Kour, 2020). For this reason, cybersecurity in railroad transportation systems poses unique challenges that can make it difficult to manage effectively. Therefore, it is important to continuously monitor the system and implement detection processes for ensuring security of railway transportation systems.

Legacy Infrastructure: Many railroad systems still rely on legacy infrastructure with outdated technologies that were not originally designed with cybersecurity in mind. Legacy infrastructure may pose significant challenges in terms of cybersecurity and retrofitting or upgrading these systems can be complex and costly (Pita, 2020). First, legacy systems often use outdated technologies and may lack modern security features. They were typically designed and implemented before cybersecurity became a central concern, making them more susceptible to vulnerabilities. Also, older systems may have limited or no built-in security controls, such as encryption, secure authentication mechanisms, or robust access controls. This makes it easier for attackers to exploit vulnerabilities. Lastly, integrating legacy systems with newer technologies or security solutions can be challenging due to compatibility issues. This can hinder the implementation of comprehensive security measures across the entire infrastructure. To address these challenges, organizations with legacy infrastructure must carefully plan and implement strategies to enhance the cybersecurity posture of their older systems. This may involve a combination of system upgrades, security retrofits, and, in some cases, a phased transition to more modern and secure technologies. Morey et al. (2022) proposed a solution that uses emerging technologies and digitalization, where automated and connected intelligent transport systems facilitate smart traffic management, using autonomous trains operating with legacy rail operations and infrastructure. However, the authors pointed out that it will be imperative to consider the impact of autonomy on policies, regulations, and standards, which will need to be carefully analyzed to incorporate autonomous trains and mixed fleet operations (Morey et al., 2022).

Interconnected Systems: Railroad systems are highly interconnected with other systems from different vendors. For example, railroad systems connect with highway traffic signaling systems with state and local highway authorities (Moore et al., 2015), and train inspection systems such as wheel impact load detector (WILD) and weight in motion. Soderi (2023) categorized those systems into three groups: railway infrastructure, rolling stocks, and railway operations. Such highly interconnected systems increase vulnerabilities and make it difficult to secure the system. The rail organizations rely on the supplier's internal vulnerability and patch management processes to identify and fix software bugs, including backdoors (Pita, 2020). A cyberattack on one infrastructure is likely to cause a domino effect, in which infrastructures are damaged one after another (Menashri & Baram, 2015). For example, any type of cyberattack on the power supply could lead to power outages, compromise safety, affect operations and maintenance, and damage infrastructure (Kour, 2020). To address these challenges, López-Aguilar et al. (2022) suggested developing the Internet of Things (IoT) and Wireless Sensor Networks (WSNs) with security layers to control malicious attacks. Soderi et al. (2023) proposed a cybersecurity assessment procedure and demonstrated virtual scenarios in which each vulnerability can be tested, and its impact and risk assessed. The large complexity of highly interconnected railway transportation systems entails several issues and challenges.

Size of Railroad Network: Railroad networks cover most of the country, and it includes tracks and stations that are spread out geographically. The U.S. rail network is among the most extensive in the world, comprising more than 140,000 miles of track (Berman, 2023). This makes it difficult to monitor and protect its infrastructure physically and electronically. Critical railway cybersecurity refers to the comprehensive and essential measures implemented to protect the information technology (IT) and operational technology (OT) systems within the railway industry from potential cyber threats and attacks (Soderi et al., 2023). Pita (2020) stated that the diverse array of technologies, protocols, and functionalities employed in rail systems poses challenges in crafting effective cybersecurity policies and standards and pointed out that while certain controls like centralized authentication and digital signatures are generally suitable for servers and workstations, they may not be necessary or applicable to process-level architectures relying on Programmable Logic Controllers (PLCs) designed to control the railway executive devices operation (Kornaszewski, 2018). Also, railroad systems require non-stop access to real-time data which in turn leads to higher costs associated with maintenance and service downtime and therefore increased vulnerability (Thaduri et al, 2019). Logistical and security problems of physically accommodating enormous volumes of passengers and freight, along with the reality that security breaches could result in public safety risks (Thaduri et al, 2019). Additionally, Pita (2020) pointed out that Operational Technology (OT)-specific protocols like Modbus and Distributed Network Protocol 3 (DNP3) are widely used in rail systems but lack inherent security features. Additionally, the niche nature of the industry makes it difficult to recruit and retain cybersecurity experts with knowledge of both railway operations and information security. Therefore, it is important to modify cybersecurity strategies that are widely used in other industries to reflect the characteristics of rail systems. Pita (2020) proposed the development and implementation of tailored safeguards to ensure the uninterrupted provision of critical services. This includes incorporating elements like Identity Management and Access Control, Protective Technology, Data Security, Awareness and Training, Processes and Procedures, among others.

Human Risk Factors: Security technologies, such as cryptography, firewalls, and authentication, help to protect infrastructure against cyberattacks. However, Human factor is often not considered important. Social engineering such as spear phishing, baiting, pretexting has been effective to breach security via people interactions (Ghafir et al., 2018). Lack of security awareness in employees can create vulnerabilities in railroad systems.

11.4.2 Effective mitigation strategies against cyber threats in railways

López-Aguila et al. (2022) provide a thorough literature review on cybersecurity within railway systems, and the authors classified controlling of cybersecurity methods into two groups: (1) Enhanced systems for security by proposing techniques to improve the railway infrastructure from an information security perspective and (2) Users' cybersecurity awareness on information security in the railway infrastructure.

Enhanced Systems for Ensuring Security: This approach focusses on building more secure systems in the railway industry. All trains should constantly and reliably perform self-monitoring actions and report their position without any infrastructure support (López-Aguila et al., 2022). Lazarescu and Poolad (2022) provide a topology based on Wireless Sensor Network (WSN) prototypes designed for low-power timely train integrity reporting in unreliable conditions. Sikora et al. (2020) propose AI-based surveillance systems for railway crossing traffic. The proposed AI system uses image inputs such as pedestrian presence, vehicle presence, vehicle trajectory, railway crossings, railway warnings and signaling systems to detect dangerous situations at railway crossings in real-time. The main benefit of the proposed system lies in its ability to conduct real-time detection, achieved through the utilization of accelerated image processing techniques and deep neural networks (Sikora et al., 2020). However, this poses significant social and ethical challenges due to the necessity of collecting massive amounts of data. Blockchain is another technology that can be used to secure the data. Mu et al. (2020) proposed a blockchain-based security solution that adopted a set of policies where users' security keys are associated with a policy set that restricts users' rights. As previously stated, railway systems are highly interconnected, which makes it difficult to address their security. Falahati and Shafiee. (2022) address this issue, especially in the context of Balises network. Balises are electronic components placed between the rails that allow vehicle–ground communications based on radio frequency (López-Aguila et al., 2022). Falahati and Shafiee. (2022) implemented a system to secure Balises network that detects attacks and operation failures. The size of network databases within the railway system is large and needs to be protected. Wu et al. (2020) proposed a scheme to ensure secure access that enables the vehicle to provide high Quality of Service (QoS) in the subway WiFi environment.

Increasing Cybersecurity Awareness: Improving cybersecurity awareness efforts will constitute crucial steps in controlling human risk factors. Kour and Karim (2021) discussed cybersecurity awareness risk for railways workforce management environment. There exists a gap in cybersecurity awareness and the authors provide a set of recommendations to improve this gap. Pita (2020) suggested to secure senior management buy-in to raise cybersecurity awareness by emphasizing the potential impacts on safety, integrity, and operational availability in the event of a cyberattack. Pita (2020) recommended forming a cybersecurity steering committee including senior management, board members, Heads of Engineering, Head of Safety, and a Chief Information Security Officer (CISO) for fostering a cybersecurity culture. In forming such committees, collaboration with experienced cybersecurity experts would be extremely important considering that the expertise of such senior management is usually limited. Integrating cybersecurity risk management into the organization-wide risk management strategy ensures that system owners and managers incorporate cybersecurity into their engineering activities (Pita, 2020).

11.5 Conclusion

As transportation systems evolve, the need for robust cybersecurity measures becomes imperative. To embrace these advancements, a comprehensive understanding of current security challenges is essential. This chapter explores cybersecurity concerns in air, automobile, and railway transportation systems, addressing sector-specific threats and challenges. Adopting appropriate strategies is crucial to ensuring the security of these critical systems under the cyber risks. Airport security includes the techniques and methods used to protect passengers, staff, aircraft, and airport property from malicious harm, crime, terrorism, and other threats. It is a combination of measures, and human and material resources, to safeguard civil aviation against acts of unlawful interference. The modern era has been one of increasing use of electronics for both engine management and entertainment systems. Some contemporary developments are the proliferation of front and all-wheel drive, the adoption of the diesel engine, and the ubiquity of fuel injection. As a result, there has been a corresponding increase in cybersecurity threats. Railroads not only increased the speed of transport; they also dramatically lowered its cost. However, the trend towards enhanced security in the rail industry involves a comprehensive approach that includes the identification of critical assets, network segmentation, advanced control measures, continuous monitoring, and the adoption of new technologies.

References

Berman, N. (2023). How the U.S. Rail System Works. Available Online: https://www.cfr.org/backgrounder/how-us-rail-system-works (accessed on 3/24/24)

Bigio, R. (2022) Cybersecurity Risk Modeling (CyRM) | FAA. Available Online: https://www.faa.gov/air_traffic/technology/cas/cytf (accessed on 1/7/24)

Brand, M. (2006). Grand Canyon Crash of '56 led to FAA. Available Online: Grand Canyon crash of '56 lead to FAA 2006: NPR.org (accessed on 1/7/24)

Cai, Z., Wang, A., Zhang, W., Gruffke, M., & Schweppe, H. (2019). 0-days & mitigations: roadways to exploit and secure connected BMW cars. *Black Hat USA, 2019*(39), 6.

Cybellum. (2024). Automotive Cyber Security: Secure products across their entire lifecycle. Available Online: https://cybellum.com/automotive/ (accessed on 1/18/24)

Charette, R. N. (2009). This car runs on code. *IEEE spectrum, 46*(3), 3.

Chen, I. C., Hsu, S. K., Wu, T. J., Yen, L. H., Lee, Y., Lin, D. Y., . . . & Su, G. W. (2013). RDSP: A Railway Decision Support Platform for Integrating and Bridging Existed Legacy Systems. In *ASME/IEEE Joint Rail Conference* (Vol. 55300, p. V001T05A001). American Society of Mechanical Engineers.

Chernov, A. V., Butakova, M. A., & Karpenko, E. V. (2015, November). Security incident detection technique for multilevel intelligent control systems on railway transport in Russia. In *2015 23rd Telecommunications Forum Telfor (TELFOR)* (pp. 1–4). IEEE.

Dickson S., (2020) FAA Cybersecurity Strategy | FAA. Available Online: https://www.faa.gov/about/plansre ports/faa-cybersecurity-strategy (accessed on 1/8/24)

Elkhail, A. A., Refat, R. U. D., Habre, R., Hafeez, A., Bacha, A., & Malik, H. (2021). Vehicle security: A survey of security issues and vulnerabilities, malware attacks and defenses. *IEEE Access, 9*, 162401–162437.

Elwell, D. K., (2018) Before the Committee on Transportation and Infrastructure Subcommittee on Aviation; concerning Implementation of the FAA Reauthorization Act of 2018. Available Online: https://www.faa.gov/testimony/committee-transportation-and-infrastructure-subcommittee-aviation-concerning (accessed on 1/9/24)

FAA (2020). FAA NextGen Annual Report for Fiscal Year 2020. Available Online: https://www.faa.gov/sites/ faa.gov/files/2022-06/NextGenAnnualReport-FiscalYear2020.pdf (accessed on 1/8/24)

FAA (2022), FAA Awards $4.4 Million in Drone Research Grants to Seven Universities. Available Online: https://www.faa.gov/newsroom/faa-awards-44-million-drone-research-grants-seven-universities (accessed on 1/6/24)

FAA (2024). FAA NextGen Today, March 24, 2024. Available Online: https://www.faa.gov/nextgen/today (accessed on 3/24/24)

Falahati, A., & Shafiee, E. (2022). Improve safety and security of intelligent railway transportation system based on Balise using machine learning algorithm and fuzzy system. *International Journal of Intelligent Transportation Systems Research*, 1–15.

Francillon, A., Danev, B., & Capkun, S. (2011). Relay attacks on passive keyless entry and start systems in modern cars. In *Proceedings of the Network and Distributed System Security Symposium (NDSS)*. Eidgenössische Technische Hochschule Zürich, Department of Computer Science.

Gao. (2020) Aviation Cybersecurity: FAA Should Fully Implement Key Practices to Strengthen Its Oversight of Avionics Risks. Available Online: https://www.gao.gov/products/gao-21-86 (accessed on 1/11/24)

Ghafir, I., Saleem, J., Hammoudeh, M., Faour, H., Prenosil, V., Jaf, S., . . . & Baker, T. (2018). Security threats to critical infrastructure: the human factor. *The Journal of Supercomputing, 74*, 4986–5002.

Hyttinen, J., Ussner, M., Österlöf, R., Jerrelind, J., & Drugge, L. (2024). *Estimating Tire Pressure Based on Different Tire Temperature Measurement Points* (No. 2024-01-5002). SAE Technical Paper.

Israel21C. (2024). Cyberattacks On Cars Increased 225% In Last Three Years. Available Online: https://www.israel21c.org/cyberattacks-on-cars-increased-225-in-last-three-years/ (accessed on 1/ 18/24).

Kornaszewski, M. (2018). Microprocessor technology and programmable logic controllers in new generation railway traffic control and management systems. *Archives of Transport System Telematics, 11*(2), 18–23.

Kour, R. (2020). *Cybersecurity in railway: a framework for improvement of digital asset security* (Doctoral dissertation, Luleå University of Technology).

Kour, R., & Karim, R. (2021). Cybersecurity workforce in railway: its maturity and awareness. *Journal of Quality in Maintenance Engineering, 27*(3), 453–464.

Lazarescu, M. T., & Poolad, P. (2020). Asynchronous resilient wireless sensor network for train integrity monitoring. *IEEE Internet of Things Journal*, 8(5), 3939–3954.

López-Aguilar, P., Batista, E., Martínez-Ballesté, A., & Solanas, A. (2022). Information Security and Privacy in Railway Transportation: A Systematic Review. *Sensors*, 22(20), 7698.

Menashri, H., & Baram, G. (2015). Critical infrastructures and their interdependence in a cyberattack–the case of the US. Military and Strategic Affairs, 7 (1), 22.

Microsoft (2016). MS Power Point-16, VnV Processes in Cybersecurity. Available Online: https://www.faa.gov/sites/faa.gov/files/2022-02/16VnVProcessesinCybersecurity.pdf (accessed on 1/5/24)

Morales, H., (2022) Cyber Enterprise Architecture (EA) | FAA. Available Online: https://www.faa.gov/air_traffic/technology/cas/ea (accessed on 1/12/24)

Moore, A., Zebell, P., Koonce, P., & Meusch, J. (2015, March). A Method to Verify Railroad Interconnect With Highway Traffic Signal Systems. In *ASME/IEEE Joint Rail Conference* (Vol. 56451, p. V001T03A006). American Society of Mechanical Engineers.

Morey, E. J., Galvin, K., Riley, T., & Wilson, R. E. (2022). Application of soft systems methodology to frame the challenges of integrating autonomous trains within a legacy rail operating environment. *Systems Engineering*.

Mu, Y.; Rezaeibagha, F.; Huang, K. Policy-Driven Blockchain and Its Applications for Transport Systems. IEEE Trans. Serv. Comput. 2020, 13, 230–240.

Olagunju. T. (2022). Cybersecurity Testing | Federal Aviation Administration. Available Online: https://www.faa.gov/air_traffic/technology/cas/ct (accessed on 1/8/24)

Pangarkar T. (2023) Automotive Cyber Security Statistics: New Way to Drive Secure. Available Online: https://scoop.market.us/automotive-cyber-security-statistics/ (accessed on 3/24/24)

Pita, A.M. Real-World Cyber Security Challenges in Rail Systems. Available online: https://railsystemsaustralia.com.au/wp-content/uploads/2020/02/Real-World%20Cyber%20Security%20Challenges%20in%20Rail%20Systems_final.pdf (accessed on 1/4/2024).

Rouf, I., Miller, R., Mustafa, H., Taylor, T., Oh, S., Xu, W., . . . & Seskar, I. (2010). Security and privacy vulnerabilities of {In-Car} wireless networks: A tire pressure monitoring system case study. In *19th USENIX Security Symposium (USENIX Security 10)*.

Roy, S. and Sridhar, B. (2021) Cyber- Threat Assessment for the Air Traffic Management System: A Network Controls Approach. Available Online:https://ntrs.nasa.gov/api/citations/20180000393/downloads/20180000393.pdf (accessed on 1/5/24)

Rupp, M., Smirnoff, P., and Scholten, U. (2021) Cybersecurity & Air Traffic Control: Revisiting Techniques Used in Cyber-Attacks and Cyber-Defense. Available Online:https://www.skyradar.com/blog/cybersecurity-and-air-traffic-control-a-general-reminder-of-the-techniques-used-in-cyber-attacks-and-cybersecurity (accessed on 1/3/24)

Shabshab, S. C., Lindahl, P. A., Leeb, S. B., & Nowocin, J. K. (2020). Autonomous demand smoothing for efficiency improvements on military forward operating bases. *IEEE Transactions on Power Delivery*, 35(5), 2243–2251.

Sikora, P., Malina, L., Kiac, M., Martinasek, Z., Riha, K., Prinosil, J., . . . & Srivastava, G. (2020). Artificial intelligence-based surveillance system for railway crossing traffic. *IEEE Sensors Journal*, 21(14), 15515–15526.

Soderi, S., Masti, D., & Lun, Y. Z. (2023). Railway cyber-security in the era of interconnected systems: a survey. *IEEE Transactions on Intelligent Transportation Systems*.

Terekhov V. Protecting Airport Data Privacy & Control from Cyber Threats: Navigating GDPR. Available Online: https://attractgroup.com/blog/aviation-cybersecurity-strategies (accessed on 3/24/24)

Thaduri, A., Aljumaili, M., Kour, R., & Karim, R. (2019). Cybersecurity for eMaintenance in railway infrastructure: risks and consequences. *International Journal of System Assurance Engineering and Management, 10,* 149–159.

Wu, Y., Ye, D., Wei, Z., Wang, Q., Tan, W., & Deng, R. H. (2018). Situation-aware authenticated video broadcasting over train-trackside WiFi networks. *IEEE Internet of Things Journal, 6*(2), 1617–1627.

Zhang, F., Clarke, D., & Knoll, A. (2014). LiDAR based vehicle detection in urban environment. In *2014 International Conference on Multisensor Fusion and Information Integration for Intelligent Systems (MFI)* (pp. 1–5). IEEE.

Emmanuel C. OGU

12 Towards robust policy frameworks for securing cyber-physical systems in healthcare

12.1 Introduction and background

The pervading influence of cyber-physical systems (CPSs) in the domain of healthcare has been lauded by several past and recent inquiries; especially for the effectiveness and efficiency that CPSs bring to various medical and healthcare tasks. A cyber-physical system (CPS) is essentially a "complex system that integrates sensing, computation, control and networking into physical processes and objects over the Internet" (Duo et al., 2022, p. 784). These systems have found applications in various multidisciplinary domains, and the global healthcare sector features several such systems like autonomous wearable and implantable medical electronic devices like drug-releasing pumps, pacemakers, hearing aids, defibrillators, pacemakers, and diagnostic equipment that measures, monitors, and records nervous and cardiovascular functions.

Systems like these can seamlessly integrate physical processes with computation/digitization, and information communication technologies (ICT) (Aguida et al., 2020); thereby making them partly physical systems, and partly cyber systems (Duo et al., 2022). Within this context, ICT refers to the integration of systems, protocols, and processes with communication networks to be able to collect, process, transmit, store and retrieve artefacts of data and information. Modern cyber-physical devices are manufactured with embedded chipsets and are designed to operate as supervisory control and data acquisition (SCADA) systems that can be wirelessly read, administered, and controlled using remote commands and procedure calls (Sheng et al., 2021).

Indeed, the architecture and design of CPSs makes them susceptible to a broad range of cyber-attacks, regardless of the sector where they are being used. Such attacks have been known to include ransomware attacks, information theft, injection and replay attacks, denial of service (DoS), distributed DoS, and jamming attacks that target sensors and actuators (Duo et al., 2022). These are to highlight a few. Generally, these attacks seek to either cause such systems to malfunction (Lenk, n.d., citing Radcliffe, 2011; Saeed et al., 2023), compromise their availability for critical use cases (Winder, 2024), alter the data and information they carry to misinform operations, or steal the sensitive data and information that they process and transmit (Gates, 2024). However, within the healthcare sector where the stakes are comparatively higher, such incidents could result in a broad range of undesirable consequences that could include regulatory sanctions (Lee & Choi, 2021), reputational damage, huge financial liabilities (Greenlee, 2023), or even loss of life (Neprash et al., 2023).

https://doi.org/10.1515/9783111289069-012

As the debates about global health security continue to assume a central focus, particularly in the wake of the CoViD-19 pandemic, it is necessary to consider the ways in which cybersecurity – particularly as it pertains to the applications of cyber-physical and other integrated ICT systems in modern healthcare delivery – intersects with global health security. Moreso, it is also important to consider what policy measures might be necessary to boost further progress in this regard. This is the focus of this research.

12.2 Health security, e-Health, and cyber-physical systems in healthcare

The discourse of health security (HS) has assumed a rather contemporaneous nature. Particularly as the realities of epidemics and pandemics such as the Ebola outbreak, the Zika virus, and more recently, the CoViD-10 global outbreak, draw global attention to "the health issues that challenge diplomacy and human security, and [the need to] mobilise the necessary resources to ensure lasting change[s]" (Davies & Kamradt-Scott, 2018). In the wake of the CoViD-19 pandemic, the World Health Organization (WHO) drew attention to a parallel pandemic that seemed to have ridden on the waves of CoViD – the pandemic of cybersecurity incidents in healthcare (WHO, 2020). At scale, recent research, and reports by Amos (2024), Neprash et al. (2023), and Miller (2022), among others, have drawn attention to the relationship between increased cyber-attacks and an increase in patient mortality rates. Indeed, the global patient mortality numbers linked to cyber-attacks over the past few years have gradually increased from a few dozens, into several scores, and now in the hundreds. Could we be looking at a dimension of global health security that may not be receiving the right measure of attention, yet?

The period of the last decade has seen the popularisation of the term "e-Health". It is an umbrella term that is essentially used in reference to a broad array of health systems, technologies, protocols, and services that are digitised and cyber-enabled. The WHO has defined eHealth as "the cost-effective and secure use of information and communications technologies in support of health and health-related fields, including health-care services, health surveillance, health literature, and health education, knowledge and research." (WHO, n.d.b). Over the years, e-Health has evolved to feature the deployment of a wide range of information and communication technologies (ICTs) (including mobile telephony, artificial intelligence, voice recognition, speech translation, video conferencing, wired & wireless communication, cybernetics, digital sensing & imaging, computational analytics, bioinformatics/biomedical informatics), supported by electronic devices, for various applications in Healthcare (Ogu, 2021).

Today, e-Health record databases make it possible to provision and transfer patient data across far distances for analysis and evaluation by teams of medical experts that are geographically dispersed (Tsai et al., 2020); electronic diagnostic systems and services enable patients to be diagnosed correctly of various symptomatic disease conditions without being physically present at a healthcare facility, through telemedicine (Haleem et al., 2021); computer-assisted prescription systems help healthcare workers to select the most effective and safest drug and treatment regimen for patients based on diagnostic reports (Chongthavonsatit et al., 2021; Rogero-Blanco et al., 2021); innovative drug delivery systems help to manage the health of patients in critical-care situations involving diseases like cancer and life-threatening tumours (Hari et al., 2023; Lai et al., 2022); and, cyber-physical systems make remote monitoring possible, in order to mitigate the shortcomings of care-givers and healthcare professionals (Ramasamy et al., 2022). These are to mention a few.

However, these eHealth innovations and implementations have not been without challenges, deficiencies, and insufficiencies. The recent spates of high-profile cyber incidents that have continued to target and disrupt eHealth systems and services bear testament to the fact that if not properly regulated, eHealth systems, technologies, protocols, and services could pose new challenges for health security in general (Federal Office for Information Security, n.d.). Patient data security and privacy, denial of service, system infiltration and hijacks, free and easy-to-use Metasploit and reverse engineering and backtracking tools, malware injection and attacks, and cyberterrorism, all represent the contemporary realities of cybersecurity that could to truncate the benefits of eHealth in the modern digital era.

12.2.1 Cyber-attacks to cyber-physical systems

The critical applications of cyber-physical systems make them viable targets for malicious actors (Mussington, 2021). In particular, the data they transmit and work with, the physical actions they activate, the critical domains where they operate, and the implications of malfunction or failure all present attractive considerations for hijack, infiltration, and theft to cybercriminals; with rewards that have real-world value and consequences (Mussington, 2021). Within the healthcare domain, two contexts of application pose a relevant focus: multimodal remote patient monitoring systems (El-Rashidy et al., 2021; Shaik et al., 2023), and autonomous drug delivery systems (Hari et al., 2023; Lai et al., 2022).

Multimodal remote patient monitoring systems (MRPMSs) offer several utilities for healthcare. Compared to alternative manual systems, MRPMSs make it possible for the health status of patients suffering chronic and acute illnesses or (infectious) diseases to be monitored from remote stations, without the physical presence of healthcare staff at the patient's bedside (Shaik et al., 2023). Using high-precision biomedical sensor devices, these systems collect real-time data regarding patients physiology (such as vitals, motion/movement, psychological state, sleep patterns, organ imagery, and various other biomarkers), then an electronic micro-control unit aggregates the data and wirelessly transmits it to healthcare providers or professionals at a remote station, who interpret the data, make diagnostic decisions, and decide on appropriate medical actions when necessary (Boikanyo et al., 2023; Shaik et al., 2022; Shaik et al., 2023). This is essentially a high-level description of the operations of MRPMSs.

Similarly, autonomous drug delivery systems (ADDSs) offer transformative potential for overcoming the challenges of traditional drug delivery using manual methods, especially in situations when "the active pharmaceutical ingredient (API) has dose-limiting side effects, a narrow therapeutic window and/or a short half-life that makes maintaining the proper drug concentration difficult" (Baryakova et al., 2023). These systems apply micro and nano robotic mechanisms to improve the efficiency of drug delivery, particularly in critical situations that are characterised by targeted precision, urgency, reachability, complexity, and risk of infection – ultimately aiming to achieve "therapeutic efficacy while minimising side effects" (Das & Sultana, 2024, p. 2). ADDSs are generally classified based on "their *route of medication administration* (for example, oral, transdermal, intravenous, intramuscular, subcutaneous, transmucosal), the *device type* (for example, injectable microparticle depot, extended-release oral formulation, intravaginal ring) or the *drug release profile* afforded by the system (pulsatile, first-order, sustained, zero-order or stimuli-responsive)" (Baryakova et al., 2023). At a high-level, the operations of ADDSs involve the use of chip-controlled robotic propulsion-driven delivery systems (featuring sensors, actuators, and nano controllers) that modulate the sustained-release of a particular drug at a particular concentration to a particular site, tissue, or cell of the body (Baryakova et al., 2023; Das & Sultana, 2024).

Both MRPMSs and ADDSs pervade the global healthcare sector today, with critical applications across different contexts. With the Internet of Medical Things (IoMT) revolution, it has become possible to integrate and interconnect such systems to "gather, analyse, and transmit health data", in a way that enables "remote patient monitoring, diagnosis, and treatment" (Huang et al., 2023). Indeed, such devices have now been seen to pose "significant risks as they are ubiquitous in anaesthesia and Intensive Care and range from ventilators, infusion pumps, monitoring equipment to implantable devices and specific organ support", with the propensity of causing "irreparable harm to a patient or caregiver" (Cartwright, 2023, p. 1124).

While there are no existing reports of actual cyber-attacks specifically targeting either MRPMSs or ADDSs as at the time of this research, there are several pointers to the reality that successful cyber-attacks to such systems could compromise safety and directly endanger human life, even at scale (Anusha et al., 2023). These include: (a) low level attacks targeting underlying chipset technology to steal sensitive information, after the manner of *"Spectre & Meltdown"* (Nosek & Szczypiorski, 2022); (b) ransomware attacks targeting the availability of CPSs, and crippling operations (Benmalek, 2024); (c) other malware attacks that seek to achieve various malicious outcomes across CPS deployments (Yu et al., 2022); (d) signal-jamming attacks targeting the sensor, control, and actuator mechanisms of CPSs towards a denial of service (Huang et al., 2021); and (e) false data injection attacks seeking to compromise the integrity of CPS deployments (Padhan & Turuk, 2022). These are to highlight a few.

However, it is also important to highlight some of the remarkable progress that has been made in the security of healthcare CPSs in recent times. Much research has been committed towards the detection and impact mitigation of various types of attacks in CPSs (Alrowais et al., 2023), such as: denial of service attacks (Sharma et al., 2023), distributed denial of service attacks (Gao & Yang, 2022), blackhole and greyhole attacks (Javed et al., 2023), SQL injection attacks (Silva et al., 2023), malware attacks (Oswal et al., 2023), deception attacks (Barchinezhad et al., 2024; Cai & Koutsoukos, 2023), and advanced persistent threats (Li & Chen, 2024), among others. Also, several approaches have been proposed for enhancing the architectural security and reliability of healthcare CPSs, using technologies like blockchain (Kumar et al., 2023), artificial intelligence (Chandani et al., 2023), and others.

12.3 Security of cyber-physical systems in healthcare: Efforts of the WHO

In May 2005, the World Health Assembly (WHA) of member states of the World Health Organization launched the Global Observatory for eHealth (GOe). Recognizing the revolutionary capabilities provided by eHealth for transforming the efficiency, responsiveness, cost, quality, equity, sustainability, and reach of healthcare services and systems across the world, the GoE was designed to study the evolution and impact of eHealth in various countries, and to strengthen healthcare systems by providing information and guidance to national governments and international organisations for effectively standardising and regulating deployments of eHealth in various jurisdictions (WHO, n.d.a; WHO, 2019).

Indeed, the recommendations and resolutions of the WHA and the GOe have pointed member states in the right directions with regards to policies and strategies for the effective governance of eHealth, as well as the creation of enabling environments for capacity development and extension for healthcare professionals, and systematic support partnerships to enhance various applications of eHealth (including TeleHealth, mHealth, big data, etc.). However, the recommendations did not provide blueprints to guide the efforts of member states on specific courses of action, illuminate areas of focus, and unpack dimensions of foreseen difficulty with regards to implementing the recommendations proffered. This is understandable, especially considering the realities of the digital divide, the capacity and priorities of healthcare systems and financing, and the need to balance the responsibilities of regulation against the utilities of innovation (WHO, 2019).

Between 2010–2015, the third global survey on eHealth undertaken by the GoE focused on the extent to which legal frameworks protect patient privacy in EHRs [electronic health records] as health care systems move towards delivering safer, more efficient, and more accessible health care (GOe, 2016). With 125 countries participating in the survey, it represents one of the relatively recent and global surveys on eHealth and its legal support frameworks. Amongst other discoveries, the survey underscored the necessity of a comprehensive legal framework for eHealth, to guide and regulate the way healthcare information and services is transferred, provisioned, and used between healthcare professionals and patients. The report also focused on the concerns for rights of usage (appropriate use, authorised use, and misuse), privacy & confidentiality, professional liability for remote healthcare, procurement of eHealth tools (electronic health records (EHRs), telemedicine systems, monitoring systems, and other medical devices), system interoperability of medical devices, as well as the harmonisation of standards and compliance requirements in the procurement and usage of eHealth tools (GOe, 2016).

Today, "many e-health technologies are already widely used, including electronic medical records (eMRs), electronic health records (eHRs), applications for health practice for mobile health (m-health), remote service provision through telecommunications (telehealth and telemedicine), electronic health information systems (eHIS) and systems for medication, chronic disease and other clinical management, electronic learning, and decision support. Social media and big data are also used for health service matters" (WHO, 2019, p. 6). Thus, considering that the threats, risks, and challenges to eHealth systems and deployments are not exclusive or peculiar to regions or jurisdictions, it is important to underscore the pain points in eHealth implementations, particularly as it bothers on cyber-physical systems, to chart a progressive path forward on a global scale. This is particularly crucial as foregoing explanations in this research already reveal how cyber-physical systems in healthcare differ remarkably from other e-health technologies.

12.4 Healthcare cyber-physical systems: Portended challenges for policy & regulation, and implications

Haque et al. (2014) present a taxonomy of modern cyber-physical systems used in healthcare. As one of the relatively highly referred publications on the subject, it has laid the foundations for numerous subsequent research in this area. As shown in Figure 12.1, this taxonomy visualises healthcare cyber-physical systems as a complex integration of several composites: applications, architecture, sensor devices & equipment, data management modules, computation subsystems, communication capabilities, security structures

& constructs, and control/actuation subsystems. Thus, this taxonomy is adopted to reflect upon the portended challenges and implications for policy and regulation of CPSs, across four panels of consideration as they bother on CPSs: design complexities that impact on cybersecurity and economics; policy insufficiencies that could affect cybersecurity; operations that complicate the task of cybersecurity; and modes of application and use that exacerbate traditional challenges of cybersecurity. The recommendations of the GOe are then highlighted as pathways for mitigating these challenges.

12.4.1 Application

Across the global healthcare sector, CPSs are deployed across an array of application areas, which could either restrict the independence of users (patients/relations/healthcare personnel) in controlled applications; or not, in assisted applications (Haque et al. 2014). As previously elucidated in this research, these applications could broadly include electronic medical records (eMRs), electronic health records (eHRs), applications for health practice for mobile health (m-health), remote service provision through telecommunications (telehealth and telemedicine), electronic health information systems (eHIS) and systems for medication, chronic disease monitoring & control, and other clinical management, as well as electronic learning, and decision support systems that integrate social media, big data, and artificial intelligence capabilities (WHO, 2019). These are to highlight a few.

Oftentimes, the engineering, development, and deployment of CPSs for various healthcare applications come with added complexities and challenges to existing systems and frameworks. These challenges generally bother on integrability, interoperability, and (backward) compatibility between legacy and new applications (Montori et al., 2024). In part, this is due to contingencies that may not be fully comprehensible until after deployment, as well as variations in technical requirements that could perpetuate inconsistencies and result in redundant subsystems. Ultimately, this creates additional vulnerabilities that could threaten the utility of the system within and across application domains, creating loopholes in existing policy frameworks. To mitigate this challenge, the GOe recommends the standardisation and harmonisation of the processes and practices that underlie the procurement of eHealth tools (GOe, 2016). This would provide an opportunity to consider how new applications would integrate and operate within existing frameworks. However, broader compliance across the sector would prove necessary for the progressive effectiveness of this recommendation.

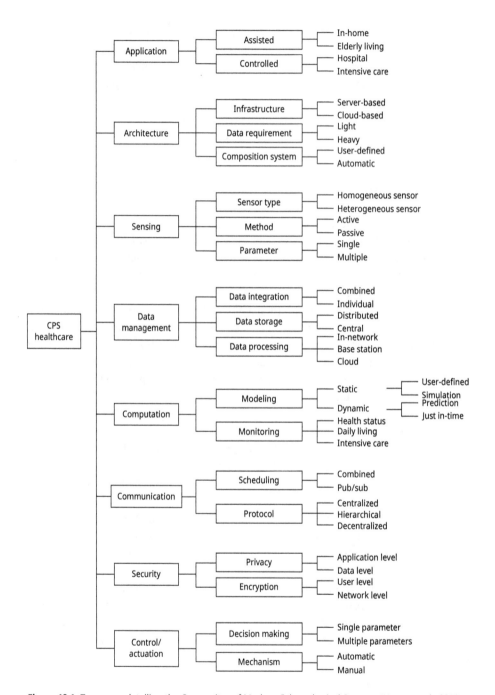

Figure 12.1: Taxonomy detailing the Composites of Modern Cyber-physical Systems (Haque et al., 2014).

12.4.2 Architecture

In ensuring the quality of service/operation, and optimum performance of CPSs in various application areas and domains, various architectural blueprints are relied upon. These architectures, which infrastructure are either hardware- (server-) or software- (cloud-) based, take cognizance of the domain/area of application, the requirements & parameters for data that would be handled by the architecture (whether heavy- or light-weight), and the various composites that must come together to power such an architecture (which may be user-defined, or pre-programmed) (Haque et al., 2014). Existing research by Rajkumar et al. (2010), Ullah et al. (2019), and Wang et al. (2011), among others, have proposed architectures for CPSs, even describing they could be applied to healthcare. These architectures generally feature subsystems for communication and sensing, computation and security, real-time scheduling & resource management, cloud integration for smart healthcare, information network capabilities, event detection and data analysis, spatiotemporal analysis, data sharing and synchronisation, amongst other innovative features.

However, as with many such nascent technologies that lack standardisation and proactive regulation, the early stages of development are often more focused on competitive innovation and operational utility, such that the need to ensure due diligence across all critical dimensions is often undermined. This often results in architectural features that could bring about solutions that offer various independent utilities and prospects within their individual scopes; but which might ultimately be un-integrable. This could lead to arrays of complexities and resultant vulnerabilities that may be imposed because of variations in the components, techniques, and subsystems, which could cascade through multi-type, and multi-parameter applications (Haque et al., 2014). In the end, the long-observed situation manifests, wherein policy and regulation would struggle to keep up with the unforeseen lapses that have been created by rapid innovation and development needs (European Parliamentary Research Service, 2016; Tanneeru, 2009).

Considering these, the GOe recommends interoperability standards to help mitigate the challenge of integrating various system architectures and dealing with emergent and underlying system complexities, with respect to procurement of composite systems, and architectures. However, in the event that the techniques and approaches to designing and enhancing such systems are not equally regulated by policy, the situation could result in stunted growth for global eHealth, by widening an already-existing gap between eHealth innovations, tools and systems that are being invented, and their acceptance/adoption across the global healthcare sector due to interoperability, ethical, security, or humanitarian concerns (GOe, 2016).

12.4.3 Sensing and data management

It is important that the data that are sensed and collected by CPSs must be in such a form that is able to meet the user and system requirements. Thus, an efficient strategy must be in place to manage, process and store these data. Since these data are often gathered from multiple distributed sensors and sensor networks, Haque et al. (2014) suggest that the information accumulated should be aggregated or integrated (from across combined or individual sources) in such a manner that allows for easy transmission and communication. The data should also be stored in real-time databases that could either be centralised, distributed, or hybridised, and could be queried to ascertain the current state of the system or entity that they represent or monitor, within reasonable logic and time constraints. In addition, the data is to be processed in real-time to be able to meet response time and arrival deadlines for critical applications, by leveraging efficient computation and communication mechanisms (Haque et al., 2014).

In line with this proposition, existing research by Rizwan et al. (2018) proposes a data management and computing framework for healthcare CPSs that integrates modern internet of things (IoT) and big data technologies for efficient sensing & communication, security & computation, and resource management with real-time scheduling. Similarly, Zhang et al. (2017) propose a healthcare CPS that incorporates cloud computing and big data technologies for assisted data management, using a "unified standard for a data collection layer, data management layer, and data-oriented service layer for distributed storage and parallel computing" (Zhou et al., 2018, p. 52184).

However, as Verma (2018) discovered, modern applications of CPSs in healthcare and medicine continue to pose challenges for data management, storage, and processing; especially as it concerns the huge amounts of datasets that are constantly being collected by various sensing devices around the world. The continuous streams and flows of these data can effectively threaten and inundate backbone processing and communication infrastructure. The critical, high-value nature of the information that are contained in these datasets also pose a focus of interest for several actors. All these increase the susceptibility of these data and information to the risks and concerns of privacy and security (D'Addona et al., 2018); thereby necessitating circumspect policy provisions for regulating the way these data are collected, analysed, processed, stored, accessed, and used.

Indeed, the constant collection of critical and high-value health data & information in large volumes of continuous streams by cyber-physical monitoring systems increase the susceptibility of these data and systems to the risks and concerns of privacy and security. In addition, the failure of such systems to satisfy minimum computing requirements and remain up to date with system upgrades and fixes pose limitations to efficiency, security, reliability, and availability, which could be exploited for malicious purposes. Also, scheduling conflicts could arise because of the heterogeneity of communication protocols used by various sensor devices, which could affect the ability of CPSs to deliver and communicate required information within rigid and critical response-time constraints.

Considering these, the GOe emphasises the criticality of data for the effective functioning of modern eHealth systems and services, without recommending what types of patient data can be collected by eHealth systems and tools, and what types cannot (GOe, 2016). The GOe also does not recommend approaches and best practices regarding how these data would be aggregated, integrated, and computed by lower-level computing systems and devices for secure and effective manipulation, and transmission (GOe, 2016). There are also no recommendations regarding unified communication protocols that are robust enough to deliver outputs to various sub-system destinations within critical response-time deadlines (GOe, 2016). Indeed, member states reported major barriers and limitations with respect to how the data collected by different eHealth services and systems can be aggregated and integrated reliably, safely, and securely. This could hamper critical applications of eHealth, which often rely on real-time and up-to-date data that is portable and understandable across various eHealth systems and platforms.

12.4.4 Computation

Haque et al. (2014) highlight the necessity of reliable computation for healthcare CPSs. CPSs rely on an efficient (static or dynamic) modelling of the system to understand its computational needs. This is particularly important due to the large networks and mechanisms for sensing, control, communication, feedback, and response that are involved in the operations of CPSs, as well as the multiple environments and variables that characterise different application domains. Computation in this regard also relates to the complexities that are imposed by the scope of monitoring that is carried out by the CPS, which differs for applications in health status monitoring, daily living monitoring, and intensive care monitoring. In light of these, a number of computational models, paradigms, and approaches have been proposed and experimented for CPSs in healthcare, including: parallel computing (Zhou et al., 2018); real-time computing (Rizwan et al., 2018); soft computing (Atif et al., 2018); edge-cognitive computing (Chen et al., 2018); fog computing (Devarajan & Ravi, 2018), (Vijayakumar et al., 2018); and cloud computing (Wang et al., 2011), to mention a few.

However, in many cases, the effective and efficient functioning and integration of these computing paradigms into the design and implementation of modern CPSs come with requirements for hardware, bandwidth, operating system, instruction set, etc.; wherein the failure to satisfy these minimum requirements could pose limitations to efficiency, reliability, and availability that could be exploited for malicious purposes.

12.4.5 Communication and security

Communication is the fulcrum of modern CPSs. It powers its core utilities for applications in healthcare. It could involve communicating the sensed data to the storage & processing servers and repositories, routing data between participating networks, or communicating processed information to observation centres or terminals domiciled in remote healthcare facilities. Indeed, modern CPSs would be dysfunctional without communication infrastructure and capabilities that are effective, accurate, secure, localised/ubiquitous, real-time/on-demand, and just-in-time, depending on the application area. Haque et al. (2014) opine that effective scheduling (mapping communication tasks to limited time resources, through synchronous and/or asynchronous approaches with concurrency control), and protocols (rules of engagement for various participating CPS devices, modules, & sub-systems, which could be centralised, hierarchical, decentralised, or hybridised) are indispensable for effective communication in modern CPSs.

Thus, Lee et al. (2018) have proposed a communication model for cyber-physical systems that uses an efficient heterogeneous network-routing method to allow participating devices in a CPS communication network to interact using heterogeneous protocols, based on a dynamic search and control mechanism. Also, Leong et al. (2018) propose a scheduling apparatus for solving problems associated with estimating "the states of multiple remote, dynamic processes" in sparsely distributed, large-scale wireless sensor networks of CPSs. The approach relies on solving a Markov decision problem (MDP) by applying a deep reinforcement learning algorithm – known as Deep Q-Network – which is immediately scalable and model-free.

However, the challenge with communication within CPSs has to do with its featuring of sensitive data in transit while it is outside the security perimeters of both the sender and receiver, and susceptible to malicious encounters within the communication medium or channel. In addition, the heterogeneity of participating CPS sensors, each with a communication protocol that is best-suited to its application, can create deep-running conflicts for schedulers & scheduling algorithms, which could affect the ability of CPSs to deliver and communicate required information in a timely manner. The implication of these challenges for policy and regulation has to do with considerations for safeguarding sensitive data while it is in transit and outside the security custody of both sender and receiver. It also has to do with considerations for standardising the requirements and expectations of communication infrastructure that power the operations of CPSs.

Furthermore, the critical and high-value nature of data and information that are usually involved in the operations of CPSs means that the security and safeguarding of such data and information is crucial. This is important considering the legal and ethical consequences for the breach or misuse of such sensitive data and information. Haque et al. (2014) identify two key components of security: privacy and confidentiality (particularly for data at rest), and encryption (particularly for data in motion/transit). In line with these, many approaches to security for CPSs have been proposed. For example, Ali et al. (2023), Dalal et al. (2023), Kanagala (2023), Rivadeneira et al. (2024), and Yang et al. (2023) have proposed frameworks for preserving privacy in CPSs, using technologies such as blockchain, machine learning, artificial intelligence, and game theory. Similarly, Lima et al. (2023), Pranav et al. (2024), and Tiwari et al. (2023) have proposed encryption models and cryptographic approaches for reliable data security in CPSs; while Javed et al. (2019), Mohammed et al. (2024), and Shi et al. (2024) have proposed integrated forms of these.

However, the task of security continues to feature two dilemmas. The first has to do with the difficulty in foreseeing all possible angles and dimensions of risks and vulnerabilities to security during the design and implementation stages of CPSs, to put in place circumspect and resilient security policies & frameworks for effectively deterring threats and attacks. This inadvertently leaves soft spots in systems, infrastructures and environments that could be exploited by malicious adversaries to compromise security (Al-Mhiqani et al., 2018). The second being the reality that the extent to which security (and policy) can be effectively deployed is constrained by the usability requirements of the systems (Lessa & Etoribussi, 2023). That is, complex security affects system usability; and for the non-technical users (patients, patient relatives, and clinicians/health professionals) that typically interface with CPSs, security complexities could create dangers and bottlenecks for critical applications.

The recommendations of the GOe emphasise the criticality of security, privacy, and confidentiality of patient's healthcare data across all adoptions and applications of eHealth systems and tools; as well as the attending liability implications (GOe, 2016). However, there are other aspects of eHealth operations that also have implications for health policy, such as best practices for the physical security of the eHealth systems and deployment environments, as well as the security of underlying infrastructure from threats posed by insiders and malicious outsiders (Ogu, 2021).

12.4.6 Control/actuation

Owing to the high-volume of patient data that modern CPSs accumulate, they are expected to intelligently analyse this data to make effective decisions and take emergency action in critical applications. However, the ethical concerns of rogue (unauthorised or unnecessary) actions and false alarms (positives or negatives) that could endanger the lives of patients continue to challenge the success of CPSs in this regard. Thus, many modern CPSs rather alert caregivers and clinicians when the monitored biomarkers exceed acceptable thresholds, by triggering an alarm (Haque et al., 2014). However, the alarm mechanism, which could be manually operable or automatically configured, is prone to misinterpreting one or more of the decision-making parameters for various reasons, and sending off false alarms; or alternatively, alarm systems could also be hacked to achieve the same event (Keoh, 2018).

Repeated occurrences of false alarms can fatigue and tire out caregivers/clinicians, thereby compromising the quality of care administered. It could also impact on perceptions of trust, security, and reliability of CPSs, even as the attack surface broadens (Samarpita et al., 2023). Hence, it is important for health policy to provide guidance for the future of control and actuation for CPSs in healthcare, especially considering security, ethical, and humanitarian concerns regarding machine-human interface for critical applications.

12.5 Recommendations

Standardisation remains one crucial challenge to the wider progress and adoption of CPSs. This lack of standardisation in the operations, processes and procedures of CPSs in healthcare impact the *availability* (being able to function optimally and deliver results, even while under attack or experiencing faults); *safety* (not posing possible or imminent risk of harm or hazard); *reliability* (being able to generate results with expected correctness & accuracy); *resilience* (being able to operate and provide services even in the presence of intrinsic and extrinsic difficulties and incapacitations); and *security* (being able to provide safeguards against incursions) (Gunes et al., 2014). It has, therefore, created, and perpetuated inconsistencies and grey areas across various application domains of CPSs, thereby leaving gaps in many policy frameworks that aim to secure the uses and applications of CPSs.

Thus, there is the need for standardisation in the operations, processes, procedures, and applications of CPSs, even before they enter critical domains such as healthcare. This would help to ensure coherence and cohesiveness of various innovative solutions and developmental approaches that emerge to advance the applications of the technology within the domain. For instance, one aspect might be to consider the minimisation of the proximal distance for various sensing and communication resource capabilities that enable cyber-physical systems. This is because distance is known to impose additional vulnerabilities to data in transit, including, but not limited to, tampering/altering, re-routing, obfuscation, tapping, and corruption.

Another area of focus for health security policies and regulations should be to settle exactly what types of data would be collectable by CPSs, the volume of such data that would be sufficient for a particular use/result by a CPS, the nature and security requirements of the databases and repositories where such data and information can be stored, the manner in which such data and information would be transmissible, and the human participants that would have access to such data. Engineers and manufacturers of healthcare CPSs would, therefore, need to consider the question of necessity of such intended data to the efficient functioning of the system, and how exactly the system would manipulate and apply such data for effective decision support.

In addition, Dey et al. (2018) recommend a rethinking of the impact that core computing abstractions could have on the design and operations of CPSs. They suggest incremental improvements based on advances that have been made in the areas of formal verification, simulation and emulation techniques, certification techniques, software engineering processes, software component technologies, and design patterns. It is important to consider this to be a critical area of focus for HSPs, especially in light of the state-of-the-art of rootkits and other computing malware that are able to truncate and subvert system computation processes and affect results in ways that could be life-threatening for critical applications. Thus, policies and regulations need to align the scope of clinical testing, modelling, and simulations of healthcare CPSs to comply with the minimum requirements for efficient computation, while also reflecting the modern realities of cybercriminal activities and attacks, especially of the politically motivated kinds that could have unlimited resource bases.

12.6 Conclusion

Brazell (2014) has emphasised the need for a transdisciplinary approach to dealing with security issues in CPSs, because "cybersecurity is headed toward a more multidisciplinary approach" (Ritchie, 2017). This is crucial to achieving policy robustness for securing critical applications of cyber-physical systems (such as healthcare) in order that health security policy frameworks are able to present a more circumspect scope for regulating CPSs in various application areas of healthcare. Indeed, the policy and regulatory recommendations of the GOe and the WHO largely present strong foundations for the global development of eHealth. However, without clear pointers on the specific areas of difficulty that arise in trying to operationalize these recommendations within the jurisdictions of member states, there is the tendency for confusion, complexities, conflict, and redundancy to arise.

Thus, this research has laid a foundation for future research by uncovering and elucidating the key areas where policy frameworks could be challenged in trying to secure, regulate, and safeguard the use of cyber-physical systems across various application domains, and particularly for critical applications such as various aspects of eHealth. Future research seeking to recommend reviews and enhancements, or evaluate the readiness and robustness of various jurisdictional and trans-jurisdictional policies and legislations aimed at regulating eHealth, and managing the involvement of CPSs for healthcare (as well as other) applications would be able to leap off the theoretical foundations laid by this research.

References

Aguida, M. A., Ouchani, S., & Benmalek, M. (2020). A review on cyber-physical systems: models and architectures. In *2020 IEEE 29th International Conference on Enabling Technologies: Infrastructure for Collaborative Enterprises (WETICE)* (pp. 275–278). IEEE. https://doi.org/10.1109/WETICE49692.2020.00060

Ali, A., Al-Rimy, B. A. S., Almazroi, A. A., Alsubaei, F. S., Almazroi, A. A., & Saeed, F. (2023, August 14). Securing secrets in cyber-physical systems: A cutting-edge privacy approach with consortium blockchain. *Sensors, 23*(16), 7162. https://doi.org/10.3390/s23167162

Al-Mhiqani, M. N., Ahmad, R., Yassin, W., Hassan, A., Abidin, Z. Z., Ali, N. S., & Abdulkareem, K. H. (2018). Cyber-security incidents: A review cases in cyber-physical systems. *International Journal of Advanced Computer Science and Applications, 9*(1), 499–508. https://doi.org/10.14569/IJACSA.2018.090169

Alrowais, F., Mohamed, H. G., Al-Wesabi, F. N., Al Duhayyim, M., Hilal, A. M., & Motwakel, A. (2023, May). Cyber attack detection in healthcare data using cyber-physical system with optimised algorithm. *Computers and Electrical Engineering, 108*, 108636. https://doi.org/10.1016/j.compeleceng.2023.108636

Amos, Z. (2024, January 8). *The Link Between Health Care Cyberattacks and Patient Mortality*. The Journal of mHealth. Retrieved April 9, 2024, from https://thejournalofmhealth.com/the-link-between-health-care-cyberattacks-and-patient-mortality/

Anusha, R., Vijayashree, J., Jayashree, J., & Yousuff, M. (2023). CPS support IoMT cyber attacks, security and privacy issues and solutions. In *Cyber-Physical Systems for Industrial Transformation* (pp. 157–175). CRC Press.

Atif, M., Latif, S., Ahmad, R., Kiani, A. K., Qadir, J., Baig, A., Ishibuchi, H., & Abbas, W. (2018). Soft Computing Techniques for Dependable Cyber-Physical Systems. *arXiv preprint arXiv:1801.10472*, 1–19. https://arxiv.org/pdf/1801.10472.pdf

Barchinezhad, S., Haghighi, M. S., & Puig, V. (2024, March). Identification and analysis of stochastic deception attacks on cyber physical systems. *Journal of the Franklin Institute, In Press*, 106774. https://doi.org/10.1016/j.jfranklin.2024.106774

Baryakova, T. H., Pogostin, B. H., Langer, R., & McHugh, K. J. (2023, March 27). Overcoming barriers to patient adherence: The case for developing innovative drug delivery systems. *Nature Reviews Drug Discovery, 22*(5), 387–409. https://doi.org/10.1038/s41573-023-00670-0

Benmalek, M. (2024). Ransomware on cyber-physical systems: Taxonomies, case studies, security gaps, and open challenges. *Internet of Things and Cyber-Physical Systems, 4*, 186–202. https://doi.org/10.1016/j.iotcps.2023.12.001

Boikanyo, K., Zungeru, A. M., Sigweni, B., Yahya, A., & Lebekwe, C. (2023, July). Remote patient monitoring systems: Applications, architecture, and challenges. *Scientific African, 20*, e01638. https://doi.org/10.1016/j.sciaf.2023.e01638

Brazell, J. B. (2014). The Need for a Transdisciplinary Approach to Security of Cyber Physical Infrastructure. In S. Suh, U. Tanik, J. Carbone, & A. Eroglu (Eds.), *Applied Cyber-Physical Systems* (pp. 5–14). Springer. https://doi.org/10.1007/978-1-4614-7336-7_2

Cai, F., & Koutsoukos, X. (2023, October). Real-time detection of deception attacks in cyber-physical systems. *International Journal of Information Security, 22*(5), 1099–1114. https://doi.org/10.1007/s10207-023-00677-z

Cartwright, A. J. (2023, April 24). The elephant in the room: Cybersecurity in healthcare. *Journal of Clinical Monitoring and Computing, 37*(5), 1123–1132. https://doi.org/10.1007/s10877-023-01013-5

Chandani, P., Rajagopal, S., Bishnoi, A. K., & Verma, V. (2023, July 11). Cyber-Physical System and AI Strategies for Detecting Cyber Attacks in Healthcare. *International Journal of Intelligent Systems and Applications in Engineering, 11*(8s), 55–61. https://ijisae.org/index.php/IJISAE/article/view/3021

Chen, M., Li, W., Hao, Y., Qian, Y., & Humar, I. (2018, September). Edge cognitive computing based smart healthcare system. *Future Generation Computer Systems, 86*, 403–411. https://doi.org/10.1016/j.future.2018.03.054

Chongthavonsatit, N., Kovavinthaweewat, C., Yuksen, C., Sittichanbuncha, Y., Angkoontassaneeyarat, C., Atiksawedparit, P., & Phattharapornjaroen, P. (2021, March 19). Comparison of accuracy and speed in computer-assisted versus conventional methods for paediatric drug dose calculation: A scenario-based randomised controlled trial. *Global Pediatric Health, 8*, 2333794X21999144. https://doi.org/10.1177/2333794X21999144

D'Addona, D. M., Rongo, R., Teti, R., & Martina, R. (2018). Bio-compatible cyber-physical system for cloud-based customizable sensor monitoring of pressure conditions. *Procedia CIRP, 67*, 150–155. https://doi.org/10.1016/j.procir.2017.12.245

Dalal, S., Poongodi, M., Lilhore, U. K., Dahan, F., Vaiyapuri, T., Keshta, I., Aldossary, S. M., Mahmoud, A., & Simaiya, S. (2023, June). Optimised LightGBM model for security and privacy issues in cyber-physical systems. *Transactions on Emerging Telecommunications Technologies, 34*(6), e4771. https://doi.org/10.1002/ett.4771

Das, T., & Sultana, S. (2024, January 03). Multifaceted applications of micro/nanorobots in pharmaceutical drug delivery systems: A comprehensive review. *Future Journal of Pharmaceutical Sciences, 10*(1), Article 2. https://doi.org/10.1186/s43094-023-00577-y

Davies, S. E., & Kamradt-Scott, A. (2018, October 21). Health security policy and politics: Contemporary and future dilemmas. *Australian Journal of International Affairs, 72*(6), 492–494. https://doi.org/10.1080/10357718.2018.1537357

Devarajan, M., & Ravi, L. (2019, December). Intelligent cyber-physical system for an efficient detection of Parkinson disease using fog computing. *Multimedia Tools and Applications, 78*, 32695–32719. https://doi.org/10.1007/s11042-018-6898-0

Dey, N., Ashour, A. S., Shi, F., Fong, S. J., & Tavares, J. M. (2018, March 10). Medical cyber-physical systems: A survey. *Journal of Medical Systems, 42*(4), Article 74. https://doi.org/10.1007/s10916-018-0921-x

Duo, W., Zhou, M., & Abusorrah, A. (2022, April 26). A survey of cyber attacks on cyber physical systems: Recent advances and challenges. *IEEE/CAA Journal of Automatica Sinica, 9*(5), 784–800. https://doi.org/10.1109/JAS.2022.105548

El-Rashidy, N., El-Sappagh, S., Islam, S. R., El-Bakry, H. M., & Abdelrazek, S. (2021, March 29). Mobile health in remote patient monitoring for chronic diseases: Principles, trends, and challenges. *Diagnostics, 11*(4), 607. https://doi.org/10.3390/diagnostics11040607

European Parliamentary Research Service. (2016). *Ethical Aspects of Cyber-Physical Systems: Scientific Foresight study*. European Union. https://www.europarl.europa.eu/RegData/etudes/STUD/2016/563501/EPRS_STU%282016%29563501_EN.pdf

Federal Office for Information Security. (n.d.). *eHealth – Cyber Security in Healthcare Bild-Dokument für das Frontend*. Federal Office for Information Security – Deutschland. Retrieved April 9, 2024, from https://www.bsi.bund.de/EN/Themen/Unternehmen-und-Organisationen/Standards-und-Zertifizierung/E-Health/e-health.html

Gao, R., & Yang, G. H. (2022, March). Distributed multi-rate sampled-data H∞ consensus filtering for cyber-physical systems under denial-of-service attacks. *Information Sciences, 587*, 607–625. https://doi.org/10.1016/j.ins.2021.12.046

Gates, L. (2024, Jan-Feb). Cyber Attacks on Interoperable Electronic Health Records: A Clear and Present Danger. *Mo Med, 121*(1), 6–9. https://www.ncbi.nlm.nih.gov/pmc/articles/PMC10887471/

GOe. (2016, December 15). *Global diffusion of eHealth: Making universal health coverage achievable: Report of the third global survey on eHealth*. WHO | IRIS Home. Retrieved April 09, 2024, from https://iris.who.int/bitstream/handle/10665/252529/9789241511780-eng.pdf

Greenlee, M. (2023, August 16). *Cost of a data breach: Healthcare industry impacts.* Security Intelligence. Retrieved March 17, 2024, from https://securityintelligence.com/articles/cost-of-a-data-breach-2023-healthcare-industry-impacts/

Gunes, V., Peter, S., Givargis, T., & Vahid, F. (2014, December 30). A survey on concepts, applications, and challenges in cyber-physical systems. *KSII Transactions on Internet & Information Systems, 8*(12), 4242–4268. https://www.itiis.org/digital-library/manuscript/894

Haleem, A., Javaid, M., Singh, R. P., & Suman, R. (2021). Telemedicine for healthcare: Capabilities, features, barriers, and applications. *Sensors International, 2,* 100117. https://doi.org/10.1016/j.sintl.2021.100117

Haque, S. A., Aziz, S. M., & Rahman, M. (2014, April 27). Review of cyber-physical system in healthcare. *International Journal of Distributed Sensor Networks, 10*(4), 1–20. https://doi.org/10.1155/2014/217415

Hari, S. K., Gauba, A., Shrivastava, N., Tripathi, R. M., Jain, S. K., & Pandey, A. K. (2023, January). Polymeric micelles and cancer therapy: An ingenious multimodal tumour-targeted drug delivery system. *Drug Delivery and Translational Research, 13*(1), 135–163. https://doi.org/10.1007/s13346-022-01197-4

Huang, C., Wang, J., Wang, S., & Zhang, Y. (2023, November 07). Internet of medical things: A systematic review. *Neurocomputing, 557,* 126719. https://doi.org/10.1016/j.neucom.2023.126719

Huang, Y., Xiong, Z., & Zhu, Q. (2021). Cross-layer coordinated attacks on cyber-physical systems: A lqg game framework with controlled observations. In *Proceedings of the 2021 European Control Conference (ECC)* (pp. 521–528). IEEE. https://doi.org/10.23919/ECC54610.2021.9654874

Javed, M., Tariq, N., Ashraf, M., Khan, F. A., Asim, M., & Imran, M. (2023, November 23). Securing Smart Healthcare Cyber-Physical Systems against Blackhole and Greyhole Attacks Using a Blockchain-Enabled Gini Index Framework. *Sensors, 23*(23), 9372. https://doi.org/10.3390/s23239372

Javed, Y., Felemban, M., Shawly, T., Kobes, J., & Ghafoor, A. (2019). A Partition-Driven Integrated Security Architecture for Cyber-Physical Systems. *arXiv preprint arXiv:1901.03018,* 1–11. https://arxiv.org/ftp/arxiv/papers/1901/1901.03018.pdf

Kanagala, P. (2023, February). Effective cyber security system to secure optical data based on deep learning approach for healthcare application. *Optik, 272,* 170315. https://doi.org/10.1016/j.ijleo.2022.170315

Keoh, S. L. (2018, June 15). *Cyber-Physical Systems Are at Risk.* InfoSecurity Magazine. Retrieved April 11, 2024, from https://www.infosecurity-magazine.com/next-gen-infosec/cyberphysical-systems-risk-1/

Kumar, M., Raj, H., Chaurasia, N., & Gill, S. S. (2023). Blockchain inspired secure and reliable data exchange architecture for cyber-physical healthcare system 4.0. *Internet of Things and Cyber-Physical Systems, 3,* 309–322. https://doi.org/10.1016/j.iotcps.2023.05.006

Lai, X., Liu, X. L., Pan, H., Zhu, M. H., Long, M., Yuan, Y., Zhang, Z., Dong, X., Lu, Q., Sun, P., Lovell, J. F., Chen, H. Z., & Fang, C. (2022, March 10). Light-triggered efficient sequential drug delivery of biomimetic nanosystem for multimodal chemo-, antiangiogenic, and anti-mdsc therapy in melanoma. *Advanced Materials, 34*(10), 2106682. https://doi.org/10.1002/adma.202106682

Lee, H., Lee, J., Nam, S., & Park, S. (2018, May 20). Efficient Heterogeneous Network-Routing Method Based on Dynamic Control Middleware for Cyber-Physical System. *Journal of Sensors, 2018,* Article ID 3176967. https://doi.org/10.1155/2018/3176967

Lee, J., & Choi, S. J. (2021, July 06). Hospital productivity after data breaches: difference-in-differences analysis. *Journal of Medical Internet Research, 23*(7), e26157. https://doi.org/10.2196/26157

Lenk, W. (n.d.). *Wireless Mobile Medical Devices | Electrical and Computer Engineering Design Handbook.* edu.tufts.sites. Retrieved March 17, 2024, from https://sites.tufts.edu/eeseniordesignhandbook/2015/wireless-mobile-medical-devices/

Leong, A. S., Ramaswamy, A., Quevedo, D. E., Karl, H., & Shi, L. (n.d.). Deep Reinforcement Learning for Wireless Sensor Scheduling in Cyber-Physical Systems. *arXiv preprint arXiv:1809.05149,* 1–9. https://arxiv.org/pdf/1809.05149.pdf

Lessa, L., & Etoribussi, A. G. (2023). Usability of Security Mechanisms of E-Health Applications: Cases From Ethiopia. In *Fraud Prevention, Confidentiality, and Data Security for Modern Businesses* (pp. 37–56). IGI Global. https://doi.org/10.4018/978-1-6684-6581-3.ch002

Li, L., & Chen, W. (2024, February 29). ConGraph: Advanced Persistent Threat Detection Method Based on Provenance Graph Combined with Process Context in Cyber-Physical System Environment. *Electronics, 13*(5), 945. https://doi.org/10.3390/electronics13050945

Lima, P. M., Carvalho, L. K., & Moreira, M. V. (2023, April). Ensuring confidentiality of cyber-physical systems using event-based cryptography. *Information Sciences, 621*, 119–135. https://doi.org/10.1016/j.ins.2022.11.100

Miller, M. (2022, December 28). *The mounting death toll of hospital cyberattacks.* Politico. Retrieved April 9, 2024, from https://www.politico.com/news/2022/12/28/cyberattacks-u-s-hospitals-00075638

Mohammed, M. A., Lakhan, A., Zebari, D. A., Abd Ghani, M., Marhoon, H. A., Abdulkareem, K. H., Nedoma, J., & Martinek, R. (2024, March). Securing healthcare data in industrial cyber-physical systems using combining deep learning and blockchain technology. *Engineering Applications of Artificial Intelligence, 129*, 107612. https://doi.org/10.1016/j.engappai.2023.107612

Montori, F., Tatara, M. S., & Varga, P. (2024, February 12). Dynamic Execution of Engineering Processes in Cyber-Physical Systems of Systems Toolchains. *IEEE Transactions on Automation Science and Engineering*, (Early Access). https://doi.org/10.1109/TASE.2024.3362132

Mussington, D. (2021, October 06). *Cyber-Physical Security in an Interconnected World.* Security Magazine. Retrieved April 9, 2024, from https://digitaledition.securitymagazine.com/october-2021/cyber-physical-cover-feature/

Neprash, H., McGlave, C., & Nikpay, S. (2023, November 17). *Ransomware attacks on hospitals: Study outlines patient impact.* STAT News. Retrieved March 17, 2024, from https://www.statnews.com/2023/11/17/hospital-ransomware-attack-patient-deaths-study/

Neprash, H., McGlave, C., & Nikpay, S. (2023, November 17). *Ransomware attacks on hospitals: Study outlines patient impact.* STAT News. Retrieved April 9, 2024, from https://www.statnews.com/2023/11/17/hospital-ransomware-attack-patient-deaths-study/

Nosek, M., & Szczypiorski, K. (2022). An Evaluation of Meltdown Vulnerability. In *Proceedings of the 2022 9th International Conference on Wireless Communication and Sensor Networks* (pp. 35–41). ACM. https://doi.org/10.1145/3514105.3514112

Ogu, E. C. (2021). *Cybersecurity for eHealth: A simplified guide to practical cybersecurity for non-technical healthcare stakeholders & practitioners.* Routledge. https://doi.org/10.1201/9781003254416

Oswal, S., Shinde, S. K., & Vijayalakshmi, M. (2023). Deep Learning-Based Anomaly Detection in Cyber-Physical System. In *Big Data Analytics in Intelligent IoT and Cyber-Physical Systems* (pp. 59–71). Springer Nature Singapore. https://doi.org/10.1007/978-981-99-4518-4_4

Padhan, S., & Turuk, A. K. (2022, August). Design of false data injection attacks in cyber-physical systems. *Information Sciences, 608*, 825–843. https://doi.org/10.1016/j.ins.2022.06.082

Pranav, G. K., Mishra, Z., & Acharya, B. (2024). Lightweight Cryptographic Solutions for Resource-constrained Devices in Cyber-Physical Systems. In *Intelligent Security Solutions for Cyber-Physical Systems* (1st ed., pp. 66–88). Chapman and Hall/CRC.

Ramasamy, L. K., Khan, F., Shah, M., Prasad, B. V. V. S., Iwendi, C., & Biamba, C. (2022, January 29). Secure smart wearable computing through artificial intelligence-enabled internet of things and cyber-physical systems for health monitoring. *Sensors, 22*(3), 1076. https://doi.org/10.3390/s22031076

Ritchie, A. L. (2017, August 03). *Improving Security Science Through Collaboration.* Carnegie Mellon School of Computer Science. Retrieved April 12, 2024, from https://www.cs.cmu.edu/news/improving-security-science-through-collaboration

Rivadeneira, J. E., Borges, G. A., Rodrigues, A., Boavida, F., & Silva, J. S. (2024, April). A unified privacy preserving model with AI at the edge for Human-in-the-Loop Cyber-Physical Systems. *Internet of Things, 25*, 101034. https://doi.org/10.1016/j.iot.2023.101034

Rizwan, P., Babu, M. R., Balamurugan, B., & Suresh, K. (2018). Real-time big data computing for internet of things and cyber physical system aided medical devices for better healthcare. In *2018 Majan International Conference (MIC)* (pp. 1–8). IEEE. https://doi.org/10.1109/MINTC.2018.8363160

Rogero-Blanco, E., Del-Cura-González, I., Aza-Pascual-Salcedo, M., García de Blas González, F., Terrón-Rodas, C., Chimeno-Sánchez, S., García-Domingo, E., López-Rodríguez, J. A., & group MULTIPAP. (2021, May 13). Drug interactions detected by a computer-assisted prescription system in primary care patients in Spain: MULTIPAP study. *European Journal of General Practice, 27*(1), 90–96. https://doi.org/10.1080/13814788.2021.1917543

Saeed, A., AlShafea, A., Foton, A., & Saeed, A. B. (2023, February 02). Pacemaker Malfunction in a Patient With Congestive Heart Failure and Hypertension. *Cureus, 15*(2), e34574. https://doi.org/10.7759%2Fcureus.34574

Samarpita, S., Mishra, R., Satpathy, R., & Pati, B. (2023). Security Issues and Privacy Challenges of Cyber-Physical System in Smart Healthcare Applications. In *Big Data Analytics in Intelligent IoT and Cyber-Physical Systems* (pp. 73–87). Springer Nature Singapore. https://doi.org/10.1007/978-981-99-4518-4_5

Shaik, T., Tao, X., Higgins, N., Gururajan, R., Li, Y., Zhou, X., & Acharya, U. R. (2022, December 05). Fedstack: Personalized activity monitoring using stacked federated learning. *Knowledge-Based Systems, 257*(12), 109929. https://doi.org/10.1016/j.knosys.2022.109929

Shaik, T., Tao, X., Higgins, N., Li, L., Gururajan, R., Zhou, X., & Acharya, U. R. (2023, March/April). Remote patient monitoring using artificial intelligence: Current state, applications, and challenges. *Wiley Interdisciplinary Reviews: Data Mining and Knowledge Discovery, 13*(2), e1485. https://doi.org/10.1002/widm.1485

Sharma, A., Rani, S., Shah, S. H., Sharma, R., Yu, F., & Hassan, M. M. (2023, May 12). An efficient hybrid deep learning model for denial of service detection in cyber physical systems. *IEEE Transactions on Network Science and Engineering, 10*(5), 2419–2428. https://doi.org/10.1109/TNSE.2023.3273301

Sheng, C., Yao, Y., Fu, Q., & Yang, W. (2021, February 11). A cyber-physical model for SCADA system and its intrusion detection. *Computer Networks, 185*, 107677. https://doi.org/10.1016/j.comnet.2020.107677

Shi, Z., Oskolkov, B., Tian, W., Kan, C., & Liu, C. (2024, July). Sensor Data Protection Through Integration of Blockchain and Camouflaged Encryption in Cyber-Physical Manufacturing Systems. *Journal of Computing and Information Science in Engineering, 24*(7), 071004. https://doi.org/10.1115/1.4063859

Silva, M., Ribeiro, S., Carvalho, V., Cardoso, F., & Gomes, R. L. (2023). Scalable Detection of SQL Injection in Cyber Physical Systems. In *Proceedings of the 12th Latin-American Symposium on Dependable and Secure Computing* (pp. 220–225). ACM. https://doi.org/10.1145/3615366.3625075

Tanneeru, M. (2009, November 17). *Can the law keep up with technology?* CNN. Retrieved April 10, 2024, from http://edition.cnn.com/2009/TECH/11/17/law.technology/index.html

Tiwari, D., Mondal, B., Singh, S. K., & Koundal, D. (2023, August). Lightweight encryption for privacy protection of data transmission in cyber physical systems. *Cluster Computing, 26*(4), 2351–2365. https://doi.org/10.1007/s10586-022-03790-1

Tsai, C. H., Eghdam, A., Davoody, N., Wright, G., Flowerday, S., & Koch, S. (2020, December 04). Effects of electronic health record implementation and barriers to adoption and use: A scoping review and qualitative analysis of the content. *Life, 10*(12), 327. https://doi.org/10.3390/life10120327

Verma, D. (2018). CPS-heart: Cyber-physical systems for cardiovascular diseases. In *Proceedings of the Workshop Program of the 19th International Conference on Distributed Computing and Networking* (pp. 26–30). ACM. https://doi.org/10.1145/3170521.3170548

Vijayakumar, V., Malathi, D., Subramaniyaswamy, V., Saravanan, P., & Logesh, R. (2019, November). Fog computing-based intelligent healthcare system for the detection and prevention of mosquito-borne diseases. *Computers in Human Behavior, 100*, 275–285. https://doi.org/10.1016/j.chb.2018.12.009

Wang, J., Abid, H., Lee, S., Shu, L., & Xia, F. (2011). A secured health care application architecture for cyber-physical systems. *arXiv preprint arXiv:1201.0213*, 1–8. https://arxiv.org/ftp/arxiv/papers/1201/1201.0213.pdf

WHO. (2019, December 05). *Regional action agenda on harnessing e-health for improved health service delivery in the Western Pacific*. World Health Organization (WHO). Retrieved April 9, 2024, from https://iris.who.int/bitstream/handle/10665/330700/9789290618959-eng.pdf

WHO. (2020, April 23). *WHO reports fivefold increase in cyber attacks, urges vigilance*. World Health Organization (WHO). Retrieved April 9, 2024, from https://www.who.int/news/item/23-04-2020-who-reports-fivefold-increase-in-cyber-attacks-urges-vigilance

WHO. (n.d.a). *Global Observatory for eHealth – Global Observatory for eHealth*. World Health Organization (WHO). Retrieved April 09, 2024, from https://www.who.int/observatories/global-observatory-for-ehealth

WHO. (n.d.b). *WHO EMRO | eHealth | Health topics*. EMRO. Retrieved April 09, 2024, from https://www.emro.who.int/health-topics/ehealth/

Winder, D. (2024, February 13). *Ransomware Attack Takes 100 Hospitals Offline*. Forbes. Retrieved March 17, 2024, from https://www.forbes.com/sites/daveywinder/2024/02/13/ransomware-attack-takes-100-hospitals-offline/?sh=4aa0931312c5

Yang, M., Feng, H., Wang, X., Wu, X., Wang, Y., & Ren, C. (2023, May 21). Data pricing with privacy loss compensation for cyber-physical systems: A Stackelberg game based approach. *Internet Technology Letters*, Online First, e443. https://doi.org/10.1002/itl2.443

Yu, Z., Gao, H., Wang, D., Alnuaim, A. A., Firdausi, M., & Mostafa, A. M. (2022, July 01). SEI2RS malware propagation model considering two infection rates in cyber–physical systems. *Physica A: Statistical Mechanics and its Applications*, *597*, 127207. https://doi.org/10.1016/j.physa.2022.127207

Zhang, Y., Qiu, M., Tsai, C. W., Hassan, M. M., & Alamri, A. (2017, March). Health-CPS: Healthcare Cyber-Physical System Assisted by Cloud and Big Data. *IEEE Systems Journal*, *11*(1), 88–95. https://doi.org/10.1109/JSYST.2015.2460747

Zhou, X., Gou, X., Huang, T., & Yang, S. (2018, September 12). Review on Testing of Cyber Physical Systems: Methods and Testbeds. *IEEE Access*, *6*, 52179–52194. https://doi.org/10.1109/ACCESS.2018.2869834

Contributors

Jose M. Bernik
Bank of America, USA

Krista N. Engemann
Accenture, USA

Kurt J. Engemann
Iona University, USA

Todd Fitzgerald
Cybersecurity Collaborative, USA

Chris Hetner
NACD, USA

Saquib Hyat-Khan
Johns Hopkins University
and AppliedTechonomics, USA

Phillip King-Wilson
Quantar Solutions Limited, UK

Robert McKinney
Point72, USA

Holmes E. Miller
Muhlenberg College, USA

Calvin Nobles
University of Maryland-Global Campus, USA

Emmanuel C. Ogu
Babcock University, Nigeria

Robert Richardson
Iona University, USA

Nikki Robinson
IBM and Capitol Technology University, USA

Heechang Shin
Iona University, USA

Ore Soluade
Iona University, USA

Jason A. Witty
USAA, USA

https://doi.org/10.1515/9783111289069-013

Index

https://doi.org/10.1515/9783111289069-014

Developments in managing and exploiting risk

The objective of this multi-volume set is to offer a balanced view to enable the reader to better appreciate risk as a counterpart to reward, and to understand how to holistically manage both elements of this duality. Crises can challenge any organization, and with a seemingly endless stream of disruptive and even catastrophic events taking place, there is an increasing emphasis on preparing for the worst. However, being focused on the negative aspects of risk, without considering the positive attributes, may be shortsighted. Playing it safe may not always be the best policy, because great benefits may be missed.

Analyzing risk is difficult, in part because it often entails events that have never occurred. Organizations, being mindful of undesirable potential events, are often keenly averse to risk to the detriment of capitalizing on its potential opportunities. Risk is usually perceived as a negative or downside, however, a commensurate weight should also be given to the potential rewards or upside, when evaluating new ventures. Even so, too much of a good thing may create unintended consequences of risk, which is also an undesirable situation. *Developments in Managing and Exploiting Risk* provides a professional and scholarly venue in the critical field of risk in business with emphasis on decision-making using a comprehensive and inclusive approach.

Vol. 1: Safety Risk Management: Integrating Economic and Safety Perspectives. Edited by Kurt J. Engemann and Eirik B. Abrahamsen

Vol. 2: Project Risk Management: Software Development and Risk. Edited by Kurt J. Engemann and Rory V. O'Connor

Vol. 3: Organizational Risk Management: Managing for Uncertainty and Ambiguity. Edited by Krista N. Engemann, Kurt J. Engemann and Cliff Scott

Vol. 4: Socio-Political Risk Management: Assessing and Managing Global Insecurity. Edited by Kurt J. Engemann, Cathryn F. Lavery and Jeanne Sheehan

Vol. 5: Cybersecurity Risk Management. Enhancing Leadership and Expertise. Edited by Kurt J. Engemann and Jason A. Witty

https://doi.org/10.1515/9783111289069-015

www.ingramcontent.com/pod-product-compliance
Lightning Source LLC
Jackson TN
JSHW051956131224
75386JS00006B/376